The Rights and Obligations of States in Disputed Maritime Areas

YOURI VAN LOGCHEM

CAMBRIDGE
UNIVERSITY PRESS

CAMBRIDGE
UNIVERSITY PRESS

University Printing House, Cambridge CB2 8BS, United Kingdom

One Liberty Plaza, 20th Floor, New York, NY 10006, USA

477 Williamstown Road, Port Melbourne, VIC 3207, Australia

314–321, 3rd Floor, Plot 3, Splendor Forum, Jasola District Centre, New Delhi – 110025, India

103 Penang Road, #05–06/07, Visioncrest Commercial, Singapore 238467

Cambridge University Press is part of the University of Cambridge.

It furthers the University's mission by disseminating knowledge in the pursuit of education, learning, and research at the highest international levels of excellence.

www.cambridge.org
Information on this title: www.cambridge.org/9781108830102
DOI: 10.1017/9781108909051

First published 2021

A catalogue record for this publication is available from the British Library.

Library of Congress Cataloging-in-Publication Data
NAMES: Logchem, Youri van, author.
TITLE: The rights and obligations of states in disputed maritime areas / Youri van Logchem, Swansea University.
DESCRIPTION: Cambridge, United Kingdom ; New York, NY : Cambridge University Press, 2021. | Includes bibliographical references and index.
IDENTIFIERS: LCCN 2021013829 (print) | LCCN 2021013830 (ebook) | ISBN 9781108830102 (hardback) | ISBN 9781108821629 (paperback) | ISBN 9781108909051 (ebook)
SUBJECTS: LCSH: Maritime boundaries. | Boundary disputes. | Jurisdiction, Territorial. | Territorial waters. | Contiguous zones (Law of the sea) | Continental shelf – Law and legislation.
CLASSIFICATION: LCC KZA1686 .L64 2021 (print) | LCC KZA1686 (ebook) | DDC 341.4/48–dc23
LC record available at https://lccn.loc.gov/2021013829
LC ebook record available at https://lccn.loc.gov/2021013830

ISBN 978-1-108-83010-2 Hardback

Contents

Preface and Acknowledgements

A significant number of disputed maritime areas remain in all parts of the world, including in the Aegean Sea (i.e. between Greece and Turkey), in the Mediterranean Sea (e.g. between Cyprus and Turkey, and Israel and Lebanon), and in Southeast Asia and the broader East-Asian region (between different combinations of claimant States, including China, Japan, Malaysia, Vietnam, South Korea, and the Philippines). Disputed maritime areas inevitably emerged due to the expansion of the limits of coastal State jurisdiction, for example, due to coastal States having entitlements to an exclusive economic zone of 200 nautical miles (nm) or concerning a continental shelf to a minimum of 200 nm. During the time that a maritime boundary has not been delimited, there are competing sovereignties, sovereign rights, and/or jurisdictional competences of at least two neighbouring coastal States over the same maritime area. Unilateral acts that are within the authority of the coastal State, and when they are undertaken in disputed maritime areas with the authorisation of only one of the claimant States – such as conducting work related to hydrocarbons, taking unilateral protective measures as regards the marine environment, and law enforcement measures – frequently lead to conflict between the States concerned. Considering the large number of disputed maritime areas that remain unresolved, several of which are long-standing, of great complexity, and regularly ignite conflicts, makes examining the issue of the rights and obligations of States prior to delimitation both necessary and timely. The central aim of this book is to discuss, from the perspective of international law, the rights and obligations of States (i.e. claimants and third States) in disputed maritime areas. A particular emphasis is placed on those areas in relation to which neighbouring coastal States have not able to agree on cooperative arrangements or a modus vivendi has not been developed to regulate activities that are undertaken in a disputed maritime area.

The topic of what the rights and obligations are of States in disputed maritime areas has kept me occupied for almost a decade now, and this book essentially forms the culmination of my research and thinking on the subject, although questions for further research do remain. My research on the topic started as a PhD student at the Netherlands Institute for the Law of the Sea (NILOS) at Utrecht University, which led to the successful defence of my PhD thesis in January 2019. This book is a heavily adapted version of my PhD manuscript. While several publications, whether from my own hand or by others, have touched on an aspect of the rather vast and complex issue of the rights and obligations of States in disputed maritime areas, none of these provides the broad coverage that this book has set out to achieve. The research for the book was completed in December 2020. Therefore, subsequent developments and materials made publicly available after that date, including those relating to *Somalia* v. *Kenya*, were not considered.

Over the years, there have been many people who contributed to the completion of the book in some shape or form. On the non-academic side, the support of my family and relatives, that started well before I began writing this book, requires special mention, particularly that of my parents and brother. From the academic side, special thanks is reserved for Fred Soons and Alex Oude Elferink, who were my two PhD supervisors at NILOS and whose (academic) guidance, substantive input on the PhD thesis, and other publications that were produced in the meantime, as well as after the completion of the PhD journey, have greatly contributed to this book. My special thanks also go to Erik Jaap Molenaar whose comments on my completed PhD manuscript have certainly added to the quality of this book. Gratitude is also owed to David Anderson. Our collaboration on a book chapter has been enormously helpful in further shaping my own ideas in relation to the issue of the rights and obligations of States in disputed maritime areas and has also been vital in writing the book. I am also grateful to Michael Wood and Robert Beckman for their help and stimulating conversations we had on the subject matter. I would also like to thank Jill Barrett, Marco Benatar, Douglas Burnett, Robin Churchill, Catherine Redgwell, Cedric Ryngaert, Clive Schofield, Nico Schrijver, Yoshinobu Takei, and Seline Trevisanut for their input. I am grateful to my current employer, Swansea University, for giving me a sabbatical that enabled me to finish the book. Further, I must thank my colleagues at the Institute of International Shipping and Trade Law (IISTL) for their continuous support. Also, the support of Tom Randall at Cambridge University Press and his belief in the book project from an early stage have been essential in the publication of this book.

And, to save the most important and influential one for last, thank you Jessica (Schechinger) for your continuous support and substantive input in terms of commenting on my writings and for lending your editing skills. Without you, the completion of this book was unlikely to have ever happened.

Cases

Aegean Sea Continental Shelf (Greece v. *Turkey)* (Interim Measures) [1976] ICJ Rep 3

Aegean Sea Continental Shelf (Greece v. *Turkey)* (Jurisdiction) [1978] ICJ Rep 3

Anglo-Iranian Oil Co. Case (Interim Measures) [1951] ICJ Rep 89

Application of the International Convention on the Elimination of All Forms of Racial Discrimination (Georgia v. *Russian Federation)* (Preliminary Objections) [2011] ICJ Rep 70

Arbitral Award of 31 July 1989 (Guinea-Bissau v. *Senegal)* (Provisional Measures) [1990] ICJ Rep 64

Arbitration between Barbados and the Republic of Trinidad and Tobago [2006] XXVII RIAA 147

Award of the Arbitral Tribunal in the Second Stage of the Proceedings between Eritrea and Yemen (Maritime Delimitation) [1999] XXII RIAA 335

Case Concerning the Continental Shelf (Libyan Arab Jamahiriya/Malta) [1985] ICJ Rep 13

Case Concerning the Delimitation of the Maritime Boundary between Guinea-Bissau and Senegal (Guinea-Bissau v. *Senegal)* [1995] ICJ Rep 423

Certain Activities Carried Out by Nicaragua in the Border Area (Costa Rica v. *Nicaragua)* (Provisional Measures) [2011] ICJ Rep 6

Certain Activities Carried Out by Nicaragua in the Border Area (Costa Rica v. *Nicaragua)* and *Construction of a Road in Costa Rica along the San Juan River (Nicaragua* v. *Costa Rica)* (Judgment) [2015] ICJ Rep 665

Chagos Marine Protected Area Arbitration (Mauritius v. *United Kingdom)* Arbitral Award of 18 March 2015

Conciliation Commission on the Continental Shelf Area between Iceland and Jan Mayen: Report and Recommendations to the Governments of Iceland and Norway [1981] XXVII ILM 1

Continental Shelf (Tunisia/Libyan Arab Jamahiriya) (Judgment) [1982] ICJ Rep 18

Delimitation of Maritime Areas between Canada and France [1992] XXI RIAA 265

Delimitation of the Maritime Boundary between Guinea and Guinea-Bissau [1985] XIX RIAA 149

Delimitation of the Maritime Boundary in the Atlantic Ocean (Ghana/Côte d'Ivoire) (Provisional measures) [2015] ITLOS Rep 146

Delimitation of the Maritime Boundary in the Bay of Bengal (Bangladesh/Myanmar) [2012] ITLOS Rep 4

Delimitation of the Maritime Boundary in the Gulf of Maine Area (Canada/United States of America) [1984] ICJ Rep 246

Dispute Concerning Delimitation of the Maritime Boundary between Ghana and Côte d'Ivoire in the Atlantic Ocean (Ghana/Côte d'Ivoire) (Judgment) [2017] ITLOS Rep 4

Electricity Company of Sofia and Bulgaria (Request for the Indication of Interim Measures of Protection) [1939] PCIJ Series A/B No. 79, 194

Fisheries Case (United Kingdom of Great Britain and Northern Ireland v. *Norway)* [1951] ICJ Rep 116

Fisheries Jurisdiction (Federal Republic of Germany v. *Iceland)* (Request for the Indication of Interim Measures of Protection) [1972] ICJ Rep 30

Fisheries Jurisdiction (United Kingdom of Great Britain and Northern Ireland v. *Iceland)* (Request for the Indication of Interim Measures of Protection) [1972] ICJ Rep 4

Fisheries Jurisdiction (United Kingdom of Great Britain and Northern Ireland v. *Iceland)* [1974] ICJ Rep 3

Frontier Dispute (Burkina Faso/Republic of Mali) (Provisional Measures) [1986] ICJ Rep 3

Gabčíkovo-Nagymaros Project (Hungary v. *Slovakia)* [1997] ICJ Rep 7

Grisbadarna Case (Norway v. *Sweden)* (Award) [1909] 11 RIAA 155

Guinea/Guinea-Bissau: Dispute Concerning Delimitation of the Maritime Boundary [1986] XXV ILM 251

In the Matter of an Arbitration between Guyana and Suriname (Guyana v. *Suriname)* [2007] XXX RIAA 1

In the Matter of an Arbitration Pursuant to an Agreement dated 3 October 1996 between the Government of the State of Eritrea and the Government of the Republic of Yemen (Eritrea/Yemen) [1998] XXII RIAA 211

In the Matter of the Bay of Bengal Maritime Boundary Arbitration (Bangladesh v. *India)* PCA Case 2010–16

In the Matter of the South China Sea Arbitration (Philippines v. *China)* [2016] XXXIII RIAA 166

Islands of Palmas Case (The Netherlands/United States) [1928] 2 RIAA 831
Lac Lanoux Case [1957] 7 RIAA 281
Land and Maritime Boundary between Cameroon and Nigeria (Cameroon v. *Nigeria; Equatorial Guinea Intervening)* [2002] ICJ Rep 303
Land Reclamation in and around the Straits of Johor (Malaysia v. *Singapore)* (Provisional Measures) [2003] ITLOS Rep 10
Legality of the Threat or Use of Nuclear Weapons (Advisory Opinion) [1996] ICJ Rep 226
Legal Status of Eastern Greenland (Denmark v. *Norway)* (Request for the Indication of Interim Measures of Protection) [1933] PCIJ Rep. Series A/B No. 55, 157
Legal Status of Eastern Greenland (Denmark v. *Norway)* (Judgment) [1933] PCIJ Rep. Series A/B No. 53, 39
Maritime Delimitation and Territorial Questions between Qatar and Bahrain (Qatar v. *Bahrain)* [2001] ICJ Rep 40
Maritime Delimitation in the Area between Greenland and Jan Mayen (Denmark v. *Norway)* [1993] ICJ Rep 38
Maritime Delimitation in the Black Sea (Romania v. *Ukraine)* [2009] ICJ Rep 61
Maritime Delimitation in the Caribbean Sea and the Pacific Ocean (Costa Rica v. *Nicaragua)* [2018] ICJ Rep 139
Maritime Delimitation in the Indian Ocean (Somalia v. *Kenya)*
Maritime Dispute (Peru v. *Chile)* [2014] ICJ Rep 3
Passage through the Great Belt (Finland v. *Denmark)* (Provisional Measures) [1991] ICJ Rep 12
Pulp Mills on the River Uruguay (Argentina v. *Uruguay)* (Provisional Measures) [2007] ICJ Rep 3
Pulp Mills on the River Uruguay (Argentina v. *Uruguay)* (Judgment) [2010] ICJ Rep 14
Railway Traffic between Lithuania and Poland (Advisory Opinion) [1931] PCIJ Series A/B No. 42 108
Responsibilities and Obligations of States with Respect to Activities in the Area (Advisory Opinion) [2011] ITLOS Rep 10
Southern Bluefin Tuna Case between Australia and Japan and between New Zealand and Japan (Award on Jurisdiction and Admissibility) [2000] XXIII RIAA 4
Sovereignty over Pulau Ligitan and Pulau Sipadan (Indonesia/Malaysia) [2002] ICJ Rep 625
Territorial and Maritime Dispute (Nicaragua v. *Colombia)* [2012] ICJ Rep 624
Territorial and Maritime Dispute between Nicaragua and Honduras in the Caribbean Sea (Nicaragua v. *Honduras)* [2007] ICJ Rep 659
The 'Enrica Lexie' Incident (Italy v. *India)* (Provisional Measures) [2015] ITLOS Rep 24

Treaties and Legislation

Agreement between the Government of Malaysia and the Government of the Kingdom of Thailand on the Constitution and Other Matters Relating to the Establishment of the Malaysia–Thailand Joint Authority (13 May 1990)

Agreement between Japan and the Republic of Korea Concerning the Establishment of a Boundary in the Northern Part of the Continental Shelf Adjacent to the Two Countries (with Map and Agreed Minutes) (30 January 1974), 1225 UNTS 103

Agreement on Provisional Arrangements for the Delimitation of the Maritime Boundaries between the Republic of Tunisia and the People's Democratic Republic of Algeria (11 February 2002) 2238 UNTS 197 52 *LoSB* 41

Articles on the Responsibility of States for Internationally Wrongful Acts, International Law Commission, Yearbook 2001/II(2) (ARSIWA)

Charter of the United Nations (24 October 1945), 1 UNTS XVI (UN Charter)

Convention on the Continental Shelf (29 April 1958), 499 UNTS 311 (1958 CSC)

Convention on the Territorial Sea and the Contiguous Zone (29 April 1958), 516 UNTS 205 (1958 CTS)

Exchange of Notes Dated 18 October 2001 and 31 October 2001 between the Government of Ireland and the Government of the United Kingdom of Great Britain and Northern Ireland Constituting an Agreement Pursuant to Article 83 Paragraph 3 of the United Nations Convention on the Law of the Sea 1982 on the Provisional Delimitation of an Area of the Continental Shelf (31 October 2001), 2309 UNTS 21

Manila Declaration on the Peaceful Settlement of Disputes of 1982, General Assembly Resolution A/RES/37/10 (15 November 1982) (Manila Declaration)

Memorandum of Understanding between the Kingdom of Thailand and Malaysia on the Delimitation of the Establishment of a Joint Authority for the Exploitation of the Resources of the Sea-bed in a Defined Area of the

Continental Shelf of the Two Countries in the Gulf of Thailand (24 October 1979), 1291 UNTS 245

Optional Protocol of Signature Concerning the Compulsory Settlement of Disputes, Geneva (29 April 1958), 450 UNTS 169

Statute of the International Court of Justice (26 June 1945), 33 UNTS 993 (ICJ Statute)

Timor Sea Treaty (20 May 2002), 2258 UNTS 3

Treaty between the Federal Republic of Nigeria and the Democratic Republic of São Tomé e Príncipe on the Joint Development of Petroleum and Other Resources, in Respect of Areas of the Exclusive Economic Zone of the Two States (21 February 2001) 50 *LoSB* 43

United Nations Convention on the Law of the Sea (10 December 1982), 1833 UNTS 3 (LOSC)

Vienna Convention on the Law of Treaties (23 May 1969), 155 UNTS 331

Abbreviations

AJIA	Australian Journal of International Affairs
AJIL	American Journal of International Law
ARSIWA	Articles on the Responsibility of States for Internationally Wrongful Acts
AsJIL	Asian Journal of International Law
AusYIL	Australian Yearbook of International Law
AYIL	Asian Yearbook of International Law
BIICL	British Institute of International and Comparative Law
BYIL	British Yearbook of International Law
CIJ	China: An International Journal
CILJ	Cambridge International Law Journal
CJCL	Chinese Journal of Comparative Law
CJFAS	Canadian Journal of Fisheries and Aquatic Sciences
CJIL	Chinese Journal of International Law
CJIRD	Caribbean Journal of International Relations & Diplomacy
COLR	China Oceans Law Review
CSA	Contemporary Southeast Asia
CSC	1958 Convention on the Continental Shelf
CTS	1958 Convention on the Territorial Sea and the Contiguous Zone
CUP	Cambridge University Press
DLJ	Dalhousie Law Journal
EEZ	exclusive economic zone
EJIL	European Journal of International Law
EU	European Union
FEER	Far Eastern Economic Review
FILJ	Fordham International Law Journal
GJIA	Georgetown Journal of International Affairs

HAQ	Harvard Asia Quarterly
HIGJ	The Hague Institute for Global Justice
HILJ	Harvard International Law Journal
HJIL	Houston Journal of International Law
HYIL	Hague Yearbook of International Law
IA	International Affairs
IBRU	International Boundaries Research Unit
ICJ	International Court of Justice
IJIL	Indian Journal of International Law
ICLQ	International & Comparative Law Quarterly
IELR	International Energy Law Review
IGCC	Institute on Global Conflict and Cooperation
ILA	International Law Association
IJECL	International Journal of Estuarine and Coastal Law
IJMCL	International Journal of Marine and Coastal Law
ILC	International Law Commission
ILS	Issues in Legal Scholarship
IPEL	Suriname International Petroleum Exploration Ltd
ISAS	Institute of Southeast Asian Studies
ITLOS	International Tribunal for the Law of the Sea
JCSAA	Journal of Current Southeast Asian Affairs
JCSL	Journal of Conflict and Security Law
JEAIL	Journal of East Asia and International Law
JENRL	Journal of Energy & Natural Resources Law
JIA	Journal of International Affairs
JISWA	Journal of Interamerican Studies and World Affairs
JIWLP	Journal of International Wildlife Law & Policy
JTMS	Journal of Territorial and Maritime Studies
JWELB	Journal of World Energy Law & Business
JYIL	Japanese Yearbook of International Law
KIOST	Korean Institute of Ocean Science and Technology
KJILCL	Korean Journal of International Law and Comparative Law
km	kilometres
LJIL	Leiden Journal of International Law
LOSC	1982 United Nations Convention on the Law of the Sea
LOSI	Law of the Sea Institute
MIMA	Malaysian Institute of Maritime Affairs
MJIL	Melbourne Journal of International Law
MJILT	Maryland Journal of International Law & Trade
MP	Marine Policy

MSILR	Michigan State International Law Review
MSR	marine scientific research
NBR	The National Bureau of Asian Research
NIDS	The National Institute for Defense Studies
NJIL	Nordic Journal of International Law
nm	nautical miles
NRCCDFO	National Research Council of Canada and Department of Fisheries and Oceans
NWCR	Naval War College Review
NYUJILP	New York University Journal of International Law and Policy
OCLJ	Ocean and Coastal Law Journal
ODIL	Ocean Development and International Law
OUP	Oxford University Press
PCA	Permanent Court of Arbitration
PCIJ	Permanent Court of International Justice
PSJLIA	Penn State Journal of Law & International Affairs
SCJIL	Santa Clara Journal of International Law
SJILS	Stanford Journal of International Law Studies
SSI	Strategic Studies Institute
TILJ	Texas International Law Journal
TJOGEL	Texas Journal of Oil, Gas and Energy Law
UBCLR	University of British Columbia Law Review
UCLJLJ	UCL Journal of Law and Jurisprudence
UMIALR	University of Miami Inter-American Law Review
UN	United Nations
UNSC	United Nations Security Council
UNCLOS I	First Conference on the Law of the Sea (1958)
UNCLOS III	Third Conference on the Law of the Sea (1973–1982)
VCLT	Vienna Convention on the Law of Treaties
VJIL	Virginia Journal of International Law
VJTL	Vanderbilt Journal of Transnational Law
VLR	Vermont Law Review
YIMEL	Yearbook of Islamic and Middle Eastern Law
ZaöRV	Zeitschrift für ausländisches öffentliches Recht und Völkerrecht

1

Introduction

The second half of the twentieth century witnessed a significant rise in disputed maritime areas, because of the expansion of the limits of coastal State authority.[1] As a result, conflicts inevitably emerged between coastal States that are in close geographical proximity to each other.

To first sketch some background to disputed maritime areas, how they arise needs to be understood. Most coastal states will make claims that are based on full entitlements to maritime zones, encompassing, for instance, the whole 200 nautical mile (nm) exclusive economic zone (EEZ) or continental shelf[2] and a 12 nm territorial sea[3] subject to delimitation, in case of an overlap.[4] Entitlements to maritime zones derive from land territory, and, in turn, the maritime zones to which a territory is entitled follow from having title over that particular piece of territory, be it mainland or a high-tide feature. Geographers have calculated that, because of this tremendous expansion of coastal State authority[5] in the past 50–60 years, about 400 'maritime areas of overlapping entitlements'[6] arose. An area of overlapping maritime entitlements exists when a maritime area has not been delimited, but where potentially a maritime boundary can be determined, due to States having entitlements to maritime zones that overlap in the same area. Often there are two States having overlapping entitlements, but for instance in

[1] I Shearer, 'The Limits of Maritime Jurisdiction' in CH Schofield et al. (eds.), *The Limits of Maritime Jurisdiction* (Martinus Nijhoff, 2014) 51, 52–53; RR Churchill and VA Lowe, *The Law of the Sea* (Manchester University Press, 1999) 147–148.

[2] Chapter 5 below.

[3] Chapter 4 below.

[4] CH Schofield, 'The El Dorado Effect: Reappraising the "Oil Factor" in Maritime Boundary Disputes' in CH Schofield et al. (eds.), *The Limits of Maritime Jurisdiction* (Martinus Nijhoff, 2014) 111, 115.

[5] This umbrella term includes sovereignty, sovereign rights, and jurisdiction.

[6] DH Anderson, *Modern Law of the Sea* (Martinus Nijhoff, 2008) 7.

semi-enclosed seas, characteristic of which is their geographical congestion, there may be more States involved.

Defining the geographical scope of what can be considered the 'maritime area of overlapping claims' or 'disputed area' will normally be a matter of comparing the legislation of the neighbouring States, or transmitted communications through diplomatic channels detailing the extent of claims to maritime zones. When boundary negotiations commence, the States at the table will often lay out where, in their view, the (future) boundary should come to lie: from then onwards, both sides are likely to adhere to this position up until the time when a compromise is reached. If there is a divergence in the positions of States over the maritime boundary, comparing these lines on a map of the area shows what parts are subject to their overlapping claims, revealing at the same time the disputed maritime area. For example, in their pleadings before an Arbitral Tribunal, Guyana and Suriname both set out where the boundary in their respective views should be. Subsequently, the Tribunal identified the area lying in between these indicated boundaries as the 'disputed area', with regard to which it was called upon to effect a delimitation.[7]

Maritime boundaries have often not been determined by States, neither by way of a negotiated boundary agreement between the coastal States nor by a delimitation effected by an international court or tribunal. Considering that international law does not oblige States to agree on the final delimitation of their disputed maritime areas,[8] a significant amount of time may elapse before States are able to delimit a maritime boundary by negotiation or adjudication.[9] Therefore, at present a considerable number of areas lack a maritime boundary, either completely or partly – the latter only delimits a given part of a potential maritime boundary, leaving its remainder undetermined. A maritime boundary may also be incomplete because it terminates at a certain point to avoid a high-tide feature over which title is disputed, and the maritime zones that may be measured therefrom, coming into play; or the delimited maritime boundary will terminate at a point where another coastal State claims to have an entitlement in addition to the States that have agreed to the delimitation.

When presented as a continuum, the existence of disputed maritime areas can be valued differently by the States concerned: ranging from being considered largely unimportant, or that the area is seen to be satisfactorily regulated by a modus vivendi or other cooperative arrangement, to a disputed

[7] *In the Matter of an Arbitration between Guyana and Suriname (Guyana* v. *Suriname)* [2007] XXX RIAA 1, 77–111 [281]–[400].

[8] *North Sea Continental Shelf (Federal Republic of Germany/Denmark; Federal Republic of Germany/Netherlands)* (Judgment) [1969] ICJ Rep 3, 33 [46].

[9] N Klein, 'Provisional Measures and Provisional Arrangements in Maritime Boundary Disputes' (2006) 21(4) *IJMCL* 423, 426.

maritime area being 'fraught with difficulty and sensitivity'.[10] Authors and international courts and tribunals have actively promoted cooperation, including agreements on permissible activities.[11] However, whatever the merits for claimant States to conclude a cooperative arrangement may be, international law only requires States to make serious efforts to this end.[12] But even if States are willing to negotiate on cooperative arrangements, their successful conclusion is often a far from straightforward exercise.[13] They may also be unwilling to cooperate with each other in the period prior to delimitation, for instance, due to historically troublesome bilateral relations. For example, Myanmar and Bangladesh, in disputed parts of the Bay of Bengal, were unwilling to cooperate in relation to mineral resources, and decided to await delimitation before starting with their development.[14] Hence, a significant number of disputed maritime areas will inevitably be left ungoverned by cooperative arrangements; and regularly there is little reason for optimism that such arrangements will be successfully created in the future. Agreed cooperative arrangements are also often not all-inclusive, meaning that conflicts can still arise in bilateral relations, independent of the setting up of these arrangements.

Varying degrees of conflict between claimant State can occur when one of the States concerned undertakes an act falling under the authority of the coastal State in relation to their disputed area, without the prior consent of the other claimant(s).[15] Conflicts created in bilateral relations, because of States acting unilaterally with regard to a disputed maritime area, by authorising or undertaking acts that are under a coastal State's authority, are not a recent phenomenon. Their appearance is linked to States starting to claim larger areas of maritime space adjacent to their coasts.[16] Disputes can, for example, arise if a claimant State authorises fishing, seismic work, drilling, or marine scientific research (MSR). In addition, disputes can be created if a State enforces its national legislation in a disputed maritime area; if it

10 K Highet, 'Maritime Boundary Disputes and Settlement' in M Kusuma-Atmadja et al. (eds.), *Sustainable Development and Preservation of the Oceans: The Challenges of UNCLOS and Agenda 21* (LOSI, 1997) 745, 746.

11 *Guyana* v. *Suriname* (n. 7) 130 [460]; Arbitral Award of 31 July 1989 *(Guinea-Bissau* v. *Senegal)* (Provisional Measures) [1990] ICJ Rep 64.

12 Chapter 5, Section 5.3.3 below.

13 M Hayashi, 'The 2008 Japan–China Agreement on Cooperation for the Development of East China Sea Resources' in MH Nordquist and JN Moore (eds.), *Maritime Border Diplomacy* (Martinus Nijhoff, 2012) 35, 36.

14 Chapter 8, Section 8.1.3 below.

15 IMA Arsana, 'Mending the Imaginary Wall between Indonesia and Malaysia: The Case of Maritime Delimitation in the Waters off Tanjung Berakit' (2011) 13(1) *Wacana* 1, 15.

16 MT Kamminga, 'Building "Railroads on the Sea": China's Attitude towards Maritime Law' (1974) 59 *China Quarterly* 544, 553–554.

takes certain unilateral measures in relation to the marine environment; or if it licenses acts that fall under coastal State authority to be undertaken by a third State, most often its nationals, within a disputed area.[17]

If one of the claimant States concerned decides to authorise an act that falls within the authority of the coastal State in relation to a disputed area, such a unilateral act will usually trigger an act of unilateralism in response. Providing some reaction may sometimes be necessary for a State to protect its claims, or to avoid accusations of having acquiesced in the other State's claim over a maritime area.[18] A variety of responses, which by their nature are unilateral acts as well, can be identified, ranging from a diplomatic protest to law enforcement.[19]

Generally, unilateral actions that are catalysts for conflict between claimants are related to exploring for, or exploiting, mineral resources or fisheries in disputed territorial sea, EEZ, or continental shelf areas.[20] Once incidents caused by unilaterally authorising or undertaking acts that are under a coastal State's authority have unfolded, it often follows that States reassert their claims to maritime zones. Although these incidents are most often in the form of an action followed by a reaction, and a new need to respond is created by a new unilateral action, an incident can also set in motion a more vicious action–reaction cycle that can only be broken if one of the States concerned abandons this unilateral practice.[21]

That a single act of unilateralism can breed new ones, combined with an overall deterioration of bilateral relations, is confirmed by the following example: after Guyana allowed an oil rig to be placed within a disputed maritime area, with the aim of commencing with exploratory drilling, Suriname put a halt to this conduct by sending its naval vessels. Both States contended that the other had acted in contravention of international law, including the obligations included in Articles 74(3) and 83(3) of the 1982 United Nations Convention on the Law of the Sea (LOSC or the Convention),[22] during

[17] Chapter 2, Section 2.3 below.

[18] DH Anderson and Y van Logchem, 'Rights and Obligations in Areas of Overlapping Maritime Claims' in S Jayakumar et al. (eds.), *The South China Sea Disputes and Law of the Sea* (Edward Elgar, 2014) 192, 210.

[19] CH Schofield, 'Blurring the Lines: Maritime Joint Development and the Cooperative Management of Ocean Resources' (2009) 8(1) *ILS* 1, 4; Y van Logchem, 'Lawful Responses to Unilateral Activities in Maritime Areas of Overlapping EEZ or Continental Shelf Claims' Paper Presented at KIOST-Columbia Joint Project on East Asian Ocean Law and Policy: Coastal State Jurisdiction & Law Enforcement: From Sovereign Rights to Disputed Zones, 12–13 November 2020 (on file with author), 1.

[20] Chapter 8 below.

[21] Y van Logchem, 'The Scope for Unilateralism in Disputed Maritime Areas' in CH Schofield et al. (eds.), *The Limits of Maritime Jurisdiction* (Martinus Nijhoff, 2014) 175.

[22] United Nations Convention on the Law of the Sea, 1833 UNTS 3.

the incident.[23] A similar sequence of events arose in the Bay of Bengal between Bangladesh and India after the CGG *Symphony*, operated by a company incorporated in a third State (Australia) and licensed by India, started seismic work unilaterally in disputed waters off South Talpatty/New Moore Island. Subsequently, the seismic vessel was forced to put a stop to its planned operation by Bangladesh. Thereafter, a diplomatic controversy arose between Bangladesh and India.[24]

1.1 OBJECTIVES

As there are many disputed maritime areas, some of which are long-standing, of great complexity,[25] and regularly ignite conflicts,[26] addressing the issue of the rights and obligations of States prior to delimitation is both pressing and topical. Such an analysis is even timelier considering that, in certain disputed maritime areas, States are increasing their level of unilateral activity, by frequently authorising or undertaking acts that are under coastal State authority.[27] Predictions have been made that, because of certain States taking such acts unilaterally, they are on a trajectory towards armed conflict.[28]

The central aim of this book is to lay out, from the perspective of international law, the rights and obligations of States (i.e. claimants and third States) in disputed maritime areas, that is areas that have not been delimited. A particular emphasis is placed on areas in which States have not been able to agree on cooperative arrangements, and where a modus vivendi has not been developed to regulate activities that are undertaken in a disputed maritime area. In terms of terminology, a 'disputed maritime area'[29] includes those areas in relation to which neighbouring States have advanced overlapping claims,

23 *Guyana* v. *Suriname* (n. 7).

24 'Indian Ships Leave Bangladeshi "Territorial Waters"', *BBC Monitoring South Asia – Political*, 28 December 2008; J Bissinger, 'The Maritime Boundary Dispute between Bangladesh and Myanmar: Motivations, Potential Solutions, and Implications' (2010) 10 *Asia Policy* 103, 109.

25 V Becker-Weinberg, *Joint Development of Hydrocarbon Deposits in the Law of the Sea* (Springer, 2014) 93.

26 J Gao, 'Joint Development in the East China Sea: Not an Easier Challenge than Delimitation' (2008) 23(1) *IJMCL* 39, 41, 75.

27 YH Song, 'The Potential Marine Pollution Threat from Oil and Gas Development Activities in the Disputed South China Sea/Spratly Area: A Role That Taiwan Can Play' (2008) 39(2) *ODIL* 150, 151.

28 Chapter 3, Section 3.1 below.

29 Y van Logchem, *Disputed Maritime Areas: The Rights and Obligations of States under International Law* (PhD Thesis, Faculty of Law, Utrecht University, 2018) 5–6.

be it concerning the territorial sea, contiguous zone, EEZ, (extended) continental shelf, or a combination thereof.

Competing claims to jurisdiction, sovereign rights, or sovereignty of coastal States, carrying with them a right to be acted upon, are at the root of problems being possibly created in bilateral relations if one of the coastal States concerned acts unilaterally in relation to a disputed maritime area. Despite the negative reaction that a unilateral act falling under the authority of the coastal State can prompt from another claimant, a crucial question logically precedes this: is this unilateral act of a claimant State, against which the response is formulated, lawful from the perspective of international law? However, if shown to be unlawful under international law, another question automatically follows: how can a claimant that is faced with the unlawful unilateral act respond lawfully thereto? This book will also assess the legal parameters for responding to the other State's unilateral conduct, or that of its nationals, in disputed maritime areas. A State can react, amongst others, through law enforcement, issuing a diplomatic protest or take the matter to international adjudication. Apart from that, because entitlements to maritime zones come with related obligations for coastal States regarding certain issues, they may also be obligated to take certain (unilateral) measures in disputed areas. For instance, as regards fisheries conservation, as well as protecting the marine environment generally, coastal States have several obligations under the LOSC, which will apply, at first glance, with equal force in disputed maritime areas.[30]

A remark about the use of terminology concerning 'unilateralism' is necessary. Unilateral acts, activities, or actions are broadly interpreted in this book, as encompassing both those acts by States that are rights based and those that are born out of an obligation under international law. More specifically, these include any unilateral steps relating to the development of mineral resources, be it concessioning or conducting a seismic survey, exploratory drilling, or exploitation; fisheries; MSR; navigational issues; laying and maintaining submarine cables and pipelines; measures taken to protect the marine environment; proclaiming national legislation pertaining to a disputed area; but also law enforcement measures; or other responses (e.g. diplomatic demarches) that can be formulated in the event of a claimant being faced with a unilateral act that is under the authority of the coastal State.[31]

Also, the word 'unilateralism', or a variant thereof, including 'acting unilaterally', will be generally employed in a more neutral sense here, in that it

[30] Chapter 2, Sections 2.3.3 and 2.3.5 below.
[31] Van Logchem (n. 19) 3, 9–10.

signifies activities that fall under the authority of the coastal State, and are undertaken without the consent of (all) claimant coastal States. More specifically, 'unilateralism' has different referents in the context of States undertaking acts unilaterally within disputed maritime areas: it can refer to taking certain actions by a claimant State or a third State, but most often one of its nationals will act, without having obtained the prior consent of the other State claiming the same maritime area. In a broad sense, acts by a claimant State or a third State that are not under the authority of the coastal State can be lawfully undertaken in a disputed maritime area under international law.[32] Most acts that are placed under the authority of the coastal State, conversely, cannot be lawfully undertaken without the prior consent of the coastal State(s). Defining acts of unilateralism as not being inherently problematic is moreover appropriate considering that international law sometimes requires States to act regarding a disputed maritime area.[33]

A more 'positive' connection between conducting an activity that falls under the authority of the coastal State unilaterally[34] and the subsequent materialisation of a willingness to address the maritime boundary dispute temporarily or conclusively has been established as well.[35] Yet, there is no general causality between conducting such an act unilaterally and the successful conclusion of a delimitation agreement, submitting a dispute to third-party dispute settlement, or concluding cooperative arrangements. More often, the opposite is true, in that agreeing on maritime delimitation or a cooperative arrangement will be made more difficult; this, in turn, may indicate a breach of international law.[36]

The jurisdictional uncertainty, which is inherent in disputed maritime areas, also affects third States, and their nationals, which leads to two questions. First, how must the nationals of third States proceed according to international law when they want to conduct activities, that fall under the authority of the coastal State, in disputed maritime areas? Second, what are the obligations that third States and their nationals have concerning such areas? Conducting activities in the framework of MSR, laying and maintaining submarine cables and pipelines, applying for concessions for mineral resource exploration, or fishing, all offer examples of activities in relation to which

32 Chapter 2, Section 2.4 below.

33 Anderson and Van Logchem (n. 18) 210.

34 'Attorney: Expect More Maritime Disputes with Deep Offshore E&P', *Natural Gas Week*, 2 November 2009.

35 TL McDorman, 'Extended Jurisdiction and Ocean Resource Conflict in the Indian Ocean' (1988) 3(3) *IJECL* 208, 217.

36 Chapter 9, Sections 9.1–9.2 below.

difficulties may be encountered by third States and private actors if these are undertaken in disputed maritime areas. Here a general division is made between activities that fall under the authority of a coastal State (e.g. activities in relation to mineral resources) and those that do not (e.g. navigation, to some extent). A relevant aspect is that the scope that remains for third States, or their nationals, to act in a disputed area, varies with the maritime zone involved, because of various degrees of authority over activities being attributed to the coastal State.

Ideally, international law provides clear obligations and rules for States (both claimant and third States) regarding disputed maritime areas. Closely aligned to this is that ideally there would be clear rules on when a claimant can enforce its laws and regulations in relation to other States in disputed areas.[37] Does the current state of international law live up to these ideals, in that it provides a clear answer to what rights *can*, and which obligations *must*, be exercised by States in relation to disputed maritime areas?[38]

In terms of the methodology used in this book, it has predominantly involved desktop research of traditional international legal sources, for example treaty law, case law, and literature. Relevant state practice, mainly in the form of incidents that have occurred in disputed maritime areas, has been analysed to develop a better understanding of the issues involved and has been used to determine whether certain customary rules exist under international law.[39] To provide the most complete picture of acts undertaken unilaterally in disputed waters, examples have been collected from two types of disputes: first, where a dispute on title to land territory underpins the disputed maritime area; and, second, where a disputed area is created by neighbouring coastal States claiming maritime zones from the baselines of mainland territory or high-tide features over which they have an undisputed title.

Collecting State practice proved difficult in respect of some activities in disputed areas, with there being little or no information in the form of actual practice publicly available. Because at times only a smaller sample could be collected, more cautious conclusions were reached regarding the (un)lawfulness of certain categories of unilateral activity which fall under the authority of the coastal State from the view of international law. In relation to certain activities, such as MSR, it can be safely assumed that these take place within disputed maritime areas. However, attempts to obtain information for this book, by trying to obtain information from State officials on unilateral MSR,

37 Van Logchem (n. 21) 192–195.

38 Chapter 9 below.

39 Chapter 8 below.

were difficult and often without result. One reason for this is that unilateral activities undertaken in the framework of MSR, or incidents following therefrom, are generally not publicised by States. Interviews with government officials to obtain a more comprehensive insight into the difficulties that are created by disputed maritime areas have been conducted. However, since they turned out to shed little light on the issue at hand, the results thereof have only been rarely used in the writing of this book.

The visibility and the amount of publicly available State practice vary with the type of unilateral activity that falls under coastal State authority involved. More specifically, three aspects are relevant. First, the regularity with which conflicts have arisen between claimant States over a category of unilateral activity. Second, the likeliness of incidents coming to light is influenced by the sensitivity of a particular act: the more sensitive an act is – that is the more severely it affects the other claimant's rights, position, or interests – the greater the risk of prompting its reaction, thereby enhancing the probability of an incident being reported. Third, the amount of information that surfaces in relation to activities that are under the authority of the coastal State and are being authorised or undertaken unilaterally, will exhibit geographical variations.[40] In addition, international courts and tribunals have decided few cases in which activities unilaterally undertaken in disputed areas figured prominently. However, two categories of cases where an international court or tribunal has had to deal with the lawfulness of States acting unilaterally, in that acts which are under a coastal State's authority were authorised or undertaken, in a disputed area are: first, in the context of requests for interim measures of protection[41]; and, second, in delimitation cases.[42] Nonetheless, a significant measure of insight has been gathered from secondary sources, such as news reports and scholarly articles. However, this book, of course, does not claim to be an exhaustive reproduction of State practice in relation to disputed maritime areas.

1.2 OUTLINE

Before the rules of international law, drafted specifically with a view to disputed maritime areas, are addressed, Chapter 2 first provides the necessary background. It looks at how such areas became a common feature of the

[40] Van Logchem (n. 29) 7–8.

[41] *Aegean Sea Continental Shelf (Greece* v. *Turkey)* (Interim Measures) [1976] ICJ Rep 3; *Guinea-Bissau* v. *Senegal* (Provisional Measures) (n. 11).

[42] *Guyana* v. *Suriname* (n. 7); *Delimitation of the Maritime Boundary in the Bay of Bengal (Bangladesh/Myanmar)* [2012] ITLOS Rep 4; *Delimitation of the Maritime Boundary in the Atlantic Ocean (Ghana/Côte d'Ivoire)* (Provisional Measures) [2015] ITLOS Rep 146.

international legal landscape and the different types of disputed maritime areas that have emerged in practice. Chapter 2 also lays out in broad strokes the distinction between when a State has undisputed title over territory, which is used to claim maritime zones from its base points, and where an underlying land territory over which title is disputed is involved.[43] The latter is explored further in Chapter 7. Attention is next given to identifying the problems that can arise in bilateral relations because of the existence of disputed maritime areas, depending on whether it is an issue between claimants (or one of its nationals and the other claimant) or between a third State (or its nationals) and a claimant. At the core of difficulties experienced by these two types of States is the following: what is the range of activities that fall within the authority of the coastal State that may be undertaken (unilaterally) by States, and what are the obligations that States have, in relation to disputed maritime areas? Chapter 2 also discusses a limited range of examples from State practice. This is expanded upon later, in Chapter 8, with an emphasis on examples of where activities when undertaken within disputed areas under the licence of one claimant State, have prompted the other claimant to respond. In addition, in Chapter 2, the potential need to respond to a unilateral act, in so far as it concerns an act that is under coastal State authority, by the other claimant State is examined, as a lack of a response from a coastal State to an act that has not been licensed by it might be seen as having acquiesced in the other State's claim over the area concerned.

In Chapter 3, the general rules of international law that apply in disputed maritime areas are examined. Depending on the characteristics of the disputed maritime area involved, these general rules of international law apply either alongside the rules contained in the LOSC or sometimes in isolation. Chapter 3 also looks into whether unilateral acts which are under coastal State authority, that have been undertaken in disputed maritime areas, can become entwined with threats to international peace and security; such claims have been made by certain States, some of which approached the United Nations Security Council (UNSC), seeking declarations that through such unilateral conduct in a disputed maritime area international peace and security was put in jeopardy.

Then, in Chapter 4, the international legal regime in respect of disputed territorial sea and contiguous zone areas, consisting of the legal framework as developed under the 1958 Convention on the Territorial Sea and the

43 K Kittichaisaree, *The Law of the Sea and Maritime Boundary Delimitation in South-East Asia* (Oxford University Press, 1987) 140.

Contiguous Zone (1958 CTS),[44] as well as the LOSC, are assessed. The primary focus is on whether an interim rule seeking to govern the conduct of States pending territorial sea or contiguous zone delimitation can be deduced from the relevant provisions that are contained in these two treaties.

At the heart of Chapter 5 is the most frequently occurring category of disputed maritime areas: that is, where the claims of coastal States to the same EEZ or continental shelf area overlap. Discussing these two types of overlapping claims simultaneously follows their development at the Third United Nations Conference on the Law of the Sea (UNCLOS III), resulting in the identical delimitation provisions that were ultimately included in the LOSC; that is Articles 74 and 83. This Chapter 5 analyses the international treaty law regimes that are applicable to disputed EEZ areas (i.e. the LOSC) and continental shelf areas (i.e. the 1958 Convention on the Continental Shelf (1958 CSC) and the LOSC).

Chapter 6 reviews the available case law of international courts and tribunals that is relevant for the question of the rights and obligations of States in disputed maritime areas. It begins with two cases covering issues related to unilaterally conducting activities that are under coastal State jurisdiction in disputed areas, and which involved requests for interim protection decided by the International Court of Justice (ICJ or the Court) prior to the entry into force of the LOSC: *Aegean Sea Continental Shelf* (Interim Measures) and *Guinea-Bissau* v. *Senegal* (Provisional Measures).[45] Next, the relevant case law from the period after the entry into force of the LOSC is examined. Special emphasis is placed on the *Guyana* v. *Suriname* case, which was decided by an Arbitral Tribunal established pursuant to Annex VII LOSC. In addition to this case, one International Tribunal for the Law of the Sea (ITLOS) case, that is *Ghana/Côte d'Ivoire*,[46] and one ICJ case, that is *Somalia* v. *Kenya*,[47] are discussed to the extent that they touch on the issue of the rights and obligations of States in disputed maritime areas. Those cases involving requests for measures of interim protection are then analysed to determine their general relevance for clarifying the obligations that States have in respect of disputed EEZ and continental shelf areas.

[44] Convention on the Territorial Sea and the Contiguous Zone, Geneva, 29 April 1958, in force 10 September 1964, 516 UNTS 205 (1958 CTS).

[45] *Guinea-Bissau* v. *Senegal* (Provisional Measures) (n. 11); *Aegean Sea Continental Shelf* (Interim Measures) (n. 41).

[46] *Ghana/Côte d'Ivoire* (Provisional Measures) (n. 42); *Dispute concerning Delimitation of the Maritime Boundary between Ghana and Côte d'Ivoire in the Atlantic Ocean (Ghana/Côte d'Ivoire)* (Judgment) [2017] ITLOS Rep 4.

[47] *Maritime Delimitation in the Indian Ocean (Somalia* v. *Kenya).*

At the core of Chapter 7 lie mixed disputes, referring to the situation where two States have made competing claims to title over the same high-tide feature or mainland territory, and use the same base points to make claims to maritime zones, whereby disputed maritime areas are created in the process. The chapter seeks to shed light on the issue of what the rights and obligations of claimants are in disputed waters located off disputed land territory.

Chapter 8 focuses on State practice, with an emphasis on acts that are under the authority of the coastal State being undertaken unilaterally by States in disputed maritime areas, due to which a conflict has arisen in bilateral relations. A disclaimer is in order here. Differences arise in two ways when analysing State practice: first, the aggregate of State practice is not always that extensive; and, second, the amount of information available in relation to particular categories of acts is uneven.[48] The chapter is structured along the lines of several different types of activities which fall under the authority of the coastal State that are conducted in disputed areas: that is, activities related to mineral resources, fisheries, and data gathering.

The final chapter, Chapter 9, adopts a bird's eye view perspective on the issue of rights and obligations of States in disputed maritime areas. At the core of this chapter lies the issue of whether the applicable international law is sufficiently precise. Connected to this, it assesses the extent to which rights and obligations can be uniformly defined along the full spectrum of disputed maritime areas. It concludes that, rather, a differential is involved, changing and tailoring the extent of these rights and obligations to match the disputed area in question. Finally, it will be discussed whether international law contributes to conflicts between claimant States, or between a third State, or its nationals, and a claimant State in respect of a disputed maritime area, or whether it prevents this. If not, who is at fault, the international legal framework or States that do not act in accordance therewith?

48 Section 1.1 above.

2

Disputed Maritime Areas: Setting the Scene

Disputed maritime areas are many and are not exclusively concentrated in certain parts of the world.[49] In comparing different continents, significant variations are revealed concerning the number of such areas that remain unresolved. For instance, in (South East and East) Asia and Africa[50] more disputed maritime areas remain than in Europe or South America.[51] In a further comparison, disputed EEZ and continental shelf areas are more voluminous than disputed territorial sea areas.[52]

Northeast Asia is an example of a region that has a high density of disputed maritime areas,[53] some of which are underpinned by a dispute on title to territory. None of the coastal States of the region (i.e. China, Japan, North Korea, the Russian Federation, Taiwan – not generally accepted to be a State – and South Korea) can claim full entitlements to maritime zones, as allowed for under the LOSC, without creating an overlap of its claims with a neighbour. Due to their inability to agree on delimitation, or, alternatively, on cooperative arrangements, conflicts over unilateral activities related to mineral resources, fisheries, or MSR have intermittently flared up between these coastal States.[54]

49 HM Al Baharna, 'Legal Implications of Maritime Boundary Disputes (with Special Reference to the Gulf)' (1994) 1(1) *YIMEL* 68, 70.

50 'Protracted Boundary Disputes Delay Africa Oil Searches' (2000) 15(3) *Hart's Africa Oil and Gas* 1.

51 R van de Poll and CH Schofield, 'A Seabed Scramble: A Global Overview of Extended Continental Shelf Submissions' Conference Paper, Contentious Issues in UNCLOS – Surely Not?, Monaco, 25–27 October 2010 (on file with author).

52 Y van Logchem, 'Exploration and Exploitation of Oil and Gas Resources in Maritime Areas of Overlap: The Falklands (Malvinas)' in J Vidmar and R Kok (eds.), *HYIL* (Brill, 2017) 29, 42.

53 AG Oude Elferink, *The Law of Maritime Boundary Delimitation: A Case Study of the Russian Federation* (Martinus Nijhoff, 1994) 320–322.

54 X Zhang, 'International Law in Managing Unsettled Maritime Boundaries: A Report on the Sino-Japanese Dispute over the East China Sea' in MH Nordquist and JN Moore (eds.), *Maritime Border Diplomacy* (Martinus Nijhoff, 2012) 309, 315.

The sketched situation illustrates concisely the types of issues discussed in this chapter. It is organised along three lines: first, what developments have created disputed maritime areas; second, their different variants; and, third, the legal issues that may arise from the existence of disputed maritime areas.

To begin with, this chapter will set the scene by sketching the general background to disputed maritime areas in Section 2.1. Insight is also provided into the actual number of such areas that exist globally. Then, Section 2.2 canvasses the different variants of disputed areas and the specific questions of international law that may arise, which vary with the type of disputed maritime zone involved. After completing this overview, the problems and legal issues presented for claimant coastal States and third States by disputed maritime areas will be addressed in Sections 2.3 and 2.4. Two central themes are apparent for them: for claimant States, the *extent* to which rights can, and obligations have to, be exercised; and, for third States, or their nationals, *how* to exercise rights that may have been obtained from one claimant State, and what obligations they must observe when acting, or seeking to act, by acting on rights and freedoms directly attributed to them under international law, in a disputed area. Issues may arise across the full range of activities that fall under the authority of the coastal State when these are undertaken, or are planned to be undertaken, within disputed maritime areas with the approval from one claimant State: that is, inter alia, concerning energy resources, placing installations, fisheries, and marine data collection. Section 2.3.6 examines the potential need to respond to such unilateral acts which are all, to varying degrees, under the authority of the coastal State, by the other claimant State. Section 2.5 concludes setting the scene for what follows, highlighting some of the main issues that arise from States having disputed maritime areas.

2.1 SKETCHING THE BACKGROUND

Under the early law of the sea, which applied until the mid-twentieth century, coastal States could exercise sovereignty over the territorial sea; regularly, although State practice was not uniform, this sovereignty would extend to the 3 nm limit.[55] Because, at the time,[56] the entitlements of coastal States to the territorial sea overlapped only incidentally, conflicts between

[55] V Prescott and CH Schofield, *The Maritime Political Boundaries of the World* (Martinus Nijhoff, 2005) 9; Churchill and Lowe (n. 1) 77–78.

[56] PC Irwin, 'Settlement of Maritime Boundary Disputes: An Analysis of the Law of the Sea Negotiations' (1980) 8(2) *ODIL* 105, 106.

neighbouring States over unilateral conduct in disputed maritime areas arose more rarely than was later the case as the limits of coastal State authority expanded. Issues involving conducting unilateral activities that are under coastal State authority in such areas were completely absent from the case law of international courts and tribunals for quite some time, only to first emerge in the *Aegean Sea Continental Shelf* (Interim Measures) case in the 1970s.[57] In legal writings of the time, equally little if anything was said on the issue of the rights and obligations of States in disputed maritime areas. Neither was this issue addressed in a way as it is now in treaty law, amongst others, in relation to disputed EEZ or continental shelf areas by virtue of Articles 74(3) and 83(3) LOSC.[58]

The expansion of the limits of coastal State sovereignty, sovereign rights, and/or jurisdiction that took place in the second half of the twentieth century led to a sharp increase in the number of disputed maritime areas.[59] Estimates of the number of such areas remaining in the international landscape, being usually confined to the 200 nm limit, vary, ranging from 100[60] to somewhere around 250.[61] Once States that have only enacted legislation claiming that they have an EEZ or a continental shelf extending to a maximum of 200 nm,[62] or that their territorial sea extends to the 12 nm limit, give an account of the extent of their claims, the actual number of disputed maritime areas can change, however. In addition, the fact that high-tide features may be entitled to maritime zones up to 200 nm,[63] or even beyond that, has contributed to a heightened interest amongst States in establishing title over such features. This concurrently motivated some States to reinforce their claims to title over high-tide features, whereby also new life was breathed into disputes lying dormant for years.[64] Their future settlement, in combination with the fact that these features might be fully entitled islands, provides an additional category of situations that can create new instances of areas of

57 *Aegean Sea Continental Shelf* (Interim Measures) (n. 41).

58 Chapter 5, Section 5.3 below.

59 Prescott and Schofield (n. 55) 217.

60 'Oceans and the Law of the Sea: Report of the Secretary-General', UN General Assembly 65th session, UN Doc. A/56/58 (9 March 2001) [42].

61 Prescott and Schofield (n. 55) 217, 245; J Donaldson and A Williams, 'Understanding Maritime Jurisdictional Disputes: The East ChinaSea and Beyond' (2005) 59(1) *JIA* 135, 141.

62 I Papanicolopulu, 'Some Thoughts on the Extension of Existing Boundaries' in R Lagoni and D Vignes (eds.), *Maritime Delimitation* (Brill, 2006) 223, 228–229.

63 Article 121(2) LOSC.

64 CH Park, 'The Sino-Japanese-Korean Resources Controversy and the Hypothesis of a 200-Mile Economic Zone' (1975) 16 *HILJ* 27, 42.

overlapping maritime claims.[65] Climate change may also create new maritime boundary disputes or exacerbate those that currently exist.[66] In this vein, receding ice cover in the Beaufort Sea, which is disputed between Canada and the United States, has functioned as a lure for commencing commercial activities, creating problems in their own right.[67]

In about half of the around 400 cases where a maritime boundary can be determined, within 200 nm that is, the States concerned have been able to come to delimitation,[68] many of which were settled without memorable difficulties.[69] A significant portion of the overlapping maritime claims that have yet to be resolved fall within the category of 'friendly overlapping claims', however.[70] This means that calm will often prevail between the States concerned, because they will refrain from engaging in activities that fall under the authority of the coastal State unilaterally,[71] or only engage in conduct that fails to alarm the other claimant,[72] or that minor differences have arisen between them, which were easily resolved through diplomacy.

Historically, however, certain disputed maritime areas have proved to be extremely complex and sensitive matters; this includes those in the East China Sea, the South China Sea, the Eastern Mediterranean Sea, and the Aegean Sea. These maritime boundary disputes are likely to remain, at least in the near future, as progress in the direction of settling these conclusively, or to shelve the delimitation issue temporarily by entering into cooperative arrangements, has been minimal or even non-existent.[73] Three reasons for this lack of progress are that the States concerned have remained firmly entrenched in their own positions as to where the boundary should lie, that they remain convinced that the area exclusively belongs to them, or that there are

65 T Davenport et al., 'Conference Report' Conference on Joint Development and the South China Sea, Organised by the Centre for International Law, National University of Singapore, 16–17 June 2011, 11.

66 'Climatic Change as a Security Issue', *The Straits Times*, 21 April 2007; J Lusthaus, 'Shifting Sands: Sea Level Rise, Maritime Boundaries and Inter-State Conflict' (2010) 30(2) *Politics* 113, 114–117.

67 Chapter 8, Section 8.1.5 below.

68 JW Donaldson, 'Oil and Water: Assessing the Link between Maritime Boundary Delimitation and Hydrocarbon Resources' in CH Schofield et al. (eds.), *The Limits of Maritime Jurisdiction* (Martinus Nijhoff, 2014) 127, 134.

69 TA Mensah, 'Joint Development Zones as an Alternative Dispute Settlement Approach in Boundary Delimitation' in R Lagoni and D Vignes (eds.), *Maritime Delimitation* (Martinus Nijhoff, 2006) 143, 145.

70 Anderson (n. 6) 7.

71 T Davenport, 'Southeast Asian Approaches to Maritime Boundaries' (2014) 4(2) *AsJIL* 309, 314.

72 Prescott and Schofield (n. 55) 344.

73 CH Schofield, 'Parting the Waves: Claims to Maritime Jurisdiction and the Division of Ocean Space' (2012) 1(1) *PSJLIA* 40, 45.

underlying disputes on title to territory. Complicating matters further is that the States involved in these complex maritime boundary disputes have regularly exhibited a tendency to unilaterally undertake acts that are within a coastal State's authority.

The exact dimension of a disputed maritime area within the 200 nm limit can be sometimes fraught with difficulty, however (e.g. when only one State has formulated its position on the maritime boundary or when the other claimant views a claim as being excessive). When States are located adjacent or opposite to each other within a distance of 24 or 400 nm measured from the relevant baselines, somewhere within this distance their entitlements to maritime zones overlap. However, the area of overlapping claims or disputed area will remain unclear in the absence of a further definition as to the extent of their claims by the States themselves. Determining with precision the dimension of the areas of overlapping claims in the South China Sea remains complicated because of China refraining from properly defining its claims.[74] If States' positions on where the maritime boundary lies have been made clear, but differ, a comparing of these lines on a map will show concurrently the parts that are subject to their overlapping claims and, at the same time, will shed light on the disputed maritime area; this is the area falling between the boundaries indicated by the States concerned.[75]

Difficulties may also emerge in distinguishing whether the area where claimants (seek to) act is part of a disputed territorial sea area (where there are overlapping sovereignty claims) or a disputed EEZ/continental shelf area (where there are overlapping sovereign rights and jurisdictions).[76] For example, it might be challenging to distinguish between acts constituting piracy or armed robbery at sea, due to it being unclear whether that part of the ocean where the offence was committed is a disputed territorial sea or EEZ area.[77] However, in practice this will often concern smaller sea areas.

Combating terrorism can also be more challenging whenever such acts occur in disputed maritime areas; however, the need for it to be repressed has

74 'Alarm Bells over South China Claims', *The Straits Times*, 30 August 2011.

75 SD Murphy, 'Obligations of States in Disputed Areas of the Continental Shelf' in T Heidar (ed.), *New Knowledge and Changing Circumstances in the Law of the Sea* (Brill, 2020) 183, 185–187.

76 DR Rothwell, 'Maritime Regulation and Enforcement: The Legal Framework for the South China Sea' in TT Thuy and LT Trang (eds.), *Power, Law, and Maritime Order in the South China Sea* (Lexington, 2015) 197, 210.

77 CH Schofield and KD Ali, 'Combating Piracy and Armed Robbery at Sea: From Somalia to the Gulf of Guinea' in R Warner and S Kaye (eds.), *Routledge Handbook of Maritime Regulation and Enforcement* (Routledge, 2016) 277, 285.

fuelled individual claimants to taking action.[78] Also, claimants have been increasingly willing to act unilaterally to prevent the use of disputed maritime areas as routes for illegal immigration, thus avoiding these areas becoming havens for committing illicit acts.[79]

Closely connected to the arising of disputed maritime areas is the general possibility of conflict emerging between claimants being enhanced as well: that is, when activities that fall within a coastal State's authority are undertaken unilaterally in such areas. This possibility is further exacerbated by the fact that such areas have become more intimately connected to the core interests of coastal States.[80] Practices exist in certain disputed areas, for example, in the South China Sea and the Mediterranean Sea where coastal States – irrespective of having a long history of conflict as a result of their unilateral actions – are increasing their level of unilateral activity, in that acts that are under coastal State authority are authorised or undertaken with greater regularity.[81]

2.2 LEGAL BASES FOR A CLAIM OVER A MARITIME AREA BY A STATE

Usually, disputed maritime areas will emerge in one of two situations – either when States claim maritime zones in a sea area separating the coasts of opposite States that is less than twice the width of the maximum entitlements they enjoy to maritime zones or when States are located adjacent to each other. Overlapping claims of States can arise: (1) between their mainland coasts; (2) between the coasts of different high-tide features; and (3) between a high-tide feature and a mainland coast.[82]

Two categories of legal bases for a claim over a maritime area by a State, subsequently resulting in overlapping claims whereby a disputed maritime

78 VL Forbes, *Indonesia's Maritime Boundaries* (MIMA, 1995) 37; D Rosenberg, 'The Rise of China: Implications for Security Flashpoints and Resource Politics' in CW Pumphrey (ed.), *The Rise of China in Asia: Security Implications* (SSI, 2002) 229, 247–248.

79 FX Bonnet, *Geopolitics of Scarborough Shoal* (Irasec's Discussion Papers, 2012) 19–20; 'St Kitts – Nevis Forms Maritime Boundary Dispute Committee', *CUOPM*, 24 February 2011.

80 E Milano and I Papanicolopulu, 'State Responsibility in Disputed Areas on Land and at Sea' (2011) 71(3) *ZaöRV* 587, 591.

81 G Xue, 'Deep Danger: Intensified Competition in the South China Sea and Implications for China' (2011–2012) 17(2) *OCLJ* 307, 320; CH Schofield and I Townsend-Gault, 'Brokering Cooperation Amidst Competing Maritime Claims: Preventative Diplomacy in the Gulf of Thailand and South China Sea' in A Chircop et al. (eds.), *The Future of Ocean Regime Building: Essays in Tribute to Douglas M. Johnston* (Martinus Nijhoff, 2009) 643, 664–665.

82 D Ortolland and J-P Pirat, *Atlas Géopolitique des Espaces Maritimes: Frontieres, Energie, Transports, Piraterie, Peche et Environment* (Editions Technip, 2010) 66.

area is created, can be distinguished.[83] First, and this is the most common category, where an overlap is the result of adjacent or opposite States claiming maritime zones from the baselines of mainland territory or high-tide features over which they have undisputed title. Second, where an unresolved dispute on title to territory lies at the heart of a disputed maritime area being created (i.e. 'mixed disputes').

In about 22 per cent of cases, a disputed maritime area is underpinned by a dispute on title to territory.[84] Then, the overlap of claims is caused by States claiming title over the same mainland territory or high-tide feature, and sovereignty, sovereign rights and/or jurisdiction over their related maritime zones.[85] Abu Musa Island (Iran and the United Arab Emirates);[86] Dokdo/Takeshima (South Korea and Japan); and Mayotte Island (Comoros and France) are examples of situations where disputes on title to territory and disputed waters concurrently exist.[87] Mixed disputes are layered: the primary focus in such a situation will be on which State has title over the mainland territory or high-tide feature, then moving on to the subsidiary issue of the delimitation of the disputed waters adjacent to the land territory. Due to these specificities, questions do arise around the applicability of the LOSC to the disputed waters created as a result, and prior to resolving the dispute on title to territory.[88]

Different variants have emerged in practice where there are overlapping claims to maritime zones by States *simpliciter*. First, adjacent States may have overlapping claims to internal waters. An example thereof is that Myanmar and Thailand have yet to delimit their internal waters off the coast of the Thai province of Ranong and the Myanmar coast.[89] Fishing activities within these disputed internal waters have been a source of conflict between Myanmar and Thailand.[90]

83 Van Logchem (n. 52) 38–40.

84 Prescott and Schofield (n. 55) 246.

85 H Nasu and DR Rothwell, 'Re-Evaluating the Role of International Law in Territorial and Maritime Disputes in East Asia' (2014) 4(1) *AsJIL* 55, 73–74.

86 D Momtaz, 'La Délimitation Du Plateau Continental Du Golfe Persique: Une Entreprise Inachevée' in L del Castillo (ed.), *Law of the Sea, From Grotius to the International Tribunal for the Law of the Sea: Liber Amicorum Judge Hugo Caminos* (Brill, 2015) 685, 686–688.

87 Ortolland and Pirat (n. 82) 117.

88 Chapter 7, Section 7.1 below.

89 MA Myoe, 'Myanmar's Maritime Challenges and Priorities' in JH Ho and S Bateman (eds.), *Maritime Challenges and Priorities in Asia: Implications for Regional Security* (Routledge, 2012) 83, 90.

90 'Maritime Dispute – Burma Wants to Hold Talks on Ranong Naval Clash', *Bangkok Post*, 15 January 1999.

Second, States that are adjacent will have overlapping claims over the territorial sea because the land boundary terminates on the coast. Also, States that are located opposite and less than 24 nm apart may have overlapping claims to the territorial sea. There are several examples of disputed territorial sea areas, including the Beaufort Sea, where the claims of the United States and Canada overlap; the Aegean Sea involving Greece and Turkey;[91] and the Bay of Kotor, where overlapping territorial sea claims have been made by Croatia and Montenegro.[92]

Third, if the distance between the opposite coasts of two States is less than 48 nm, or where the coasts are adjacent, a concurrent need *may* arise to delimit the overlapping territorial sea and contiguous zone claims of neighbouring coastal States: that is, delimiting disputed contiguous zone areas *simpliciter*, or, alternatively, if the other State does not claim a contiguous zone, to an EEZ.

Fourth, if the distance between the relevant baselines of opposite States is less than 400 nm, there might be disputed EEZ as well as continental shelf areas. There are currently around 200 areas in relation to which States have made overlapping claims to EEZ areas (sometimes to fishery zones) or to continental shelf areas.[93]

Fifth, overlapping extended continental shelf areas can occur as well; that is, beyond the 200 nm limit. As regards disputed extended continental shelf areas, the provision in Articles 74(3) and 83(3) LOSC should apply with equal force. This is because the extended continental shelf is part of the continental shelf of the coastal State, and in relation to which the same delimitation rule provided in paragraph 1 of these provisions is relevant.

Sixth, overlapping claims to archipelagic waters may exist, but these only seem to be possible when there is an underlying dispute on title to land territory.

In a variation on the theme, disputed maritime areas can also be located in enclosed or semi-enclosed seas. Two examples of seas that are currently still largely disputed, and that meet the classification of a semi-enclosed sea, are the South China Sea and the Adriatic Sea. When there is agreement on a sea having the status of an enclosed or semi-enclosed sea,[94] Article 123 LOSC

[91] T Scovazzi, *Maritime Delimitations in the Mediterranean Sea* (*Cursos Euromediterráneos Bancaja de Derecho Internacional*, Vol. VIII/IX, 2004/2005) 461–463.

[92] D Arnaut, 'Adriatic Blues: Delimiting the Former Yugoslavia's Final Frontier' in CH Schofield et al. (eds.), *The Limits of Maritime Jurisdiction* (Martinus Nijhoff, 2014) 145, 154–155.

[93] Prescott and Schofield (n. 55) 217.

[94] H Djalal, *Preventive Diplomacy in Southeast Asia: Lessons Learned* (The Habibie Center, 2003) 38–39.

carries some relevance in the context of protecting the marine environment (and with regard to MSR and, possibly, fisheries), requiring States to 'coordinate' between them when exercising their rights and obligations under the LOSC concerning these subjects.[95] This is no different in relation to disputed maritime areas that may exist in enclosed or semi-enclosed seas, as the condition for Article 123 LOSC to apply is if a State borders such a sea.

2.3 CLAIMANT STATES AND DISPUTED MARITIME AREAS

Whenever claims to maritime zones overlap, certain rights and obligations will be incumbent on the coastal States concerned. These rights and obligations are not in any way hypothetical or conditional in that their existence would be dependent on the maritime boundary having been delimited.[96] However, for claimant States there is uncertainty around two different aspects: first, the extent to which they are permitted to exercise coastal State authority in disputed areas; and, second, the (extent of the) obligations imposed on claimants, and which need to be performed in relation to such areas.[97]

Having a valid claim, that is derived from the international law of the sea, underlies the possibility for claimant coastal States to undertake or regulate activities under coastal State sovereignty or jurisdiction in a disputed maritime area.[98] However, the crux of the matter, pending delimitation, lies in the fact that there are concurrent claims to sovereignty, sovereign rights, and/or jurisdiction of coastal States in relation to the same area.[99] Equal weight must be attributed to States' entitlements and related rights; that is, as long as an international court or tribunal has not pronounced itself on their respective strengths and assuming that the claims of States to maritime zones are not excessive, meaning that these claims at a minimum rest on a prima facie basis of international law. If that is the case, a State cannot claim to have a superior entitlement compared to that of the other claimant State, which would allow it

95 N Hong, *UNCLOS and Ocean Dispute Settlement: Law and Politics in the South China Sea* (Routledge, 2012) 71, 92; K Zou, 'Managing Biodiversity Conversation in the Disputed Maritime Areas: The Case of the South China Sea' (2015) 18(1) *JIWLP* 97, 99–100.

96 JI Charney, 'The Delimitation of Ocean Boundaries' in DG Dallmeyer and L DeVorsey Jr (eds.), *Rights to Oceanic Resources* (Martinus Nijhoff, 1989) 25, 29.

97 V Prescott, *The Gulf of Thailand: Maritime Limits to Conflict and Cooperation* (MIMA, 1998) 17.

98 Becker-Weinberg (n. 25) 95–96.

99 Anderson and Van Logchem (n. 18) 198.

to regulate and manage a disputed maritime area at the expense of the State with the 'weaker' entitlement.[100]

The entitlements of two States with adjacent or opposite coasts to a continental shelf, and sovereign rights in relation thereto, are exclusive, ipso facto and ab initio. The sovereignty that a coastal State has over its territorial sea, or the sovereign rights within a claimed EEZ, similarly implies exclusivity. However, pending the final delimitation, and because of an overlap of claimed entitlements, the exact extent of the coastal States' entitlements to a territorial sea, EEZ, and continental shelf, as well as related sovereignty, sovereign rights, and/or jurisdiction, is uncertain in geographic terms. When States think along the lines of that having claimed entitlements it implies an unfettered ability to act on their rights or sovereignty, because of this exclusivity aspect, difficulties invariably emerge. For instance, conducting a unilateral act that is within the authority of the coastal State in what can be considered the disputed area by claimant A may lead to an infringement of the sovereignty, sovereign rights, and/or jurisdiction of claimant B, which will regularly provoke a reaction from the latter.

In fact, there is a certain deceptiveness in the use of the word 'exclusive' in this context: although an entitlement shapes the possibility for a coastal State to act regarding the disputed maritime area, none of the claimants has such exclusivity in the real sense of the word; pending delimitation, the exercise of authority by the coastal State shall be qualified. Nor can this element of exclusiveness be read as that no limits must be observed in the extent to which an entitlement and related sovereignty, sovereign rights, and/or jurisdiction may be used by a coastal State prior to the delimitation of a disputed maritime area. The uncertainty over the exact extent to which each coastal State's entitlement and related rights extends in geographic terms entails that the exercise of coastal State authority is qualified by rules of international law, which require coastal States to exercise restraint in relation to a disputed area. Limitations to this end will inter alia flow from the combination of Articles 74(3) and 83(3) LOSC[101] and other obligations of international law.[102] It is only after delimitation (either by way of an agreement or a judicial settlement) that the exercise of the entitlement and related sovereignty, sovereign rights, and/or jurisdiction of coastal States to maritime zones is no longer subject to limitations flowing from the requirement to exercise restraint pursuant to international law.

100 'Dispute between Vietnam and China Escalates over Competing Claims in South China Sea', *The New York Times*, 11 June 2011.

101 Chapter 5, Section 5.3 below.

102 Chapter 3, Sections 3.2–3.11 below.

This raises the question of to what extent a claimant State can 'use' or 'act upon' its claimed entitlement and related sovereignty, sovereign rights, and/or jurisdiction in a disputed maritime zone: would it be able to unilaterally authorise or undertake activities that are under coastal State authority in a disputed maritime area, regardless of there being an overlap with the other State's entitlement?

Usually, claimant States – and third States or their nationals – will (wish to) go forward with undertaking activities falling under the authority of the coastal State, or requesting or providing authorisation thereto, in the period before delimitation.[103] Some of the typical questions that may arise in the relation between claimant States are: can a claimant allow mineral resources to be explored or exploited without the prior consent of the other claimant?; can a claimant unilaterally conduct or authorise activities in the framework of MSR?; can it unilaterally allow installations, or pipelines, to be placed on the seabed that are, for instance, used for activities concerning mineral resources?; can a claimant State, when faced with a violation of its national laws and legislation that extend to a disputed maritime area, enforce these laws against the other claimant (or a third State, or its nationals) for a breach thereof?; or can a claimant unilaterally adopt protective measures concerning fisheries and the marine environment?

Practice shows, however, that, in relation to all those activities, some measure of conflict has arisen in bilateral relations because of these acts being, or authorised to be, undertaken in disputed maritime areas.[104] The following serves as an example in relation to the laying of pipelines: a plan to allow the 'Nord-stream' pipeline to pass through an area located south off the coast of the Danish island of Bornholm, as originally intended, was abandoned due to the disputed status of these waters. More specifically, Poland's strong opposition to the construction of the pipeline led to the route being adjusted so that the disputed area was avoided.[105]

As the actual usage of disputed maritime areas increased, so have conflicts between claimants over activities over which they can conjointly exercise authority as a coastal State. Because of this concurrent existence of coastal State authority, the other claimant that is faced with the unilateral conduct of a claimant State, or an act carried out under the latter's prior consent, will often feel legitimised to respond by, inter alia, enforcing its national laws and regulations against the (private) actor undertaking the activity. Such a response can set in motion a cycle of subsequent actions and reactions between claimant States, through which the maritime boundary dispute is aggravated incrementally.[106]

103 Arsana (n. 15) 15.
104 Chapter 8 below.
105 Ortolland and Pirat (n. 82) 70.
106 Van Logchem (n. 21) 175.

Most often, however, these incidents are in the form of an action followed by a reaction, and a new need to respond is created by a new unilateral action that is subject to the authority of the coastal State.[107] Were the other claimant to abstain from reacting, the acting State is likely to take the position that the former has recognised the superiority of the latter's claim. To avoid this, providing some reaction against the other State's unilateral conduct may therefore sometimes be necessary for a State; that is, to protect its claims, or to avoid accusations of having acquiesced in the other State's claim over a maritime area. For example, after announcing an intention by the other claimant to award concessions for mineral resource activity in relation to a disputed area, or when actual work on such bases is being undertaken, protesting can be warranted.[108]

A separate line of enquiry is to what extent claimants are called upon to positively take certain actions (because they have related obligations) in connection with their disputed area, as a matter of international law (of the sea) and due to possessing an entitlement to maritime zones, for instance with the aim of fisheries conservation or protecting the marine environment. The rights of coastal States to maritime zones are counterbalanced by obligations that are imposed on them pursuant to Part XII LOSC, including in relation to the marine environment. For instance, Article 192 LOSC places coastal States under a general obligation to protect the marine environment. This obligation is not conditional on a maritime area having been delimited. Looking at the language of Article 192, 'States' is mentioned in a general sense and without any further qualification. Hence, coastal States whose claims overlap over the same area are not excused from taking protective measures aimed at the marine environment of disputed areas in order to inter alia combat pollution, pursuant to Article 194 LOSC.[109]

2.3.1 *Mineral Resources*

Coastal States have sovereign rights and jurisdiction over mineral resources in the EEZ and continental shelf.[110] They also have discretionary authority with respect to the mineral resources contained in the shelf's subsoil; for instance, coastal States are allowed to postpone development, possibly indefinitely, or to

107 Ibid.

108 Anderson and Van Logchem (n. 18) 210. This view is later echoed by AHA Hsiao, 'Unilateral Actions and the Rule of Law in Maritime Boundary Disputes' (2016) 22 *AYIL* 237, 239.

109 I Townsend-Gault, 'Maritime Cooperation in a Functional Perspective' in CH Schofield (ed.), *Maritime Energy Resources in Asia: Legal Regimes and Cooperation* (NBR Special Report, 2012) 7, 10.

110 Article 76(1)(4) LOSC.

select petroleum companies to conduct work concerning these resources.[111] Except with regard to marine pollution, the factual exploitation of mineral resources from the continental shelf by the coastal State is not further circumscribed in the LOSC, leaving it to the discretion of the coastal State to decide on the methods used in this regard or the quantities that may be extracted from the seabed.[112] Implicit in this is the assumption that there is one coastal State which can inter alia exclusively authorise such activities, or engage in it itself, to the exclusion of other States. This exclusivity is reinforced in Article 77(2) LOSC, providing that mineral resources in the seabed can only be explored and exploited by the coastal State, or with its approval.

Drilling into the continental shelf is also placed under the jurisdiction of coastal States in Article 81 LOSC. Its inclusion in the Convention has led to the argument that, prior to a final delimitation, claimants must abstain from authorising exploratory or exploitation drilling in relation to a disputed continental shelf area, as well as not give concessions in respect thereto.[113] Contrary to this conclusion, Article 81 deals only with drilling during the phase of exploitation, and not with exploratory drilling. Even if its reach could be extended to cover exploratory drilling in disputed continental shelf areas as well, whether it can be upheld that such drilling breaches Article 81 LOSC depends on a particular understanding of the exclusivity aspect of the rights that coastal States possess in the continental shelf, being as follows: these rights must be completely shielded from infringement prior to delimitation, because of it being unclear to which extent a coastal State's sovereign rights reach prior to the final delimitation.[114] This is where 83(3) LOSC, particularly the obligation not to hamper or jeopardise that is contained therein, comes into play.[115]

Most of the untapped mineral resource deposits are located in disputed maritime areas, obtaining a significant relevance for coastal States as a result.[116] A few examples combining (rumours of) the presence of mineral resources in

111 S Oda, *International Control of Sea Resources* (Martinus Nijhoff, 1989) 167.

112 RR Bundy, 'Natural Resource Development (Oil and Gas) and Boundary Disputes' in GH Blake et al. (eds.), *Peaceful Management of Transboundary Resources* (Martinus Nijhoff, 1995) 23, 39.

113 V Becker-Weinberg, 'Joint Development Agreements of Offshore Hydrocarbon Deposits: An Alternative to Maritime Delimitation in the Asia-Pacific Region' (2011) 13(1) *COLR* 60, 91; H Fox et al., *Joint Development of Offshore Oil and Gas: A Model Agreement for States with Explanatory Commentary* (BIICL, 1989) 33.

114 Chapter 5, Section 5.1 below.

115 Ibid. Section 5.3.

116 CH Schofield, 'No Panacea? Challenges in the Application of Provisional Arrangements of a Practical Nature' in MH Nordquist and JN Moore (eds.), *Maritime Border Diplomacy* (Martinus Nijhoff, 2012) 151, 158.

great quantities with these resources being located in disputed areas are the East China Sea,[117] the South China Sea,[118] and the Arctic.[119] Two effects can be detected if mineral resources are present, or their presence is perceived, in a disputed maritime area: that is, either the road to delimitation or the setting up of cooperative arrangements is made easier[120] or, conversely, more difficult;[121] the latter, however, being frequently the case.

Mineral resource activity in disputed maritime areas is a matter that is often fraught with difficulties. Revenues that can be earned from offshore development,[122] accompanied by a willingness of States to engage in conduct to that end, also in disputed maritime areas, make the potential for conflict between coastal States all too clear, however.[123] Such conflict is not of recent origin, having effectively emerged ever since States started to claim vaster areas of sea adjacent to their coasts.[124] For example, unilateral conduct in relation to disputed continental shelf areas of the South China Sea already led to conflict in the 1970s.[125] However, the regularity and intensity with which conflict is created by States acting unilaterally with respect to mineral resources in disputed maritime areas might well have been lower in the past, only to be enhanced as time went on.[126]

Attracting foreign participation from the petroleum industry to engage in activity in disputed areas has sometimes become increasingly difficult as well.[127] This is despite the fact that developing partnerships with foreign oil companies has been assumed to be in the best interests of a claimant State for

[117] NA Ludwig and MJ Valencia, 'Oil and Mineral Resources of the East China Sea' (1993) 30(4) *GeoJournal* 381.

[118] G Xue, 'The South China Sea: Competing Claims' in CH Schofield et al. (eds.), *The Limits of Maritime Jurisdiction* (Martinus Nijhoff, 2014) 225, 227.

[119] United States, 'National Security Presidential Directive/NSPD – 66; Homeland Security Presidential Directive/HSPD – 25', 12 January 2009, G.2, available at www.nsf.gov/geo/plr/opp_advisory/briefings/may2009/nspd66_hspd25.pdf.

[120] MJ Valencia and M Miyoshi, 'Southeast Asian Seas: Joint Development of Hydrocarbons in Overlapping Claim Areas' (1986) 16(3) *ODIL* 211, 218.

[121] DM Ong, 'South-East Asian State Practice on the Joint Development of Offshore Oil and Gas Deposits' in GH Blake et al. (eds.), *The Peaceful Management of Transboundary Resources* (Martinus Nijhoff, 1995) 77, 78–79.

[122] Klein (n. 9) 426.

[123] JI Charney and LM Alexander (eds.), *International Maritime Boundaries*, Vol. 1 (Martinus Nijhoff, 1993) xix, xxiii.

[124] I Townsend Gault, 'Petroleum Development Offshore: Legal and Contractual Issues' in N Beredjick and T Wälde (eds.), *Petroleum Investment Policies in Developing Countries* (Kluwer, 1989) 101, 129.

[125] Kamminga (n. 16) 553–554.

[126] Milano and Papanicolopulu (n. 80) 590.

[127] L Buszynski and I Sazlan, 'Maritime Claims and Energy Cooperation in the South China Sea' (2007) 29(1) CSA 143, 166.

several reasons.[128] First, it would confer a measure of legitimacy upon a State's claim over a maritime area, if it is successful in attracting investments from the foreign petroleum industry.[129] Second, to enter into joint ventures with foreign petroleum companies is commercially attractive.[130] Third, it supplies third States with a stake in a maritime boundary dispute.[131] Securing the participation of petroleum companies incorporated in larger and more powerful States is considered particularly attractive. This is because it would protect the State authorising the unilateral conduct from the other claimant taking physical steps against these companies, due to their being incorporated in powerful third States, which are likely to offer their nationals protection when faced with such a reaction from the other claimant. Asymmetries that might exist in the technological capabilities of individual claimants to enter into activities related to mineral resources in disputed maritime areas can also be overcome by involving foreign petroleum companies, which bring their own capital as well as technology. This may explain why incidents that have arisen in such areas cross-cut any lines in terms of the wealth, size, and power of the States concerned.[132]

Whatever the positive effects of attracting foreign investments, an opposite trend is seen in certain disputed maritime areas: that is, the claimant States have become more restrained in offering and activating licences for blocks located therein.[133] The motivation behind this restraint may be to avoid a negative reaction from the other claimant. One reason to avoid this is that if a petroleum company, while operating in a disputed area, were forced to abandon its work by the other claimant, the company might try to invoke force majeure to be released from its obligations towards the licensing State.

In broad terms, two categories of unilateral conduct in connection with mineral resources in disputed maritime areas can be distinguished: granting concessions to prospect, drill, or develop these resources; and conducting actual work on these bases.[134] Their relation can be framed as that granting concessions constitutes the preparatory phase: after the activation of

128 DJ Dzurek, 'Boundary and Resources Disputes in the South China Sea' in EM Borgese and N Ginsburg (eds.), *Ocean Yearbook*, Vol. 5 (Brill, 1985) 254, 263.

129 JD Ciorciari and JC Weiss, 'The Sino-Vietnamese Standoff in the South China Sea' (2012) 13 (1) *GJIA* 61, 64.

130 Buszynski and Sazlan (n. 127) 156.

131 Ibid. 157.

132 Chapter 8, Section 8.1 below.

133 C Yiallourides, 'Oil and Gas Development in Disputed Waters under UNCLOS' (2016) 5(1) *UCLJLJ* 593, 81–85.

134 MJ Valencia, 'Asia, the Law of the Sea and International Relations' (1997) 73(2) *IA* 263, 270.

a concession, conduct in relation to mineral resources in disputed maritime areas is meant to be subsequently undertaken.[135]

As mineral resource development will progress through different phases, several different activities can be identified under this broad umbrella. Chronologically speaking, it starts with initial assessments on the plausibility that deposits of mineral resources exist, for example, by conducting a hydrographic survey, next is seismic work, and then it moves on to drilling, and ultimately the extraction of the mineral resources from the seabed through exploitation drilling. As one progresses through these stages, the marine environment will be put incrementally at risk with the acts involved causing increasing damage; however, the actual risk of damage varies with the type of activity concerned.[136]

Auctioning concession areas that are located within a disputed maritime area by a coastal State can, without taking subsequent acts on this given basis, function as a catalyst for difficulties in bilateral relations. An example is when India opened a tender process, and indicated its willingness to entertain bids from the petroleum industry for obtaining exploration rights in relation to the area in dispute with Bangladesh, the latter contested the lawfulness thereof.[137] The act of granting a concession by a coastal State signifies a claim of entitlement to the maritime area covered by it.[138] Concessions that apply to disputed waters will usually include a disclaimer informing concessionaires of the area being disputed, and the difficulties that this might possibly entail for them.[139]

There are many examples of States awarding concessions that are located in a disputed area, also regularly without subsequent disputes arising, making it a common phenomenon.[140] For instance, Liberia and Sierra Leone have awarded concessions pertaining to a disputed maritime area, and allowed data to be gathered on these bases, all without protest.[141] However, there is also significant contrary State practice, in that awarding concessions by the

135 Ibid.

136 C Morales Siddayao, 'Oil and Gas on the Continental Shelf: Potentials and Constraints in the Asia-Pacific Region' (1984) 9(1–2) *Ocean Management* 73, 95.

137 M Habibur Rahman, 'Delimitation of Maritime Boundaries: A Survey of Problems in the Bangladesh Case' (1984) 24(12) *Asian Survey* 1302, 1308.

138 *Guyana* v. *Suriname* (n. 7) Suriname's Rejoinder 84 [3.124].

139 M Waibel, 'Oil Exploration around the Falklands (Malvinas)' *EJIL: Talk! Blog*, 13 August 2012.

140 MJ Valencia, 'Joint Jurisdiction and Development in Southeast Asian Seas: Factors and Candidate Areas' (1985) 10(3–4) *Energy* 573, 576.

141 *Report on the Obligations of States under Articles 74(3) and 83(3) of UNCLOS in respect of Undelimited Maritime Areas* (BIICL, 2016) 86–87 (BIICL Report).

other State[142] prompts protests.[143] An example is that, after both Colombia and Venezuela started to give concessions to the petroleum industry concerning their disputed continental shelf area in the Gulf of Venezuela, difficulties began to mount between them.[144] The act of attributing rights to the petroleum industry in relation to a disputed continental shelf area, through granting concessions, is considered unlawful by some authors;[145] often, however, these statements are framed along normative lines, rather than focusing on the current state of international law.[146]

Two advantages follow when States refrain from taking unilateral steps enabling mineral resource exploration to be undertaken in disputed maritime areas. First, conflicts between claimants are more likely to be prevented. And, second, a coastal State's rights exclusive character will be left intact in that after delimitation, and in relation to those areas falling on its own side of the boundary, it will have complete discretion over the formulation of its energy policy, concessioning or other activities connected to mineral resources. In this vein, the policy of the United States has been not to entertain any bids that have been put in by the petroleum industry in relation to its disputed maritime areas.[147]

With regard to seismic work, the main question that arises is the following: can one State seek to clarify the potential of the mineral resources of a disputed area through conducting a seismic survey unilaterally, or by providing authorisation to that end to a private actor?[148] The uncertainty prevailing over the true extent of mineral resources in a disputed maritime area can often be traced back to the fact that all the States concerned, or one of them, consider seismic work to be unlawful.[149] For example, Myanmar and India both took the position that seismic work cannot lawfully be undertaken in their disputed

142 DJ Dzurek, 'Southeast Asian Offshore Disputes' in EM Borgese and N Ginsburg (eds.), *Ocean Yearbook*, Vol. 11 (Brill, 1994) 157, 163–164.

143 Chapter 8, Section 8.1 below.

144 LN George, 'Realism and Internationalism in the Gulf of Venezuela' (1988–1989) 30(4) *JISWA* 139, 149; V VanBuren, 'The Colombia-Venezuela Maritime Boundary Case: Proposal for a Joint Development Zone in the Gulf of Venezuela' (2006) 1 *TJOGEL* 68, 83–84.

145 U Leanza, 'The Delimitation of the Continental Shelf of the Mediterranean Sea' (1993) 8(3) *IJMCL* 373, 394.

146 VD Degan, 'The Value of the Manila Declaration on International Dispute Settlement in a Case in which the Philippines is a Party' (2012) 11(1) *CJIL* 5, 6.

147 A Roach, 'Maritime Boundary Delimitation: United States Practice' (2013) 44(1) *ODIL* 1, 5.

148 Y van Logchem, 'The Status of a Rule of Capture under International Law of the Sea with regard to Offshore Oil and Gas Resource-Related Activities' (2018) 26(2) *MSILR* 195, 232–235.

149 NA Owen and CH Schofield, 'Disputed South China Sea Hydrocarbons in Perspective' (2012) 36(3) *MP* 809.

maritime area, leaving its resource potential unclear up until after delimitation.[150]

Allowing seismic work to be undertaken unilaterally would perceivably place the claimant collecting the information in an advantageous position compared to the other State. Often, however, because seismic work leads to a more marginal interference with the other State's rights, meaning that the resulting prejudice to rights can be financially remedied *ex post facto* (that is, after delimitation), the lawfulness thereof is assumed.[151] Yet the lawfulness of the activation of a licence enabling seismic work to proceed can be questioned on the following grounds. First, it regularly ignites conflict between claimants, ranging from verbal spats to the sending of naval vessels to put a stop to a unilateral seismic activity.[152] And, second, though that information is gathered by unilateral means, a knowledge imbalance is created, because it is not equally at the disposal of the other claimant, whereby reaching delimitation between the States concerned may be made more difficult.[153] An example where conflict was engendered is when in 1991 a consortium of petroleum companies, incorporated in third States but operating only under Malaysia's concession, prompted a protest by Vietnam.[154] This is however not invariably the case, as seismic work can just as well be undertaken without protest from the other claimant – for example, Suriname and Guyana both considered such work to be a lawful unilateral use of a disputed continental shelf area.[155] In light of this diversity, a latent danger is that, while conducting a seismic survey, the petroleum company may be forced to cease its activities by the other State, which may lead to damages being incurred; that is, in terms of lost business as well as the loss of its investments.[156]

After promising areas for containing in situ mineral resources have been identified through seismic surveying, the true viability of these resources will need to be further confirmed through exploratory drilling into a discovered field.[157]

Coastal States will regularly agree to a moratorium on drilling in a disputed area pending the result of negotiations or the outcome of judicial

150 'New Energy Frontier', *Daily Mirror (Sri Lanka)*, 10 March 2011.

151 Chapter 9, Section 9.3.3.1 below.

152 Chapter 8, Section 8.1 below.

153 S Fietta, '*Guyana/Suriname*' (2008) 102(1) *AJIL* 119, 127.

154 Dzurek (n. 142) 163–164.

155 Chapter 6, Section 6.3.1 below.

156 G Burn et al., 'Legal Issues in Cross-Border Resource Development' (2015) 8(2) *JWELB* 154, 167; PHF Bekker, 'Maritime Boundary Disputes Risk Investment in Offshore Energy Projects' (2005) 21(11) *Natural Gas & Electricity* 10.

157 F Jahn et al., *Hydrocarbon Exploration and Production* (Elsevier, 2008) 547.

proceedings.[158] Once negotiations started between Malaysia and Vietnam over delimiting their maritime boundary in the Gulf of Thailand,[159] Petronas postponed its unilateral activities there, against which Vietnam had earlier protested. Furthermore, the two States, in setting some ground rules to apply during several rounds of delimitation talks at their first meeting in 1991, agreed to maintain the status quo ante regarding mineral resources.[160]

Clarification was sought by Romania regarding the accuracy of a report that Ukraine had approved drilling off the coast of Serpent Island in the Black Sea while proceedings were underway before the ICJ in 2007.[161] According to Romania, while drilling had to be abjured within the disputed area prior to the Court delivering its final ruling, seismic work could be undertaken *pendente litis*.[162] Also, after arbitral proceedings were initiated by the Philippines against China, the Philippines suspended all drilling in the South China Sea.[163]

Outside the context of when a delimitation dispute is being adjudicated, or when delimitation negotiations are ongoing, unilateral drilling in a disputed maritime area tends to be similarly controversial, regularly leading to the other claimant formulating a counter-response when drilling, or an attempt thereto, is detected. Two effects follow from unilateral exploratory drilling, making it seemingly unlawful: first, it would lead to the rights of the other claimant(s) becoming endangered with irreparability; and, second, it might be caught under the obligation not to hamper or jeopardise under Articles 74(3) and 83(3) LOSC.[164]

Moving to the stage of unilateral exploitation within a disputed maritime area can be regarded as being more unlikely; but, as the maritime boundary dispute between Ghana and Côte d'Ivoire illustrates, it is not unthinkable either.[165] An important practical limitation to a State being able to move to the stage of production is that oil and gas fields which have been discovered have a lead-in time of approximately ten years before they are able to produce.[166] This

158 Bundy (n. 112) 27–28.
159 NH Thao, 'Joint Development in the Gulf of Thailand' (1999) *IBRU Boundary and Security Bulletin* 79, 81.
160 NH Thao, 'Vietnam's First Maritime Boundary Agreement' (1997) *IBRU Boundary and Security Bulletin* 74, 75.
161 'Romania Asks Ukraine to Explain Drilling off Disputed Island', *BBC Monitoring European*, 22 November 2007.
162 Ibid.
163 'Philippines Halts Exploration in "Disputed" Sea', *Jakarta Post*, 3 March 2015; 'RPT-The Philippines Suspends Reed Bank Drilling in S. China Sea – Philex Unit', *Reuters*, 3 March 2015.
164 Churchill and Lowe (n. 1) 192.
165 *Ghana/Côte d'Ivoire* (Judgment) (n. 46) 173 [651].
166 CH Schofield, 'What's at Stake in the South China Sea? Geographical and Geopolitical Considerations' in R Beckman et al. (eds.), *Beyond Territorial Disputes in the South China Sea: Legal Framework for the Joint Development of Hydrocarbon Resources* (Edward Elgar, 2013) 11, 39.

provides the other claimant with ample time and opportunity to learn of any intention to exploit mineral resources unilaterally and to protest thereafter,[167] resulting, normally, in the abandonment of further exploitation efforts within the disputed area. This is reinforced by State practice, showing that claimants will usually detect drilling quite early, often even before it has started, and will subsequently protest, or, if the drilling has begun, they will prevent the licensed oil company from completing its work. Nevertheless, there are examples where one claimant has claimed that the other has started with unilaterally exploiting mineral resources from a disputed maritime area – often, however, it is difficult to verify the accuracy of such claims.[168] For example, the Democratic Republic of Congo claimed that Angola had unilaterally started with producing mineral resources from their disputed continental shelf area.[169] A further example is that Somalia accused Kenya of having made a start with appropriating mineral resources from their disputed maritime area – which Kenya denied.[170]

2.3.2 *Placing Installations*

One aspect of the rights that a coastal State has over the EEZ is having jurisdiction over installations (Article 60 LOSC).[171] More generally, installations and structures that are used in connection with mineral resources fall under the jurisdiction of the relevant coastal State.

Installations can be deployed and used for the purpose of exploring or exploiting mineral resources from the seabed, and to generate energy from alternative sources, including ocean currents and wind, but they are also employed during MSR projects. The regime contained in the LOSC governing MSR applies to research installations that a (third) State seeks to use in researching a disputed maritime area.[172]

Difficulties regularly emerge, however, in connection with the erection of installations that are perceived to start work concerning mineral resources within disputed maritime areas.[173] There are few examples in State practice where activities undertaken in relation to alternative energy resources in

167 IFI Shihata and WT Onorato, 'Joint Development of International Petroleum Resources in Undefined and Disputed Areas' in GH Blake et al. (eds.), *Boundaries and Energy: Problems and Prospects* (Kluwer, 1988) 433, 448.

168 K Zou, 'Joint Development in the South China Sea: A New Approach' (2006) 21(1) *IJMCL* 83, 86.

169 BIICL Report (n. 141) 87.

170 *Somalia* v. *Kenya* (n. 47) Somalia's Memorial 127 [8.1].

171 Churchill and Lowe (n. 1) 261.

172 Article 258 LOSC.

173 Chapter 8, Section 8.1 below.

disputed maritime areas have led to conflict in bilateral relations. However, when an energy company opted to approach only the German government for prior consent to build an offshore wind farm in a disputed part of the Ems Estuary, a diplomatic controversy arose with the Netherlands.[174] While Germany was contemplating issuing a licence for building the wind farm, the Dutch government was not notified or consulted by Germany.[175]

2.3.3 *Fisheries*

Various types of problems may arise if claimant States fail to bring fisheries under the reach of a cooperative arrangement, and when, in their absence, fishery activities are licensed to be undertaken in a disputed maritime area. This ranges from conflicts between fishing fleets, to disputes on the diplomatic level between States.[176] For instance, Estonia and Latvia became embroiled in an 'outright fish war' prior to EEZ delimitation.[177] In fact, a string of effects can be set in motion through unilateral fishing activities that will affect not only fish stocks or the States having disputed areas but also humans, finding its pinnacle in that food security is put in peril as a result.[178] Fisheries can also have effects on non-target species and the broader marine ecosystem; for instance, due to particular fishing techniques being employed (e.g. bottom fishing or dynamite fishing).

Inherent in the notion of the sovereign rights that coastal States have over the EEZ is that they have a right of exclusive access to any of the fish species contained therein. As a corollary, any fishing activities conducted by nationals of a different State require the coastal State's consent.[179] Accompanying these rights are various obligations concerning fisheries, including inter alia that coastal States, through adopting conservation and management measures based on the best scientific research available, must prevent the over-exploitation of fisheries (Article 61(2) LOSC). Measures taken in this regard must ensure that fishing populations and harvested species can continue to produce the maximum sustainable yield (Article 61(3) LOSC). Other relevant

174 S van Dinter, 'De Zeegrenzen ten Noorden van het Eems-Dollardgebied' (2011) 13 *Niewsbrief Integraal Beheer Noordzee*.

175 'Bizarrer Streit um Nordsee-Windpark – Rotoren in der Rätselzone', *Süddeutsche Zeitung*, 10 August 2011.

176 TN Dang, 'Turn Disputed Fishing Grounds Into "Grey Zone"', *The Straits Times*, 17 June 2011.

177 E Franckx, 'Fisheries in the South China Sea: A Centrifugal or Centripetal Force' (2012) 11(4) *CJIL* 727, 737.

178 R Pomeroy et al., 'Fish Wars: Conflict and Collaboration in Fisheries Management in Southeast Asia' (2007) 31(6) *MP* 645, 646.

179 *North Sea Continental Shelf* (n. 8) 22 [19].

obligations are the following: that the living resources within a coastal State's EEZ must be utilised optimally (Article 62(1) LOSC); that States having claimed EEZ areas are obliged to cooperate in relation to shared and straddling fish stocks (Article 63 LOSC); and that pursuant to Article 64 LOSC a similar obligation exists to cooperate concerning highly migratory fish stocks.

China has invoked these obligations to justify proclaiming laws and regulations pertaining to living marine resources[180] in the disputed South China Sea areas.[181] After the Hainan province enacted legislation in which pressing concerns such as protecting fish stocks and their ability to rejuvenate, for instance by setting catch limitations, were addressed,[182] and pursuant to which a prior consent requirement was set in relation to conducting fishery surveys in areas of the disputed South China Sea, other claimant States protested. China claimed that enacting this piece of legislation was necessary to ensure that the obligations it has under the LOSC were being carried out, including obligations arising thereunder in connection with fisheries and protection of the marine environment. Similarly, in an attempt to break a downward trend of fish stocks collapsing in disputed parts of the Gulf of Tonkin, China decided to limit the locations where fishing activities by its nationals could be undertaken: fishermen were prohibited from fishing beyond the provisional equidistance boundary.[183]

Any limitations and obligations that can be recognised to exist concerning fisheries in undisputed EEZ areas apply without deviation in disputed EEZ areas as well. However, an important difference is that, in disputed areas, there are at least two coastal States that have similar and shared obligations regarding fisheries located in the same area, which they will both need to comply with. Of course, this complicates matters for coastal States, for instance as to how they can exercise their obligations effectively. Taking successful conservation efforts in relation to fish stocks in disputed maritime areas has been premised on cooperation between the coastal States concerned;[184] the mobility of certain fish stocks enhances this need.[185] For example, as fish populations

180 Over tuna fisheries in the South China Sea, the Western and Central Pacific Fisheries Commission exercises de facto competence.

181 'Foreign Ministry Spokesperson Hua Chunying's Regular Press Conference on January 9, 2014', available at www.fmprc.gov.cn/mfa_eng/xwfw_665399/s2510_665401/2511_665403/t1117017.shtml.

182 'The South China Sea: Hai-handed', *The Economist*, 13 January 2014.

183 G Xue, 'Improved Fisheries Co-Operation: Sino-Vietnamese Fisheries Agreement for the Gulf of Tonkin' (2006) 21(2) *IJMCL* 217, 221.

184 JS Kang, 'The United Nation Convention on the Law of the Sea and Fishery Relations between Korea, Japan and China' (2003) 27(2) *MP* 111, 116.

185 S Borg, 'The Conservation of Marine Living Resources under International Law: The 1982 United Nations Convention on the Law of the Sea and Beyond' in D Attard et al. (eds.), *IMLI*

plummeted in the Gulf of Thailand, concerns have been expressed that, without cooperation between the coastal States concerned, they may become fully depleted.[186] Also, without cooperation, conservation measures taken by one coastal State are likely to be undermined by the actions of another State;[187] this, in turn, can lead to conflicts in bilateral relations.[188]

While the presence of fish stocks in disputed maritime areas can bring claimant States to conclude cooperative arrangements designed to manage this living resource more responsibly, they, conversely, can exert a dividing effect between States in that they are a source of conflict if fishery activities do occur. Competition between the fishermen of the claimant States may arise in relation to a disputed area, in turn almost invariably leading to the overfishing of fish stocks.[189] The two elements of competition and overfishing are regularly interrelated in the following way: fishermen of the respective claimants will increase their fishing efforts in disputed areas up to a point where the fish stocks are being put at risk or actually become depleted.[190] An example illustrating this relationship is the East China Sea, where collapsing fish stocks, combined with their inability to recover, ultimately led to fishermen of the States of the East China Sea turning to unlawful fishing practices. Faced with this, other coastal States of the East China Sea took enforcement measures against fishermen resorting to such practices.[191] A similar pattern is visible in the Gulf of Thailand, where fishing activities have created a conflict between Malaysia, Vietnam, and Thailand.[192]

The exploitation of fish stocks in disputed maritime areas does not require sizable investments – and neither is a great deal of (technical) expertise or advanced gear required.[193] Fishermen inadvertently wandering into disputed

Manual on International Law, Vol. I: The Law of the Sea (Oxford University Press, 2014), 342–343.

186 CH Schofield and M Tan-Mullins, 'Maritime Claims, Conflicts and Cooperation in the Gulf of Thailand' in EM Borgese et al. (eds.), *Ocean Yearbook*, Vol. 22 (Brill, 2013) 75, 79–80.

187 JM Van Dyke, 'The Republic of Korea's Maritime Boundaries' (2003) 18(4) *IJMCL* 509, 536.

188 Roach (n. 147) 5; TL McDorman, *Salt Water Neighbours: International Ocean Law Relations between the United States and Canada* (Oxford University Press, 2009) 72.

189 Franckx (n. 177) 728; S Wu, *Solving Disputes for Regional Cooperation and Development in the South China Sea: A Chinese Perspective* (Chandos, 2013) 164–165.

190 Prescott and Schofield (n. 55) 216; JI Charney, 'Central East Asian Maritime Boundaries and the Law of the Sea' (1995) 89(4) *AJIL* 724, 746.

191 MJ Valencia and Y Amae, 'Regime Building in the East China Sea' (2003) 34(2) *ODIL* 189, 193; R Emmers, *Resource Management and Contested Territories in East Asia* (Palgrave Macmillan, 2013) 39.

192 'Thais and Viets to Set Aside Dispute', *The Straits Times*, 1 April 1997.

193 L Brilmayer and N Klein, 'Land and Sea: Two Sovereignty Regimes in Search of a Common Denominator' (2000–2001) 33(3) *NYUJILP* 703, 753.

areas are also a possibility.[194] Two approaches can be taken by States concerning fisheries in disputed maritime areas. One is that they may pursue repressive approaches, for instance, by prohibiting fishing in disputed maritime areas and imposing penalties for non-compliance. But, even if claimant States were to agree not to fish in their disputed maritime areas, there might still be a need for them to cooperate: that is, when the distributional range of fish stocks extends beyond the disputed maritime areas and into their undisputed maritime zones. The second approach is preventative in nature. An example is, if a claimant State's fishing vessels are equipped with satellite-based vessel monitoring systems (VMS), this mitigates any difficulties in actively controlling and influencing the fishing activities of its nationals in relation to a disputed maritime area.[195] However, if a State does not equip its vessels with VMS, then, even if a claimant would refrain from licensing fishing activities, there may be some continuous measure of fishing activity,[196] thus keeping intact the risk of a subsequent conflict between claimant States.[197]

Basing himself on a finding from the *Icelandic Fisheries Jurisdiction* cases, where the ICJ declined to put a stop to ongoing fishing activities within a unilaterally extended fisheries zone, and applying it by analogy to disputed maritime areas,[198] Dang has argued that the lawfulness of certain fishing activities in disputed areas can be upheld.[199] Apart from the peculiarities of the *Icelandic Fisheries Jurisdiction* cases, which preclude what was held in these cases being applied by analogy to disputed maritime areas,[200] in order to assess to what extent undertaking fishing activities in disputed areas is permissible, Article 74(3) LOSC combined with the significant obligations coastal States have concerning fisheries and the wider marine environment impose limitations thereon.[201]

Fishing within a disputed area can also be a perilous undertaking for fishermen. Occasional reports exist of individual fishermen being shot at by enforcement officials of the other claimant State, because of unlawfully conducting fishing activities in a disputed area, damaging property,

194 RW Smith, 'A Geographical Primer to Maritime Boundary-Making' (1982) 12(1–2) *ODIL* 1, 11; Anderson (n. 6) 418.

195 'Fish War Crisis Brings Thai and Malaysian PMs to the Table', *Financial Times* (London), 14 December 1995; 'Thais and Viets' (n. 192).

196 Churchill and Lowe (n. 1) 199.

197 RR Churchill, 'Fisheries Issues in Maritime Boundary Delimitation' (1993) 17(1) *MP* 44, 45.

198 Chapter 9, Section 9.3.3.2 below.

199 TN Dang, 'Fisheries Co-operation in the South China Sea and the (Ir)relevance of the Sovereignty Question' (2012) 2(1) *AsJIL* 59, 71–72.

200 Chapter 3, Section 3.4 below.

201 Churchill and Lowe (n. 1) 199.

and causing bodily harm, sometimes even resulting in casualties.[202] Other effects are that a claimant starts more regular patrols of these fishing grounds, or begins providing its fishing vessels with an (armed) escort. All this is to ensure that the fishing activities of its nationals can continue uninterrupted.[203] However, when State A takes enforcement measures, for example by boarding vessels and arresting fishermen, against claimant State B's vessels for fishing activities in its disputed area, and then prosecuting these and the crew in State A, public opinion in (flag) State B can become inflamed,[204] or can create a significant conflict at the diplomatic level.

Claimant States sometimes actively encourage their fishermen to start fishing within disputed territorial sea or EEZ areas. For example, China has claimed that other claimants of the South China Sea actively encourage their fishermen to start fishing in disputed waters, in particular Vietnam.[205] China has also reportedly encouraged vessels flying the Chinese flag to penetrate further into the disputed areas of the East China Sea to begin fishing activities;[206] this prompted a protest by Japan. Further, Guinea-Bissau claimed that Senegal encouraged its national fishermen to increase fishing efforts in the disputed EEZ area in an attempt to fortify its claim over the area.[207] These Senegalese fishermen were subsequently arrested and brought to port by Guinea-Bissau for violating its EEZ rights. Another example is Somalia, which in its pleadings before the ICJ claimed that Kenya had encouraged its fishermen to increase their fishing efforts in the disputed EEZ area, whereby Somalia's sovereign rights were damaged in a permanent manner and international responsibility had been incurred by Kenya.[208] It may be that lying behind engaging in such practices is the misplaced belief that this will strengthen a State's claim over the disputed area. These encouragements to intensify fishing effort in a disputed area can have detrimental effects on two fronts, putting their lawfulness into question: they may lead to overfishing, which would inter alia breach Article 61(2) LOSC, and they can create a conflict between the coastal

202 PC Yuan, 'China's Sovereignty over Its Offshore Oil and the New Law of the Sea' (1985) 10(3–4) *Energy* 525, 531; 'Tension in Asia over Wealth under the Sea', *The New York Times*, 19 May 1996.

203 'China Starts Regular Patrols of South China Sea', *Xinhua*, 25 April 2010.

204 'China Accuses Vietnam in South China Sea Row', *BBC News*, 10 June 2011.

205 D Zha, 'China's Exploitation of the South China Sea Resources: The Case of Hainan Province' (2000) 15 *Research Institute Working Paper, Asia Pacific Series IUJ* 3, 13.

206 AD Ba, 'Staking Claims and Making Waves in the South China Sea: How Troubled Are the Waters?' (2011) 33(3) CSA 269, 277.

207 *Guinea-Bissau* v. *Senegal* (Provisional Measures) (n. 11) 68 [17].

208 *Somalia* v. *Kenya* (n. 47) Somalia's Memorial 143 [8.34].

States concerned, which may, for example, breach the prohibition of hampering or jeopardising, as is laid down in Article 74(3) LOSC.

2.3.4 *Marine Data Collection*

'Marine data collection' is a generic term that applies to a wide range of activities, including activities conducted in the framework of MSR and military or hydrographic surveys.[209] These acts being carried out with a common aim of obtaining knowledge about the sea are also undertaken in disputed maritime areas. For instance, a 'hydrographic vessel' belonging to the Portuguese Navy (prior to Guinea-Bissau gaining its independence) operated on several occasions, over a period of eleven years, in parts of a territorial sea area – and perhaps beyond the outer limit of the territorial sea – that were also claimed by what was then France (which after gaining its independence is now Guinea), with the goal of collecting data from the disputed area.[210] These activities never prompted France to protest.[211]

Gathering data on a disputed maritime area has however sparked incidents in bilateral relations. For example, in the Aegean Sea, Greece and Turkey clashed over unilateral activities through which data were sought to be collected on the disputed continental shelf area.[212] Conducting activities in the framework of MSR in disputed parts of the South China Sea has been singled out as one of the themes interlinking with the bevy of other issues (e.g. territorial sovereignty issues and security) adding complexity to these disputes.[213] After Vietnam and the Philippines agreed to jointly undertake an MSR project in disputed areas of the South China Sea,[214] China protested: without its prior consent, the project could not be lawfully undertaken.[215]

One broad explanation underlying the anxiety that some claimants exhibit when it comes to data gathering from disputed maritime areas, and despite appearing relatively harmless, is that States regularly treat each other's

209 R Pedrozo, 'Close Encounters at Sea: the USNS Impeccable Incident' (2009) 62(3) *NWCR* 101, 106–107.

210 KA McLlarky, 'Guinea/Guinea-Bissau: Dispute Concerning Delimitation of the Maritime Boundary, February 14, 1985' (1987) *MJILT* 93, 94.

211 *Delimitation of the Maritime Boundary between Guinea and Guinea-Bissau* [1985] XIX RIAA 149, 161–162 [29].

212 *Aegean Sea Continental Shelf* (Interim Measures) (n. 41).

213 'Calmer Sea Will Benefit All', *China Daily*, 7 September 2011.

214 R Amer and NH Thao, 'A New Legal Arrangement for the South China Sea' (2009) 40(4) *ODIL* 333, 338.

215 R Amer and NH Thao, 'Vietnam's Border Disputes: Legal and Conflict Management Dimensions' (2005–2006) 12 *AYIL* 111, 122.

unilateral acts with general suspicion, regardless of the type of act involved.[216] A second explanation is that collecting information, in the form of conducting a survey or activities within the framework of MSR, is perceived by some coastal States as being a front for research into the presence of natural resources.

The distinction between what constitutes 'activities conducted in the framework of MSR' and other 'data gathering activities' takes on a heightened importance in two respects. First, in assessing the relevant legal framework whenever such activities are undertaken in disputed maritime areas. And, second, certain data gathering activities, including hydrographic surveying, in so far as they occur beyond the 12 nm limit of the territorial sea,[217] cannot be brought under the rules that are applicable to activities taking place in the framework of MSR. In fact, they constitute a category of activity that is beyond the authority of the coastal State; this means that it can be freely engaged in within disputed maritime areas as well.[218]

China and the United States, as a third State, clashed on several occasions over the latter's naval vessels being driven away from disputed areas of the South China Sea while conducting hydrographic surveys.[219] However, these incidents are not necessarily linked to the area in question being disputed; rather, these conflicts seem to be rooted in different views that the two States have with respect to the rights of other States in the EEZ of the coastal State.[220]

Complicating matters is the fact that Part XIII LOSC does not define MSR.[221] Within the territorial sea, undertaking a MSR project is under the sovereignty of the coastal State; this is inter alia indicated by the fact that, if a vessel were to conduct this activity during its passage, it could no longer be regarded as innocent (Article 19(j) LOSC). Similarly, all MSR projects in the EEZ require the consent of 'the coastal State' under Article 246 LOSC. Its

[216] Valencia and Amae (n. 191) 196.

[217] Articles 19(2)(j) and 21(1)(g) LOSC.

[218] A Roach and RW Smith, *Excessive Maritime Claims* (Brill, 2012) 435–436; AHA Soons, *Marine Scientific Research and the Law of the Sea* (Kluwer, 1982) 157.

[219] A Dupont and CG Baker, 'East Asia's Maritime Disputes: Fishing in Troubled Waters' (2014) 37(1) *The Washington Quarterly* 79, 89; MJ Valencia, '"The Impeccable incident" Truth and Consequences' (2009) 5(2) *China Security* 22.

[220] Z Haiwen, 'Is It Safeguarding the Freedom of Navigation or Maritime Hegemony of the United States? – Comments on Raul (Pete) Pedrozo's Article on Military Activities in the EEZ' (2010) 9(1) *CJIL* 31, 36.

[221] Soons (n. 218) 118–125; KY You, 'The Law and Practice Relating to Marine Scientific Research in Northeast Asia' in MH Nordquist et al. (eds.), *The Law of the Sea Convention: US Accession and Globalization* (Brill, 2012) 492, 494.

paragraph 3, however, stipulates that consent shall normally be given by the coastal State for research that 'increases scientific knowledge of the marine environment for the benefit of all mankind'.

The issue of requesting consent takes on a particular relevance with respect to undertaking acts in the framework of MSR in disputed areas, as the position might be taken that the prior consent of all claimant coastal States concerned needs to be obtained before such a research activity can commence. This is because, depending on the maritime zone involved, the coastal State has exclusive jurisdiction or sovereignty over MSR.[222] In this vein, China has taken the position that the lawfulness of activities conducted in the framework of MSR in its disputed maritime areas is completely dependent on its prior consent.[223] Contrary to this position, it has been held by some authors that conducting MSR in disputed maritime area with the consent of only one claimant State is lawful:[224] that is, activities undertaken in the framework of MSR, but not concerning mineral resources.

2.3.5 *The Marine Environment*

The marine environment in a range of disputed maritime areas is being put in jeopardy with alarming rapidity.[225] A reason for this is that most claimant coastal States will overwhelmingly focus on the *rights* they purportedly have in disputed areas, whereas exercising obligations in relation to protecting the marine environment are regularly not that high on the agenda.[226] The South China Sea is an example of where sources polluting the marine environment are plenty. Pollution emanating from land-based resources and from seabed activities[227] has had tangible negative effects on the marine environment of its disputed sea areas.[228] Another source of pollution is tankers used for transporting oil, disposing their waste into the disputed waters of the South China Sea.[229] Also, in the Gulf of

222 Article 246 LOSC.
223 Amer and Thao (n. 215) 122.
224 Valencia and Miyoshi (n. 120) 213.
225 NC Hoi and VH Dang, 'Building a Regional Network and Management Regime of Marine Protected Areas in the South China Sea for Sustainable Development' (2015) 18(2) *JIWLP* 128, 129.
226 I Townsend-Gault, 'Compliance with the United Nations Convention on the Law of the Sea in the Asia-Pacific Region' (1999) 33(2) *UBCLR* 227, 229, 231.
227 Song (n. 27) 151, 162–167.
228 S Tonnesson, 'China and the South China Sea: A Peace Proposal' (2000) 31(3) *Security Dialogue* 307, 314, 322.
229 MJ Valencia, 'The South China Sea: Prospects for Marine Regionalism' (1979) 2(2) *MP* 98, 95–96.

Thailand, pollution emanating from different sources, detrimentally affecting the marine environment of the disputed area, has given cause for concern.[230]

Claimant States have in a way a shared obligation to preserve and protect the marine environment of a disputed maritime area, and to protect it from damaging and polluting activities in the period preceding delimitation. Nonetheless, disputed maritime areas have been argued to 'constrain' claimant States from 'fully exercising environmental jurisdiction'.[231] This incompleteness seems to tie in with the assumption that there is an inherent uncertainty as to who is to be considered the coastal State, and therewith who would come to bear the positive obligations towards the marine environment exclusively.

To deny the application of the obligation to protect the marine environment in disputed maritime areas, for example, as laid down in Part XII LOSC is misplaced, however. Looking inter alia at the language of Article 192, it refers to 'States' without any qualification. In fact, most of the obligations existing in Part XII LOSC are not connected to a particular maritime zone or to one coastal State. Yet, there is an enhanced need for cooperation between claimants in order for any measures to be as effective as they can be; these can otherwise be undermined, thereby losing much of their effectiveness.[232] Conflict does sometimes emerge when a State takes necessary protective measures relating to the marine environment of a disputed maritime area. For instance, renewing a ban by China aimed at replenishing fish stocks has consistently been protested by Vietnam and the Philippines.[233] There is, however, growing recognition of the importance of protecting the marine environment of disputed maritime areas in international case law. The aspect of avoiding the marine environment from being affected by unilateral conduct was crucial in the Tribunal's appraisal of whether a unilateral act hampers or jeopardises pursuant to Articles 74(3) and 83(3) LOSC in *Guyana* v. *Suriname*: if the negative effects on the marine environment surpass a certain threshold, the unilateral act is caught under this negative obligation.[234]

230 Schofield and Tan-Mullins (n. 186) 82–83.

231 A Chircop, 'Regional Cooperation in Marine Environmental Protection in the South China Sea: A Reflection on New Directions for Marine Conservation' (2010) 41(4) *ODIL* 334, 338.

232 Schofield (n. 116) 157; Van Dyke (n. 187) 519–539.

233 TN Dang, 'China's Fishing Ban in the South China Sea: Implications for Territorial Disputes' (2011) *RSIS Commentaries* (S Rajaratnam School of International Studies, 9 June 2011) 89; Z Sun, 'South China Sea: Reducing the China-Vietnam Tension' (2011) *RSIS Commentaries* (S Rajaratnam School of International Studies, 8 August 2011) 107.

234 *Guyana* v. *Suriname* (n. 7) 132–133, 137 [467] [470] [480].

2.3.6 *Responding – or Not – to a Unilateral Act*

Practice shows that, when a coastal State is confronted with an act falling under the authority of the coastal State that is authorised or undertaken unilaterally by the other coastal State, a willingness to respond regularly will arise.[235] Three motivations for a State to produce such a response are:[236] first, a State's desire to assert its own position; second, a State feeling compelled to respond in order to shield its interests, sovereignty, sovereign rights, and/or jurisdiction from infringement; and, third, to avoid claims of silence in relation to a unilateral act, that is subject to the authority of the coastal State, having led to acquiescence.[237]

Acquiescence is inferred from the silence or inaction of a State in a situation where taking some action was called upon, in order not to mitigate the legal strength of its claim.[238] By protesting, a State can pre-empt claims of having acquiesced.[239] A protest can also prevent the formation of a new customary rule. Whether a State has acquiesced in another State's claim after previously keeping silent over a period of time is intimately linked to the circumstances surrounding the situation, however, and thus impossible to generalise. An illustration of the role that the notion of acquiescence may play in disputed maritime areas is supplied by Ghana in its maritime boundary dispute with Côte d'Ivoire, where it argued unsuccessfully that Côte d'Ivoire had acquiesced in its conduct in relation to mineral resources located in a disputed continental shelf area, by not protesting against it.[240] Another example is China's annual imposition of a moratorium on fisheries, against which both the Philippines and Vietnam protested due to a fear that failing to do so could be construed as acquiescence.[241]

'Hypersensitivity' is almost invariably exhibited when claimant A is faced with unilateral conduct that is under the authority of the coastal State from claimant B, prompting it to respond.[242] This suggests that a failure to respond

235 Van Logchem (n. 21) 175.

236 Ibid. 192–195.

237 BH Oxman and JF Murphy, *Nonviolent Responses to Violence-Prone Problems: The Cases of Disputed Maritime Claims and State-Sponsored Terrorism* (The American Society of International Law Studies in Transnational Legal Policy, 1991) 3.

238 NSM Antunes, 'Acquiescence' in R Wolfrum (ed.), *The Max Planck Encyclopedia of Public International Law* (Oxford University Press, 2008), online edition, 3.

239 G Fitzmaurice, 'The Law and Procedure of the International Court of Justice, 1951–54: General Principles and Sources of Law' (1953) 30 *BYIL* 1, 28–29, 42–43.

240 *Ghana/Côte d'Ivoire* (Judgment) (n. 46) 47, 64 [130] [189].

241 'At UN Assembly, Philippines Decries Expansionist Territorial Claims in Region', *UN News Centre*, 29 September 2014.

242 IC MacGibbon, 'The Scope of Acquiescence in International Law' (1954) 313 *BYIL* 143, 181–182.

may more easily be seen as acquiescence when a claimant is faced with such unilateral actions in disputed maritime areas – however, there is a shortage of case law to back this view. Claimants may remain oblivious to the fact that the other claimant has undertaken an activity within a disputed area without its prior consent until after the fact, but this is only more rarely the case. Yet Sweden only protested after learning that Norway had completed its drilling in a disputed continental shelf area.[243] Far more often, however, claimants will monitor with great care the movements and actions of other States in disputed areas; a claimant, upon detecting an act that is felt to infringe upon its interests, position, or rights, is then likely to somehow respond.

The reaction of a claimant State to the conduct of the other claimant in a disputed area can relate to both lower-sensitivity activities (e.g. MSR or laying and maintaining submarine cables)[244] and to those that are generally regarded as controversial, particularly activities concerning mineral resources or fishing. Assuming the activity is under the authority of the coastal State, which varies with the maritime zone involved, the ways in which a claimant State can respond to unilateral conduct can be effectively organised along two lines: by diplomatic means (e.g. negotiating, protesting, and submitting the dispute to third-party dispute settlement) or by taking physical measures (e.g. law enforcement or the sending of naval vessels).[245]

The differences that exist between law enforcement and protesting are significant. When placed on a continuum, law enforcement can be put at the end almost opposite to deciding on protesting against unilateral action that is subject to the authority of the coastal State via diplomatic demarches.[246] Law enforcement is an example of a reaction that is much more invasive in terms of the effect caused to another State's rights as well as the possible conflict that may subsequently be engendered in bilateral relations. As State practice illustrates, taking enforcement measures in a disputed maritime area often proves seriously controversial, however.[247] Although difficult to quantify, with increasing pace, claimant States may nowadays feel less restrained in

243 R Lagoni, 'Interim Measures Pending Maritime Delimitation Agreements' (1984) 78(2) *AJIL* 345, 364.

244 Y van Logchem, 'Submarine Telecommunication Cables in Disputed Maritime Areas' (2014) 45(1) *ODIL* 107.

245 Y van Logchem, 'The Rights and Obligations of States in Disputed Maritime Areas: What Lessons Can Be Learned from the Maritime Boundary Dispute between Ghana and Côte d'Ivoire?' (2019) 52(1) *VJTL* 121, 128.

246 US Department of State, *Gulf of Thailand: Maritime Jurisdictional Disputes and Anti-Piracy Activities* (Geographic Research Study, 1984) 4.

247 Van Logchem (n. 21) 192–195.

taking enforcement action when faced with unilateral conduct, which is under the authority of the coastal State, by the other claimant State.[248]

At the low end of the scale of available responses for a State if it wants to object to a particular action or reaction by the other State in relation to a disputed area is protesting[249] through diplomatic demarches.[250] A protest constitutes a unilateral act that is undertaken by a State in relation to a disputed area,[251] which can make clear that a dispute has materialised under international law.[252] Protests issued through diplomatic demarches can take different forms: whereas some coastal States will focus on the unlawfulness of the unilateral act that is subject to coastal State authority undertaken within a disputed maritime area from the perspective of international law, other States will protest by pointing to the exclusive usage they are argued to have over the area concerned.[253] Only more rarely will States protest by invoking the provisions contained in the LOSC, including Articles 74(3) and 83(3).[254] Far more often, States will rely on general rules of international law, or turn to the justification of their actions or reactions based on exclusivity. Falling in the latter category are China, Japan, and the Philippines, which tend to formulate their position on the basis of being entitled to have exclusive use of a disputed area.[255] Vietnam, in responding to an oil rig that was moved under the sole authorisation of China into a disputed maritime area to begin exploratory drilling, assumed the role of the 'relevant coastal State' that enjoys exclusive jurisdiction over the area concerned: the area where the drilling was

[248] I Papanicolopulu, 'Enforcement Action in Contested Waters: the Legal Regime' Paper Presented at 6th IHO-IAG ABLOS Conference: Contentious Issues in UNCLOS – Surely Not?, 2010 (on file with author), 1.

[249] IC MacGibbon, 'Some Observations on the Part of Protest in International Law' (1953) 30 *BYIL* 293, 298–299.

[250] Oxman and Murphy (n. 237) 1; NSM Antunes, 'Estoppel, Acquiescence and Recognition in Boundary Dispute Settlement' (2000) 2(8) *IBRU Boundary & Territory Briefing* 1, 3.

[251] C Eick, 'Protest' in R Wolfrum (ed.), *The Max Planck Encyclopedia of Public International Law* (Oxford University Press, 2008), online edition, 1.

[252] I Brownlie, *African Boundaries: A Legal and Diplomatic Encyclopaedia* (University of California Press, 1979) 13.

[253] 'Vietnam Holds Live-Fire Navy Drill Amid China Spat', *The Associated Press*, 13 June 2011; 'Dispute between Vietnam and China' (n. 100)

[254] AG Oude Elferink, 'Arguing International Law in the South China Sea Disputes: The Haiyang Shiyou 981 and USS Lassen Incidents and the *Philippines* v. *China Arbitration*' (2016) 31(2) *IJMCL* 205, 210.

[255] A Kanehara, 'A Legal and Practical Arrangement of Disputes Concerning Maritime Boundaries Pending Their Final Solution and Law Enforcement: A Japanese Perspective' in NA Martínez Gutiérrez (eds.), *Serving the Rule of International Maritime Law: Essays in Honour of Professor David Joseph Attard* (Routledge, 2010) 95, 100.

to begin fell squarely within Vietnam's EEZ, being removed 120 nm from its mainland coast.[256] Despite the fact that States can employ language under which it is argued that the other State, rather than acting in a disputed maritime area, has undertaken an act in an area that is under the exclusive jurisdiction of the other State,[257] as a part of their 'diplomatic and political strategy',[258] none of the States involved can claim to have exclusive usage of a disputed maritime area prior to its delimitation.[259] That is, of course, assuming that the States concerned have made claims over the same area that, at a minimum, rest on a prima facie basis of international law.

States can also invoke various responses simultaneously. Protests are sometimes combined with a visible show of 'force', by dispatching a State's naval vessels. For instance, unilateral seismic work by India in the Bay of Bengal motivated Bangladesh to respond along two lines: it protested through diplomatic channels and it dispatched its naval vessels to the area concerned.[260] After China wanted to start capitalising on two earlier finds of mineral resources in the disputed East China Sea,[261] and against which Japan protested, Japan bolstered its naval presence in the disputed maritime area.[262] Thereafter, China sent its naval vessels to an area in relation to which it sought to start development.[263]

Vessels that seek to begin operations in disputed maritime areas can be escorted by vessels that are within that State's government service. Government vessels are regularly used by coastal States to escort other vessels as a precaution, which may deter the other claimant from sending its own naval vessels. Guyana, for example, provided seismic vessels that it authorised to start operations in an area which Suriname also claimed with coastguard vessels for protective purposes.[264] However, government vessels being present

256 'China's Illegal Placement of Haiyang Shiyou 981 Oil Rig in the Exclusive Economic Zone and Continental Shelf of Viet Nam, and the Sovereignty of Viet Nam over the Hoang Sa Archipelago', Bangkok, 4 July 2014, available at www.vietnamembassy-thailand.org/en/nr070521165843/nr070725012202/ns140704195817.

257 Arsana (n. 15) 15.

258 Kanehara (n. 255) 100.

259 Leanza (n. 145) 394.

260 Chapter 8, Section 8.1.3 below.

261 J Gao, 'A Note on the 2008 Cooperation Consensus between China and Japan in the East China Sea' (2009) 40(3) *ODIL* 291, 294.

262 CH Schofield and I Townsend-Gault, 'Choppy Waters Ahead in "a Sea of Peace Cooperation and Friendship"?: Slow Progress Towards the Application of Maritime Joint Development to the East China Sea' (2011) 35(1) *MP* 25, 29; SS Harrison, 'Seabed Petroleum in Northeast Asia: Conflict or Cooperation' in SS Harrison (ed.), *Northeast Asia: Conflict or Cooperation* (Woodrow Wilson International Center for Scholars: Asia Program, 2005) 3, 3–4.

263 'Chinese Warships Make Show of Force at Protected Gas Rig', *The Japan Times*, 10 September 2005.

264 *Guyana* v. *Suriname* (n. 7) Guyana's Memorial 62 [4.50]–[4.52].

within a disputed area may also be in reaction to a previously undertaken unilateral act that falls within the authority of a coastal State. For example, a visit by the naval vessels of Bangladesh to a disputed part of the Bay of Bengal led to an oil rig licensed by Myanmar having to abandon its work and withdrawing from the area concerned.[265]

The decision of a coastal State to send its naval vessels to a disputed maritime area may signify a State's desire to show that it has a claim to the area concerned, and its willingness to act against perceived infractions of its rights and interests by other States. Malaysia after having awarded two concessions located in disputed parts of the Celebes Sea received a diplomatic protest from Indonesia.[266] While pursuing diplomatic efforts,[267] they both decided to increase the number of their warships within the area.[268] Positioning additional warships was viewed by both as quite a natural reaction to another claimant's unilateral act taken in relation to a disputed area.[269]

Claimants are also strengthening their navies, enabling them to patrol disputed areas more vigorously. Both Guyana and Suriname decided to give a financial injection to their navies in the wake of the incident with the CGX drilling rig licensed by only Guyana.[270] Greater naval capabilities, coupled with a greater willingness to take law enforcement measures in disputed maritime areas, may enhance the likelihood of conflict arising due to these States operating with greater regularity in close proximity to each other.

Alternatively, a State that is faced with a unilateral act falling under the authority of a coastal State within a disputed maritime area, which it believes to breach international rules, could engage in countermeasures, in accordance with the rules on international responsibility.[271] This State may take countermeasures with the intention to persuade the State that acted unilaterally, by authorising or undertaking an act that is under coastal State authority, to cease its unlawful act and to induce compliance with its international obligations. Countermeasures may involve an action that may itself be a violation of international law. However, their unlawfulness can be

265 Bissinger (n. 24) 109.
266 'Malaysia Urges Indonesia to Use Diplomacy in Maritime Disputes', *BBC Monitoring Asia Pacific*, 4 March 2005.
267 Ibid.
268 'Patrolling Warships Not Sign of Conflict, Says Syed Hamid', *Malaysia General News*, 11 March 2005.
269 Ibid.
270 'Guyana, Suriname Must Share Rich Oil Source, UN Tribunal Rules', *The Associated Press*, 21 September 2007.
271 Articles on Responsibility of States for Internationally Wrongful Acts, ILC *Yearbook* 2001/II(2) (ARSIWA).

precluded, as it may be considered as a lawful response to the first perceived wrongful act against which the countermeasure is directed. Chapter II of Part III of the Articles on State Responsibility (ARSIWA) sets various conditions that must be met for countermeasures to be lawful.[272] These conditions entail both procedural and substantive requirements. Falling within the category of procedural requirements is that taking a countermeasure must be preceded by a request for suspension of the alleged wrongful act, and an invite to start negotiations must be extended.[273] As to the substance of countermeasures, they may inter alia not be punitive in nature, must be proportional, and their effects must be reversible to the greatest extent possible. A countermeasure is predicated on the fact that there has been a prior wrongful act. Here lies a potential risk for the State that resorts to a countermeasure: what if its subjective assessment that a unilateral act, although falling within the authority of a coastal State, was unlawful is incorrect? Then, that State itself may be held responsible for a violation of international law, with no circumstances precluding the wrongfulness of the act. Another potential difficulty, which a State may need to consider when taking countermeasures, is that the lawfulness of engaging a countermeasure in response to a unilateral activity undertaken regarding a disputed EEZ/continental shelf area can be assessed through the lens of Articles 74(3) and 83(3) LOSC, particularly whether that countermeasure would hamper or jeopardise a final delimitation.

Other lawful options that may be available to States that seek to respond to an act falling under coastal State authority in a disputed area are retorsion and law enforcement, the latter refers to a State enforcing its laws through policing activities. When a claimant alleges that an activity is unlawful, it may resort to retorsion, which constitutes a reaction to another State's act which does not interfere with the latter State's rights under international law.[274] This thus refers to an action which might be seen to be unfriendly by the other State, in that it may negatively impact the bilateral relations of the States concerned, but which is lawful under international law.

Law enforcement can be seen as a reaction to the other claimant's conduct, that is either undertaken by itself or for which it has given authorisation to a private actor, in relation to a disputed maritime area, and which the enforcing State regards as having adversely affected its rights and/or interests.[275]

[272] Ibid. 31[3], 75[4].

[273] Ibid. 136[3].

[274] T Giegerich, 'Retorsion' (2011) in R Wolfrum (ed.), *The Max Planck Encyclopedia of Public International Law* (Oxford University Press, 2008), online edition, 1.

[275] Van Logchem (n. 21) 192–195.

Two preliminary conditions need to be met before considering whether taking enforcement measures in a given situation is lawful: first, the vessels used must meet the criteria of government vessels set out under the international law of the sea; and, second, the unilateral conduct against which the claimant State wants to exercise law enforcement powers must be within coastal State authority.[276]

Two interlinked questions for coastal States related to acts occurring in a disputed maritime area can be recognised: first, do States have the right to adopt laws and regulations in relation to a particular type of activity when it is undertaken in a disputed area?; and, second, can they take enforcement measures in case these proclaimed laws and regulations are breached by a State or private actor operating in a disputed area without that coastal State's consent?[277] Claimant States regularly enact legislation, pertaining to activities that are under the authority of the coastal State, whose reach extends to disputed maritime areas. This creates the possibility for a claimant to act against the other State, or a private actor operating solely with the latter's prior consent, that moves into the disputed area and starts certain operations there.

Conflict almost invariably follows whenever claimant A exercises law enforcement over claimant B,[278] or a private actor licenced by it, possibly reducing the chances that the States concerned reach a diplomatic solution to the dispute or the underlying delimitation issue. Tensions that have arisen between the States of the South China Sea over arresting and prosecuting the other State's vessels and nationals for fisheries offences, without consent of the flag State or State of nationality, confirm this.[279] Because of this effect, the circumstances under which reacting through law enforcement will be considered lawful may be reduced.[280]

Arresting nationals of the other claimant can also lead to nationals of the enforcing State being subjected to enforcement measures as a reaction. To illustrate this, after Indonesia arrested seven Malaysian fishermen for fishing in a disputed territorial sea area, and tried to take them into one of its ports, Malaysia arrested three Indonesian enforcement officials for engaging in unlawful enforcement within what Malaysia perceived to be its territorial sea.[281]

276 Rothwell (n. 76) 211.

277 P Jimenez Kwast, 'Maritime Law Enforcement and the Use of Force: Reflections on the Categorisation of Forcible Action at Sea in the Light of the *Guyana/Suriname* Award' (2008) 13(1) *JCSL* 49, 69.

278 'China Accuses Vietnam in South China Sea Row', *BBC News*, 10 June 2011.

279 Anderson and Van Logchem (n. 18) 193–194.

280 Chapter 6, Section 6.9 and Chapter 9, Section 9.3.3.4 below.

281 'Arrests at Sea Raise Tensions with Malaysia', *The Jakarta Globe*, 16 August 2010; Arsana (n. 15) 11.

Although infrequent, taking enforcement measures does not necessarily lead to heated diplomatic exchanges or a counter-response from the other claimant. Indonesian fishing vessels operating in an area disputed with Palau have been regularly arrested and brought to what to them is a foreign port for prosecution and the imposition of a fine.[282] Somewhat surprisingly perhaps, Indonesia, reportedly, has not made 'significant objections' to its fishermen being arrested.[283]

Importantly, the right of a coastal State to enforce its laws and regulations, which have been proclaimed in accordance with international law, in a particular maritime zone exists de jure.[284] However, the crux of the matter is whether a claimant State is allowed to act upon its de jure right to take law enforcement measures when faced with a breach of its laws and regulations in a disputed maritime area, and if so, in what way. The problem of law enforcement is that, when a claim over a maritime zone by State A will be disputed by claimant State B, the possibility to engage in law enforcement there by State A will automatically be contested as well.[285]

Two considerations are relevant in determining whether a claimant would be allowed to take enforcement measures against the other claimant, or a private actor operating under the licence of the latter, in a disputed EEZ/continental shelf area. First, whether a substantive right to enforce exists under general international law and national legislation; and, second, whether a particular enforcement measure would be in conformity with Articles 74(3) and 83(3) LOSC.[286] Views have varied over the lawfulness of law enforcement in disputed areas, ranging from that it cannot be considered lawful because of the other State's rights becoming threatened with irreparability[287] to that having rights over a maritime area also brings along with it a power to act against an infringement thereof.[288]

A difficulty is that the dividing line between what constitutes law enforcement and a threat to use force may be difficult to draw, and rather often a more subtle difference exists between them in practice. For instance, arresting a vessel if it has committed a certain offence will be accompanied by a threat to use force

282 V Prescott and G Boyes, 'Undelimited Boundaries in the Pacific Ocean Excluding the Asian Rim' (2000) 2(8) *IBRU Maritime Briefing* 1, 35.
283 Ibid.
284 Van Logchem (n. 244) 116.
285 Jimenez Kwast (n. 277) 69; Schofield and Townsend-Gault (n. 81) 669.
286 Milano and Papanicolopulu (n. 80) 623–624.
287 SP Kim, *Maritime Delimitation and Interim Arrangements in North East Asia* (Martinus Nijhoff, 2004) 58–59; YH Tran, 'The South China Sea Arbitral Award: Legal Implications for Fisheries Management and Cooperation in the South China Sea' (2017) 6(1) *CILJ* 87, 92.
288 Papanicolopulu (n. 248) 2; Van Logchem (n. 21) 193–194.

if the arrest is resisted. On its own, the fact that a measure of force has been used cannot automatically lead to the conclusion that an enforcement action within a disputed maritime area is unlawful.[289] Complicating matters in assessing its lawfulness is that there is no provision in the LOSC that explicitly addresses law enforcement within a disputed maritime area. In disputed EEZ or continental shelf areas, if a claimant State contemplates law enforcement action, Articles 74(3) and 83(3) LOSC, particularly in the form of the obligation not to hamper or jeopardise, will constitute the relevant rule, however.

2.4 THIRD STATES, THEIR NATIONALS, AND DISPUTED MARITIME AREAS

Whenever the claims of coastal States to maritime zones are based on international law, the claimants involved have related sovereignty over a disputed maritime area; the absence of a delimited maritime boundary does not change this. This implies that third States cannot engage in a broader range of activities in the disputed maritime area than they would be allowed to undertake had the maritime area been delimited.[290] Disputed maritime areas are certainly not residual areas of the high seas, or a *res nullius*.[291]

Two entwined aspects determine the extent to which third States can undertake acts in disputed maritime areas: first, the type of activity concerned, and, second, the authority that a coastal State has over that activity under international law in its maritime zones. Coastal States will also have jurisdiction in certain matters notwithstanding the rights of third States, for example, regarding marine pollution caused by shipping. An implication of this is as follows: given that wilfully polluting on a serious scale by a vessel flagged to a third State renders the passage non-innocent (Article 19(2)(h) LOSC), if this occurs within disputed territorial sea areas, claimants can act against the polluting foreign vessel.

Although third States have no claim or entitlement to a disputed maritime area, the rights and freedoms that third States have in undisputed waters, for example, navigational rights and freedoms, exist with equal force alongside the sovereignty, sovereign rights, and/or jurisdiction of coastal States in relation to disputed waters. There is another side to this argument, however: that is, those limitations that exist as to exercising rights by third States in undisputed maritime areas will apply mutatis mutandis to disputed maritime areas.

[289] Chapter 6, Section 6.9 and Chapter 9, Section 9.3.3.4 below.

[290] Charney (n. 96) 29.

[291] Townsend-Gault (n. 109) 10; *Ghana/Côte d'Ivoire* (Judgment) (n. 46) 155 [578].

With respect to shipping issues, a coastal State has jurisdiction irrespective of the rights of third States, however. That being said, third States may engage, for example, in the freedom of navigation in disputed EEZ or continental shelf areas,[292] but subject to the qualifications recognised under the LOSC.[293] In addition, vessels of third States can make use of their right of innocent passage in disputed territorial sea areas.[294] However, China claimed that the United States threatened regional peace and security by having one of its warships navigate in disputed waters close to the Spratly Islands.[295] It is, however, not clear what the legal implications are of a State acting in a way whereby regional peace and security are argued to be undermined.

In practice, the rights and freedoms that third States have are mostly exercised by private actors, rather than by the State itself. In this vein, a distinction is drawn between, first, the conducting of activities by third States in disputed maritime areas through which they exercise rights attributed to them directly, and, second, the activities of third States, or their nationals, that fall under the authority of the coastal State, and from which the prior consent of none or only one of the claimant States has been secured. This distinction is critical with different legal questions being involved.

A negative effect that disputed maritime areas may have for third States in exercising rights attributed to them directly is the following: these States may be confronted with an accumulation of requirements, which may be conflicting, or be of questionable lawfulness. Although navigational rights and freedoms remain untouched in disputed territorial seas, EEZ, and above continental shelf areas,[296] claimants do occasionally try to prohibit vessels flying the flags of other States from entering such areas. Illustrative in this respect is when Colombia sought to close the waters off the coasts of certain disputed high-tide features in the Caribbean Sea in 2005. Then, it designated these disputed waters as 'Areas to be Avoided' for reasons of navigational safety and the protection of the marine environment.[297] Beyond influencing the navigational rights of third States, Colombia's designation was controversial given that Nicaragua claimed title over the islands as well, and both States

292 Article 87 (1)(c) LOSC.
293 Articles 87(2) and 88 LOSC.
294 Article 17 LOSC.
295 'China Protests US Ship Near South China Sea Island', *Al Jazeera*, 11 August 2017.
296 Lagoni (n. 243) 365.
297 International Maritime Organization, NAV 51/3/10, Sub-Committee on Safety of Navigation, 51th session, 22 March 2005.

viewed the cays as being part of their continental shelf, since they are less than 200 nm from their mainland coasts.[298]

Another example is that the existence of a disputed maritime area can create a difficult environment for conducting activities in relation to submarine cables, in that work related thereto may be significantly inconvenienced. This is a type of activity that in principle gives rise to practical problems in the relationship between claimant(s) and a private actor, the submarine cable industry.[299] The need to secure multiple permits or other forms of consent from claimant States, often translating into extra costs, delays and administrative acts are some of the issues that submarine cable companies face when they seek to operate in disputed areas.[300] For instance, after several submarine cable systems located in disputed sea areas of East Asia were damaged following the Hengchun earthquake of 2006, their repair was delayed by the fact that various permits had to be obtained from the claimants.[301]

Setting a permit requirement for submarine cable activities beyond the limit of disputed territorial sea areas is problematic from the view of international law. Nonetheless, certain claimant States do impose such a requirement, which are regularly underpinned by submarine cables being perceived as a suitable vehicle to strengthen a coastal State's claim over a disputed maritime area.[302] As a result, the submarine cable industry needs to be aware of and comply with the laws and regulations of all claimant States, if it wants to, for example, avoid being subjected to enforcement measures. In order to prevent difficulties from arising, the industry has adopted the strategy of providing notification whenever a submarine cable system is to pass through a disputed EEZ or continental shelf area.[303]

In respect of acts that fall within the authority of the coastal State, third States, or their nationals, can encounter difficulties in two distinct phases: first, when they seek to start operations (i.e. in the phase of planning activities), and, second, when the activity takes place within such an area (i.e. the execution phase). Uncertainty exists for third States, particularly their nationals who will mainly be the ones that conduct work in another State's disputed maritime area, over what activities they can undertake pursuant to the consent of one claimant State in a disputed maritime area.

298 Fox et al. (n. 113) 185.
299 Van Logchem (n. 244) 107.
300 T Davenport, 'Submarine Communications Cables and Law of the Sea: Problems in Law and Practice' (2012) 43(3) *ODIL* 201, 211–212.
301 Van Logchem (n. 244) 113.
302 Ibid. 107, 115.
303 Ibid. 114.

The main issues confronting third States are concentrated on the notion of prior consent. More specifically, a third State or a national thereof that wants to undertake an activity which is under the authority of the coastal State within a disputed area is faced with the following question: must all coastal States be approached for their prior consent, or would the consent of only one of them suffice to commence such an activity lawfully? To illustrate this with an example, Article 77(1) LOSC attributes an exclusive right to the coastal State to explore and exploit the natural resources of the continental shelf. The legal implication of this is that a third State, or its national(s), cannot start exploiting, drilling, or conducting seismic work in relation to mineral resources of a disputed shelf area without the prior consent of one or perhaps all coastal States concerned. This line of reasoning can mutatis mutandis be applied to fisheries and activities in the framework of MSR, which are both types of activity falling under the authority of the coastal State. If a third State, or a private actor incorporated in a third State, requests consent from only one coastal State, this can result in significant complications; for example, it may be forced by the other claimant to halt an MSR project or fishing activities. Research institutions of third States that want to engage in activities in the framework of MSR in disputed maritime areas are amongst those facing the question of whether prior consent is required from all coastal States concerned. If a research institution were to begin a research activity with the prior consent of only one coastal State, it might prompt the other State to intervene in its work.

For petroleum companies that are incorporated in third States, it is of crucial importance to identify which coastal State they need to approach to obtain a concession for drilling, or seismic work; this is because the industry will not obtain concessions from multiple coastal States.[304] Large investments will need to be made by the petroleum industry to be able to begin with the exploration or exploitation of mineral resources.[305] A licensing State cannot guarantee, however, that, upon the discovery of commercially viable deposits, the petroleum company that had made the discovery can also start exploiting the disputed area.[306] This forces petroleum companies to depart from their usual modus operandi: that is, to obtain the exclusive right to extract mineral resources.[307] Also, there is a serious risk of losing an investment when a petroleum company decides to begin operations in a disputed maritime area pursuant to a licence from a claimant; an investment might be lost if the

304 M Byers, *International Law and the Arctic* (Cambridge University Press, 2013) 57.

305 Morales Siddayao (n. 136) 84–85.

306 'Shell Hopes Brunei, Malaysia, Indonesia Resolve Maritime Disputes Soon', *Agence France Presse*, 14 June 2005.

307 'Unocal Awarded Disputed Block by Indonesia', *World Markets Analysis*, 9 November 2004.

concession area, after delimitation, is located on the other State's side of the boundary. Petroleum companies are regularly involved in difficulties when acting in a disputed maritime area with only one coastal State's prior consent,[308] perhaps even having grown accustomed to experiencing some level of interference in their work. The reason lying behind these difficulties is that the exploratory rights were obtained from a claimant State whose claim is disputed by the other claimant; consequently, the petroleum company's concession will be disputed as well.[309] An example of this is that, after learning that Thailand had given a concession to Amoco covering a disputed area, Kampuchea (now Cambodia) gave a general warning to petroleum companies that they 'will be responsible for all the consequences which may arise from their illegal actions'.[310]

Similar economic considerations are at play with regard to fishing activities in disputed areas. Assuming all coastal States concerned would permit foreign vessels to fish in a disputed area, to obtain multiple fishing licences as a vessel flagged to a third State, seems economically unattractive. Usually, if a coastal State does permit foreign vessels to fish in its undisputed EEZ, for example, a fee for access will be charged. Applied to disputed areas, this means that payment of double fees will be required.

A different situation, although rare in State practice, is that a third State might be on the receiving end of a protest from a claimant if one of its nationals decides to undertake certain activities in a disputed maritime area without having obtained prior consent from all of the coastal States concerned. For example, if a petroleum company that is incorporated in a third State decides to engage in an activity in a disputed area with a licence from one claimant State, the third State – being the one where the petroleum company is incorporated – might be caught in the middle. This occurred when Vietnam concessioned several Indian petroleum companies to conduct mineral resource activities in continental shelf areas, which were the subject of a dispute between China and Vietnam.[311] China lodged a protest not only with Vietnam but also with India, accusing the latter of seeking to make itself an intractable part of the South China Sea disputes, which China considered unlawful from the view of international law.[312] Further, China cautioned

308 'China Pushes the Boundaries', *Oil & Gas Journal*, 2 August 2010.

309 H Groves, 'Offshore Oil and Gas Resources: Economics, Politics and the Rule of Law in the Nigeria-Sao Tome E Principe Joint Development Zone' (2005) 59(1) *JIA* 81, 83–84.

310 CW Dundas, 'The Impact of Maritime Boundary Delimitation on the Development of Offshore Mineral Deposits' (1994) 20(4) *Resources Policy* 273.

311 'India Downplays Chinese Objections to Oil Foray in South China', *The Economic Times*, 21 September 2011.

312 Wu (n. 189) 160.

India not to allow its petroleum companies to undertake work under concessions which they had been granted earlier in the disputed continental shelf area.[313]

Assuming the decision has been made to go forward with the project, in the phase of undertaking a type of activity that is under the authority of the coastal State within a disputed area, problems can arise if not all coastal States have been approached; that is, inter alia if the (national of a) third State has favoured one of these States, by approaching it exclusively for its prior consent and not the other claimant. Alternatively, a third State, or its nationals, can also notify a claimant of their intention to start work under the consent of the other claimant, prior to a unilateral undertaking. However, merely giving notification that an activity that falls under the authority of the coastal State is to proceed in a disputed maritime area might be insufficient in the view of the State being notified, possibly prompting it to respond.

Even when a third State has approached all coastal States involved, there is still no guarantee that the activity can proceed unhindered. The possibility of having to abandon an activity, for example an MSR project in the EEZ, is present if a claimant State decides to withdraw its earlier given consent; for example, because it has learned that it was not exclusively approached for its prior consent. This last possibility seems less prevalent with respect to the petroleum industry operating in disputed maritime areas, as petroleum companies will only obtain a concession from one of the coastal States concerned.[314] However, it is not merely a hypothetical concern for companies based in third States, having been issued with a concession by a claimant State to start exploration or exploitation activities for mineral resources in a disputed area, to be forced to abandon their operations prior to when they began or while operating in such an area.[315] In fact, State practice quite regularly demonstrates that foreign petroleum companies have had to abandon or postpone their planned or actual activities in disputed maritime areas under pressure from another coastal State.[316]

313 'China Warns India on South China Sea Exploration Projects', *The Hindu*, 15 September 2011; 'Oil Riches Pile on China Doorstep as Clashes Delay Drilling', *Bloomberg*, 11 November 2011.

314 CH Park, 'Oil under Troubled Waters: The Northeast Asia Sea-Bed Controversy' (1973) 14(2) *HILJ* 212, 226.

315 International Crisis Group, *Stirring up the South China Sea* (Asia Report, 2012) 25.

316 S Tonnesson, 'Could China and Vietnam Resolve the Conflicts in the South China Sea?' in YH Song and Z Keyuan (eds.), *Major Law and Policy Issues in the South China Sea: European and American Perspectives* (Routledge, 2014) 207, 212; Chapter 8 below.

2.5 CONCLUDING REMARKS

Two developments have raised the visibility and importance of disputed maritime areas: first, the marked growth of coastal State sovereignty, sovereign rights, and/or jurisdiction; and, second, the creation of disputed waters as a result of States making claims to maritime zones from high-tide features.[317] Legal issues connected to disputed maritime areas, such as their delimitation and the rights and obligations of States pending delimitation, have also become increasingly important as a result.

As the number of disputed maritime areas increased, so did the potential for conflict between States. Two (often combined) detrimental effects, which also suggest there having been a breach of international law, often exist in bilateral relations if claimant States act unilaterally, by authorising or undertaking conduct that falls under the authority of the coastal State, in relation to their disputed maritime area. First, it can impede the chances of successful delimitation; and, second, it might prompt the other State to respond, whereby the maritime boundary dispute is exacerbated as a result.[318]

At the heart of possible conflicts occurring is that, in the absence of delimitation, there will be competing sets of sovereignty, sovereign rights, and/or jurisdiction of two States over the same area, which commonly imply exclusivity. Entitlements and rights of claimant States in relation to a disputed maritime area coexist and there is no hierarchical order; that is, if the claims of States to maritime zones are not excessive, and an international court or tribunal has not pronounced itself on the respective strengths of these entitlements and related rights. Claimant States are likely to operate from a similar assumption: activities falling under the authority of the coastal State invariably require its prior consent before they may be undertaken in disputed areas. A coastal State's authority must be determined by reference to two distinct aspects. First, it varies with the type of maritime zone involved. A general distinction can be drawn between maritime zones that are under the sovereignty of a coastal State, for example the territorial sea, and those that are within coastal State jurisdiction, like the EEZ and the continental shelf. Second, a coastal State's authority is dependent on the type of activity; this aspect is also relevant in respect of acts undertaken unilaterally by another State (either the other claimant, a third State, or its nationals) in a disputed maritime area.

317 Section 2.1 above and Chapter 7 below.

318 UK Jenisch, '10 Jahre Neues Internationales Seerecht – Eine Billanz des UN-Seerechtsübereinkommens 1994–2004' (2006) 28(2) *Natur und Recht* 79, 82.

Separate problems and questions arise depending on whether an issue arises between claimants (or one of its nationals and the other claimant) or between a third State (or its nationals) and a claimant. However, a common denominator can be detected as to what may lie at the core of difficulties experienced by these two types of States: what is the range of activities that may be undertaken (unilaterally) by States, and what are the obligations that States have in relation to disputed maritime areas? The notion of prior consent, and the degree to which it must be secured, if at all, prior to acting in relation to a disputed maritime area plays a pivotal role in this regard.

Three variations can be identified in relation to the extent of prior consent being required. First, there are activities which are not subject to the authority of the coastal State and which will not require prior consent; this means that these activities do not need to be pre-announced nor is there a duty of notification. Coastal States cannot exclude third States, and their nationals, to undertake acts that fall outside of the authority of the coastal State within a disputed area. The other side of the coin is that acts which are placed within coastal State authority cannot be undertaken by a third State without obtaining prior consent from the coastal State(s). Second, some activities which are within a coastal State's authority may be undertaken pursuant to a licence from one claimant. And, third, the undertaking of some activities that are under the authority of the coastal State will depend on securing consent from all of the claimants concerned. Whether all acts undertaken in disputed maritime areas can be categorised neatly according to the aforementioned schematisation is, however, doubtful. This is because local variations may require different degrees of prior consent.[319] It is important to emphasise, particularly considering that amongst claimant States there seems to be less recognition thereof, that the range of coastal States' obligations relating to inter alia the marine environment and fisheries apply with equal force in their disputed maritime areas; the only difference is that there are concurrent obligations of the States concerned over the same maritime space in the period prior to delimitation.

319 Chapter 9, Section 9.3.2 below.

3

Disputed Maritime Areas: General Rules of International Law

Those provisions of the LOSC, specifically drafted with disputed maritime areas in mind, including Article 15 and Articles 74(3) and 83(3), which are discussed in Chapters 4 and 5 may be limited in their sphere of operation: that is because certain overlapping claim scenarios that arise in practice are beyond the reach of these provisions.[320] Furthermore, not all States that have disputed maritime areas have become a party to the LOSC, including Israel, Turkey, the United States, and Venezuela.[321] Assessing what the applicable international law is in disputed maritime areas for those States that are not a party to the LOSC is not without difficulties. For example, this is the case for Israel's unilateral acts that have been undertaken in relation to mineral resources in an area that is disputed with Lebanon.[322] Due to Israel not being party to the Convention, and as far as the disputed EEZ/continental shelf area is concerned, Articles 74(3) and 83(3) might not be directly applicable, unless the provision therein reflects a customary rule.[323]

Both considerations underline the need to map out what general rules of international law will apply across the complete range of disputed maritime areas. By way of a preface, it can be observed that the gist of Articles 74(3) and 83(3) (in that it calls on States to cooperate and abstain from certain acts) mirrors some other rules of international law that may already be binding on States with regard to disputed maritime areas, irrespective of a State having

320 T Davenport, 'The Exploration and Exploitation of Hydrocarbon Resources in Areas of Overlapping Claims' in R Beckman et al. (eds.), *Beyond Territorial Disputes in the South China Sea: Legal Framework for the Joint Development of Hydrocarbon Resources* (Edward Elgar, 2013) 93, 113.

321 With the exception of Turkey, the other three remaining States (Israel, the United States, and Venezuela) are parties to the 1958 Conventions.

322 Chapter 8, Section 8.1.13 below.

323 Chapter 5, Section 5.3.10 below.

become a party to the LOSC. Certain other non-conventional rules of international law will be applicable to disputed maritime areas – this can be in addition to rules contained in the LOSC or separate therefrom, depending on whether the overlapping claims scenario falls under its scope. Essentially, there are two sources of international law from which non-conventional rules can be derived: customary international law and general principles of international law; each will be explored in this chapter.

However, this chapter begins in Section 3.1 with whether, as a result of unilateral conduct in disputed maritime areas, a situation can be created that surpassed the threshold of international peace and security being put in jeopardy. Coastal States, in order to have the existence of such a threat recognised, have approached the UNSC on several occasions, seeking declarations from it to that effect. Next, Sections 3.2–3.10 explore whether a bevy of principles – the common denominator of which is that States need to exercise some form of restraint – operate in disputed maritime areas and what their status is: that is, that no irreparability is caused to the other State's rights; that a dispute is not aggravated or extended; that States are to uphold the existing status quo, prior to delimitation; that States are required to act in good faith; that their actions do not amount to an abuse of rights; and that due regard must be shown to the rights and obligations of other States. A treaty obligation to exercise restraint already exists in the form of the obligation not to hamper or jeopardise in Articles 74(3) and 83(3) LOSC, which is regularly referred to as the obligation of 'self-restraint', requiring claimant States to show due diligence.[324] However, the question arises whether, separate from this treaty-based obligation, an obligation of restraint can be derived from customary international law, or whether it operates as a general rule of international law. Before rounding off this chapter, the possibility of engaging international responsibility, if certain unilateral activities that fall within a coastal State's authority have been undertaken in disputed areas resulting in a breach of international law, is discussed in Section 3.11.

3.1 UNILATERALISM IN DISPUTED MARITIME AREAS: THREATS TO PEACE AND SECURITY?

When a State undertakes an act under the authority of the coastal State unilaterally with regard to a disputed maritime area, bilateral relations are

324 Milano and Papanicolopulu (n. 80) 604, 638; KH Wang, 'Bridge over Troubled Waters: Fisheries Cooperation as a Resolution to the South China Sea Conflicts' (2001) 14(4) *The Pacific Review* 531, 538.

regularly detrimentally affected.[325] Beyond that, such unilateral acts have been attributed wider negative effects in that they have been linked to threats to peace and security manifesting directly or indirectly: that is, these acts will result in armed confrontations or conflicts, or pose threats to peace and security in their own right. But can unilaterally authorising or undertaking an act that falls under the authority of the coastal State within a disputed maritime area, and the reaction it may prompt from the other claimant, lead to putting international peace and security at risk?

As regards certain regions, including the Mediterranean Sea[326] and the South China Sea,[327] a relationship has been drawn between maritime boundary disputes and armed conflict: that is, these can become entwined if a claimant State continues to take acts unilaterally, by authorising or undertaking conduct which is under coastal State authority in disputed maritime areas, whereby conflict with another coastal State is provoked. An illustration of the fact that armed conflict may arise is that certain States have been close to taking military action against the other claimant, which was motivated by unilateral acts that fall within a coastal State's authority relating to a disputed maritime area; this was reported to be the case between Bangladesh and Myanmar,[328] and between Greece and Turkey.[329]

Judge Higgins sought to dispel the view that maritime boundary disputes and threats to peace and security are different types of disputes that exist without any contact between them.[330] Along similar lines, the Venezuelan Ambassador to the Organization of American States, speaking before its Council, stated that a causal relationship existed between unilateral action by Colombia and international peace and security having been threatened as a result; this was because it prompted Venezuela to react.[331] A further example is Nicaragua, which took the position that, because its own naval vessels operated alongside those of Colombia and Honduras in a maritime area that

325 Chapter 8 below.

326 M Wählisch, 'Israel-Lebanon Offshore Oil & Gas Dispute – Rules of International Maritime Law' (2011) 15(31) *ASIL Insights* 1–2.

327 IJ Storey, 'Beyond Territorial and Maritime Disputes: The South China Sea as a Center of Global Rivalry or Platform for Prosperity?' in TT Thuy and LT Trang (eds.), *Power, Law, and Maritime Order in the South China Sea* (Lexington Books, 2015) 349, 352.

328 Bissinger (n. 24) 109.

329 M Pratt and CH Schofield, 'Cooperation in the Absence of Maritime Boundary Agreements: The Purpose and Value of Joint Development' in B Öztürk (ed.), *2000 Proceedings of the International Symposium, 'The Aegean Sea, 2000'* (Turkish Marine Research Foundation, 2000) 152.

330 Speech by HE Judge Rosalyn Higgins, President of the ICJ, at the Tenth Anniversary of the ITLOS, 29 September 2006.

331 'Venezuela Says Colombia Threatened Peace', *Associated Press*, 21 August 1987.

was claimed by all three of them, a situation was likely to be triggered that would come to undermine international peace and security.[332] Also, as a consequence of the Philippines seeking to have other States acknowledge that opening disputed areas for consideration was lawful, China argued that the way was being paved for a threat to international peace and security to manifest.[333]

In its pleadings in the *Aegean Sea Continental Shelf* (Interim Measures) case, Greece went to great pains to argue that there was a nexus between conducting seismic work unilaterally and the reaction it would prompt, thereby a threat to international peace and security would automatically emerge – this motivated Greece to also bring the maritime boundary dispute to the attention of the UNSC. Adding fuel to the fire was that, while the ICJ was considering indicating interim measures of protection, Turkey decided to increase its exploration activities with respect to disputed areas of the Aegean Sea.[334] In reviewing this situation, Judge Stassinopoulos maintained, in his dissenting opinion, that a threat to international peace and security had formed.[335] Yet, a reluctance sometimes exists in the case law to merge unilateral conduct in a disputed maritime area and the creation of a threat to international peace and security. For example, Judge ad hoc Thierry, in the interim measures phase in the dispute between Guinea-Bissau and Senegal, concluded that the threat posed by unilaterally undertaken acts that are under coastal State jurisdiction in a disputed EEZ area was that their bilateral relations were seriously aggravated, but fell short of international peace and security being threatened.[336] But has the UNSC ever recognised that undertaking an act within a disputed maritime area unilaterally, and the reaction it may prompt from the other claimant, led to international peace and security having been endangered?

3.1.1 *Greece and Turkey*[337]

After convening an emergency session upon the request of Greece in 1976, the UNSC expressed concerns over Turkey's unilateral seismic work

332 'Nicaragua Bars Honduran and Colombian Trawlers', *Word Markets Analysis*, 17 December 1999.

333 Degan (n. 146) 6.

334 *Aegean Sea Continental Shelf* (Interim Measures) (n. 41) 37 (Dissenting Opinion of Judge Stassinopoulos).

335 Ibid.

336 *Guinea-Bissau* v. *Senegal* (Provisional Measures) (n. 11) 81 (Dissenting Opinion of Judge Thierry); Chapter 6, Section 6.2 below.

337 For more on Greece and Turkey, Chapter 6, Section 6.1 and Chapter 8, Section 8.1.13 below.

in disputed parts of the Aegean Sea, but little beyond that. This is aside from enumerating some general rules of international law that the two States must observe in their bilateral relations. In the preamble to its Resolution, the UNSC began by emphasising that Greece and Turkey needed to exhibit mutual respect for each other's rights and obligations under international law.[338] It continued by stating that Greece and Turkey must do their utmost to avoid undertaking acts unilaterally that aggravate their dispute so as not to frustrate the prospect of the peaceful settlement of their maritime boundary dispute. In the first two paragraphs of the operative part of its Resolution, the UNSC clarified that a further aggravation and extension of the dispute could be forestalled if Greece and Turkey were to observe mutual restraint.[339] Combined with this, they had to make efforts – the UNSC suggested conducting direct negotiations – to defuse the tension that had developed between the two States because of the Turkish unilateral exploratory work.[340]

The roles were reversed in 1987, when Turkey complained to the UNSC about Greece planning to authorise one of its concessionaires to drill in a disputed part of the Aegean Sea.[341] The activation of a concession was argued by Turkey to be irreconcilable with the 1976 Resolution of the UNSC. In a letter submitted to the UNSC, Greece pointed to a discrepancy between Turkey's position on paper and its actual behaviour in practice. This was because Turkey's claim as to the existence of an obligation of absolute restraint that existed under international law in respect of a disputed continental shelf area conflicted with its having granted a number of concessions located in their disputed area, and in relation to which exploration was due to proceed shortly.[342] In the same letter, Greece denied that drilling of its own was to proceed in the short term: it was only in the process of acquiring a majority share in the North Aegean Petroleum Company.[343] The UNSC was apparently satisfied with the assurance given by Greece that the drilling was not to be undertaken in the near future, as it took no further action.

338 UNSC Resolution 395, UN Doc. S/RES/395, 25 August 1976.

339 Ibid.

340 Ibid.

341 Letter dated 23 March 1987 from the Permanent Representative of Turkey to the United Nations addressed to the Secretary-General, UN Doc. S/18759, 23 March 1987.

342 Letter dated 27 March 1987 from the Permanent Representative of Greece to the United Nations addressed to the Secretary-General, UN Doc. S/18766, 27 March 1987.

343 Ibid.

3.1.2 *Cyprus and Turkey*

Both Cyprus and Turkey sought on multiple occasions to have the UNSC pronounce that acts undertaken by the other disputant in relation to disputed waters off the coast of Cyprus created a threat to international peace and security. Most of the protests of the Turkish Republic of Northern Cyprus centred on the island's stability and peace in the Eastern Mediterranean region being undermined as a result of the conduct of Cyprus in relation to mineral resources.[344] Another line of protest arose from Turkey, speaking on behalf of the Turkish Republic of Northern Cyprus, arguing that opening disputed areas for consideration, and conducting unilateral work there, exacerbated difficulties in reaching a negotiated settlement on both the issues of the underlying dispute on title to territory and that of the disputed waters.[345]

Cyprus claimed that Turkey took 'provocative action' in 2002, by allowing the *Piri Reis* to go into a Turkish Cypriot port after it had unlawfully researched areas of the territorial sea and continental shelf aiming to 'reveal the geological structure of the region'.[346] In late January 2007, the Cypriot government announced that it was going to make the necessary preparations to drill in a disputed continental shelf area. Turkey protested along three lines:[347] first, drilling in the disputed waters was prejudicial to settling the underlying dispute on title to territory between the two States; second, Cyprus lacked the jurisdiction to unilaterally authorise petroleum companies to drill, as it would breach the rights of the Turkish population on the island; and, third, Cyprus exacerbated the dispute to a point where international peace and security would be put in jeopardy.[348] Despite Turkey attempting to dissuade Cyprus from exploring for mineral resources unilaterally, Cyprus decided to relaunch a tender for thirteen blocks located in their disputed area.[349] This was, according to Turkey, aimed at creating a fait accompli to the latter's detriment.[350]

344 Letter dated 2 February 2007 from the Permanent Representative of Turkey to the United Nations addressed to the Secretary-General, UN Doc. A/61.727-S/2007/54, 2 February 2007.

345 'A Gassy Problem', *Hurriyet Daily News*, 7 August 2011.

346 Letter dated 28 May 2002 from the Permanent Representative of Cyprus to the United Nations addressed to the Secretary-General, UN Doc. A/56/966-S/2002/587, 28 May 2002.

347 Identical letters dated 31 January 2007 from the Permanent Representative of Cyprus to the United Nations addressed to the Secretary-General and the President of the Security Council, UN Doc. A/61/726-S/2007/52, 2 February 2007.

348 Letter dated 8 August 2007 from the Permanent Representative of Turkey to the United Nations addressed to the Secretary-General, UN Doc. A/61/1027-S/2007/487, 10 August 2007.

349 Letter dated 23 July 2007 from the Permanent Representative of Turkey to the United Nations addressed to the Secretary-General, UN Doc. A/61/1011-S/2007/456, 23 July 2007.

350 Ibid.

Renewed attempts were made some six months later in 2007 by Cyprus to undertake activities in relation to mineral resources in the disputed area.[351] In its strongly worded protest, Turkey made it clear that it was willing to invoke forceful means if necessary, which, according to Cyprus, created a threat to international peace and security.[352]

On 26 November 2008, Turkey once again complained to the UNSC about the unlawfulness of Cyprus' unilateral acts in relation to mineral resources.[353] This was followed by a period of relative calm. Tensions resurfaced between the two States on 29 October 2013,[354] when Cyprus claimed that Turkey had reserved parts of its continental shelf area for conducting seismic work.[355] Both the issuing of a warning and conducting seismic work were considered to be unlawful by Cyprus, calling on Turkey to abort its ongoing work and to refrain from its initiation in the future.[356]

Later, it became clear that the unilateral seismic activity had begun well before Cyprus had protested, as the *Barbaros Hayreddin Paşa*, while being accompanied by a navy frigate, had already completed part of its planned seismic work in the territorial sea.[357] Notwithstanding the protest by Cyprus, Turkey's seismic work continued for almost four months.[358] A short time thereafter, Turkey identified another area in which it wanted to begin seismic work – Cyprus, however, had already concessioned a number of petroleum companies in relation to the area and it thereby protested.[359] In fact, Cyprus had authorised drilling under one of these concessions, as a well was being drilled at the time, prompting a protest from Turkey.[360]

351 Letter dated 6 August 2007 from the Permanent Representative of Cyprus to the United Nations addressed to the Secretary-General, UN Doc. A/61/1020-S/2007/474, 7 August 2007.

352 'Cyprus President Says Exploratory Drilling for Offshore Oil and Gas Deposits to Begin Soon', *The Washington Post*, 13 September 2011.

353 Letter dated 26 November 2008 from the Permanent Representative of Turkey to the United Nations addressed to the Secretary-General, UN Doc. A/63/574-S/2008/741, 28 November 2008.

354 Letter dated 29 October 2013 from the Permanent Representative of Cyprus to the United Nations addressed to the Secretary-General, UN Doc. A/68/555-S/2013/634, 29 October 2013.

355 Ibid.

356 Letter dated 5 December 2013 from the Permanent Representative of Cyprus to the United Nations addressed to the Secretary-General, UN Doc. A/68/644-S/2013/720, 5 December 2013.

357 Ibid.

358 Letter dated 13 February 2014 from the Permanent Representative of Cyprus to the United Nations addressed to the Secretary-General, UN Doc. A/68/759, 18 February 2014.

359 Ibid.

360 Note Verbale dated 13 November 2014 from the Permanent Mission of Cyprus to the United Nations addressed to the Secretary-General, UN Doc. A/69/582, 14 November 2014.

3.1.3 *Libya and Malta*

The positioning of an oil rig by Malta, and conducting exploratory drilling into a disputed continental shelf area, led Libya to send its naval vessels in an attempt to put a stop to the drilling.[361] Following this attempt, Malta complained to the UNSC in September 1980, arguing that Libya's reaction to the drilling threatened international peace and security. Malta's complaint centred on the reaction of Libya being directed against a lawful undertaking in an area that fell squarely within Malta's exclusive jurisdiction;[362] the area was located in much closer proximity to the Maltese coast. More specifically, acts undertaken by Libya, and which threatened international peace and security, were the following, according to Malta: several Libyan warships surrounding the oil rig; one of the Libyan warships attaching itself to the 'buoys of the Italian drilling contractor';[363] ordering the oil rig to terminate its work; uttering additional threats to use force; arresting an Italian representative of the petroleum company; and threatening to use force against other petroleum companies holding concessions from Malta.[364]

Malta's position was effectively built on two pillars: first, the exploratory drilling was lawful because it had been undertaken on Malta's own side of the equidistance boundary – this position was derived from Article 6 1958 CSC;[365] and, second, that Malta possessed the inherent right to drill within the disputed area.[366] The fact that the Libyan government had received a prior notification of the drilling nine months prior, and no protest was received from Libya, reinforced the strength of Malta's contention, so it argued.[367]

After bringing the situation to the attention of the UNSC, Malta requested an assurance from Libya that it would refrain from harassing or threatening its

361 Letter dated 17 November 1981 from the Permanent Representative of Malta to the United Nations addressed to the President of the Security Council, UN Doc. S/14756, 17 November 1981.

362 Letter dated 8 December 1981 from the Permanent Representative of Malta to the United Nations addressed to the President of the General Assembly, UN Doc. S/14782, 9 December 1981.

363 Letter dated 11 September 1980 from the Permanent Representative of Malta to the United Nations addressed to the President of the Security Council, UN Doc. S/14170, 12 September 1980.

364 S/14756 (n. 361); Letter dated 1 September 1980 from the Permanent Representative of Malta to the United Nations addressed to the President of the Security Council, UN Doc. S/14140, 1 September 1980.

365 Chapter 5, Section 5.2 below.

366 Letter dated 4 September 1980 from the Permanent Representative of Malta to the United Nations addressed to the President of the Security Council, UN Doc. S/14147, 4 September 1980.

367 S/14140 (n. 364).

concessionaires to use force while they were operating in the disputed area on future occasions. Libya claimed that the dispute posed no actual threat to international peace and security, thereby placing the matter outside of the purview of the UNSC.[368] The accusation by Malta that Libya was to blame for the conflict was turned on its head by the latter: Malta should have abstained from drilling in relation to the disputed continental shelf area.[369] Malta's attempt to have the UNSC intervene in the matter was with the aim of ensuring that Malta could put its claimed rights to use in the disputed area and be protected from a future use of force, or being threatened therewith, as 'a small and unarmed country'. However, the UNSC declined to pronounce itself on whether the acts of Libya posed a threat to international peace and security.[370]

As Libya kept on delaying the ratification of an earlier agreed settlement agreement, Malta responded in two other ways: first, it accused Libya of employing stalling tactics; and, second, it declared that Libya's claim that, pending delimitation by the ICJ, no drilling could be undertaken unilaterally, was baseless and was 'viewed with grave concern'.[371] Malta in light of the previous history between the two States, where Libya threatened to use force against an oil rig operating in their disputed area and its tardiness in ratifying the settlement agreement, was unwilling to accept this rule.[372] To now introduce a limitation on the possibility for Malta to conduct drilling, rather than five years earlier when Malta expressed its intention thereto, could no longer be considered 'equitable' as it had become increasingly urgent to proceed with this type of activity.[373]

As time passed, Malta grew increasingly frustrated with the stance of Libya,[374] again requesting the UNSC to intervene by, inter alia, condemning Libya for 'its show of force' with regard to the oil rig that moved into their disputed area and began work in 1981, which 'could have led to international

368 Letter dated 11 November 1981 from the Permanent Representative of the Libyan Arab Jamahiriya to the United Nations addressed to the President of the Security Council, UN Doc. S/14752, 12 November 1981; Letter dated 3 September 1980 from the Permanent Representative of the Libyan Arab Jamahiriya to the United Nations addressed to the President of the Security Council, UN Doc. S/14145, 3 September 1980.

369 Ibid.

370 S/14782 (n. 362).

371 Letter dated 23 January 1981 from the Permanent Representative of Malta to the United Nations addressed to the Security Council, UN Doc. S/14343, 23 January 1981.

372 Letter dated 14 January 1981 from the Permanent Representative of the Libyan Arab Jamahiriya to the United Nations addressed to the President of the Security Council, UN Doc. S/14331, 14 January 1981.

373 S/14343 (n. 371).

374 Letter dated 18 June 1981 from the Permanent Representative of Malta to the United Nations addressed to the Security Council, UN Doc. S/14558, 18 June 1981.

hostilities in an already explosive Mediterranean'.[375] According to Malta, there was a continuous threat of peace and security becoming jeopardised: when Libya would be confronted with future unilateral drilling, it would be committed to respond in the same way.[376] Once again, the UNSC did not comment on whether a threat to international peace and security had manifested as alleged by Malta.[377]

3.2 PEACEFUL SETTLEMENT OF MARITIME BOUNDARY DISPUTES

A generally accepted maxim of international law, and a rule of customary international law, is that a peaceful settlement must be brought about, which applies whenever a maritime boundary dispute arises between coastal States or when conflicts are brought about by its absence, for instance because of acts of unilateralism.[378] More specifically, when an international dispute arises, States must seek to settle their differences in a way that does not endanger international peace and security.

Acting in a manner which is otherwise inconsistent with the principles enshrined in the UN Charter,[379] as laid down in various places in the UN Charter (Articles 1(3), 2(3)(4), 13(1)(b), and 55), and reiterated in a number of other multilateral treaties, including Articles 279 and 301 LOSC,[380] is considered to be an unlawful means to settle a dispute; this includes using or threatening to use force. There is also a general mention of the principles of non-use of force and peaceful settlement in the Declaration on Principles of International Law concerning Friendly Relations and Co-operation amongst States (Friendly Relations Declaration),[381] offering a more complete expression of the contents of the principles anchored in the UN Charter.[382] One of its main objectives was to clarify the scope and contents of the principles

375 Letter dated 21 July 1981 from the Permanent Representative of Malta to the United Nations addressed to the President of the Security Council, UN Doc. S/14595, 22 July 1981.

376 S/14756 (n. 361); Letter dated 2 November 1981 from the Acting Permanent Representative of Malta to the United Nations addressed to the President of the Security Council, UN Doc. S/14743, 3 November 1981.

377 'Libya and Malta Seek Ruling', *The New York Times*, 31 July 1982.

378 CD Gray, *International Law and the Use of Force* (Oxford University Press, 2008) 30.

379 Charter of the United Nations, San Francisco, 24 October 1945, 1 UNTS XVI.

380 Jimenez Kwast (n. 277) 59.

381 Declaration on Principles of International Law concerning Friendly Relations and Co-operation among States in Accordance with the Charter of the United Nations General Assembly Resolution 2625 (XXV), 24 October 1970.

382 R Rosenstock, 'The Declaration of Principles of International Law Concerning Friendly Relations: A Survey' (1971) 65(5) *AJIL* 713, 715.

contained in the UN Charter, by taking into account subsequent developments.[383] The Friendly Relations Declaration's relevant elaboration of the principle obliging States to seek a peaceful settlement of their dispute, and that in this search acts aggravating their dispute must be avoided, reads as follows: 'States parties to an international dispute, as well as other States, shall refrain from any action that may aggravate the situation to endanger the maintenance of international peace and security, and shall act in accordance with the purposes and principles of the United Nations.'[384] The reference to the non-aggravation of a dispute resulting from the unilateral actions of States is directly connected to avoiding the emergence of a situation posing a threat to international peace and security,[385] whereby a high threshold is introduced.

In the fourth paragraph of the Friendly Relations Declaration, the category of boundary disputes is addressed, where it is designated as 'as special case of the general prohibition set forth in the first paragraph'.[386] It is phrased in the following terms:

> Every State has the duty to refrain from the threat or use of force to violate the existing international boundaries of another State or as a means of solving international disputes, including territorial disputes and problems concerning frontiers of States.

Although the Friendly Relations Declaration fails to mention that this obligation is directly related to both terrestrial and maritime boundaries, the term 'international boundaries' can be read as to encompass maritime boundaries as well. This view is supported by the ICJ's decision in the *Aegean Sea Continental Shelf* (Jurisdiction) case, where the language used in the context of the Friendly Relations Declaration, that of 'frontiers', was interpreted by the ICJ to similarly encompass maritime boundary disputes.[387] There, the ICJ held that the phrase 'territorial status' also applied to the continental shelf, lending credence to the assumption that maritime boundary disputes are included within the scope of the Friendly Relations Declaration.[388] Moreover, it is questionable whether the abovementioned provision in the Friendly Relations Declaration was meant to give an exhaustive enumeration as to the types of disputes covered by this obligation: 'territorial disputes and problems concerning frontiers of States', signified by

383 I Sinclair, 'The Significance of the Friendly Relations Declaration' in V Lowe and C Warbrick (eds.), *The United Nations and the Principles of International Law* (Routledge, 1994) 1, 25.
384 First paragraph of the Friendly Relations Declaration (n. 381).
385 Section 3.1 above.
386 Rosenstock (n. 382) 718.
387 *Aegean Sea Continental Shelf (Greece v. Turkey)* (Jurisdiction) [1978] ICJ Rep 3, 31–37, [76]–[90].
388 Anderson and Van Logchem (n. 18) 223.

the word 'including', can be read as examples of international disputes that may arise, and wherein the principle of the non-use of force or threat of force equally applies.

3.3 EXERCISING RESTRAINT

There is some mention in international law discourse of the existence of an 'obligation of restraint' that applies in disputed maritime areas,[389] which can refer to three different aspects: first, to the treaty obligation not to hamper or jeopardise in Articles 74(3) and 83(3) LOSC, which is sometimes colloquially referred to as an 'obligation of restraint';[390] second, that as a matter of a general rule of international law States must practise restraint; and, third, that a customary rule obligating States to exercise restraint in disputed maritime areas has come into being as the result of the existence of State practice combined with an *opinio juris*.[391] An example from State practice where the notion of restraint was invoked by a State was when Vietnam accused China of breaching the restraint it is required to observe pursuant to international law, by stopping and arresting Vietnamese fishing vessels in a disputed area.[392]

Regional commitments of States emphasising the importance of restraint in relation to their disputed maritime areas, which serves to mitigate the chances of conflict and to shape a climate in which their maritime boundary disputes could be settled amicably, also exist.[393] A notable example is the Declaration on the Conduct of Parties in the South China Sea (Declaration).[394] Running as a common thread through this Declaration is that States have committed themselves to settle disputes peacefully, and to that end must abstain from complicating or escalating their maritime boundary disputes by acting unilaterally, by authorising or undertaking acts that are under coastal State authority.[395] Although of a non-binding nature, the Declaration refers to international law and includes elements related to the obligations of the coastal States of the South China Sea. More specifically, its point 4, which,

389 BIICL Report (n. 141) 28, 136.

390 Ibid. 122.

391 Ibid. 28, 136.

392 'Vietnam Raises Survey Ship Incident at Singapore Security Dialogue', *BBC Monitoring Asia Pacific – Political*, 7 June 2011.

393 1992 ASEAN Declaration on the South China Sea, Adopted by the Foreign Ministers at the 25th ASEAN Ministerial Meeting in Manila, Philippines, on 22 July 1992.

394 YH Song, 'The South China Sea Declaration on Conduct of Parties and Its Implications: Taiwan's Perspective' (2003) 129 *Maritime Studies* 13, 17.

395 S Wu and H Ren, 'More Than a Declaration: A Commentary on the Background and Significance of the Declaration on the Conduct of the Parties in the South China Sea' (2003) 2(1) *CJIL* 311.

aside from mentioning 'friendly consultations and negotiations', reiterates the obligations of States to settle disputes through peaceful means and to abjure from the use or threat to use force. This is followed by point 5, which reads as follows:

> The Parties undertake to exercise self-restraint in the conduct of activities that would complicate or escalate disputes and affect peace and stability including, among others, refraining from action of inhabiting on presently uninhabited islands, reefs, shoals, cays, and other features and to handle their differences in a constructive manner.

In view of the language employed in this point 5, States of the South China Sea must exercise mutual restraint to avoid aggravating a dispute.[396] The words used are 'complicate' or 'escalate', rather than the more commonly used terms 'aggravation' and 'extension'; but their gist is similar.

How helpful this reference to restraint is has been questioned, with the Declaration failing to single out particular conduct that would meet this threshold,[397] thereby leaving the material reach of this self-restraint largely undefined.[398] Nonetheless, the converse side of this is that the text is flexible and malleable, meaning that it covers the full range of activities having an effect of complicating or escalating a maritime boundary dispute.

The Declaration was initially received with great enthusiasm.[399] But this enthusiasm subsided due to a perceived low observation rate thereof, as examples derived from State practice where there was a perceived lack of observed restraint began to accumulate.[400] After China authorised an oil rig to be placed in a maritime area disputed with the Philippines, the latter's Foreign Secretary invoked the Declaration to argue that the unilateral act breached its terms.[401] The roles were reversed, however, when the Philippines, in the wake of opening tracts for bidding in a disputed part of the South China Sea and inviting the petroleum industry to put in bids,[402] received a protest from China in which it indicated that this breached the principle of restraint, as laid down

396 Amer and Thao (n. 214) 338–339.

397 WN Duong, 'Following the Path of Oil: The Law of the Sea or Realpolitik – What Good Does Law in the South China Sea Territorial Conflicts' (2006–2007) 30(4) *FILJ* 1098, 1173.

398 Amer and Thao (n. 214) 338.

399 NH Thao, 'The 2002 Declaration on the Conduct of Parties in the South China Sea: A Note' (2003) 34(3–4) *ODIL* 279; D Tan, 'The Diaoyu/Senkaku Dispute: Bridging the Cold Divide' (2006) 5(1) *SCJIL* 134, 164–165, 168.

400 BS Glaser, 'Armed Clash in the South China Sea' (2012) 14 *Council on Foreign Relations: Center for Preventive Action* 5.

401 'Philippines to Propose No Action to Raise Tension in Sea Disputes', *Reuters*, 29 July 2014.

402 Degan (n. 146) 10.

in point 5 of the Declaration.[403] China also invoked the Declaration to protest against the 'Joint Oceanographic and Marine Scientific Research Expedition' planned to be jointly undertaken by Vietnam and the Philippines. In its protest, China argued that the States of the South China Sea have committed themselves not to undertake activities in the framework of MSR pursuant to the Declaration; this type of activity would breach the restraint States are required to observe.[404] Attempts to give teeth to this Declaration, being considered the logical next step, have failed so far, however,[405] primarily because the States of the South China Sea accuse each other of unilaterally undertaking acts that violate the principle of restraint.[406]

The Norwegian prime minister, prior to the LOSC coming into force, commented on the state of the international law that is applicable to disputed continental shelf areas, stating that self-restraint is required to be observed by claimants in connection therewith.[407] Without States making explicit what the legal basis is for them exercising restraint, this can potentially be retraced to a large number of sources of international law: general rules of international law (e.g. non-aggravation or non-extension of a dispute or not to threaten irreparability of the other State's rights) or conventional law (e.g. the obligation not to hamper or jeopardise under Articles 74(3) and 83(3) LOSC). Further complicating matters is that the motives underlying exercising restraint by a State in relation to a disputed area can be heterogeneous, or difficult to pinpoint, and may not necessarily be born out of a desire not to breach the applicable international law.[408] In its oral pleadings before the ITLOS, Ghana alluded to the same problem: when States exercise restraint in disputed maritime areas, as was alleged by Côte d'Ivoire to be a general requirement of international law, there is often no way of knowing whether the reason underlying this restraint is paragraph 3 of Article 83 LOSC[409] – or rather that there is an alternative motivation on the part of the State concerned for observing restraint in relation to a disputed area. A coastal State's decision to exercise restraint with regard to a disputed area could be driven by financial

403 'Manila Rejects New Chinese Claim to Territory Just 50 Miles Away from Philippine Province', *The Washington Post*, 14 November 2011.

404 Adopted by the Foreign Ministers of ASEAN and the People's Republic of China at the 8th ASEAN Summit in Phnom Penh, Cambodia, on 4 November 2002.

405 I Storey, 'Kudos for Progress but More Needs to be Done', *The Straits Times*, 30 July 2011.

406 'Vice Foreign Minister of PRC Fu Ying's Interview with the Straits Times and Lianhe Zaobao', 10 September 2012, available at www.chinaembassy.org.sg/eng/xwdt/t967803.htm.

407 RR Churchill and G Ulfstein, *Marine Management in Disputed Areas: The Case of the Barents Sea* (Routledge, 1992) 87.

408 Oude Elferink (n. 254) 210.

409 *Ghana/Côte D'Ivoire* (Judgment) (n. 46) Oral Proceedings (ITLOS/PV.17/C23/3) 29.

motivations. In this vein, if a coastal State were to act unilaterally in relation to mineral resources in a disputed maritime area, and if this were to provoke a conflict with another claimant, foreign petroleum companies might be scared off, leading them to abandon previously adopted commitments, or making them highly reluctant to take on new ones.[410] Alternatively, it could be politically convenient for a coastal State to observe restraint, or that the State in question lacks the technological capabilities to proceed, for example, with work in relation to mineral resources in a disputed area.

Another issue is whether observing restraint by a claimant State with regard to a disputed maritime area by, for example, not giving and activating concessions equals acquiescence.[411] Along these lines, Indonesia sought to construe Malaysia's licensing practice in the Celebes Sea (not extending beyond a particular point) as representing acquiescence in the boundary suggested by Indonesia.[412] International courts and tribunals have not accepted the contention advanced by claimant A that the restraint exercised by claimant B, in that the latter refrained from engaging in particular acts beyond a particular point of a disputed maritime area, or generally abstained from acting in relation thereto, constituted recognition, that is acquiescence.[413] These acts of restraint have rather been interpreted in a positive light: the restraint was born out of a desire not to negatively influence the ongoing dispute, through adding complications or extending its duration.[414] In a similar vein, in determining whether Honduras and Nicaragua tacitly agreed to a maritime boundary by not giving concessions beyond a particular line, the ICJ tied this to the need for observing restraint as required under international law;[415] in terms of prudency, the ICJ applauded this. A similar position emerged from an earlier case dealt with by the ICJ between Indonesia and Malaysia over Pulau Ligitan and Pulau Sipdan, where abstaining from actively concessioning was interpreted as the State being prudent by observing the necessary restraint.[416]

But how to view claims that there is an obligation of restraint under international law, should its existence be considered fact or fiction? To use

[410] Buszynski and Sazlan (n. 127) 166.
[411] X Li, 'Time Right to Develop S China Sea Resources', *Global Times*, 20 October 2011.
[412] T Areej et al., 'The Dispute between Malaysia and Indonesia over the ND6 and ND7 Sea Blocks: A Malaysian Perspective' (2015) 8(1) *JEAIL* 171, 180–181.
[413] *Territorial and Maritime Dispute between Nicaragua and Honduras in the Caribbean Sea (Nicaragua* v. *Honduras)* [2007] ICJ Rep 659, 735–736 [254]; *Sovereignty over Pulau Ligitan and Pulau Sipadan (Indonesia/Malaysia)* [2002] ICJ Rep 625, 664 [79].
[414] Ibid.
[415] Ibid. *Nicaragua* v. *Honduras.*
[416] *Indonesia/Malaysia* (n. 413) 664 [79].

the words 'obligation of restraint' as a colloquial short form to refer to the obligation not to hamper or jeopardise under Articles 74(3) and 83(3) LOSC does not raise any significant issues. Quite a different matter is whether an obligation of restraint, having a standing of its own, does operate as a general rule of international law in disputed maritime areas. More aptly put, the obligation of restraint is a patchwork of different strands of international law, which are at one in imposing on coastal States an obligation to observe a measure of restraint. While some of these have the status of a general rule of international law, others are treaty-based. This includes the obligation not to aggravate or extend a dispute, the obligation not to cause irreparable prejudice to the rights of the other State, and – tailored specifically to disputed EEZ/continental shelf areas – the treaty obligation not to hamper or jeopardise delimitation. In terms of scope of application, the obligation not to hamper or jeopardise encompasses the broadest range of unilateral acts falling within the authority of the coastal State, due to its setting the lowest threshold in order to assume a breach thereof.[417] As a result, acts aggravating or extending a dispute, or causing irreparable prejudice to rights, would automatically breach Articles 74(3) and 83(3) LOSC.

The measure of restraint that a claimant must observe in respect of a disputed maritime area cannot be defined *in abstracto*, rather it varies according to the given locality and the type of activity concerned.[418] Similarly, Ghana in its maritime boundary dispute with Côte d'Ivoire argued that an assessment whether a unilateral act falling under the jurisdiction of the coastal State has an effect of hampering or jeopardising must be made in the context of the particular situation.[419] State practice supported taking such a case-oriented approach, providing a highly diversified picture that is as follows: while unilateral seismic work has created a significant conflict in certain disputed maritime areas, in other disputed areas, however, the generally considered more invasive act of unilateral drilling has not led to conflicts in bilateral relations.[420] In fact, the aspect of the specific circumstances that exist in a disputed maritime area renders distinguishing between lawful and unlawful acts *in abstracto* a problematic exercise.[421] Hence, there is a need for the malleability of the applicable international law to determine the actual restraint that must be observed in relation to a disputed maritime area by an individual claimant. One possible variable is that the larger and more

[417] Chapter 5, Section 5.3.4 below.
[418] Chapter 9, Section 9.3.2 below.
[419] *Ghana/Côte d'Ivoire* (Judgment) (n. 46) Reply of Ghana 151–152 [5.38].
[420] Ibid.
[421] Chapter 9, Section 9.3 below.

powerful the State, the greater is its responsibility in observing restraint in disputed maritime areas.[422]

3.4 IRREPARABLE PREJUDICE TO RIGHTS

Usually, when dealing with maritime boundary disputes,[423] international courts and tribunals will have jurisdiction to prescribe interim measures of protection whenever the situation so requires, or upon the explicit request of one of the parties to a dispute. The primary aim of interim measures procedures is to ensure that the rights of the parties to a dispute are preserved prior to that a judgment on the merits is delivered, and that it is not rendered inconsequential by unilateral measures taken by the States concerned. A central question in the case law on interim protection is that there must be an imminent and real threat of irreparability to the rights of the other State, in order for an international court or tribunal to prescribe interim measures of protection.[424]

In its decision in the *Aegean Sea Continental Shelf* (Interim Measures) case, the ICJ considered that an emerging threat of irreparability existed concerning the other State's sovereign rights if a State were to appropriate mineral resources from a disputed continental shelf area, to undertake exploratory drilling, and to move installations into such an area.[425] The continued relevance of this concept of irreparable prejudice is demonstrated by the fact that, in its award in *Guyana* v. *Suriname*, the Tribunal invoked the principle of irreparable prejudice to rights by analogy in clarifying the content of Articles 74(3) and 83(3) LOSC.[426] Since then, not threatening irreparable prejudice to rights has effectively become the threshold that needs to be exceeded in order for international courts and tribunals to assume the unlawfulness of a unilateral act, falling under the jurisdiction of the coastal State, within a disputed maritime area.[427]

Concerning law enforcement in disputed areas, the following argument (mainly derived from the *Icelandic Fisheries Jurisdiction* cases) has been presented: taking enforcement measures against the other claimant State, usually a private actor operating with its consent, invariably threatens the

422 'US to South China Sea Claimants: Set Good Example', *The Philippine Star*, 30 July 2014.

423 Van Logchem (n. 21) 194–195.

424 *Pulp Mills on the River Uruguay (Argentina* v. *Uruguay)* (Provisional Measures) [2007] ICJ Rep 3, 13 [32]; *Ghana/Côte d'Ivoire* (Provisional Measures) (n. 42) 155 [41]; *The 'Enrica Lexie' Incident (Italy* v. *India)* (Provisional Measures) [2015] ITLOS Rep 24, 197 [87].

425 *Aegean Sea Continental Shelf* (Interim Measures) (n. 41) 10 [30].

426 Chapter 6, Section 6.6 below.

427 BIICL Report (n. 141) 37–38.

latter State's rights with irreparability, hence rendering it unlawful.[428] At the heart of the *Icelandic Fisheries Jurisdiction* cases was Iceland's unilateral extension of its exclusive fisheries jurisdiction from 12 to 50 nm, which prompted Germany and the United Kingdom to request interim measures of protection from the ICJ. They argued that this unilateral extension violated international law, resulting in a decrease of high seas areas where their fishermen were able to fish freely and making them a target of law enforcement by Iceland. To prevent this, both Germany and the United Kingdom requested the ICJ to indicate interim measures of protection with the following aim: Iceland had to be forbidden *pendente litis* from taking enforcement measures against vessels flying the flags of Germany and the United Kingdom within the newly and unlawfully extended zone. The Court acceded to this request.[429] However, contrary to the view that the *Icelandic Fisheries Jurisdiction* cases illustrate the unlawfulness of law enforcement in disputed areas,[430] they contain two peculiarities which preclude an analogous application of what was held in these cases to disputed maritime areas.[431] First, the cases were dealt with on the eve of the expansion of the entitlements of coastal States to maritime zones; and, second, the Icelandic unilateral claim did not create a maritime area subject to the overlapping claims of coastal States.

3.5 NON-AGGRAVATION OR NON-EXTENSION OF A DISPUTE

The principle of States having to refrain from aggravating or extending a dispute, in the main, requires them to observe a measure of restraint. It has a close connection with other principles of international law: that is, disputes need to be settled peacefully, States must refrain from the use of force, act in good faith, and not abuse their rights.[432] An example of a State invoking the notions of non-aggravation and non-extension is Turkey, when it accused Cyprus of having aggravated their dispute by conducting seismic work when faced with protests from the Turkish Republic of Northern Cyprus, and while negotiations on the underlying territorial dispute were ongoing.[433]

428 Dang (n. 199) 73–74.
429 *Fisheries Jurisdiction (United Kingdom of Great Britain and Northern Ireland* v. *Iceland)* (Request for the Indication of Interim Measures of Protection) [1972] ICJ Rep 4, 17.
430 BIICL Report (n. 141) 74.
431 But see N Klein, 'Provisional Measures and Provisional Arrangements' in AG Oude Elferink et al. (eds.), *Maritime Boundary Delimitation: The Case Law* (Cambridge University Press, 2020) 117, 132.
432 Van Logchem (n. 52) 61–62.
433 A/63/574-S/2008/741 (n. 353).

In terms of its origin, aggravating or extending a dispute first surfaced in 1939 in the decision in *Electricity Company of Sofia and Bulgaria*. One of the common threads in the order of the PCIJ was related to preventing a State's rights from being prejudiced, and that the final resolution of a dispute was not made more difficult. In the operative part of the order, the PCIJ, after laying out the foundation for this view, stated 'that no step of any kind is taken capable ... of aggravating or extending the dispute submitted to the Court.'[434] In this respect, the PCIJ indicated that it was merely giving expression to a principle that had gained universal acceptance by international courts and tribunals and in treaty law.[435] The PCIJ, by concluding that there was a general principle of not aggravating or extending a dispute under international law, must have seen it either as a universal principle, which later became embodied in Article 41 ICJ Statute, or as being inherent in the judicial function.[436] Subsequently, not aggravating (or not extending) a dispute disappeared from the case law for some years.[437] Thereafter, it made a revival in the requests of some States for interim measures of protection before the ICJ, starting with the *Anglo-Iranian Oil Co.* case in 1951,[438] and since then it has been a regular component in decisions of the ICJ and other international courts and tribunals.

The place that the principle of not aggravating or extending a dispute has occupied in indicated interim measures by international courts and tribunals varies in two ways – the defining difference being the importance attributed to this principle as the underlying rationale for the decision on whether relief *pendente litis* can be offered. Its first application is that interim measures of protection can be indicated with not aggravating or extending the dispute being the sole *ratio decidendi*.[439] The order in the *Case concerning the Frontier Dispute* has become the *casus classicus* for arguing for the existence of a threat of a dispute being aggravated or extended, as *simpliciter* sufficient to indicate interim measures of protection.[440] The second application is that interim

434 *Electricity Company of Sofia and Bulgaria* (Request for the Indication of Interim Measures of Protection) [1939] PCIJ Series A/B No. 79 194, 199.

435 Ibid.

436 HWA Thirlway, 'The Indication of Provisional Measures by the International Court of justice' in R Bernhardt (ed.), *Interim Measures Indicated by International Courts* (Springer, 1994) 1, 13.

437 *Electricity Company of Sofia and Bulgaria* (n. 434) 199.

438 *Anglo-Iranian Oil Co. Case* (Interim Measures) [1951] ICJ Rep 1951 89, 93.

439 R Kolb, 'Note on New International Case-Law Concerning the Binding Character of Provisional Measures' (2005) 74(1) *NJIL* 117, 125; PJ Goldsworthy, 'Interim Measures of Protection in the International Court of Justice' (1974) 68(2) *AJIL* 258, 261.

440 *Frontier Dispute (Burkina Faso/Republic of Mali)* (Provisional Measures) [1986] ICJ Rep 3, 9 [18].

measures of protection indicated with the aim of not aggravating or extending a dispute are covered under the broad umbrella of there being a threat of causing irreparability to rights. Here the overarching reason for providing interim protection was thus to avert rights becoming irreparably prejudiced. In *Pulp Mills* (Provisional Measures), the Court has regarded its power to indicate interim protection to be inexorably interwoven with the presence of an urgent necessity to prevent irreparable prejudice being done to a State's rights, prior to a final ruling on the matter having been delivered.[441]

Another key issue centres on the status of non-aggravation and non-extension under international law in a more general sense. Is their relevance confined to when the dispute is under the consideration of an international court or tribunal and measures of interim protection are indicated to that end, or does abstaining from aggravating or extending a dispute exist as a duty, outside of the context of interim measures procedures, that is as a general rule of international law?

Not aggravating or extending a dispute can be assumed to be a general rule of international law.[442] Support for the existence of such a general rule comes from the fact that, almost routinely, international courts and tribunals will call on parties to a dispute to refrain from aggravating or extending their dispute in their indicated interim measures of protection.[443] In their separate opinions in the *Aegean Sea Continental Shelf* (Interim Measures) case,[444] Judges Elias and Lachs both reiterated that, as a general rule of international law, States must refrain from taking acts that aggravate or extend their dispute.[445] Lagoni combined two sources to argue for the existence of a rule of customary international law imposing a duty on States not to aggravate or extend: first, the earlier discussed dictum of the PCIJ in *Electricity Company of Sofia and Bulgaria*; and, second, several provisions of the General Act for the Pacific Settlement of Disputes of 1928.[446] An example from State practice is that the coastal States of the South China Sea have made declarations in terms of them having to exercise restraint in order not to aggravate or extend their existing disputes.[447]

441 *Argentina* v. *Uruguay* (n. 424) 129 [62].

442 AHA Soons and N Schrijver, 'What Does International Law Say about the China–Japan Dispute over the Diaoyu/Senkaku Islands?' (2012) *HIGJ Briefing Paper* 3, 17.

443 DW Greig, 'The Balancing of Interests and the Granting of Interim Protection by the International Court' (1987) 11 *AusYIL* 108, 124.

444 *Aegean Sea Continental Shelf* (Interim Measures) (n. 41) 28 (Separate Opinion of Judge Elias); 20–21 (Separate Opinion of Judge Lachs).

445 Ibid.

446 Lagoni (n. 243) 363.

447 Djalal (n. 94) 113–125.

Additional confirmation is to be found in, inter alia, the rather widespread inclusion of these notions of non-aggravation and non-extension in various international law documents. Its inclusion in these documents was seen by the Tribunal in *Philippines* v. *China* as support for the existence of an obligation not to aggravate or extend a dispute under international law while States are involved in dispute settlement proceedings.[448] Here the Tribunal elaborated on the extensive case law that has been developed over the years by international courts and tribunals in which the general principle of not aggravating or extending a dispute was invoked.[449] Although recognising that the cases in question were interim measures procedures, which meant that they had a special character, the Tribunal went on to suggest that this general principle of not aggravating or extending a dispute does not exist in the vacuum of when interim protection is prescribed by an international court or tribunal, or when a dispute settlement process is set in train by the States concerned.[450]

Furthermore, the treaty obligation in the form of not hampering or jeopardising, as contained in Articles 74(3) and 83(3) LOSC, reinforces the status of not aggravating and extending a dispute as a general rule, by tailoring it to be applied to disputed EEZ and continental shelf areas.[451] This is even though its language – not hampering or jeopardising – is slightly different from the standard wording found in many interim measures orders, with the latter calling upon States to take no steps leading to an aggravation or extension of their dispute.[452] Nonetheless, the gist of the terms 'hamper', 'jeopardise', 'aggravate', or 'extend' is similar: reaching a particular result (i.e. delimitation or resolving a dispute) must not be made more difficult, through unilateral acts falling within coastal State jurisdiction being undertaken having one, or a combination, of these four effects.

3.6 THE PRINCIPLE OF GOOD FAITH AND THE PROHIBITION ON ABUSE OF RIGHTS

In its ruling in *North Sea Continental Shelf*, the ICJ stated that States are under an obligation to conduct delimitation negotiations in good faith,[453] but they do not need to end successfully.[454] This obligation can be extended to

448 *In the Matter of the South China Sea Arbitration (Philippines* v. *China)* [2016] XXXIII RIAA 166, 599–600 [1169]–[1170].

449 Ibid. 601 [1173].

450 Ibid.

451 Lagoni (n. 243) 363.

452 Van Logchem (n. 52) 60–62.

453 *North Sea Continental Shelf* (n. 8) 45–48 [85] [87].

454 *Land and Maritime Boundary between Cameroon and Nigeria (Cameroon* v. *Nigeria; Equatorial Guinea intervening)* [2002] ICJ Rep 303, 424 [244].

apply to when a claimant wants to enter into negotiations on delimitation or cooperative arrangements in good faith, and extends an invitation to that end; then, an obligation to start negotiations in good faith exists.[455] Another requirement derived from this principle is that, while negotiating, a State must refrain from conducting itself in a manner such that the reason for instigating the negotiations is prematurely defeated. Hence, conducting unilateral acts having a detrimental effect on the progress or outcome of talks (e.g. issuing concessions, or announcing a willingness to activate such concessions) may breach the principle of good faith. It is also relevant that both obligations in Articles 74(3) and 83(3) LOSC are underpinned by a good faith component, which widens the range of conduct that can be captured under these obligations compared to if these were obligations of result.[456]

The requirement of acting in good faith is echoed in treaty form in Article 300 LOSC, which stipulates that States should not misuse their rights; such a use would suggest that a State has acted in bad faith. Tailored to disputed areas, these basic principles of good faith and the prohibition on abuse of rights operate more broadly in the period preceding delimitation in several ways. For example, a State by starting with unilateral drilling or through taking enforcement action in response to an alleged violation of its rights has seemingly lost its willingness to negotiate in good faith on settling a dispute.[457] Also, the possibility of an abuse of right might enter into the picture if a State decides to act on its rights with regard to a disputed maritime area, by authorising an activity or starting with a physical activity unilaterally, and if that act leads to a significant conflict between the States concerned. Then, the argument can be made that the State undertaking or authorising an act on the basis of its rights would have misused them.

3.7 THE PRINCIPLE OF DUE REGARD

The concept of due regard, which is also anchored in treaty form in the LOSC (e.g. Articles 79(5) and 87(2)), is derived from the principle of good faith.[458] In *Fisheries Jurisdiction (United Kingdom of Great Britain and Northern Ireland* v. *Iceland*), the ICJ, basing itself on customary law, held that both parties to the dispute, having concurrent rights, were under an obligation to have due regard for each other's rights. This similarly applied to the period when the States

455 *Ghana/Côte d'Ivoire* (Judgment) (n. 46) 167 [628].
456 Chapter 5, Section 5.3.2.5 below.
457 BIICL Report (n. 141) 19.
458 Articles 56(2) and 58(3) LOSC.

concerned would be negotiating in good faith on settling their dispute.[459] The Tribunal in *Philippines* v. *China* went along similar lines, although with the addition that beyond having due regard for another State's rights this also extends to its obligations.[460]

When applied to disputed maritime areas, the concept of due regard has the following implication: coastal States must exercise their rights reasonably, and they must observe a measure of restraint while acting in relation thereto.[461] Having due regard will not only apply in relations between coastal States, however. Articles 56(2) and 58(3) LOSC are respectively tailored to coastal States or third States, pursuant to which these two groups of States must show mutual respect for each other's rights. In fact, Article 56(2) LOSC extends the sphere of operation of the obligation for the coastal State to exercise due regard to all 'other States'. Because of the generality of the wording, an additional requirement rests on claimant States in respect of disputed maritime areas: they must have due regard for each other's entitlements and related rights to maritime zones. However, there is a further relevant aspect: coastal States must also respect the rights and freedoms of third States in these areas.[462] This is relevant because Articles 74(3) and 83(3) LOSC do not govern issues between a claimant coastal State and a third State, or its nationals, in relation to disputed EEZ/continental shelf areas.[463] Conflicts between a coastal State and a third State created by the existence of disputed maritime areas can be mediated by whether the two groups of States have observed the required measure of 'due regard' for each other's rights, pursuant to the parallel provisions of Articles 56(2), 58(3), 87(2), and 79(5) LOSC. An example of showing due regard for the rights of coastal States, as is envisaged under Article 58(3) LOSC, is the general policy of submarine cable companies incorporated in third States sending notifications when submarine cable operations are planned to be undertaken in disputed EEZ or continental shelf areas.[464]

3.8 PRESERVATION OF THE STATUS QUO

Another notion, having a close connection to restraint, is the preservation of an existing status quo by States. Its gist, when applied to disputed maritime areas,

459 *Fisheries Jurisdiction (United Kingdom of Great Britain and Northern Ireland* v. *Iceland)* [1974] ICJ Rep 3, 20, 27, 34 [50] [62] [79].

460 *Philippines* v. *China* (n. 448) 608 [1197].

461 DH Anderson, 'Freedom of the High Seas in the Modern Law of the Sea' in D Freestone et al. (eds.), *The Law of the Sea: Progress and Prospects* (Oxford University Press, 2006) 327, 331–332; Churchill and Lowe (n. 1) 206.

462 Chapter 2, Section 2.4 above.

463 Van Logchem (n. 244) 116.

464 Ibid. 119.

is as follows: no unilateral acts falling under the authority of the coastal State may be undertaken that lead to a change in the status quo. Rosenne defined the importance of obligations imposed on States pursuant to the UN Charter in the context of areas of overlapping claims, through the same lens: they seek to avert changes being made to the existing status quo between the States concerned.[465] An example derived from State practice is when the Philippines accused China of having upset the existing status quo through taking the following steps: declining to remove Chinese vessels from Scarborough Shoal; the imposition of a moratorium on fishing; and engaging in land reclamation projects in the Spratly Islands.[466]

A status quo is not synonymous with a moratorium. The main substantive difference is that there might be certain types of acts that are under the authority of the coastal State that may be undertaken unilaterally within a disputed maritime area, because of these acts being a part of the existing status quo. For instance, if all claimants undertake seismic work, without protest, this category of unilateral activity is part of the status quo, making it a lawful use of a disputed area. In a similar vein, Ghana in its maritime boundary dispute with Côte d'Ivoire contended that economic conduct that was a part of the status quo that existed between them could not possibly hamper or jeopardise delimitation.[467] To the contrary, it is activities falling outside of the status quo that are prohibited from being undertaken without the consent of the other State. The status quo is not static; it may change its composition as time elapses or with the changing attitudes and positions of the States concerned.

A key step in operationalising this notion in a disputed maritime area is to construe the existing status quo between the States involved. At the same time, this may form the crux in its successful operationalisation: conflict might arise between claimant States over what the relevant status quo is composed of, and which is to be preserved in the period preceding delimitation.[468] Illustrating this is the positions taken by Ghana and Côte d'Ivoire in their maritime boundary dispute as to the composition of the status quo existing between them. Côte d'Ivoire sought to subject the disputed area with Ghana to a moratorium, which it deemed to be the required status quo.[469] Ghana,

465 MH Nordquist et al. (eds.), *United Nations Convention on the Law of the Sea 1982, A Commentary*, Vol. V (Martinus Nijhoff, 1989) 124.

466 'At UN Assembly' (n. 241).

467 *Ghana/Côte d'Ivoire* (Judgment) (n. 46) Reply of Ghana 137 [5.2].

468 *Passage through the Great Belt (Finland* v. *Denmark)* (Provisional Measures) [1991] ICJ Rep 12, 18–19 [28]–[30].

469 *Ghana/Côte d'Ivoire* (Provisional Measures) (n. 42) 152–153 [25].

however, construed the prevailing status quo differently: a de facto equidistant maritime boundary existed between both the parties to the dispute, meaning that Ghana could freely undertake acts in relation to mineral resources on its own side of the boundary.[470] Also, in distinguishing between permissible and impermissible unilateral acts falling under the jurisdiction of the coastal State, Suriname, in its maritime boundary dispute with Guyana, relied on the notion of the status quo,[471] which consisted of 'transitory or tolerated occasional actions',[472] and excluded acts of unilateral drilling as undertaken by Guyana.[473] Whatever the difficulties with determining the status quo, the acts that must be postponed are those through which the prevailing status quo is altered; significant in determining whether such a caused alteration is lawful in a disputed EEZ/continental shelf area are Articles 74(3) and 83(3) LOSC.[474]

3.9 THE NO-HARM PRINCIPLE

Under international law, States are required to behave as good neighbours pursuant to the principle of good neighbourliness – this is stated in the Latin maxim *sic utere tuo, ut alienum non laedas*. Good neighbourliness, which can be designated as the requirement of causing no harm, is one of the bedrocks on which a peaceful coexistence of States on the international plane is founded.[475] This principle is fairly abstract, but it encompasses more specific components, one of which is the obligation that a State having to be a good neighbour cannot use areas under its sovereignty or jurisdiction in such a way as to cause harm.[476]

On various occasions, the ICJ has endorsed the existence of this specific application of the principle of good neighbourliness. The gist of its statements was that States must 'ensure that activities within their jurisdiction and control respect the environment of other States'.[477] Article 300 LOSC, which requires

470 *Ghana/Côte d'Ivoire* (Judgment) (n. 46) Reply of Ghana 137 [5.2].

471 *Guyana* v. *Suriname* (n. 7) Suriname's Counter-Memorial 117 [7.42].

472 Ibid.

473 Ibid. Suriname's Rejoinder 28 [4.15]–[4.16]; Guyana's Reply 138–139 [5.5].

474 Chapter 5, Section 5.3 below.

475 Article 74 UN Charter.

476 Z Gao, 'The Legal Concept and Aspects of Joint Development in International Law' in EM Borgese et al. (eds.), *Ocean Yearbook*, Vol. 13 (Brill, 1997) 107, 114–115.

477 *Legality of the Threat or Use of Nuclear Weapons* (Advisory Opinion) [1996] ICJ Rep 226, 241 [29]; *Pulp Mills on the River Uruguay (Argentina* v. *Uruguay)* (Judgment) [2010] ICJ Rep 14, 55–56 [101]; *Gabčíkovo-Nagymaros Project (Hungary* v. *Slovakia)* [1997] ICJ Rep 7, 77–78 [140].

that States must exercise their rights in a way that does not abuse these rights, is geared towards a similar aim. The no-harm principle as understood in the usual sense, in that it relates to using areas that are under the sovereignty or jurisdiction of one State, does not neatly fit the situation that exists in a disputed maritime area, with there being at least two coastal States involved that lay claim to the same area. A broader interpretation of the no-harm principle, in which likewise disputed maritime areas would be encompassed, runs as follows:[478] a claimant State must refrain from activities that infringe upon a neighbouring coastal State's entitlements to maritime zones and related rights that it enjoys under international law.

Two different positions emerge when the thrust of the no-harm principle, defined in the way as set out above, is applied to disputed maritime areas. The first position is that a claimant must abstain from engaging in a unilateral act that falls within the authority of the coastal State, which might subsequently be shown to have violated international law; that is, if, after delimitation, the area is located on the side of the boundary of the other State, being the one that has not acted unilaterally.[479] This is regardless of the nature or extent of such a wrong. Understood as such, the no-harm principle in connection with a disputed continental shelf area, to which rights exist ab initio, or a disputed EEZ area, would have the de facto effect of introducing a moratorium on activities falling under coastal State jurisdiction. Support for this view concerning continental shelf areas comes from the fact that Article 77 LOSC points to the exclusivity of a coastal State's sovereign rights in relation thereto. However, when viewed in the light of international case law, and its emphasis on the fact that the rights of the other State must be threatened with irreparability in order for a unilateral act falling under the jurisdiction of the coastal State to be considered unlawful, this makes the first position seemingly more difficult to uphold.[480]

The second position based on the principle of no harm is a claimant accepting the risk that, if, after delimitation, the act turns out to have taken place on the other State's side of the boundary, it has committed a breach of international law, giving rise to international responsibility. An example of the application of the no-harm principle in this manner is visible in the ICJ's decision in *Certain Activities Carried Out by Nicaragua in the Border Area (Costa Rica* v. *Nicaragua)*, which was about a disputed mainland territory to

478 BIICL Report (n. 141) 20.

479 M Miyoshi, 'The Basic Concept of Joint Development of Hydrocarbons on the Continental Shelf' (1988) 3(1) *IJECL* 1, 10; Churchill and Ulfstein (n. 407) 89.

480 *Aegean Sea Continental Shelf* (Interim Measures) (n. 41) 10–11 [28]–[33].

which Costa Rica and Nicaragua had competing title claims. In its order,[481] the ICJ ordered both parties to the dispute to abstain from having military personnel present in the disputed territory pending the settlement of their dispute. It also found that previously undertaken acts, including dredging by Nicaragua on what turned out to be Costa Rica's territory,[482] breached international law and had to be properly compensated.[483] The ICJ tied the unlawful character of the conduct to the fact that these acts had occurred on, what could be considered in hindsight, the sovereign territory of Costa Rica.

On a *mutatis mutandis* application of what the ICJ held and when applying it to disputed continental shelf areas, this may entail that, if a claimant decides to undertake certain acts unilaterally on the basis of its inherent rights, and if it turns out that the area in question is located on the other State's side of the boundary after delimitation, a breach of international law has automatically occurred. Despite the inherent right component being absent concerning EEZ areas, the lack thereof would not alter the argument that drastically;[484] this is because, if coastal States have claimed EEZs in accordance with international law which overlap, the claimed entitlement to one, and the rights and obligations it carries with it, are not fictitious; this is even when the extent of the EEZ is unclear due to the boundary not having been delimited.

3.10 THE USE OR THREAT OF FORCE

Disputes over land boundaries have been assumed to more readily evolve into armed conflicts than their counterparts at sea.[485] Short of armed conflict, the use of force by a claimant State, or threats made as to its future use, against the other claimant or a national of a third State upon their conducting activities in disputed maritime areas are, however, not merely theoretical speculation. Complicating matters in this regard is that the dividing line between what constitutes lawful 'law enforcement' and the 'use of force' is not always easily drawn. One reason for this is that reactions taken under the pretence of law enforcement can also fall within the category of an unlawful use of force, as for

481 *Certain Activities Carried Out by Nicaragua in the Border Area (Costa Rica* v. *Nicaragua)* (Provisional Measures) [2011] ICJ Rep 6, 27–28 [86].

482 *Certain Activities Carried Out by Nicaragua in the Border Area (Costa Rica* v. *Nicaragua)* and *Construction of a Road in Costa Rica along the San Juan River (Nicaragua* v. *Costa Rica)* (Judgment) [2015] ICJ Rep 665, 703 [93].

483 Ibid.

484 But see BIICL Report (n. 141) 20; NA Ioannides, 'The Legal Framework Governing Hydrocarbon Activities in Undelimited Maritime Areas' 68(2) *ICLQ* 345, 358.

485 J Paulsson, 'Boundary Disputes into the Twenty-First Century: Why, How … and Who?' (2001) 95 *American Society of International Law Proceedings* 122; Mensah (n. 69) 145.

example *Guyana* v. *Suriname* exemplifies.[486] Nevertheless, the other side to this is that the use of force during law enforcement operations is not unlawful per se.[487]

After being confronted with plans for acts falling within the authority of the coastal State to be undertaken unilaterally within a disputed area by the other claimant State, or when a protest has been prompted as a result, certain States are quick to resort to using the threat to use force rhetoric – its gist is that a State will use (the threat of) force in an attempt to dissuade the other State from acting in disputed waters. One example is South Korea not excluding the possibility of using force against Japan, if the latter would follow through on its intentions to conduct a 'marine survey' in the disputed waters off the coast of Dokdo/Takeshima.[488] Similarly, the discovery of an oil and gas field in a disputed part of the Mediterranean Sea by Israel spurred some heated exchanges of words with Lebanon, with both sides alluding to the possibility of employing force to protect their respective rights.[489]

Practice shows that coastal States have occasionally decided to respond to unilateral acts falling under coastal State jurisdiction in a way that is seen as difficult to reconcile with the obligation not to use force or utter threats as to its use. For instance, a seismic vessel operated by a petroleum company incorporated in the United States, which was licensed by Guyana to start work off the coast of the disputed Essequibo region, was greeted by a Venezuelan naval vessel, which commanded the work to stop and instructed the seismic vessel to make its way towards a Venezuelan port for further processing.[490] Guyana's president, talking about the incident in Parliament, stated that expelling the unarmed seismic vessel from their disputed area was in fact an 'extreme use of force'.[491]

Two other examples can be given. First, after naval vessels belonging to the Philippines detected that China had demolished structures built on Mischief Reef that had been used by fishermen,[492] these Philippine naval vessels were met by Chinese naval vessels that were dispatched to the area. Subsequently,

[486] Chapter 6, Section 6.3.2 below.

[487] Chapter 9, Section 9.3.3.4 below.

[488] 'S. Korea Threatens to Use Force against Japan's Maritime Challenge', *Yonhap*, 18 April 2006; 'S. Korea Vows to Take All Measures to Protect Dokdo', *Yonhap*, 20 April 2006.

[489] 'Israel-Hezbollah Dispute over Mediterranean Resources', *Huffington Post*, 26 July 2011; 'Lebanon to Fight Israel at U.N.', *Daily Star Lebanon*, 11 July 2011.

[490] Chapter 8, Section 8.2 below.

[491] 'The Caribbean . . . a Zone of Peace', Address by Brigadier David Granger, MSS, President of the Cooperative Republic of Guyana, to the 11th Parliament, Georgetown, 9 July 2015, available at www.minfor.gov.gy/docs/otherspeeches/Address_to_Parliament_HE.pdf.

[492] S Raine, 'Beijing's South China Sea Debate' (2011) 53(5) *Survival: Global Politics and Strategy* 69, 73.

rounds of fire were exchanged between these navy vessels. Second, when China cut cables attached to vessels that Vietnam had allowed to survey disputed areas of the South China Sea, the US Senate considered this to be an unlawful use of force.[493]

In *Guyana* v. *Suriname*, Guyana sought a declaration from the Tribunal on its submission that Suriname by putting a stop to lawful drilling had breached the obligation to peacefully settle a dispute, by employing force that violated the territorial integrity of Guyana.[494] While marked disparities in wealth or power between the two States are not evident, the use of force by Suriname was seen by Guyana to be particularly controversial in light of its limited military capabilities. Suriname argued that the accusation of Guyana that its territorial integrity had been breached was premature – after all, the incident occurred in a disputed maritime area, meaning that such a contention could only succeed after a delimitation had been effected, and the area was located on Guyana's side of the established maritime boundary.[495] Apart from this argument, Suriname sought to persuade the Tribunal that its reaction was towards a lawful end as the drilling occurred within its sovereign waters, and could not be considered an unlawful use of force.[496] No instructions had been given to its naval vessels to use force against the oil rig, nor did the Surinamese naval officers harbour any intention to use force or threaten its use.[497] The only available firepower were small handguns in the possession of the naval officers for the purposes of self-defence.[498] The Tribunal in its considerations attributed no significance to the fact that the 'territorial integrity or political independence' of Guyana could not be considered breached, because the incident occurred in a disputed area. In its award, the Tribunal concluded that Suriname's reaction, being in the nature of self-help, violated, amongst others, the UN Charter, requiring States to refrain from threatening to use force.[499]

3.11 STATE RESPONSIBILITY

Questions of state responsibility may arise when a State has acted unilaterally, by authorising or undertaking acts that are under coastal State authority, in relation to a disputed maritime area. Once conduct occurs that breaches a rule

493 US Senate Resolution No. 412, 10 July 2014.
494 *Guyana* v. *Suriname* (n. 7) 120 [426].
495 Ibid. 145 [441].
496 Ibid.
497 Ibid. 143 [437].
498 Ibid.
499 Ibid. 147–148 [446].

of international law, it should be properly repaired.[500] Two conditions must be met for responsibility to be found by an international court or tribunal. First, there must be an obligation of international law that applies in the relation between the State alleging such a breach and the State that has acted in such a way as to cause injury. Second, the conduct must be attributable to the State whose (in)action has resulted in damage:[501] that is, a causal connection needs to exist between the harmful conduct in question and the damage incurred. In assessing a breach, and to engage responsibility, rules of international law provide the relevant standard against which the conduct is judged. Conduct that breaches one or both of the obligations contained in Articles 74(3) and 83(3) LOSC, or other rules of international law that are applicable to disputed areas, are in principle therefore suitable for reparation. Consider, for example, the unilateral extraction of mineral resources from the seabed of the disputed area, which can be viewed as breaching international law and could incur State responsibility: that is, if, after delimitation, the area in question is not considered to be under the exclusive jurisdiction of the extracting State.[502]

States faced with issues related to a unilateralism in disputed maritime area have exhibited a willingness to bring issues of State responsibility to the attention of international courts and tribunals, frequently requesting to be appropriately compensated for, or that, if the wrong cannot be restituted, then satisfaction should be provided.[503] In this vein, Bangladesh requested compensation from the ITLOS for the unilateral conduct of Myanmar undertaken in relation to a disputed continental shelf area, which it argued had resulted in a breach of the obligation to make every effort to reach a provisional arrangement in the sense of Articles 74(3) and 83(3) LOSC.[504] In *Guyana* v. *Suriname*, Guyana requested to be financially compensated, or to be provided with satisfaction if it was found that the wrong could not be restituted by monetary means, for the damage it had incurred, consisting of, for example, losing investments from foreign petroleum companies and being prevented from capitalising on developing its natural resources, because of Suriname's unilateral actions in the disputed area which violated Articles 74(3) and 83(3) LOSC.[505] In contrast to *Bangladesh/Myanmar*, where the claim that breaches of paragraph 3 needed to be repaired was withdrawn,[506] the Tribunal in

[500] Article 1 ARSIWA.
[501] Article 2 ARSIWA.
[502] Milano and Papanicolopulu (n. 80) 616–617.
[503] *Guyana* v. *Suriname* (n. 7) Guyana's Statement of Claim 14–15 [33].
[504] *Bangladesh/Myanmar* (n. 42) Bangladesh's Notification 6 [26].
[505] *Guyana* v. *Suriname* (n. 7) Guyana's Statement of Claim 14–15 [33].
[506] *Bangladesh/Myanmar* (n. 42) Bangladesh's Memorial 50 [4.19].

Guyana v. *Suriname* actually had to rule on whether Guyana had to be compensated, or if the wrong could not be compensated for, then satisfaction should be given. After making the finding that both parties to the dispute had violated Articles 74(3) and 83(3) LOSC, the Tribunal rejected Guyana's request for reparation. The Tribunal concluded that settling the maritime boundary dispute was itself sufficient redress for Guyana, whereby the Tribunal followed the line developed by the ICJ with regard to declaratory relief as such being sufficient as a remedy.[507]

In *Ghana/Côte d'Ivoire*, the Special Chamber dealt with whether international responsibility was incurred for breaches of Article 83 LOSC and Côte d'Ivoire's sovereign rights through Ghana's unilateral acts that fall under the jurisdiction of the coastal State. It started with the finding that the entitlement of a coastal State to a continental shelf is connected to the coastal State's coast, and that sovereign rights in relation thereto are exclusive and exist ab initio. Then, it went on to ascertain the nature of a judgment on delimitation, concluding that it is inevitably underpinned by a constitutive aspect, in that it conclusively determines which part of the disputed continental shelf area belongs to which coastal State, thereby prioritising the entitlement of one coastal State over the entitlement of the other State.[508] Given that the areas where the unilateral conduct complained of by Côte d'Ivoire occurred were considered by the Special Chamber to be under the exclusive jurisdiction of Ghana, the Chamber assessed whether international responsibility can be incurred by a claimant acting unilaterally in an area that, after delimitation, is located on that State's own side of the boundary.[509] The general thrust of the Chamber's reasoning is that, as long as a unilateral act falling under the jurisdiction of the coastal State is undertaken in a disputed maritime area claimed in good faith, no international responsibility will be incurred; this is irrespective of whether, after delimitation, the area is considered to be under the exclusive jurisdiction of the other coastal State, because of its falling on its side of the boundary. This means that a unilateral act which is under the jurisdiction of the coastal State can almost always be undertaken in relation to a disputed continental shelf area, seemingly without incurring international responsibility; this is even if the area, after delimitation, is located on the side of the boundary of the State that has not acted unilaterally.[510] From the Special Chamber's finding, a broader adverse consequence may follow,

507 'Guyana Pleased Maritime Dispute with Surinam Settled', *BBC Monitoring Latin – Political*, 23 September 2007.

508 *Ghana/Côte d'Ivoire* (Judgment) (n. 46) 158 [591].

509 Ibid. [592].

510 Ibid. 184 [19] (Separate Opinion of Judge Paik); Van Logchem (n. 245) 164–166, 176.

however: coastal States might be less willing to exercise restraint in relation to their disputed areas.[511]

3.12 CONCLUDING REMARKS

There are several obligations of international law, requiring States to exercise restraint, that apply in all disputed maritime areas, irrespective of the application of the LOSC. Claimant States are *de minimis* obliged to respect their obligations under the UN Charter: that is, not to use force, or to threaten therewith, and to peacefully settle their disputes. This means, inter alia, that States must settle their maritime boundary disputes by invoking means that do not endanger 'international peace and security'.[512] Nonetheless, the UNSC can decide to step in, by taking any measures it deems appropriate pursuant to Chapter VII UN Charter in relation to a disputed maritime area, if a threat to international peace and security emerged through unilateral conduct being undertaken. However, to date, it has never recognised this to be the case, despite being urged by States to recognise that such a threat existed.

Further minimum requirements exist under general international law, from which limitations flow as to the extent States can act in relation to a disputed maritime area. Amongst these is the 'no-harm' principle, which requires that, pending the settlement of their dispute, acts that result in the rights of the other State being infringed upon must be avoided. Further, States must act in good faith, and their actions may not amount to an abuse of rights. The requirement of due regard serves as a standard of behaviour for States in disputed maritime areas, and applies equally to any response to an alleged violation, as well as in relation to undertaken activities.

From these broad basic principles, other more specific principles arise. These include two principles that originate from procedures involving interim measures. However, they have a broader relevance beyond this specific context, applying to disputed maritime areas generally: first, acts that lead to aggravating or extending a dispute must be eschewed;[513] and, second, the rights of the other State must not be threatened with a risk of irreparability.[514]

Also relevant is the concept of keeping the status quo. However, to determine whether making an alteration to the status quo by acting unilaterally with regard to a disputed maritime area is permitted, must be viewed in, for

[511] Ibid. 176–177.
[512] Article 2(3) UN Charter.
[513] But see C Whomersley, 'The South China Sea: The Award of the Tribunal in the Case Brought by Philippines against China – A Critique' (2017) 16(3) *CJIL* 387, 419–421.
[514] Section 3.4 above.

example, the light of the obligation not to hamper or jeopardise as included in Articles 74(3) and 83(3) LOSC, in so far it concerns a disputed EEZ/continental shelf area. A breach of these aforementioned principles may result in the underlying maritime boundary dispute being exacerbated, whereby reaching a peaceful settlement is pushed further out of sight. Furthermore, both a unilateral act, falling under the authority of the coastal State, undertaken in a disputed maritime area and a response of a State to what it believes to be an unlawful act may fall within the domain of State responsibility. However, so far, international courts and tribunals that were faced with claims for financial reparation by States have deemed the settlement of the maritime boundary dispute to be satisfactory compensation.

4

Disputed Territorial Sea and Contiguous Zone Areas: Applicable Conventional Rules

Disputed territorial sea areas have, for instance, arisen between France and the United Kingdom in the Dover Strait;[515] Croatia and Slovenia in the Piran Bay;[516] Greece and Turkey in the Aegean Sea;[517] Iran, Iraq, and Kuwait in the northern part of the Persian Gulf;[518] and Israel and Lebanon in the Eastern Mediterranean Sea.[519] New needs for territorial sea delimitations may arise depending on how certain disputes over title to land territory, particularly high-tide features, are resolved – for instance, in the South China Sea, where delimiting various territorial sea boundaries between different high-tide features may be necessary when the underlying disputes over title to them are taken out of the equation.[520]

It might be the case that States have not yet attempted to delimit their territorial sea boundary because of a disagreement over land boundaries, possibly also over their terminus, or underlying disputes on title to territory. Or a modus vivendi might have developed in disputed territorial sea areas, enabling the States concerned to deal with any problems that may arise through informal consultations, and thereby preventing incidents, including those that can occur between the fishing fleets of coastal States.

515 Anderson and Van Logchem (n. 18) 194.

516 Arnaut (n. 92) 148–149.

517 D Bölükbaşi, *Turkey and Greece – The Aegean Disputes: A Unique Case in International Law* (Cavendish Publishing, 2004) 102–104.

518 JP Piscatori, 'Saudi Arabia and the Law of the Sea' in RB Lillich and JN Moore (eds.), *Role of International Law and an Evolving Ocean Law* (NWC, 1980) 633, 635.

519 W Zhang and F Zheng, 'The Offshore Oil and Gas Dispute and the Maritime Delimitation Scheme between Israel and Lebanon' (2014) 2 *COLR* 116, 134.

520 AG Oude Elferink, 'The Islands in the South China Sea: How Does Their Presence Limit the Extent of the High Seas and Area and the Maritime Zones of the Mainland Coasts' (2001) 32 (2) *ODIL* 169, 175. But see KC Fu, 'Safeguarding China's National Interests in the South China Sea: Rectification, Services, Leadership, and Maritime Delimitation' (2013) 17(1) *COLR* 12, 25.

However, there is a significant potential for a dispute between States in connection with disputed territorial sea areas.[521] This is because it is their sovereignty that overlaps over the same area, meaning that States can claim to have almost full authority over activities undertaken by other (coastal) States in the waters concerned; and that most forms of conduct by other States or their nationals will, according to the State that has an entitlement, require its prior approval. As a result, fishery activities, conduct undertaken in the framework of MSR, activities in relation to submarine cables and pipelines, and mineral resource exploration are all examples of types of activities over which the claimant States concerned will commonly assume to have the authority to regulate and manage activities of this nature within disputed territorial sea areas.

Although the frequency with which disputed EEZ or continental shelf areas that will create conflict in bilateral relations remains higher, conflicts related to disputed territorial sea areas do emerge.[522] For example, when Germany issued a licence to construct a wind farm ('Borkum Riffgat'), without consulting or notifying the Dutch government of its intentions, the latter protested.[523] Here it was unclear whether either Germany or the Netherlands, or possibly both, had to be approached by the energy industry for a licence prior to operating within the disputed territorial sea area.

Disputed contiguous zone areas may arise outside the 12 nm limit of the territorial sea. Coastal States are permitted to claim a contiguous zone (Article 33 LOSC), which lies beyond the outer limit of the territorial sea. A contiguous zone claim may not extend further than 12 nm;[524] that is, if the State opts for a 12 nm territorial sea. An apparent difficulty arises with respect to the text of Article 33 LOSC and the possibility to derive an interim rule therefrom: similar to that this provision is silent on how to delimit a disputed contiguous zone area, it prima facie does not provide an interim rule either.

This chapter begins by appraising the rules of international law that are applicable to disputed territorial sea areas. Article 15 LOSC, which seeks to deal with disputed territorial sea areas, is virtually a replica of the provision that

521 Anderson and Van Logchem (n. 18) 195–197.

522 But see D Arnaut, 'Stormy Waters on the Way to the High Seas: The Case of the Territorial Sea Delimitation between Croatia and Slovenia' in DD Caron and HN Scheiber (eds.), *Bringing New Law to Ocean Waters* (Brill, 2004) 417, 427; M Klemenčić and A Gosar, 'The Problems of the Italo-Croato-Slovene Border Delimitation in the Northern Adriatic' (2000) 52(2) *GeoJournal* 129, 136.

523 'Bizarrer Streit' (n. 175).

524 Article 33 LOSC.

was included in Article 12 1958 CTS.[525] The latter will be analysed first in Section 4.1. When compared to the text of Article 12, minor changes are made in the wording and composition of the second sentence of the final text of Article 15 LOSC. Section 4.2 retraces the origins of Article 15 LOSC by reviewing the (more limited) debates that occurred at UNCLOS III in relation to disputed territorial sea areas. The textual elements of Article 15 LOSC, with a focus on the extent to which the provision intends to regulate the period preceding delimitation, will be laid out in the same section. It will also be addressed whether other rules of international law will exert their influence either alongside the interim rule contained in this provision or, when it is inapplicable or non-existent, whether any alternative rules can be invoked as a substitute in disputed territorial sea areas. The situation where overlapping contiguous zones claims are made and the international law that is applicable thereto will be discussed in Section 4.3. Section 4.4 concludes the chapter by critically reviewing the international legal framework applicable to both disputed territorial sea areas and disputed contiguous zone areas.

4.1 ARTICLE 12 1958 CTS

In its Draft Articles of 1956, the ILC included two separate provisions on territorial sea delimitation. These drew a distinction according to whether the coasts of the States concerned were adjacent (Article 14) or opposite (Article 12) to each other.[526] Their difference in language, in that Article 12 speaks of 'failing such agreement' and Article 14 includes the phrase 'in the absence of such agreement', was abandoned in an amended version of Article 12 1958 CTS.[527] Here 'failing agreement to the contrary' became the favoured formulation for both situations.[528]

The two Draft Articles were based on the same substantive notion: territorial sea delimitation must come about through an agreement between the States concerned. Prior to delimitation, an equidistance boundary would come to divide a disputed territorial sea area, assuming that a double condition has been met: first, that delimitation negotiations must have failed; and, second,

525 *Maritime Delimitation and Territorial Questions between Qatar and Bahrain (Qatar v. Bahrain)* (Judgment) [2001] ICJ Rep 40, 94 [176].

526 ILC Yearbook (1956), UN Doc. A/CN.4/SER.A/1956/Add.1, Vol. II, 257–258.

527 Doc. A/CONF.13/5 (23 October 1957), Official Records of the United Nations Conference on the Law of the Sea, Vol. I, 94 (Norway); Doc. A/CONF.13/39 (1958), Official Records of the United Nations Conference on the Law of the Sea, Vol. III, 190 [44–45] (Norway).

528 Ibid. 191 [5–6] (Saudi Arabia), 192 [24] (the Soviet Union), 193 [39] (Indonesia).

no special circumstances are present which would require that a boundary which is at variance with equidistance should be determined.[529]

At the First United Nations Conference on the Law of the Sea (UNCLOS I), the issue of introducing an interim rule for disputed territorial sea areas was raised by Colombia,[530] the Netherlands,[531] Norway,[532] and Spain.[533] A division along the lines of the views of two groups of States was revealed: must an interim rule be sought on the basis of an equidistance boundary, or should an obligation for States to submit the maritime boundary dispute to arbitral or judicial proceedings be created?

One common thread in these latter positions was that a rule specifically tailored to deal with the period preceding territorial sea delimitation was not offered: they merely reiterated that disputes between States must be settled peacefully. Both the Netherlands and the United States recognised that the extension of the maximum limit of the territorial sea to 12 nm would be mirrored by a consequential rise in the number of disputes in relation to the territorial sea.[534] A comprehensive system of dispute settlement would have to be introduced to make sure that these disputes were settled whenever they arose.[535] Disputes over the interpretation or application of the legal rules with regard to disputed territorial sea areas could, according to the United States, be submitted unilaterally to arbitration or a different 'method of peaceful solution' for final settlement.[536] The motivation underlying the Dutch proposal, wherein a compulsory dispute settlement mechanism was introduced, was a degree of scepticism over the ability of States to settle their disputes through negotiations.[537]

Another common thread is that the proposals of Colombia, Norway, and Spain envisaged the mutatis mutandis application of the rule of equidistance[538] during the period before delimitation in the form of an

529 Ibid. 189 [36] (United Kingdom).

530 Doc. A/CONF.13/C.1/L.127 (1958), Official Records of the United Nations Conference on the Law of the Sea, Vol. III, 245 (Colombia); Doc. A/CONF.13/C.1/L.120 (1958), Official Records of the United Nations Conference on the Law of the Sea, Vol. III, 242 (Colombia).

531 A/CONF.13/5 (n. 527) 107 (the Netherlands).

532 A/CONF.13/39 (n. 527) 55 [9] (Norway); Doc. A/CONF.13/C.1/L.97 (1 April 1958), Official Records of the United Nations Conference on the Law of the Sea, Vol. III, 239 (Norway).

533 Doc. A/CONF.13/C.1/L.126 (31 March 1958), Official Records of the United Nations Conference on the Law of the Sea, Vol. III, 245 (Spain).

534 Doc. A/CONF.13/C 1/L.159/Rev. 2 (17 April 1958), Official Records of the United Nations Conference on the Law of the Sea, Vol. III, 253 (United States); A/CONF.13/5 (n. 527) 107, 110 (the Netherlands).

535 Ibid.

536 A/CONF.13/C 1/L.159/Rev. 2 (n. 534) (United States).

537 A/CONF.13/5 (n. 527) 110 (the Netherlands).

538 A/CONF.13/C.1/L.126 (n. 533) 245 (Spain).

interim rule.[539] Norway, for example, developed an interim rule whereby an equidistance boundary would come to divide the disputed territorial sea area.[540] This was regardless of whether the States concerned could claim entitlements beyond the equidistance boundary, or could show the existence of special circumstances.[541] Its reliance on a strict equidistance boundary rendered the Norwegian proposal controversial, and, as a result, was unable to attract many followers at UNCLOS I. This opposition is important, but must be placed in its proper context: the unfavourable response of these States seems to have been primarily connected to using equidistance as the main rule in delimitation.

Article 12 1958 CTS will be activated when States whose coasts are opposite or adjacent to each other have made overlapping territorial sea claims. Its language places emphasis on delimitation having to be effected by agreement; States may rely on the rule of equidistance in delimiting their territorial sea boundary. A certain deceptiveness has been attributed to the language of Article 12. While, at face value, emphasis is placed on the rule of equidistance, in the same sentence this primacy is weakened by adding a caveat: no special circumstances or a historic title must exist.[542] Similarly, in terms of an interim rule, the language of Article 12 1958 CTS points to the fact that States are prohibited from exercising sovereignty in disputed territorial sea areas beyond the equidistance boundary if there are no special circumstances or historic title.

An example derived from State practice of Article 12 1958 CTS being interpreted in this way was when in 1957 the California Oil Company approached the government of the then British Guiana (now Guyana) for a concession located in an area that was comparatively closer to the mainland coast of the Netherlands (now Suriname).[543] The United Kingdom, anticipating the codification of the ILC's Draft Articles, argued that the equidistance boundary constituted the applicable interim rule,[544] forming the basis on which the United Kingdom would be able to deal with the request of the petroleum company. Key in this assessment was whether the territorial sea area, in relation to which an interest was shown, lay on its own side of the equidistance boundary. After applying this test, the United Kingdom concluded that the concession sought by the California Oil Company concerned

539 RP Anand, *Origin and Development of the Law of the Sea* (Martinus Nijhoff, 1983) 179–180.

540 A/CONF.13/C.1/L.97 (n. 532) (Norway); A/CONF.13/39 (n. 527) 55 [9] (Norway).

541 Ibid. 190 [44]–[46] (Norway).

542 DP O'Connell and IA Shearer, *International Law of the Sea: Vol. II* (Clarendon Press, 1984) 677.

543 *Guyana* v. *Suriname* (n. 7) Guyana's Memorial 23 [3.25].

544 Ibid. 25 [3.29].

an area that would be on the Surinamese side of a hypothetical equidistance boundary, and was thus more likely to be determined to be under the latter's exclusive jurisdiction upon delimiting their disputed area. As the ILC's Draft Articles provided for the fact that the other State 'could show the existence of special circumstances', the United Kingdom deemed it necessary to be restrained in its licensing policy by not awarding new concessions in relation to areas close to or straddling this putative boundary.[545] Any other approach would, according to the United Kingdom, carry the risk of the other coastal State successfully demonstrating the existence of special circumstances, making the awarding of the concession unlawful in hindsight. By that same logic, in areas further removed from the equidistance boundary, that is on its own (the western) side, there was no restriction for the United Kingdom to award and activate licences for exploration activities.[546] The United Kingdom, believing that giving the concession would be beneficial to its negotiating position down the line,[547] put its original plans into effect and approved an amended proposal for conducting seismic work by the California Oil Company on 15 April 1958.[548] Under the terms of its concession, the company was authorised to operate in maritime areas on the western side of the equidistance boundary; on the basis thereof, exploratory activities were undertaken.[549]

4.2 ARTICLE 15 LOSC

Article 15 LOSC was agreed without much difficulty at UNCLOS III.[550] Debates over the design of an interim rule for disputed territorial sea areas were, however, infrequent,[551] and those debates that did take place during UNCLOS III were in the context of designing, at the same time, interim rules for disputed EEZ and continental shelf areas.[552]

In proposals by States at UNCLOS III, there was a general correlation between a State's preference for a particular rule of delimitation and the way

545 Ibid. Annex 17.
546 Ibid. 25 [3.29].
547 Ibid.
548 Ibid. 47 [4.21].
549 Ibid. 26–27 [3.32].
550 NSM Antunes, *Towards the Conceptualisation of Maritime Delimitation: Legal and Technical Aspects of a Political Process* (Martinus Nijhoff, 2003) 98; P Weil, *The Law of Maritime Delimitation – Reflections* (Cambridge University Press, 1989) 136; B Vukas, *The Law of the Sea: Selected Writings* (Martinus Nijhoff, 2004) 85.
551 SN Nandan and S Rosenne (eds.), *United Nations Convention of the Law of the Sea 1982: A Commentary*, Vol. II (Martinus Nijhoff, 1993) 140.
552 Chapter 5, Section 5.3.1 below.

it proposed to deal with the period before delimitation. States favouring equidistance as the main rule of delimitation often more or less automatically applied this solution to the time preceding territorial sea delimitation.[553] Typically, replicating the pattern at UNCLOS I,[554] the introduced provisions based on equity did not provide for a specific interim rule: in fact, these merely sought to ensure that peaceful means would be employed in settling disputes that would emerge from extending the territorial sea limit to 12 nm. Emphasis was placed on Article 33(1) UN Charter, providing a plethora of ways for States to peacefully settle their disputes, ranging from negotiations to judicial settlement by an international court or tribunal.

At its seventh session (1978), Negotiating Group 7 (Working Group 7 or NG7) was given the mandate to negotiate on maritime delimitation – which only a short time earlier was categorised as one of the most complex issues at UNCLOS III.[555] Territorial sea delimitation, as well as related issues, including an interim rule, was included within the range of issues NG7 was called upon to discuss.[556] Despite its broader mandate, negotiations within this group focused mainly on the EEZ and continental shelf, with a strong emphasis on designing a relevant rule of delimitation;[557] this could be explained by the fact that the available text on territorial sea delimitation was not engulfed in controversy. Two exceptions were the proposals of Morocco and the Netherlands, which sought to impose an interim rule for the territorial sea, the EEZ, and the continental shelf that was identical in content.

The main effect of the interim rule suggested by the Netherlands was that, through temporarily qualifying the entitlements of coastal States up to a point that was equidistant from their coasts (when measured from the relevant baselines) in the case of an overlap, a situation would be avoided where concurrent sets of sovereignties of coastal States existed over the same disputed territorial sea area.[558]

Very different was a proposal introduced by Morocco, whereby claimants would be subject to two obligations that were geared towards two different purposes: cooperation and abstention. First, the cooperative aspect was formed by the fact that one of the obligations aimed to stimulate uses of

553 Nandan and Rosenne (n. 551) 136.

554 Section 4.1 above.

555 ED Brown, 'Delimitation of Offshore Areas: Hard Labour and Bitter Fruits at UNCLOS III' (1981) 5(3) *MP* 172, 179.

556 Nandan and Rosenne (n. 551) 139–140.

557 Ibid. 140.

558 Doc. A/CONF.62/C.2/L.14 (19 July 1974), Official Records of the Third United Nations Conference on the Law of the Sea, Vol. III, 190–191 (the Netherlands).

bona fide claimed areas by coastal States in the transitional period before delimitation.[559] This element of cooperation in the Moroccan proposal was demonstrated by the phrase that States whose territorial sea claims overlap 'shall endeavour to reach mutually acceptable provisional arrangements'.[560] Second, constituting the aspect of abstention was the position that States must refrain from unilateral conduct that is under the sovereignty of the coastal State complicating territorial sea delimitation.[561] More specifically, two separate categories of unilateral activity were identified as complicating a delimitation: first, acts that 'could prejudge a final solution', and, second, those acts that would aggravate the maritime boundary dispute.

Substantially similar language was introduced in the final text of Articles 74(3) and 83(3) LOSC, which applied in relation to disputed EEZ and continental shelf areas.[562] Yet, to transplant the approach of paragraph 3, which is based on imposing two separate obligations on States that are tailored towards cooperation and abstention, to disputed territorial sea areas was not seriously contemplated by most delegations in UNCLOS III.[563]

Disputed territorial sea areas of States with opposite or adjacent coasts are governed by Article 15 LOSC, which represents a rule of customary international law.[564] The basic rule is that delimitation must occur by agreement – the States concerned may use the rule of equidistance in seeking an agreement. However, the presence of a historic title or special circumstances can lead to the rule of equidistance not being used.[565] Now, attention will be directed to situations where the sovereignty claims of coastal States overlap, with a view towards determining what is required of the States concerned if sovereignty is asserted over the same disputed territorial sea area.

4.2.1 *Is an Interim Rule Provided?*

Some scepticism has been expressed as to whether Article 15 LOSC offers an interim rule. At the root of this scepticism lies the fact that Article 15 is largely uninformative on this matter, as it does not provide an interim rule that is

559 R Platzöder, *Third United Nations Conference on the Law of the Sea: Documents* (Oceana, 1983) Vol. IX, 395 (NG 7/3, Morocco).

560 Ibid.

561 Ibid.

562 Chapter 5, Section 5.3 below.

563 Ibid. Section 5.3.1.

564 Antunes (n. 550) 98; Weil (n. 550) 136; *Qatar* v. *Bahrain* (n. 525) 91 [167].

565 Ibid. 94 [176]; *Nicaragua* v. *Honduras* (n. 413) 659 [280].

developed along similar lines as Articles 74(3) and 83(3) LOSC.[566] Two elements which are omitted from the text of Article 15 LOSC underlie this conclusion: first, Article 15 is silent on how claimant States can settle their conflicts created by the absence of a territorial sea boundary; and, second, it fails to give claimants explicit guidance as to how to conduct themselves in the period preceding delimitation. The aforementioned criticism suggests that, pursuant to Article 15 LOSC, the alleged primacy of the equidistance boundary line, which would be imposed on claimant States, is first and foremost conditioned on the situation that States fail to reach an agreement stipulating otherwise.[567] This would be exemplified by the wording 'failing agreement', indicating that States must have been in contact to devise an alternative solution. But is this interpretation correct?

Two textual elements prima facie stand out in appraising the extent to which Article 15 LOSC lays down an interim rule. Significant in this respect is that in the first part of the sentence mention is made of the remainder of the text of the provision being activated 'failing agreement between them to the contrary'. Hence, the emphasis is placed on 'agreement', leading to the following question: is the application of an equidistance boundary as an interim rule only envisaged if previous negotiations have failed to produce results?

According to one reading of the language used in Article 15 LOSC, it can be argued that it does not seek to provide an interim rule. Its success, however, depends on whether the phrase 'where it is necessary by reason of historic title or other special circumstances to delimit the territorial seas of the two States in a way which is at variance therewith' (emphasis added) can be interpreted as that the word 'delimiting' suggests, that a historic title or special circumstances only need to be considered in delimitation. However, to subsequently read Article 15 LOSC as a coastal State being allowed to extend its territorial sea provisionally to the equidistance boundary prior to delimitation, which can be considered an interim rule in its own right, runs into a difficulty. Because of the fact that no time limit is prescribed for starting delimitation negotiations, or to successfully agree thereon, opening negotiations, or even if negotiations have begun, these can be postponed, possibly indefinitely, which has the following effect: the equidistance boundary, regardless of whether States have entitlements beyond it, would be the de facto territorial sea boundary.

On an alternative and broad interpretation of the phrase 'failing agreement', it refers to the period where the territorial sea claims continue to overlap and

566 Nandan and Rosenne (n. 551) 143.

567 Zhang and Zheng (n. 519) 139.

States have not agreed on delimitation. The period of 'failing agreement' ceases to exist when a delimitation agreement has become binding on the coastal States having overlapping territorial sea claims. In adding this element to the second restriction found in Article 15 LOSC – that there can be no 'historic title and special circumstances' invalidating the mandatory use of an equidistance boundary – the interim rule that can be deduced from this Article 15 must incorporate both of these elements.

Taking these elements together, the offered interim rule can be defined as follows: overlapping claims to sovereignty are prevented from occurring by qualifying the territorial sea entitlements of coastal States to the line of equidistance in those areas where their coasts are less than 24 nm apart, or adjacent, and no boundary has been determined, and where there is no reason (i.e. no special circumstances or historic title) for the States concerned to claim entitlements beyond it. With an ordinary reading of this provision, the interim rule in Article 15 LOSC, restricting a State's entitlement to a territorial sea to the equidistance boundary, will thus be activated in certain situations: that is, in the absence of a historic title or special circumstances (e.g. pre-existing boundary agreements or islands that significantly alter the course of the equidistance boundary),[568] which may be alleged to exist by a claimant.[569] This is relevant in connection with the South China Sea, where the existence of a historic title (or something akin thereto) to maritime areas is claimed by China.[570] The conditionality of the equidistance boundary line as an interim rule is confirmed in the second sentence of Article 15 LOSC: 'the provisions of this paragraph' shall not apply when 'historic title or other special circumstances' are present.[571]

The authors whose thinking converges on the fact that Article 15 LOSC offers an interim rule are, however, not at one as to what its content is meant to be. Antunes interprets the interim rule of Article 15 in the following manner: 'when agreement cannot be reached, equidistance is the line beyond which, prima facie, states cannot exercise their sovereignty'.[572] Vukas construes the provided interim rule as follows: if States fail to arrive at territorial sea delimitation, a coastal State is permitted to extend its territorial sea boundary no further than the equidistance line.[573] Although both refer to the

568 *Guyana* v. *Suriname* (n. 7) 90–91 [323]–[325].
569 Nandan and Rosenne (n. 551) 135.
570 L Guoqiang, 'Claims Over Islands Legitimate', *Chinadaily.com.cn*, 22 July 2011.
571 Anderson and Van Logchem (n. 18) 196.
572 Antunes (n. 550) 98.
573 Vukas (n. 550) 85.

equidistance boundary in the absence of an agreement, on a closer reading some differences between the two discussed positions are, however, revealed.

These two views essentially address different issues: the first view focuses on exercises of sovereignty, which are limited to the equidistance boundary, whereas the second view is concerned with the extension of a State's entitlement to a territorial sea to a point that is equidistant from the coasts of the States in question. This latter view suggests that a claimant State may lay down a putative equidistance boundary to divide a disputed territorial sea area. In a sense, the view of Antunes logically follows the one of Vukas: if an equidistance boundary has been provisionally imposed on a disputed territorial sea area, it will form the outer point up to which the State can exercise acts of sovereignty. These differences in interpretation are thus not impossible to reconcile: while the territorial sea boundary remains disputed, and there are no special circumstances or historic title, neither of the claimants is allowed to exercise sovereignty beyond the provisional equidistance boundary.[574]

Some State practice provides support for the view that States having disputed territorial sea areas consider the equidistance boundary to be the applicable rule prior to delimitation. In responding to accusations of having unlawfully arrested Malaysian fishermen for fishing in a disputed territorial sea area, the president of Indonesia stated, by citing relevant parts of Article 15 LOSC, that the area was divided by a provisional equidistance boundary prior to delimitation.[575] Another example is that Croatia claimed that, while its territorial sea claim overlapped with that of Slovenia, both were not allowed to perform acts of sovereignty beyond the equidistance boundary, prior to delimitation.[576]

4.2.2 *What if Special Circumstances or a Historic Title Are Claimed?*

If a State would claim the existence of special circumstances or a historic title, because of which the application of the equidistance boundary as an interim rule is rendered void, there are no alternative provisions tailored towards disputed territorial sea areas to remedy this omission. It has been suggested to extend the reach of one or both of the two obligations contained in Articles 74(3) and 83(3) LOSC to those disputed territorial sea areas where the interim rule provided for in Article 15 LOSC is not applicable.[577]

574 Lagoni (n. 243) 350; Nandan and Rosenne (n. 551) 141.
575 Arsana (n. 15) 2.
576 Arnaut (n. 522) 434.
577 Milano and Papanicolopulu (n. 80) 612; Lagoni (n. 243) 367.

Usually, however, the activation of the two obligations of Articles 74(3) and 83(3) LOSC is considered to be contingent on the existence of overlapping EEZ/continental shelf claims.[578] Similarly, the drafters of the LOSC did not perceive widening the scope of paragraph 3 by bringing situations that are different from disputed EEZ or continental shelf areas under its sphere of operation. It was already recognised at a relatively early stage of the negotiations at UNCLOS III that equidistance was going to be the guiding rule in territorial sea delimitation. This solution was meant to cover the period preceding delimitation as well, given that States at UNCLOS III exhibited few intentions to the contrary, in that most suggestions for an interim rule to apply in disputed territorial sea areas were not at variance with equidistance.

Sometimes, however, it is not the territorial sea claims of coastal States that overlap *simpliciter*. Rather, this may be a type of overlap that will exist alongside overlapping EEZ and continental shelf claims having been made by the States concerned. Examples of where overlapping territorial sea claims are but one element in a broader delimitation dispute is the Beaufort Sea in the Arctic (involving Canada and the United States),[579] and Ambalat (involving Indonesia and Malaysia) in the Celebes Sea.[580] In such cases, difficulties might arise in distinguishing between what constitutes the disputed territorial area and the disputed EEZ/continental shelf area; this is likely to relate to only smaller parts of the disputed area concerned, however.

Substantively different interim rules are included in the LOSC to deal with disputed EEZ or continental shelf areas and disputed territorial sea areas in the period before delimitation. This has the following effect: if one of the States concerned has claimed the existence of a historic title or special circumstances in relation to the territorial sea areas, rendering the equidistance line as an interim rule not obligatory, only those areas where the EEZ/continental shelf claims overlap will be governed by the obligations of Articles 74(3) and 83(3) LOSC. Is it then prudent to accept an analogous application of paragraph 3 to the territorial sea area, by expanding its reach to the disputed maritime area as a whole? Maritime delimitation cases where single maritime boundary delimitations are increasingly becoming the norm, referring to an uninterrupted boundary that delimits the overlapping territorial sea, the EEZ

578 Chapter 5, Section 5.3.7 below.

579 Prescott and Schofield (n. 55) 526–527.

580 'Indonesia to Settle Unsolved Border Problems with Neighbouring Countries', *BBC Monitoring Asia Pacific – Political*, 27 June 2011; VL Forbes, *Indonesia's Delimited Maritime Boundaries* (Springer, 2014) 69–71.

and the continental shelf areas might perhaps be invoked to support this view.[581] Here international courts and tribunals have often assumed that Articles 74 and 83 LOSC are applicable whenever they have been called upon to determine a single maritime boundary.[582] More recently, however, the Special Chamber in *Ghana/Côte d'Ivoire* (Judgment) took a different approach: it applied Article 15 and Articles 74 and 83 LOSC separately in delimiting the maritime boundary for the territorial sea, the EEZ, and the (extended) continental shelf but concluded that the same methodology could be used throughout.[583] A further argument against the mutatis mutandis application of Articles 74(3) and 83(3) LOSC to disputed territorial sea areas is that it fails to consider the fundamentally different nature of the entitlements that overlap: in a disputed territorial sea area, there is an overlap of States sovereignties, whereas, in a disputed EEZ/continental shelf area, there is an overlap of sovereign rights, which are more limited in nature. Falling back on general rules of international law may thus be necessary to fill the gap left by the LOSC if through special circumstances or historic title being invoked, the mandatory application of the equidistance boundary as an interim rule is nullified.[584]

4.3 DISPUTED CONTIGUOUS ZONE AREAS: DOES AN INTERIM RULE EXIST?

There may be overlapping claims to contiguous zones where the States are either adjacent or opposite and less than 48 nm apart. The interim rule provided by Article 24(3) 1958 CTS stipulates that the entitlements of States to a claimed contiguous zone would automatically extend up to the equidistance boundary;[585] this means that States could exercise their contiguous zone rights up to this point exclusively prior to delimitation.[586] At first glance, this interim solution is substantively similar to the interim rule that was designed for disputed territorial sea areas, pursuant to Article 12 1958 CTS, which was later included, almost verbatim, in Article 15 LOSC. Yet there is a profound

581 *Maritime Delimitation in the Black Sea (Romania v. Ukraine)* [2009] ICJ Rep 61, 101–103 [115]–[122].

582 *Bangladesh/Myanmar* (n. 42) 55–56 [182]–[184]; *Arbitration between Barbados and the Republic of Trinidad and Tobago (Barbados v. Trinidad and Tobago)* [2006] XXVII RIAA 147, 213 [234]–[235]; *Maritime Dispute (Peru v. Chile)* [2014] ICJ Rep 3, 65 [179].

583 *Ghana/Côte d'Ivoire* (Judgment) (n. 46) 82–83, 116–117 [261]–[263] [409].

584 Chapter 3, Sections 3.2–3.10 above.

585 Article 24(3) 1958 CTS.

586 B Milligan, *Legal and Policy Options for the Provisional Joint Management of Maritime Space Subject to Overlapping Jurisdictional Claims* (PhD Thesis, Faculty of Law, University of Wollongong, 2012) 43–45.

difference between them. The moment when the equidistance boundary is activated as an interim rule for the contiguous zone was not made conditional on the absence of historic titles or special circumstances.

At UNCLOS III, the issue of an interim rule for overlapping contiguous zone claims was not addressed, for which several explanations can be given. First, it may have been because of an oversight on the part of States at UNCLOS III. Second, the intention of the drafters of the Convention may have been to leave it to the coastal States concerned to agree on a way to deal with their disputed contiguous zone area. Third, no immediate need may have been identified for designing a rule applicable thereto. This view is based on the contiguous zone being a zone of enforcement jurisdiction instead of legislative jurisdiction, meaning that there is no overlap of coastal States' laws operating in the same area. Fourth, States at UNCLOS III might have had the assumption that contiguous zone rights could be concurrently exercised in a disputed contiguous zone area without a conflict ensuing between the coastal States concerned, due to the limited nature of these rights.[587]

However, the difficulty with the aforementioned two views is the lack of assurances that indeed no difficulties will emerge between States, particularly whenever one of them enforces its proclaimed laws and regulations against the other claimant State, or in relation to an activity that has been approved by the latter in relation to a disputed contiguous zone area. Given that the contiguous zone spatially overlaps with the EEZ, whenever one is claimed, this means that, if an overlap arises, the question comes to the fore whether Article 74(3) LOSC, relating to disputed EEZ areas, cannot be applied by analogy. Due to the dissimilar rights being attributed to coastal States pursuant to these two maritime zones, the application, by analogy, of paragraph 3 of Article 74 LOSC to disputed contiguous zone areas is not appropriate, however.

4.4 CONCLUDING REMARKS

After debates at UNCLOS III ended, the equidistance rule prevailed as an interim rule for disputed territorial sea areas. An ordinary reading of Article 15 LOSC, which is an almost verbatim reproduction of Article 12 1958 CTS, provides the following interim rule: historic titles and special circumstances allow States to extend their claim beyond the equidistance boundary; in the

[587] L Caflisch, 'The Delimitation of Marine Spaces between States with Opposite or Adjacent Coasts' in R-J Dupuy and D Vignes (eds.), *A Handbook of the New Law of the Sea*, Vol. I (Martinus Nijhoff, 1991) 425, 425–426.

absence thereof, the equidistance boundary divides the area of overlapping territorial sea claims.[588]

A disagreement between States about the validity of relevant baselines can be a complicating factor in determining where the equidistance boundary line lies between States' coasts prior to delimitation, but, otherwise, the solution it provides is rather straightforward.

The interim rule provided by Article 15 LOSC is cast in unusual terms, however, that is: 'neither of the two States is entitled, failing agreement between them to the contrary, to extend its territorial sea beyond the median line'.[589] As a result, a restriction is imposed on the maximum entitlement of coastal States to a territorial sea of 12 nm: pending delimitation, their entitlements to a territorial sea are limited to the boundary that is equidistant from their coasts. A State claiming more extensive areas of territorial sea, whereby this provisional equidistance boundary line is crossed, would therefore breach international law.

But is using an equidistance boundary as an interim rule *de lege ferenda*? Its advantages manifest themselves mainly in the apparent effectiveness and simplicity of the rule; this can be retraced to there being *no* overlap of States' sovereignties over the same territorial sea area. Pending delimitation, there will be clarity as to the geographical extent of a State's sovereignty: on its own side of the putative boundary, a coastal State can exercise sovereignty, including in relation to activities being conducted by third States or their nationals; that is, inasmuch as the LOSC permits them to do so. Hence, during this interim period, the applicable legal regime is virtually identical to undisputed territorial sea areas: coastal States are entitled to exercise sovereignty over activities falling within their authority with the equidistance boundary constituting the outer point.

Using an interim rule based on the provisional equidistance boundary can have negative effects, however, as States already seeking to determine the territorial sea boundary on the basis of equidistance may gain little from making efforts to come to a final delimitation. At UNCLOS I, the Netherlands was aware of this potential difficulty and adopted the position that the use of the equidistance boundary line had to be truly temporary and had to make way for a final boundary as soon as possible.[590] Further, although not unique to disputed territorial sea areas, a general risk of escalation nevertheless remains when States are operating in close vicinity to, or on, this putative equidistance boundary dividing a disputed territorial sea area. For

588 Anderson and Van Logchem (n. 18) 196.

589 Ibid.

590 A/CONF.13/5 (n. 527) 107, 110 (the Netherlands).

instance, if a coastal State allows a seismic survey to be conducted of the area that is directly adjacent to the equidistance boundary, information on quantities of mineral resources is likely to be revealed for areas that are located on the other side of the boundary. However, claimant States must refrain from taking actions, or approving acts, that result in the sovereignty of the other State being infringed upon. Hence, seismic vessels licensed by one coastal State should refrain from gathering data on mineral resources from across the temporary equidistance boundary. If, for whatever reason, these seismic vessels must turn on the 'other side' of the boundary (where they have no licence to explore, but still enjoy the right of innocent passage), their instruments should be switched off, unless they have the permission of the 'other side' to conduct a seismic survey.

Another issue concerns the applicable interim rule in situations where overlapping claims to a territorial sea, an EEZ, and a continental shelf area are combined. If none of the States concerned has claimed the existence of a historic title or special circumstances in relation to the territorial sea area, that part will be divided by the equidistance boundary line, whereas the disputed EEZ/continental shelf areas will be governed by the obligations of Articles 74(3) and 83(3) LOSC. This may give rise to the issue of whether a part of the disputed area must be considered as territorial sea or EEZ/continental shelf.[591] The situation becomes more complex if special circumstances or a historic title has been invoked, which renders the automatic application of the equidistance boundary as an interim rule in what constitutes the disputed territorial sea area void. However, filling this gap by extending the scope of application of Articles 74(3) and 83(3) LOSC to the disputed area in its entirety is difficult to justify. But irrespective of the applicability of these treaty provisions, States that are faced with disputed territorial sea areas have the obligation under international law to exercise restraint, for example by virtue of the principle of having due regard to the rights and interests of other states and the prohibition on abuse of rights.[592]

Even though the contiguous zone is a zone of enforcement jurisdiction rather than legislative jurisdiction, difficulties could emerge between States if they have a disputed contiguous zone area. For example, if law enforcement measures are taken against actors operating there with the sole authorisation of the other claimant State. While an interim rule is provided in Article 24(3) 1958 CTS, stipulating that the entitlements of States to a claimed contiguous zone would automatically extend up to the equidistance boundary, the LOSC

591 However, the areas to which this will relate will be only marginal.

592 Chapter 3, Sections 3.2, 3.6–3.7 above.

abandoned this approach for unclear reasons. This has left a lacuna in the framework of the LOSC, as a mutatis mutandis application to disputed contiguous zone areas of the interim rule provided for disputed EEZ areas in the form of Article 74(3) is inappropriate, by virtue of dissimilar rights being attributed to coastal States pursuant to these maritime zones.

5

Disputed EEZ and Continental Shelf Areas: Applicable Conventional Rules

Overlapping claims to the same EEZ and continental shelf area regularly arise beyond the 12 nm limit; however, in contrast to the continental shelf, an EEZ must be proclaimed. In the absence of delimitation, overlapping sets of sovereign rights and jurisdictional competences of two States will exist over the same area. There are about 200 situations where claims to the same EEZ (in some cases fishery zones) or continental shelf area overlap and no boundary, or only a partial one, has been established.[593] In its judgment in the *Libya/Malta Continental Shelf* case, the ICJ designated the EEZ and the continental shelf to be customary rules.[594] While most coastal States have claimed an EEZ, there are some exceptions: for example, most States bordering the Mediterranean Sea have not claimed an EEZ, for reasons associated with fisheries and its geographical context.[595]

Section 5.1 begins with assessing the type of overlap that is created when States have made overlapping claims to EEZ areas or to continental shelf areas. In what follows, a detailed examination of the relevant conventional international rules applicable in disputed EEZ and continental shelf areas is placed at the forefront of the analysis. Particularly relevant are the two identically phrased provisions of Articles 74(3) and 83(3) LOSC, placing two separate obligations on States: first, States are exhorted to explore designing provisional arrangements; and, second, States must abstain from undertaking unilateral acts falling under the jurisdiction of the coastal State that complicate delimitation. Before examining their contents, the predecessor of the LOSC, the 1958 CSC, and its Article 6 will be addressed in Section 5.2, with

593 Chapter 2, Section 2.1 above.

594 *Case concerning the Continental Shelf (Libyan Arab Jamahiriya/Malta)* [1985] ICJ Rep 13, 33–34 [34].

595 Vukas (n. 550) 150.

a view towards ascertaining the extent to which this latter provision sets out an interim rule governing disputed continental shelf areas. This Article 6, being rather different in terms of its substance and composition than Articles 74(3) and 83(3) LOSC, places emphasis on the rule of equidistance, also, at first glance, as an interim rule guiding the conduct of States in the period before delimitation. Critical in its development was the ILC, performing nearly all of the preparatory work for UNCLOS I by completing a set of Draft Articles on the Law of the Sea in 1956.

Section 5.3 focuses on Articles 74(3) and 83(3) LOSC. It starts with an overview of their drafting history, where there were two duelling currents that could not see eye to eye on how to deal with disputed EEZ/continental shelf areas: one group of States advocated the use of the equidistance line as an interim rule, whereas the other emphasised that, unless States could agree on cooperative measures, no economic activities could be conducted. The chapter will then move to analyse the substantive elements of Articles 74(3) and 83(3) LOSC, by examining its language. Two other variants of an approach to an interim rule that is applicable in disputed EEZ or continental shelf areas have been advocated: the moratorium approach and the use of an equidistance boundary. Whether these approaches can be reconciled with the language of Articles 74(3) and 83(3) LOSC will be addressed in Sections 5.3.8 and 5.3.9. Section 5.3.10 considers the fact that not all States faced with disputed EEZ/continental shelf areas are a party to the LOSC, which underlines the need to appraise the customary status of Articles 74(3) and 83(3) LOSC. Section 5.3.11 discusses the following: in light of the high number of disputed EEZ/continental shelf areas, paragraph 3 is perceivably of great importance in dealing with these areas, but does it live up to this promise? Following on from this, Section 5.3.12 addresses whether it is necessary to understand the importance of Articles 74(3) and 83(3) LOSC differently from how it is usually, that is, by moving away from placing the main emphasis on the obligation to seek cooperative arrangements. Section 5.4 concludes the chapter.

5.1 THE CHARACTERISTICS OF OVERLAPPING EEZ/ CONTINENTAL SHELF CLAIMS

It is claims to sovereign and jurisdictional rights by coastal States that overlap in relation to disputed EEZ and continental shelf areas. Coastal States are given rights over living and non-living natural resources contained within the (disputed) EEZ and continental shelf area, and over activities related to exercising these rights, including placing installations (Article 77(1)(4) LOSC). Most of the provisions of the LOSC in respect of the EEZ and continental shelf, except for the delimitation articles, that is Articles 74 and 83, have, however, been laid down under the assumption that clarity exists concerning the geographical extent of the coastal State's sovereign and jurisdictional rights. While these rights are meant to be exclusive, it is only after delimitation (i.e. when the geographical extent of a coastal State's rights is clear) that a coastal State has exclusivity, in the real sense of the word, over (the living and non-living resources of) the EEZ or continental shelf area.[596]

Prior to delimitation, there is a coexistence of competing claims to exclusivity of coastal States over the same EEZ and continental shelf area. Therefore, the adoption of a certain line of thinking in terms of exclusivity by the coastal States concerned in relation to the same disputed EEZ or continental shelf area runs into the difficulty of different States operating from the same premise:[597] activities which are under the jurisdiction of the coastal State, when they are planned to be undertaken, will be considered by both coastal States as falling within their exclusive jurisdiction, and inevitably requiring their prior consent because of their having entitlements and related rights over the area concerned. If such an act were to start within a disputed area with the licence of a claimant State, the other State may consider it imperative to respond to this act because it infringes on its exclusive sovereign rights and/or to protect its claim over the area.

The rights of coastal States to the continental shelf exist ipso facto and ab initio, with the result that, amongst others, any mineral resources in the shelf's subsoil are consequently under that State's jurisdiction.[598] There are two ways to understand the inherent right aspect of States over disputed continental shelf areas, and the effect it has on the possibility for claimants to undertake unilateral conduct in relation thereto. The key difference between them centres around the importance that must be attributed to the eventuality that, through the other State having unilaterally undertaken an act falling under coastal State jurisdiction, there might have been, after delimitation, infringements of a coastal State's rights to its continental shelf, which are meant to be exclusive.

The logic underlying the first view is that considering that coastal States' rights to the continental shelf are sovereign rights and are inherent, and cover the natural resources contained therein, prior consent must have been given by each of the States concerned before activities falling under coastal State

596 Milano and Papanicolopulu (n. 80) 589–590.

597 BH Oxman, 'Political, Strategic, and Historical Considerations' in JI Charney and LM Alexander (eds.), *International Maritime Boundaries*, Vol. 1 (Martinus Nijhoff, 1993) 3, 5.

598 MD Evans, *Relevant Circumstances and Maritime Delimitation* (Oxford University Press, 1989) 55; *North Sea Continental Shelf* (n. 8) 22, 29 [19] [39].

jurisdiction may be undertaken in a disputed continental shelf area.[599] Two aspects define the core objectives of this first view: first, avoiding, in retrospect (i.e. after delimitation), an (possible) infringement of a coastal State's rights; and, second, that the exclusivity of a coastal State's rights is fully preserved by imposing a moratorium.[600] More specifically, it avoids the situation where coastal State A will have infringed on the 'exclusive' nature of the sovereign rights of claimant State B; that is, in the event that the part of the continental shelf where the act was undertaken by State A falls after delimitation on State B's side of the boundary.

The second view, falling at the opposite end of the spectrum, is as follows: having sovereign rights as a coastal State brings with it a connected right, and an exclusive prerogative, to actively act upon them. Under this view, the time before and after delimitation are effectively treated identically.

A variant of this view is based on the position that a coastal State has an entitlement to a continental shelf that extends to, at least, 200 nm from the baselines, meaning that prior to a delimitation the coastal State is allowed to exercise its rights without limitation up to where its entitlement extends. For instance, when China claimed that Vietnam had unlawfully given a concession to British Petroleum in relation to the disputed Nam Con Son basin, Vietnam's justification was as follows: the approval of this seismic work was lawful because it related to an area within 200 nm from its mainland coast, and was thus located on its own continental shelf.[601] This defending of a State's own (re)actions and condemning the actions of another State on the basis of its closeness to the coast neglects an important aspect, however: when the other claimant has an entitlement to the same continental shelf area according to international law, a State cannot claim that its own entitlement and related rights are 'superior' to those of the other coastal State. This is unless an international court or tribunal would deliver a ruling that supports such an assertion, or in the case of excessive claims being made. Another difficulty with this view is that it is highly unlikely that the entire disputed area will be within the exclusive jurisdiction of one coastal State after delimitation. More likely is that a part of what is now a disputed maritime area will be, after delimitation, under the exclusive jurisdiction of State A while another part will fall under the exclusive jurisdiction of State B. By accepting the validity of this second

599 *Somalia* v. *Kenya* (n. 47) Somalia's Memorial 131–132 [8.11].

600 D Tas, 'Oil and Gas in the East China Sea: Maritime Boundaries, Joint Development and the Rule of Capture' (2011) 29 *IELR* 48, 59.

601 YH Song and S Tonnesson, 'The Impact of the Law of the Sea Convention on Conflict and Conflict Management in the South China Sea' (2013) 44(3) *ODIL* 235, 251.

view, a blind eye is also turned to the fact that acting on sovereign or jurisdictional rights in a disputed maritime area will often create conflict in bilateral relations, thereby lessening the chances of reaching a delimitation agreement. It is further accepted that the other State's rights may be detrimentally and irreversibly affected as a result. This is when acts which are under coastal State jurisdiction have been undertaken unilaterally in a part of the disputed continental shelf area that after delimitation is located on the other claimant's side of the boundary.

The inherency component of States' rights is not relevant in relation to the EEZ: this zone will need to be explicitly established by a State via making an explicit claim. Although States do not have inherent rights in the EEZ, an analogous application of the arguments presented above concerning the continental shelf is appropriate: when coastal States have made claims to EEZs in accordance with international law, but these overlap, creating a disputed area, their entitlements to an EEZ, and the accompanying sovereign rights and obligations, are not fictitious.

How the notion of 'exclusivity' is to be understood in the context of both disputed continental shelf and EEZ areas remains uncertain,[602] however, but part of the answer lies in the identical provision in Articles 74(3) and 83(3) LOSC, which imposes limitations on the extent to which claimants can put their rights to use, by acting unilaterally, in relation to such areas.

5.2 ARTICLE 6 1958 CSC

The importance of the issue of disputed continental shelf areas, and of finding a way to deal with them, was first recognised at the ILC's second session in 1950: the extension of coastal States' entitlements to continental shelves would lead to a consequential increase in disputes, which could be of such complexity that the States concerned would be unable to settle them themselves. Although discussions continued until 1951, the lines were already largely drawn between its members in 1950 as to how to deal with disputed continental shelf areas. Their views effectively fell into two lines of thought: either a delimitation dispute must be submitted to compulsory third-party settlement or the States concerned must settle the dispute through negotiations. However, some ILC members expressed a view that was at variance therewith, highlighting the need to design a rule that would apply pending continental shelf delimitation.

602 Chapter 9, Section 9.3.1 below.

Scelle, one of the members of the ILC, was highly critical of the conclusion contained in the Secretariat's memorandum of 1950[603] that the delimitation of 'the continental shelf should be the subject of agreement between States'.[604] Underlying this criticism were two arguments. First, a claimant could be strong-armed by the other claimant into developing the natural resources of a disputed continental shelf area against its wishes.[605] Second, the conclusion merely placed emphasis on 'agreement'; but there was no default provision that would be activated if the States concerned were unable to reach an agreement.[606] As a result, there was a certain circularity in this conclusion: after negotiations on delimitation have failed to produce a result, States can possibly continue negotiating indefinitely, due to the absence of a time limit within which the continental shelf boundary must have been delimited.

Three options were identified by Scelle to deal with disputes over the continental shelf boundary: either the dispute had to be submitted to the ICJ or arbitral proceedings or, if the States concerned could not agree to submit the dispute to adjudication, the prevalent status quo would have to be maintained.[607] A double aim would be accomplished by having States maintain the status quo pending delimitation: first, it would prevent the natural resources of the continental shelf area from being developed unilaterally; and, second, it would contribute to preserving peace between the States concerned, thereby ensuring that the issue would not increase to the level of an actual conflict. Acts involving taking, or attempting to take, exploitable resources from disputed continental shelf areas without having concluded a cooperative arrangement had to be abstained from for two reasons:[608] first, because of the change engendered in the status quo; and, second, bilateral relations would be detrimentally affected.

Although it was widely recognised within the ILC that exhorting States to find a boundary agreement was light on substance, a disagreement existed amongst its members over whether establishing a stronger obligation was appropriate. Hudson poured new wine into old wineskins by proposing that States with adjacent coasts, whose continental shelf claims overlap, should determine the boundary through agreement.[609]

603 Memorandum on the Regime of the High Seas, UN Doc. A/CN.4/32, ILC Yearbook (1951), UN Doc. A/CN.4/SER.A/1951/Add.1 (1957), Vol. II, 75.
604 ILC Yearbook (1951), UN Doc. A/CN.4/SER.A/1951 (1957), Vol. I, 288 [5].
605 Ibid. 289 [16].
606 Ibid. 288 [5].
607 Ibid. 289 [16].
608 Ibid.
609 Ibid. 290 [19].

Two other members of the ILC (El Khoury and Cordova) approached the issue of how to deal with the period prior to continental shelf delimitation from the angle that, if States were unable to successfully negotiate a boundary agreement, the continental shelf boundary was to be delimited by an international court or tribunal.[610] Following the view of Scelle, they agreed that conducting activities enabling the development of exploitable resources of the disputed seabed area was dependent on making cooperative arrangements by the States concerned.[611] Hsu, also a member of the ILC, presented States whose continental shelf claims overlap with two choices: either they start arbitral proceedings to effect a delimitation or, in the absence of such a referral, complete restraint was called for, in that a moratorium on the exploration and exploitation of the disputed continental shelf area would come into effect. Lifting this moratorium was dependent on delimitation.[612]

As discussions went on within the ILC, the introduction of compulsory dispute settlement became more widely accepted. The need for its introduction was indicated by the concern that, through extending the outer limit of the continental shelf, 'peaceful relations between States' would inevitably be strained,[613] especially if attempts at the unilateral 'exploration and exploitation of the continental shelf' were made by the States concerned in the absence of delimitation.[614] Starting arbitral proceedings to delimit a disputed continental shelf area was considered necessary to prevent disputes arising over its unilateral exploration or exploitation.[615] Alternatively, any issues brought about by the absence of a continental shelf boundary could be settled by invoking the plethora of peaceful means enumerated in Article 33 UN Charter,[616] including negotiations.[617]

Nonetheless, Cordova tried to blow new life into the idea of placing coastal States under an obligation to maintain the status quo in relation to a disputed continental shelf area.[618] His attempt was mainly practically motivated: it would enable a debate amongst delegations in UNCLOS I as to whether the development of an interim rule would be useful or not. However, the majority of the ILC members rejected Cordova's attempt to continue thinking on developing an interim rule: a future convention was to establish a mechanism for

610 Ibid. 288 [8].
611 Ibid. 291 [45].
612 Ibid. 291 [46].
613 ILC Yearbook (1953), UN Doc. A/CN. 4/8ER. A/1953/Add. 1 (1959), Vol. II, 217 [87].
614 Ibid.
615 Ibid. [90].
616 Ibid. [89].
617 Ibid. [88].
618 ILC Yearbook 1951, Vol. I (n. 604) 292 [62].

compulsory dispute settlement, ensuring that continental shelf boundary disputes would be settled conclusively and which would include the option of requesting the indication of measures of interim protection.[619] That this would have rendered designing an interim rule redundant is not completely convincing; this is because the possibility to request interim measures of protection lagged inevitably behind the establishment of the Arbitral Tribunal.

Building on the work that had been done by the committee of experts in the context of territorial sea delimitation, the ILC enunciated a substantively identical delimitation rule for situations where the claims of States with adjacent and opposite coasts to the same continental shelf area overlap.[620] The main novelty of this approach is the larger emphasis placed on the equidistance rule, as its reach was extended to also cover overlaps of claims created between adjacent coasts. Under this approach, a State's entitlement to a continental shelf was restricted to the equidistance boundary in the case of an overlap of its claims with those of another State, and in the absence of special circumstances.

During debates over the ILC's Draft Articles at UNCLOS I's Fourth Committee, it became clear that most States were firmly opposed to imposing an obligation on States to have their delimitation disputes settled by an Arbitral Tribunal.[621] Despite an apparent need to now design an interim rule that would guide the actions and reactions of States in the period preceding delimitation, this issue was in fact not brought up as talks progressed at UNCLOS I.[622]

Two possible explanations for the lack of a further debate on designing an interim rule can be given. First, UNCLOS I was generally stressed for time; and, second, delegations were unlikely to have received instructions from their governments to make efforts to ensure that a provision of this nature would be included in the final text of the convention. Arguably, this left a lacuna in the framework of the 1958 CSC in terms of an interim rule being provided; this is unless the ultimate version of Article 6 can be regarded as having filled it.

Because States at UNCLOS I failed to design a specific interim rule that applied to the period preceding delimitation, the wording of Article 6 as it stands in the 1958 CSC, referring to the equidistance boundary in the absence

619 Ibid. [63]–[64].

620 ILC Yearbook 1953, Vol. II (n. 613) 216 [81].

621 Optional Protocol of Signature concerning the Compulsory Settlement of Disputes, Geneva, 29 April 1958, in force on 30 September 1962, 450 UNTS 169.

622 AG Oude Elferink, *The Delimitation of the Continental Shelf between Denmark, Germany and the Netherlands: Arguing Law, Practicing Politics?* (Cambridge University Press, 2013) 197.

of an agreement, plays a central role in formulating the content of an interim rule; that is, assuming there is one contained therein. At first glance, and relating to an interim rule, the language of Article 6 suggests the following: a provisional equidistance boundary divides the disputed continental shelf area. Its applicability is, however, subject to a limitation: no special circumstances must have been invoked by a State that would allow it to extend its claim beyond this boundary.[623]

Article 6 1958 CSC has been interpreted as allowing coastal States to initiate steps with a view to unilaterally delimiting a disputed continental shelf area.[624] This is if delimitation negotiations have been exhausted, and that, in determining the boundary, Article 6 was followed to the letter.[625] After that, the coastal State having proclaimed an equidistance maritime boundary in accordance with the text of Article 6 1958 CSC must, however, await the reaction of the other coastal State.[626] This boundary may become final through acquiescence: that is, if the other coastal State fails to protest or alternatively does not suggest where the maritime boundary lies. Once the other claimant State protests, an international dispute will arise, which will not only need to be resolved by invoking peaceful methods[627] but will also render the unilaterally determined boundary without validity under international law. Put in its proper perspective, States can freely use this approach, whereby a State unilaterally proclaims a maritime boundary (which does not necessarily need to be based on the equidistance line) and awaits the reaction of the other coastal State, thus relying on acquiescence for the boundary to become final. But this is not a true 'interim rule', however, as the use of the equidistance boundary is tied to the viewpoints of the States involved.

Leaving aside situations where there is an explicit or tacit agreement, a separate issue is whether, in the absence thereof, the default rule is that a temporary equidistance boundary automatically comes to divide a disputed continental shelf area as an interim rule.[628] In *North Sea Continental Shelf*, Denmark and the Netherlands contended that the default rule which had to

623 ILC Yearbook 1953, Vol. II (n. 613) 216 [82]; UD Klemm, 'Allgemeine Abgrenzungsprobleme Verschiedener Seerechtlich Definierter Räume' (1978) 38 *ZaöRV* 512, 533–534.

624 CL Rozakis, 'The Greek Continental Shelf' in TC Kariotis (ed.), *Greece and the Law of the Sea* (Martinus Nijhoff, 1997) 67, 77; Weil (n. 550) 110.

625 Ibid.

626 Rozakis (n. 624) 77.

627 Ibid.

628 Kim (n. 287) 29; JM van Dyke, 'Disputes over Islands and Maritime Boundaries in East Asia' in S-Y Hong and JM van Dyke (eds.), *Maritime Boundary Disputes, Settlement Processes, and the Law of the Sea* (Brill, 2009) 39, 72.

be applied pending the continental shelf delimitation with Germany was the equidistance boundary;[629] this is unless there are 'special circumstances' allowing at least one of the States concerned to claim entitlements to continental shelf areas located beyond this boundary. As was evidenced in the licensing practice of the Netherlands from 1956 onwards, it respected the equidistance boundary in awarding licences for exploratory work for mineral resources.[630]

Both Denmark and the Netherlands in *North Sea Continental Shelf* contended that a State invoking the existence of special circumstances, as allowed for under Article 6 1958 CSC, has the concurrent onus of providing evidence of such circumstances.[631] A failure to provide evidence of their existence would activate the default rule that a disputed continental shelf area is to be divided by an equidistance boundary.[632] However, both the drafting history and the language of Article 6 1958 CSC do not support the view that a State alleging the existence of special circumstances must submit irrefutable evidence thereof.[633] At UNCLOS I, it was generally accepted that the existence, or the absence, of special circumstances in the sense of Article 6 could not be appraised by the State asserting their existence or by the State that was confronted with a claim of this nature. Rather, only an international court or tribunal could confirm their existence.[634]

In examining Article 6 1958 CSC *proprio motu* in *North Sea Continental Shelf*, the ICJ elaborated on the relation between the reference to the rule of equidistance and the absence of special circumstances, and how these aspects subsequently link to whether an equidistance continental shelf boundary is imposed on an area.[635] As far as this relation is concerned, the following question arises according to the ICJ: '[M]ust negotiations for an agreed boundary prove finally abortive before the acceptance of a boundary drawn on an equidistance basis become obligatory in terms of Article 6, if no special circumstances exist?'[636]

629 Oude Elferink (n. 622) 65.

630 *North Sea Continental Shelf* (n. 8) The Netherlands Counter-Memorial 311 [11].

631 AO Adede, 'Toward the Formulation of the Rule of Delimitation of Sea Boundaries between States with Adjacent or Opposite Coasts' (1979) 19(2) *VJIL* 207, 214; Oude Elferink (n. 622) 65.

632 E Grisel, 'The Lateral Boundaries of the Continental Shelf and the Judgment of the International Court of Justice in the North Sea Continental Shelf Cases' (1970) 64(3) *AJIL* 562, 570.

633 Caflisch (n. 587) 441.

634 ILC Yearbook (1953), UN Doc. A/CN.4/SER.A/1953 (1959), Vol. I, 131–133, [14] [17] [28] [33] [35] [39].

635 *North Sea Continental Shelf* (n. 8) 27 [34].

636 Ibid.

This *obiter dictum* has been interpreted as implying that the ICJ is of the view that, if negotiations have failed to produce any other result, the continental shelf boundary would come to consist of the equidistance boundary line.[637] However, when looking at the language of Article 6 1958 CSC, reference is made to a situation in which there are no special circumstances, requiring a boundary to be determined that is at variance with the rule of equidistance.[638] There is no mention of the need for having started negotiations as a condition to activate the remainder of the provision.

On a better view, the reference to special circumstances is only deemed relevant in the context of delimiting the continental shelf boundary, having no bearing on the formulation of an interim rule. Because Article 6 1958 CSC contains the phrase that 'in the absence of agreement, and unless another boundary line is justified by special circumstances' (emphasis added), it may be argued that no interim rule is provided. At its heart, the provision seeks to assist States in delimiting the continental shelf boundary, which is signified by the reference being made to the use of 'another boundary line'. This choice of words suggests that this part of the sentence is not meant to formulate an interim rule. Supporting this view further are the debates within the ILC, where there were at least four members who recognised the need to introduce an explicit rule to maintain the status quo within a disputed continental shelf area, but were ultimately unsuccessful in this aim.[639] Its remaining members emphasised that, through introducing an obligation to submit these disputes to judicial proceedings resulting in binding decisions, the design of an interim rule had become redundant.[640]

5.3 ARTICLES 74(3) AND 83(3) LOSC

Articles 74(3) and 83(3) LOSC lay down two obligations for claimant States that apply prior to EEZ or continental shelf delimitation. In terms of content, this provision is the same in both articles, reading as follows: 'Pending agreement as provided for in paragraph 1, the States concerned, in a spirit of understanding and cooperation, shall make every effort to enter into provisional arrangements of a practical nature and, during this transitional period, not to jeopardize or hamper the reaching of the final agreement. Such arrangements shall be without prejudice to the final delimitation.' The addressees of paragraph 3 are States whose coasts lie opposite or adjacent to each other

637 Kim (n. 287) 29.
638 Klemm (n. 623) 533.
639 ILC Yearbook 1951, Vol. I (n. 604) 291–292, [45]–[46] [62].
640 Ibid.

and have overlapping EEZ and continental shelf claims.[641] This aspect of there having to be a certain geographical relationship between the coasts of States limits the range of situations in which Articles 74(3) and 83(3) LOSC can be successfully applied.[642] Its sphere of operation is as follows: it is applicable to those activities that are conducted by, or under the authority of, claimant coastal States, or to activities over which they may conjointly exercise jurisdiction in a disputed EEZ or continental shelf area.

There are two pillars in Articles 74(3) and 83(3) LOSC.[643] First, States must make every effort to enter into provisional arrangements of a practical nature. Second, they must make every effort not to hamper or jeopardise reaching a delimitation agreement. The first pillar of paragraph 3 is encouraging in nature, in that it seeks to activate claimants to do something: that is, making every effort to successfully set up provisional arrangements in relation to a disputed EEZ/continental shelf area. At first glance, the underlying nature of this obligation is very similar to the obligation that States have under general international law to negotiate in good faith.[644]

Forming the second pillar underlying paragraph 3 is an obligation that is prohibitive in nature: the States concerned must make every effort not to act in a way that results in reaching a delimitation agreement being hampered or jeopardised.[645] This obligation can be seen as an extension of other obligations that already rest on States under international law: that is, to ensure that activities under their jurisdiction and control do not cause harm to a neighbouring State and that a State's exercise of its rights might not amount to an abuse thereof.[646] Hence, the idea of abstention, in that States must practise restraint,[647] underlies the obligation not to hamper or jeopardise. However, while this much is clear, it is less clear what the extent and the sphere of operation of this obligation is. Complicating this is the fact that Articles 74(3) and 83(3) LOSC contains no explicit elaboration as to the specific actions or reactions caught by the obligation – that is, beyond that it means to forestall those acts having an effect of hampering or jeopardising.[648]

641 HD Phan, 'Conduct of Parties in Disputed Maritime Areas: the Guyana v. Suriname Case' (2014) 54(3–4) *IJIL* 487, 492; Fietta (n. 153) 127.

642 Section 5.3.7 below.

643 R Beckman, 'Legal Framework for Joint Development in the South China Sea' in S Wu et al. (eds.), *UN Convention on the Law of the Sea and the South China Sea* (Routledge, 2014) 251, 254.

644 *Ghana/Côte d'Ivoire (Judgment)* (n. 46) Oral Proceedings (ITLOS/PV.17/C23/6) 25.

645 Ibid. 29.

646 Chapter 3, Section 3.9 above.

647 Kim (n. 287) 76; BIICL Report (n. 141) 23–24.

648 Dang (n. 199) 70.

One reason why paragraph 3 does not produce an exhaustive list of acts having the effect of hampering or jeopardising is that it seeks to apply to a wide range of maritime boundary disputes, having quite different characteristics and dynamics.[649] In fact, there is not an absolute standard that is applicable to disputed EEZ/continental shelf areas *in abstracto*: whether a unilateral act falling under the jurisdiction of the coastal State undertaken in relation thereto is unlawful according to international law directly interacts with the specific circumstances of the maritime boundary dispute involved.[650]

5.3.1 *Negotiating History*

In the early stages of the debates at UNCLOS III, a recognition emerged that the future text of the Convention should include a provision for the consequential increase in disputed EEZ and continental shelf areas and to deal with conflict between coastal States that resulted from the lack of maritime delimitation.[651] However, this was not reflected in proposals that were introduced in these early stages, which rarely touched upon the issue of an interim rule.[652] Complicating matters in designing an interim rule was that these negotiations were held within the larger context of EEZ and continental shelf delimitation; and to reach agreement thereon turned out to be one of the thorniest issues at UNCLOS III.[653]

Particularly complicating a widely acceptable package of delimitation provisions being designed was the conflicting views of two groups of States, rallying around either the principle of equidistance or equity, as the substantive delimitation rule that was to be included in paragraph 1.[654] However, the division between States in UNCLOS III was not evenly split between these positions – in fact, the majority of States did not align themselves with one of these doctrinal positions.[655] The division between States over the rule of delimitation endured for the full duration of the negotiations at UNCLOS

[649] BIICL Report (n. 141) 25.
[650] Van Logchem (n. 21) 196.
[651] Anderson and Van Logchem (n. 18) 199; Nandan and Rosenne (n. 551) 492–493.
[652] Platzöder (n. 559) 461 (NG7/39, Chairman NG7).
[653] JR Stevenson and BH Oxman, 'The Third United Nations Conference on the Law of the Sea: The 1974 Caracas Session' (1975) 69(1) *AJIL* 1, 17; G Jaenicke, 'Die Dritte Seerechtkonfernz der Vereinten Nationen: Grundprobleme im Überblick' (1978) 38 *ZaöRV* 438, 461–462.
[654] S Yanai, 'International Law Concerning Maritime Boundary Delimitation' in D Attard et al. (eds.), *The IMLI Manual on International Maritime Law Vol. I: The Law of the Sea* (Oxford University Press, 2014) 304, 310.
[655] BH Oxman, 'The Third United Nations Conference on the Law of the Sea: the Seventh Session (1978)' (1979) 73(1) *AJIL* 1, 23–24.

III, spanning nine years. It was only in its last days that a complete set of delimitation provisions, being one of the last open issues, was agreed upon.[656]

Designing an interim rule was more made difficult by the recognition of a strong interrelation between the issues of a rule of delimitation and an interim rule at UNCLOS III,[657] whereby the issue of an interim rule was caught up in the inimical talks over the rule of delimitation.[658] Although seen as an 'important part of the 'package',[659] designing an interim rule was not regarded as being of equal complexity, or of similar importance as the rule of delimitation.[660]

For most of the duration of UNCLOS III, views differed between delegations over the underlying nature of an interim rule: that is, whether it should be preventive in nature, in that a disputed EEZ/continental shelf area is divided by the equidistance boundary, or that it should seek to incentivise States to come to cooperative arrangements in relation thereto; in their absence, a moratorium would be imposed. Despite these differences, there were also shared concerns amongst States at UNCLOS III over some checks having to be placed on the scope for unilateralism in disputed maritime areas. This conviction inspired the current tone of the negative obligation not to hamper or jeopardise a final boundary agreement in Articles 74(3) and 83(3) LOSC.

As the States at UNCLOS III struggled to find an acceptable language for a provision containing an interim rule, it became increasingly clear that a fine line had to be walked between two aspects, which proved difficult to reconcile: first, not to overly burden the possibility to undertake acts which are under coastal State jurisdiction unilaterally; and, second, to limit the scope for such unilateral acts in disputed EEZ/continental shelf areas. It turned out to be rather difficult to find language for an interim rule that would overcome the suspicions of some States at UNCLOS III that a moratorium in disguise would be introduced.

States that expressed a preference for the delimitation rule of either equidistance or equity generally rallied around proposals containing interim rules that were reflective of these respective preferences. In the same vein, the Chairman of NG7, Manner, observed that, whatever the exact phrasing of an

656 *Award of the Arbitral Tribunal in the Second Stage of the Proceedings between Eritrea and Yemen (Maritime Delimitation)* [1999] XXII RIAA 335, 362 [116].

657 Oxman (n. 655) 23.

658 EL Miles, *Global Ocean Politics: The Decision Process at the Third United Nations Conference on the Law of the Sea 1973–1982* (Martinus Nijhoff, 1998) 394.

659 Evans (n. 598) 40.

660 Lagoni (n. 243) 349–350; JA de Yturriaga, *The International Regime of Fisheries: From UNCLOS 1982 to the Presential Sea* (Martinus Nijhoff, 1997) 82.

interim rule, the fact remained that its acceptability for many delegations was interwoven with the rule of delimitation due to their close connection.[661]

As negotiations progressed, it became clear that the success of finding a widely acceptable interim rule was contingent not only on reaching consensus on a rule of delimitation but also on dispute settlement, a topic in relation to which reaching an agreement proved to be quite formidable as well. In line with the recognition of most States at UNCLOS III insisting on the three issues of maritime delimitation, an interim rule, and dispute settlement being inseparable from each other,[662] efforts were then directed towards developing a comprehensive package, containing provisions on the earlier-mentioned three issues, and which would be able to count on the broad agreement of States.[663] To facilitate this aim, smaller negotiation groups were subsequently created.

One of the first issues that needed to be addressed, however, was whether the rules applicable to disputed EEZ and continental shelf areas required uniquely tailored solutions or, rather, whether they could be developed in unison. In early proposals, the rules applicable to a disputed EEZ and continental shelf area were dealt with largely separately.[664] Thereafter, the recognition grew amongst States at UNCLOS III that interim rules for the EEZ and continental shelf had to be formulated along the same substantive lines. However, Ireland continued its approach of differential treatment: it only proposed an interim rule that was tailored to be applied pending continental shelf delimitation.[665] This approach where the EEZ and the continental shelf were treated separately was abandoned by the publication of the Revised Single Negotiation Text/Part II (RSNT/Part II) of 1976.

Shortly thereafter, the first signs were already visible that there was a division between States advocating the use of an equidistance boundary as an interim rule, and those prescribing coming to a cooperative arrangement as a requirement for accessing natural resources contained within a disputed area.[666] At the second session of UNCLOS III in 1974, one of the earliest

661 Platzöder (n. 559) 461 (NG7/39, Chairman NG7); Doc. A/CONF.62/RCNG/1 (19 May 1978), Official Records of the Third United Nations Conference on the Law of the Sea, Vol. X, 125.

662 Oude Elferink (n. 53) 27–28; Y Tanaka, *Predictability and Flexibility of Maritime Delimitation* (Hart, 2006) 45.

663 Platzöder (n. 559) 432 (NG7/26, Chairman NG7); Doc. A/CONF.62/SR.126 (2 April 1980), Official Records of the Third United Nations Conference on the Law of the Sea, Vol. XIII, 13 [25] (Spain), 16 [69] (Chile).

664 Brown (n. 555) 181–182.

665 Doc. A/CONF.62/C.2/L.43 (6 August 1974), Official Records of the Third United Nations Conference on the Law of the Sea, Vol. III, 220–221 (Ireland).

666 Miles (n. 658) 394; Oude Elferink (n. 53) 34.

proposals expressing a preference for the use of the equidistance boundary as an interim rule was introduced by the Netherlands. In that same year, Ireland coined the concept of a moratorium on economic conduct that would be activated if the States concerned were unable to conclude a cooperative arrangement in relation to a disputed continental shelf area.[667] Subsequently, this division in views entrenched the debates concerning the issue of an interim rule.[668]

The Dutch proposal developed a delimitation rule along substantively different lines than an interim rule: if the States concerned failed to effect a delimitation based on equitable principles, the equidistance boundary would apply as an interim rule. Playing a critical role in its proposal was third-party dispute settlement: if States failed to negotiate a delimitation agreement, and if conciliation was equally unsuccessful, it would be mandatory to have the maritime boundary delimited by adjudication.[669] Because a significant amount of time can elapse before the final delimitation is effected, the Netherlands deemed it necessary that an interim rule would apply automatically, meaning that it had to be activated the moment that disputed EEZ or continental shelf areas emerged.[670] The content of an interim rule proposed by Greece and Japan was developed largely along the same lines: that is, a geographical line divides the area of overlapping EEZ or continental shelf claims, and forms the outer limit of where States would be allowed to exercise jurisdiction or sovereign rights prior to delimitation.[671] Competing sovereign rights and jurisdiction of different States over the same part of a disputed EEZ/continental shelf area would be removed under these proposals. This is because respective jurisdictions would be assigned to claimant States, where they can exercise their sovereign rights exclusively prior to delimitation; that is, in areas located on a State's own side of the provisional equidistance boundary.

States seeking an interim rule based on equity were strongly opposed to any proposals promoting the use of the equidistance boundary. One of the earliest proposals developed based on equitable principles was a proposal by Ireland.[672] Its intention was to ensure that States in bona fide claimed

667 A/CONF.62/C.2/L.43 (n. 665) (Ireland).

668 M Nordquist and CH Park (eds.), *Reports of the United States Delegation to the Third United Nations Conference on the Law of the Sea* (Law of the Sea Institute, 1983) 283–284.

669 A/CONF.62/C.2/L.14 (n. 558) (the Netherlands).

670 Ibid.

671 Ibid.; Doc. A/CONF.62/C.2/L.32 (31 July 1974), Official Records of the Third United Nations Conference on the Law of the Sea, Vol. III, 211 (Greece); Doc. A/CONF.62/C.2/L.31/Rev.1 (16 August 1974), Official Records of the Third United Nations Conference on the Law of the Sea, Vol. III, 211 (Japan).

672 A/CONF.62/C.2/L.43 (n. 665) (Ireland).

continental shelf areas did not unilaterally undertake activities of an exploratory or exploitative nature. Before such activities could begin, the prior approval of all the coastal States concerned needed to be secured.

South Korea drew attention to disputed maritime areas located in enclosed and semi-enclosed seas.[673] These would inevitably occur when the characteristics of these seas were combined with the extension of coastal State jurisdiction over maritime zones,[674] and were ideally settled by direct delimitation negotiations under this proposal. As negotiations could be unsuccessful, an interim rule for enclosed and semi-enclosed seas patterned along the following lines had to be introduced in conjunction: the equidistance boundary would come to divide disputed areas located in enclosed and semi-enclosed seas. This solution was not applied by analogy to 'regular' areas of overlapping claims, which had to be treated differently in the view of South Korea, in that emphasis was placed on the need for entering into cooperative arrangements, particularly whenever 'one party had difficulty in accepting the claim of the other' over a disputed EEZ or continental shelf area.[675]

In 1975, the Second Committee created an informal consultative group that dealt with the issue of maritime delimitation in its broadest sense.[676] After holding two rounds of talks, the Second Committee produced two draft provisions, which formed the basis for future discussions on an interim rule, through their inclusion in Articles 61(3) and 70(3) of the Informal Single Negotiation Text/Part II (ISNT).[677] These closely followed the thrust of the earlier proposals of the Netherlands, Japan, and Greece,[678] stipulating that, in the absence of delimitation, a coastal State was entitled to extend its EEZ or continental shelf to the equidistance boundary; this is unless 'relevant circumstances' are present, entitling a State to claim areas as part of its EEZ and continental shelf beyond the equidistance boundary.[679]

673 Chapter 2, Section 2.2 above.

674 Doc. A/CONF.62/C.2/SR.17 (26 July 1974), Official Records of the Third United Nations Conference on the Law of the Sea, Vol. III, 148 [29]–[30] (South Korea).

675 Ibid. [30].

676 Doc. A/CONF.62/C.2/L.89/Rev.1 (15 July 1975), Official Records of the Third United Nations Conference on the Law of the Sea, Vol. IV, 195, 196 [5] [17] (Rapporteur, Second Committee).

677 Doc. A/CONF.62/WP.8/Part II (ISNT 1975), Official Records of the Third United Nations Conference on the Law of the Sea, Vol. IV, 153–171.

678 Nandan and Rosenne (n. 551) 960.

679 Doc. A/CONF.62/WP.8/REV.1/Part II (ISNT 1976), Official Records of the Third United Nations Conference on the Law of the Sea, Vol. V, 164–165 (Articles 62(3), 71(3)) (RSNT/Part II).

At the fourth session of UNCLOS III, opposition swelled against Articles 61(3) and 70(3) ISNT, resulting in the decision of the Chairman of the Second Committee to abandon an approach to an interim rule based on equidistance. There were two reasons underlying that decision. First, it had become increasingly clear that compulsory dispute settlement to have disputes over EEZ/continental shelf delimitation settled by an international court or tribunal was not going to command general approval from the States at UNCLOS III.[680] Second, the approach of developing an interim rule based on equidistance had lost a great deal of its followers compared to the preceding deliberations. Concerns were being voiced that, if an interim rule on the basis of equidistance were designed without it being accompanied by an obligation to submit the underlying delimitation dispute to third-party settlement, coastal States would have little incentive to delimit their EEZ or continental shelf boundary; that is, if at least one of the coastal States concerned is already satisfied with the interim solution.[681] As a result, the putative equidistance boundary may de facto become the 'definitive' boundary.[682]

In light of these developments, the Chairman of the Second Committee considered a continuation of the discussions on an interim rule along the lines of equidistance to be unconducive to a rule to this end being introduced in the framework of the future convention.[683] He suggested an alternative solution: that is, to tie the paragraph providing an interim rule to the paragraph that would come to lay down the delimitation rule.[684] This nexus was created in the revised version of Articles 62 and 71, and subsequently in the official negotiating text (RSNT/Part II), stipulating as follows: in the absence of delimitation, claimant coastal States 'shall make provisional arrangements' by 'taking into account the provisions of paragraph 1'.[685] The implication of the phrase 'shall' being introduced in the language of Articles 62(3) and 71(3) RSNT/Part II is that States would have been placed under an obligation to successfully enter into provisional arrangements. However, because of the reference to paragraph 1, containing the vague concept of 'equitable principles',[686] these provisions failed to offer States a substantive criterion on the basis of which they could conclude provisional arrangements prior to delimitation.

680 Ibid. 153 [12].
681 Grisel (n. 632) 570.
682 Oxman (n. 655) 23.
683 Ibid.
684 RSNT/Part II (n. 679).
685 Ibid. 164–165 (Articles 62(3) and 71(3)).
686 Klemm (n. 623) 533.

In the two rounds of negotiations that followed in 1976 and 1977, progress in devising an interim rule for disputed EEZ and continental shelf areas was hardly discernible. Although at the time no provision was introduced that could count on the broad agreement from delegations, the Chairman of the Second Committee nonetheless had full confidence that such a result could be successfully brought about.[687]

At the resumed fifth session in 1976, not long after the establishment by the Second Committee of Negotiation Group No. 5, a smaller subgroup was created, which was tasked to deal (in one session) with the legal framework applicable to EEZ/continental shelf delimitation, particularly Articles 62 and 71 of the RSNT/Part II.[688] The main driving force leading to the creation of the subgroup were the continuous difficulties that were encountered in relation to designing a rule of delimitation, which hindered progress in finding a broad agreement on the content of an interim rule as well.[689]

At the sixth session in 1977, Spain introduced a proposal requiring claimant States to exercise restraint, by not crossing the equidistance line in the period prior to delimitation.[690] Its activation was linked to the condition that the States concerned could not 'agree on alternative interim measures of mutual restraint'; an example hereof is when it is agreed not to enforce one's own laws and regulations, for instance pertaining to fisheries, against the other State's nationals in the disputed maritime area. Subsequently, the Spanish suggestion was replicated in the proposal by a group consisting of eighteen more States, making up the equidistance group ('the group of nineteen').[691] Under both these proposals, the scope of application of the interim solution based on the equidistance boundary was extended to the period when delimitation was to be effected by an international court or tribunal as well.

As the two rounds of negotiations in 1976 and 1977 drew to a close, no substantive change was made to the language of the delimitation provisions in the Informal Composite Negotiation Text (ICNT). The only change effected was renumbering Articles 62 and 71 of the RSNT/Part II as Articles 74 and 83.[692]

687 Doc. A/CONF.62/L.17 (16 September 1976), Official Records of the Third United Nations Conference on the Law of the Sea, Vol. VI, 138 [46] (Chairman, Second Committee).

688 Nandan and Rosenne (n. 551) 963.

689 Doc. A/CONF.62/L.17 (n. 687).

690 R Platzöder, Third United Nations Conference on the Law of the Sea: Documents (Oceana, 1982) Vol. IV, 467 (Articles 71(2)–(3), Spain).

691 Ibid. 467 (Article 71(3), Bahamas, Barbados, Colombia, Costa Rica, Cyprus, Democratic Yemen, Denmark, Greece, Guyana, Italy, Japan, Kuwait, Malta, Norway, Spain, Sweden, Tunisia, United Arab Emirates, United Kingdom).

692 Doc. A/CONF.62/WP.10 (15 July 1977), Official Records of the Third United Nations Conference on the Law of the Sea, Vol. VIII, 17 (Article 83).

The continued inability to find a provision that was acceptable to both delimitation groups led at the seventh session in 1978 to the issue of maritime delimitation being amongst seven issues that were labelled as being utterly difficult to resolve.[693] This dichotomy between the views of the two delimitation groups was also reflected in the proposals on an interim rule, as these continued to be regularly developed in a way reflecting the preferred delimitation rule of the States concerned. At one end of the spectrum, there was a group of twenty States[694] supporting a proposal that was based on using the equidistance boundary as an interim rule. At the other end of the spectrum, there was a group of twenty-seven States seeking to incorporate the rule of equity into an interim rule. Its content was that States should enter into provisional arrangements, taking into account equitable principles, with a view to managing and conducting activities in relation to disputed EEZ and continental shelf areas.[695] Most of the other States at UNCLOS III were caught between these two extremes. Because these States did not belong to either of the delimitation groups,[696] they were, however, able to produce proposals seeking to mediate between these opposite positions, which paved the way for an ultimately acceptable text of an interim rule for disputed EEZ and continental shelf areas.

In 1978, after NG7 was established and was placed under the leadership of Manner,[697] Morocco developed a conciliatory proposal that States having bona fide overlapping EEZ or continental shelf claims were to be subject to two distinct obligations. First, States were exhorted – must 'endeavour' – to seek agreement on cooperative arrangements; and, second, they had to abstain from taking any 'measure which would prejudice a final solution'.[698] This latter obligation was further circumscribed in the Moroccan proposal, in that the States concerned had to eschew any actions that would 'prejudice a final solution in any way' as well as 'aggravate their conflict'.[699]

693 Nordquist and Park (n. 668) 211–212.

694 Platzöder (n. 559) 392 (NG7/2, Article 84[83](3), Bahamas, Barbados, Canada, Colombia, Cyprus, Democratic Yemen, Denmark, Gambia, Greece, Guyana, Italy, Japan, Kuwait, Malta, Norway, Spain, Sweden, United Arab Emirates, United Kingdom, Yugoslavia). NG7/2/Rev.1 and NG7/2/Rev.2 make no change to paragraph 3. Reproduced in Platzöder, ibid. 393–394.

695 Ibid. 402 (NG7/10, Article 83, Algeria, Argentina, Bangladesh, Benin, Congo, France, Iraq, Ireland, Côte d'Ivoire, Kenya, Liberia, Libyan Arab Jamahiriya, Madagascar, Mali, Mauritania, Morocco, Nicaragua, Pakistan, Papua New Guinea, Poland, Romania, Senegal, Syrian Arab Republic, Somalia, Turkey, and Venezuela).

696 A/CONF.62/RCNG/1 (n. 661).

697 Irwin (n. 56) 109–110.

698 Kim (n. 287) 35.

699 Platzöder (n. 559) Vol. IX, 395 (Morocco).

During the seventh session in 1978, the moratorium approach was reintroduced by Papua New Guinea, by replicating the gist of Ireland's proposal that was tabled in 1974. Under Papua New Guinea's proposal, undertaking unilateral economic activities prior to delimitation was predicated on the States concerned having entered into provisional arrangements, which followed in terms of design paragraph 1, referring to equity as a delimitation rule, to the letter.[700] A failure to design an interim rule along these lines had two implications in the view of Papua New Guinea: first, the current version of an interim rule had to be removed from the negotiating text; and, second, the search for an interim rule could be abandoned altogether.[701]

Against the background of these different proposals, the Chairman of NG7 considered the consensus to lie in the proposal of the group of States promoting equitable principles, pursuant to which States were exhorted to conclude provisional arrangements, and which he deemed to provide a reasonable prospect of a compromise.[702]

In summarising the discussions that occurred in NG7, the Chairman observed that a measure of willingness existed amongst States to clarify in greater detail what was expected of coastal States in the period preceding delimitation. One suggested approach was to place limitations on the range of lawful economic conduct in disputed EEZ/continental shelf areas.[703] Norway seeking to bring further specificity to the text, as it stood in the ICNT, identified two elements that required more in-depth discussion.[704] First, the 'duty' imposed on States to 'make provisional arrangements' should be further specified. Second, guidelines circumscribing the scope for States to exercise jurisdiction over natural resources and related acts needed to be developed. The use of the word guidelines suggests that these would have been more akin to mere suggestions than to rules of a binding nature.[705] Norway identified two approaches through which the contents of these perceived guidelines could be further developed, that is by concentrating:[706] first, on the unlawfulness of erecting installations in a disputed continental shelf area; and, second, on unilaterally taking (or attempting to take) natural resources therefrom.

The NG7 Chairman's earlier observation that States at UNCLOS III were willing to include objective elements in a provision providing an interim rule

700 Ibid. 406 (NG7/15, Art 83(3), Papua New Guinea).
701 Adede (n. 631) 223.
702 A/CONF.62/RCNG/1 (n. 661) 125.
703 Ibid.
704 Platzöder (n. 559) 406 (NG7/16, Norway).
705 But see Adede (n. 631) 223; De Yturriaga (n. 660) 82.
706 Platzöder (n. 559) 406 (NG7/16, Norway).

was not mirrored in the remainder of the seventh session. In fact, there seems to have been no further debate or elaboration on this issue.[707]

As discussions drew to a close, the Chairman of NG7 observed that the need to include an interim rule was recognised by all delegations.[708] At this time, the language of Articles 74(3) and 83(3) ICNT was not revised. This was because the Chairman considered that revising the provisions of the ICNT in accordance with the proposals that were received positively by States, including Morocco's proposal, would not have substantially improved the possibility of reaching a consensus.[709]

At the second meeting of NG7, taking place at the resumed seventh session in 1978, the issue of an interim rule was more intensively debated by the States participating in UNCLOS III.[710] The Chairman of NG7 shed some light on two issues related to the development of an interim rule:[711] first, the state of the negotiations in relation to developing an interim rule; and, second, it provided an indication of the direction in which these negotiations were progressing.[712]

After reviewing the proposal included in the ICNT, the Chairman of NG7 concluded the following: revising Articles 74(3) and 83(3) along the lines of States being placed under an obligation to enter into provisional arrangements would not improve the possibility of reaching a consensus, rather the contrary.[713] There was, however, no opposition from States at UNCLOS III to include wording that would exhort the States concerned to try to agree on cooperative arrangements.[714]

Provisional arrangements were regarded by the Chairman of NG7 as a useful instrument in avoiding the aggravation of maritime boundary disputes. This was anchored in the belief that, in the absence of such arrangements, coastal States would continue to act unilaterally, by authorising or undertaking acts that are under coastal State jurisdiction, leading to an automatic aggravation of their maritime boundary dispute. After recognising that any concluded provisional arrangements would invariably be diverse in content as well as their nature, suitable wording that would encourage States to enter into such arrangements needed to be chosen in the view of the Chairman.[715]

707 Adede (n. 631) 223.
708 A/CONF.62/RCNG/1 (n. 661) 125.
709 Ibid.
710 Nordquist and Park (n. 668) 285.
711 Platzöder (n. 559) 428–430 (NG7/24, Articles 74(3)/83(3), Chairman NG7).
712 Ibid. 428 (NG7/23, Articles 74(3)/83(3), Chairman NG7).
713 Ibid.
714 Ibid.
715 Platzöder (n. 559) 430 (NG7/24, Articles 74(3)/83(3), Chairman NG7).

States that disagreed with the position of the Chairman of NG7, however, continued to reiterate their positions that the substance of an interim rule had to align with whatever rule of delimitation was included in the final text of the Convention. This led to the reintroduction of proposals which had previously only acquired more moderate support from delegations.[716]

While there was a consensus that restraint had to be exercised by States in relation to their disputed areas, the question remained to what extent.[717] Through the introduction of more explicit rules circumscribing the remaining scope for unilateralism in disputed EEZ and continental shelf areas, certain States attempted to clarify to which extent restraint had to be observed;[718] for example, by stipulating that coastal States must observe restraint in conducting unilateral actions resulting in the 'depletion of resources or environmental damage'.[719]

In one of his observations, the Chairman of NG7 signalled that some States at UNCLOS III continued to advance the notion that, in the absence of cooperative arrangements or delimitation, a moratorium on all activities associated with natural resources would be put in effect in a disputed area.[720] Shortly thereafter, but especially at the eighth session in 1979, the tone of the debates over an interim rule based on a moratorium changed, acquiring a more negative stance, as more States started to speak out against its imposition. Several considerations prompted this change in views: the vagueness of the moratorium concept, its lack of content, and the limited operational use it would have in light of the aforementioned considerations.[721] Because of this, the Chairman suggested abandoning the discussion on an interim rule based on the moratorium approach. Despite the moratorium approach falling into disfavour, the observance of restraint by States in relation to a disputed EEZ and continental shelf area was still considered to be an essential aspect of an interim rule geared towards facilitating delimitation.[722]

In his report, the Chairman of NG7 summarised the category of proposals seeking to introduce a moratorium as seeking to prevent States from making 'unilateral arrangements'.[723] This reference has to be understood as seeking to prevent any arrangement from being imposed without the consent of the other

716 Ibid. 428 (NG7/23).
717 Ibid. 430 (NG7/24).
718 Oxman (n. 655) 23.
719 Ibid.
720 Platzöder (n. 559) 269 (NG7/45, Article 83(3), Chairman NG7).
721 Ibid. 432–437 (NG7/26).
722 Ibid. 430 (NG7/23).
723 Ibid. 433–434 (NG7/26).

claimant. Imposing such an arrangement unilaterally would be at odds with the thrust of the paragraph setting out that delimitation must come about by agreement between the States concerned.

According to the Chairman of NG7, it became increasingly clear that continuing on the same lines as set out previously, in that a solution would have to be found by developing the text of an interim rule on either the basis of equidistance or equity, was counterproductive to completing the search for such a rule.[724] Therefore, some new approaches mediating between these different approaches had to be developed.

By drawing inspiration from several suggestions having been advanced in earlier debates at UNCLOS III,[725] India, Iraq, and Morocco conjointly developed a conciliatory draft article, which was introduced in 1979. There were two components to this suggestion. First, the positive component, stipulating that adjacent or opposite coastal States, whose maritime boundary dispute was not pending before an international court or tribunal, must 'in a spirit of cooperation' make some efforts to enter into provisional arrangements.[726] Second, and this was the negative component, States were subject to a parallel obligation to eschew activities that both aggravate a situation, and jeopardise the interests of the other coastal State. As this proposal resembles quite closely the final text of Articles 74(3) and 83(3) LOSC, it has been credited for paving the way for a compromise on an interim rule being reached, or, at a minimum, being instrumental in its final design.[727] Despite the praise that the proposal received, this admiration was not shared amongst all States at UNCLOS III, as its text encountered two sorts of criticism.

First, the text conflated two separate issues: it simultaneously included the phrases 'shall' (i.e. connoting an obligation of result) and 'freely' (i.e. the absence of any form of obligation) in the same sentence. Perhaps most problematic was that these words have different and to a certain degree opposite meanings, making the extent of the obligation that was perceived to be imposed on States under this proposal unclear, ranging from there being no obligation (i.e. indicated by the word 'freely') to the existence of an absolute obligation to enter into such arrangements (i.e. as exemplified by the word 'shall').[728]

The States supporting the proposal introduced by India, Iraq, and Morocco claimed that the concurrent use of the words 'shall' and 'freely' within the

724 Ibid. 434.

725 Nordquist and Park (n. 668) 285.

726 Platzöder (n. 559) 453 (NG7/32, Article 83(3), India, Iraq, and Morocco).

727 Kim (n. 287) 36–37.

728 Adede (n. 631) 245.

proposal was not contradictory. Rather, these two words denoted different stages that the coastal States will go through, which will ultimately result in provisional arrangements being successfully concluded. The relationship between the words 'shall' and 'freely' could be framed as follows: the word 'shall' seeks to create an obligation for States to begin good faith negotiations. Depending on the success of these talks, States could 'freely' make the decision to enter into such arrangements 'in the spirit of cooperation', as contemplated under the provision.

The second line of criticism levelled at the proposal was that the insertion of language calling on States to abjure taking unilateral acts that aggravate reaching a delimitation would inevitably run into interpretational difficulties.[729] Central to this criticism were three considerations.

First, some States believed that a moratorium on economic conduct would be introduced under the guise of States being called upon to observe restraint. These concerns centred on the use of wording of 'aggravate the situation or jeopardise the interests' of claimant States, which it was argued would lead to the introduction of a de facto moratorium.[730]

Second, linking the lawfulness of a unilateral act to whether a State's interests would be impaired ran the risk of being abused, due to this being 'subject to unilateral interpretation' by the States concerned.[731]

Third, pursuant to the proposal, provisional arrangements could take two forms, which were not further elaborated upon. This kept their contents vague, meaning that either measures of mutual restraint or, alternatively, measures of mutual accommodation could be agreed upon. As a defence, the proponents of the proposal underscored that the aim was not to give an exhaustive enumeration of the types of cooperative arrangements that States could enter into;[732] rather, measures of 'mutual restraint' or 'mutual accommodation' were two examples of the forms such arrangements could take.

A proposal subsequently introduced by Mexico and Peru duplicated some of the substantive elements of the Indian, Iraqi, and Moroccan proposal, with the variation that it differs in terms of its scope of application. The Mexican/Peruvian proposal made no mention of a final settlement.[733] In the main, the Mexican/Peruvian proposal called upon States to try to conclude provisional arrangements, and not to act in a way that made reaching the delimitation more difficult.[734] It

729 Ibid.
730 Platzöder (n. 559) 461 (NG7/39, Chairman NG7).
731 Adede (n. 631) 245.
732 Ibid.
733 Platzöder (n. 559) 456 (NG7/36/Rev.1, Article 83, Mexico and Peru).
734 Ibid.

also circumscribed the period during which a provisional arrangement may be in existence, limiting its maximum duration to two years. The identified negative relation between the length of a provisional arrangement and delimitation was construed by Mexico and Peru as that the longer such an arrangement would regulate a disputed maritime area, the dimmer the prospect of a successful delimitation would become.

Reportedly, many of the delegations at UNCLOS III favourably received the proposals of Mexico/Peru and India/Iraq/Morocco.[735] However, adjusting the ICNT in accordance with the gist of these two proposals was unlikely to be welcomed by other States at UNCLOS III. There were two reasons for this: first, because of the failure of the two proposals to establish a substantive nexus between an interim rule and the rule of delimitation;[736] and, second, concerns remained over the perceived economic implications that these proposals could have for coastal States.

At the eighth session in 1979, significant difficulties remained in the search for an interim rule pertaining to disputed EEZ and continental shelf areas.[737] Now both the proposals introduced by Iran, Iraq, and Morocco, and Mexico and Peru met with a decidedly mixed response. Also, the provision proposed in the ICNT of 1977, establishing a nexus between the rule of delimitation in paragraph 1 and the interim rule of paragraph 3, in that a duty was placed on claimants to 'make provisional arrangements', attracted far more criticism than it had done hitherto.[738] The limiting impact of this provision on the extent to which coastal States could economically develop a disputed area was still a serious concern amongst certain States at UNCLOS III. Also, there were some delegations that withdrew their support for designing an interim rule; this was because they were no longer convinced of its usefulness.[739] For example, Israel sought the deletion of the interim rule from the ICNT of 1977, suggesting abandoning the search for such a rule completely,[740] as its introduction would 'do more harm than good'.[741]

In the face of dwindling support for its inclusion, the States retaining the view that an interim rule had to be made part of the package of delimitation provisions started to reintroduce all separate categories of suggestions that had

735 Ibid. 453 (NG7/32, Article 83(3), India, Iraq, and Morocco).
736 Adede (n. 631) 245.
737 CH Park, 'Offshore Oil Development in the China Seas: Some Legal and Territorial Issues' in EM Borgese and N Ginsburg (eds.), *Ocean Yearbook*, Vol. 2 (Brill, 1980) 302, 311–312.
738 A/CONF.62/WP.10 (n. 692).
739 Platzöder (n. 559) 433–434 (NG7/26, Article 83(3), India, Iraq, and Morocco).
740 Doc. A/CONF.62/C.2/SR.57 (24 April 1979), Official Records of the Third United Nations Conference on the Law of the Sea, Vol. XI, 60 [49].
741 Ibid.

been discussed in previous rounds of negotiations at UNCLOS III, and hitherto attracted varying degrees of criticism. These suggestions fell along three lines: first, exhorting States to seek provisional arrangements in accordance with equitable principles; second, adopting rules that would prohibit claimants from taking unilateral acts in disputed areas having a detrimental effect on delimitation; and, third, proposing to ban all economic activities from a disputed EEZ or continental shelf area through the introduction of a moratorium.[742]

To address the difficulties that still prevailed in finding any sort of compromise on the language used for an interim rule,[743] the Chairman of NG7 convened a 'private group' which was put directly under his direction. It received instructions to further develop the earlier tabled proposals by Mexico/Peru and India/Iraq/Morocco, which, according to the Chairman, held sufficient promise to form the basis of a modified provision of an interim rule that would be able to attract the support of many States.[744] After completing its deliberations, the group produced the following proposal:

> Pending agreement as provided for in paragraph 1, the States concerned, in a spirit of understanding and co-operation, shall make every effort with a view to entering into provisional arrangements. Accordingly, during this transitional period, they shall refrain from aggravating the situation or hampering in any way the reaching of the final agreement. Such agreements shall be without prejudice to the final delimitation.[745]

After receiving a ringing endorsement from the Chairman of NG7, the proposal was placed, without amendments, in the Chairman's summary report.[746] The vast majority of States did not share his enthusiasm, with the result that the search for an interim rule could not be brought to a close.

On becoming aware of this, the Chairman refrained from amending the language of the first revised ICNT in accordance with the private group's text. Rather, its revision was deferred to the second revised version of the ICNT (ICNT/Rev.2). Thereafter, the private group's proposal formed the basis on which negotiations over an interim rule were held at UNCLOS III – that was, between the

742 Platzöder (n. 559) 433–434 (NG7/26, Article 83(3), India, Iraq, and Morocco).
743 De Yturriaga (n. 660) 83.
744 Ibid. 83–84.
745 Platzöder (n. 559) 461 (NG7/39, Chairman NG7).
746 Ibid.

resumed eighth session in 1979 up until the issue was forwarded to the Plenary Conference in 1980.

Three modifications were made to the language of the private group's proposal, in an attempt to lay to rest any concerns over its economic implications for coastal States: first, the reference to States having to refrain from 'aggravating the situation' had to be omitted, and was replaced by 'jeopardising'; second, the wording 'in any way', which was deemed to be too broad, also had to be removed; and, third, the order of the words was slightly rearranged.

Despite these modifications, controversy remained over the decision of the Chairman of NG7 to replace the interim rule as it stood in the previous negotiation text with the suggestion of the private group in ICNT/Rev.2. In fact, this move perplexed both the Chairman of the Second Committee and the equitable principles delimitation group.[747] Their puzzlement came from the fact that at the ninth session in 1980, the degree of support from States at UNCLOS III for the compromise interim rule that was favoured by the Chairman of NG7 had greatly withered.

The equitable principles group responded by aiming to revive its own suggestion as to the content of an interim rule:[748] any provisional regime could only come about through an agreement between the claimant States, by taking into account the provisions of paragraph 1, laying down a delimitation rule based on equity. Furthermore, several States felt that to decide finally on the text of an interim rule, with the outcome of negotiations on the rule of delimitation being unclear, was akin to putting the cart before the horse.[749] However, the text in the second revision of the ICNT in 1980 withstood any attempts at change, remaining substantively unchanged in the Draft Convention.[750]

After the ninth session (1980), the Chairman of the Second Committee transferred the issue of maritime delimitation to the Plenary of the Conference, and the debate over the delimitation rule flared up once again.[751] Through

747 Doc. A/CONF.62/Wp.10/Rev.2 (11 April 1980), Official Records of the Third United Nations Conference on the Law of the Sea, Vol. VIII 20 [10] (Explanatory Memorandum).

748 Platzöder (n. 559) 403 (NG7/10, Article 83, Algeria, Argentina, Bangladesh, Benin, Congo, France, Iraq, Ireland, Côte d'Ivoire, Kenya, Liberia, Libyan Arab Jamahiriya, Madagascar, Mali, Mauritania, Morocco, Nicaragua, Pakistan, Papua New Guinea, Poland, Romania, Senegal, Syrian Arab Republic, Somalia, Turkey, and Venezuela).

749 Nandan and Rosenne (n. 551) 975; Platzöder (n. 559) 269 (NG7/45, Article 83(3), Chairman NG7).

750 Doc. A/CONF.62/L.78 (28 August 1981), Official Records of the Third United Nations Conference on the Law of the Sea, Vol. XV, 172 (Draft Convention).

751 Doc. A/CONF.62/L.51 (29 March 1980), Official Records of the Third United Nations Conference on the Law of the Sea, Vol. XII, 89 (Chairman, Second Committee).

conversations with the two delimitation groups, held by the new president of UNCLOS III at the resumed ninth and tenth session, it became clear that reaching a compromise on the rule of the delimitation of the continental shelf and the EEZ would be predicated on developing new conciliatory proposals. As a result, whether Articles 74(3) and 83(3) of the ICNT/Rev.2, in its then current form, would be included in the final text of the Convention became contingent on the success of drafting a new widely acceptable delimitation provision.[752]

At the Plenary of UNCLOS III, Iran was one of the few States that reverted to the issue of an interim rule, and its content: whatever its design, it was imperative that no moratorium on economic conduct was introduced because of its economic implications.[753] Rather on the contrary, for Iran the acceptability of an interim rule was predicated on the fact that it must allow for a degree of unilateral economic development of a disputed EEZ or continental shelf area.[754] This was necessary in order to ensure that the primary aim lying behind the introduction of an interim rule would be realised: successfully reaching a delimitation agreement.[755]

Colombia identified the provisions dealing with disputed EEZ and continental shelf areas as one of the pillars underpinning the legal system governing the oceans, and being of chief merit to the international community.[756] A particular concern for Colombia was that, through making a reservation, coastal States could not be bound by the obligation not to hamper or jeopardise, as required by Articles 74(3) and 83(3) LOSC.[757] Heavy criticism was directed by Argentina against the delimitation provisions in the ICNT/Rev.2, but Articles 74(3) and 83(3) LOSC elevated the overall meagre standing of the negotiated package.[758]

Ultimately, an agreement on the delimitation provisions, focusing on the EEZ/continental shelf boundary being equitable,[759] was reached. The interim rule, which had been devised earlier, managed to emerge out of this process unscathed, and was finally included in the final version of the Convention in Articles 74(3) and 83(3).

752 Brown (n. 555) 180.
753 Doc. A/CONF.62/SR.126, Official Records of the Third United Nations Conference on the Law of the Sea, Vol. XVI, 19 [123] (Iran).
754 Ibid.
755 Ibid.
756 Doc. A/CONF.62/SR.172, Official Records of the Third United Nations Conference on the Law of the Sea, Vol. XVI, 117 [33] (Colombia).
757 Ibid. 116 [31].
758 Doc. A/CONF.62/SR.126, Official Records of the Third United Nations Conference on the Law of the Sea, Vol. XVI, 17 [88] (Argentina).
759 Nandan and Rosenne (n. 551) 980.

5.3.2 *Textual Analysis*

Articles 74(3) and 83(3) met with a largely critical reception shortly after the text of the LOSC was adopted, and prior to its entering into force.[760] However, its language was carefully drafted.[761] In discussions over the text of paragraph 3 within either the English or French language group at UNCLOS III, there were ostensibly no differences in the views over the exact wording that was going to be included in the final version of the Convention.[762] Despite its careful drafting, the language of the paragraph is convoluted and rather open-ended; as a result, it is not very easy to construe its meaning.[763]

The inclusion of open wording in paragraph 3 of Articles 74 and 83 LOSC may have been deliberate, however: leaving its content vague has the upside that there is flexibility in this paragraph, thereby ensuring that it has a large degree of applicability in disputed EEZ and continental shelf areas. By that same token, the relevance of paragraph 3 would be preserved in the face of intricacies that can be present in individual disputed EEZ or continental shelf areas in two ways: first, a disputed maritime area will generate its own level of conflict; and, second, the lawfulness of certain unilateral acts may be viewed differently by the States concerned.[764]

Paragraph 3's primary underlying aim is more easily discernible: it seeks to steer between States having to seek cooperative arrangements and abstaining from unilateral conduct that complicates delimitation. Complicating matters, in terms of interpretation, is that the language of paragraph 3, and its main elements, have not all been the object of judicial comment. Therefore, falling back on the ordinary meaning of the wording, supplemented by the context of Articles 74(3) and 83(3), is sometimes inevitable in interpreting its meaning.[765]

Two temporal elements can be found in paragraph 3 of Articles 74 and 83 LOSC, both of which are tied to its activation, but whose meanings continue to defy uniform interpretation, however.[766] Paragraph 3 begins by introducing its first temporal element in that it is 'pending agreement as provided for in

760 Caflisch (n. 587) 495; ED Brown, *International Law of the Sea* (Dartmouth Publishing, 1994) 159.

761 Anderson and Van Logchem (n. 18) 205.

762 Oral comment by BH Oxman and T Treves at the 'UNCLOS and the South China Sea' Conference organised by the Centre for International law, National University of Singapore, Singapore, 26–28 June 2013.

763 Anderson and Van Logchem (n. 18) 205.

764 Chapter 9, Section 9.3.2 below.

765 Anderson and Van Logchem (n. 18) 205–208; Van Logchem (n. 245) 133–139.

766 Y Tanaka, 'Unilateral Exploration and Exploitation of Natural Resources in Disputed Areas: A Note on the *Ghana/Côte d'Ivoire* Order of 25 April 2015 before the Special Chamber of ITLOS' (2015) 46(4) *ODIL* 315, 316.

paragraph 1', thereby imposing two obligations on States. In the French text of the Convention, reference is made to the period where a future delimitation agreement is 'awaited' (French text: 'en attendant la conclusion de l'accord vise au paragraphe 1').[767] This phrase is directly followed by the obligation to make efforts to enter into provisional arrangements, and then the formulation of the negative obligation not to hamper or jeopardise delimitation follows. And, second, also in the first sentence of paragraph 3, the other temporal element is encountered, that is 'during this transitional period'.

5.3.2.1 Agreement

According to its text, the activation of paragraph 3 is contingent upon the existence of a situation as contemplated under Articles 74(1) and 83(1) LOSC: there has to be a need for an EEZ/continental shelf maritime boundary between the adjacent or opposite coasts of States, which is to be established by an agreement on the basis of international law.[768] Because of the link between paragraph 3 and 'agreement' in the sense of paragraph 1 of Articles 74 and 83 LOSC, it is critical to develop an understanding of what is meant by 'agreement'. A first issue that arises is whether some attempts must have been made at attaining delimitation by agreement by the States concerned, in that delimitation negotiations have been held, either in the present or in the past.

When it is clear to neighbouring States that there is an overlap in their EEZ or continental shelf claims, making apparent the need for delimitation, and they have commenced delimitation negotiations, States must negotiate in good faith.[769] As international law imposes no constraints on how long these talks may or must take, or that these must be successful,[770] States can negotiate for as long as they want to, or as long as is necessary.[771]

The word 'agreement', based on a narrower but problematic interpretation, can be linked to the fact that delimitation negotiations must have started in order for the two obligations under Articles 74(3) and 83(3) LOSC to be activated.[772] This view similarly excludes the period during which the States concerned have agreed to submit their dispute to third-party dispute settle-

[767] Anderson and Van Logchem (n. 18) 208.
[768] Section 5.3.7 below.
[769] Chapter 3, Section 3.6 above.
[770] *Cameroon* v. *Nigeria* (n. 454) 424 [244].
[771] DM Ong, 'Joint Development of Common Offshore Oil and Gas Deposits: "Mere" State Practice or Customary International Law?' (1999) 93(4) *AJIL* 771, 784.
[772] Lagoni (n. 243) 357.

ment, and when the case is being considered by an international court or tribunal – submitting a dispute to international adjudication follows after an agreement, although indirectly, has been reached. But the main problem with delaying the activation of paragraph 3 until delimitation negotiations have started lies with the fact that its obligation not to hamper or jeopardise does not exert its relevance in the period prior thereto, offering ample opportunity to the States concerned to pre-empt the success of these talks by acting unilaterally in relation to their disputed area.

The willingness of coastal States to delimit their disputed EEZ or continental shelf area, or to cooperate in relation thereto, will invariably differ from one situation to the next. Certain States will prefer to still operate within a given status quo, which may have been prevalent for a significant period of time.[773] As a further variable, the possibility that delimitation negotiations are opened between certain States may be rather remote. For instance, Vietnam's unwillingness to open delimitation negotiations with China has been retraced to the fact that it would lend undue credence to the latter's claim encompassing most of the South China Sea.[774] It might also be that continuing to operate under a provisional arrangement, or modus vivendi, may be comparatively more beneficial to a State than if it were to determine a maritime boundary. In a somewhat similar vein, South Korea may have for a long time been unwilling to replace a fishery arrangement agreed upon in 1956 with a new one, as its terms would likely be less favourable.[775] Furthermore, the absence of friendly relations between States can be a notable obstacle to negotiations being opened, thereby shelving their opening, at least until diplomatic relations are initiated or resumed.[776] However, once negotiations are opened, the obligation requiring States to make efforts to enter into provisional arrangements is applicable. When negotiations are ongoing, States may not undertake acts having the consequential effect of hampering or jeopardising reaching a delimitation agreement; undertaking acts having one of these effects could derail initiated talks or lead to counter-actions from the other coastal State. Cases where coastal States made claims of this nature against the other State are not merely theoretical. An example is when Montenegro claimed that

773 A Munton, 'Timor Plays a Waiting Game over Oil and Gas', *Canberra Times*, 2 December 2004.

774 R Amer, 'China, Vietnam and the South China Sea: Disputes and Dispute Management' (2014) 45(1) *ODIL* 17, 18; J Li and R Amer, 'Recent Practices in Dispute Management in the South China Sea' in CH Schofield (ed.), *Maritime Energy Resources in Asia: Legal Regimes and Cooperation* (NBR Special Report No. 3, 2012) 79, 98–99.

775 MG Koo, *Island Disputes and Maritime Regime Building in East Asia: Between a Rock and a Hard Place* (Springer, 2010) 178–179.

776 Hayashi (n. 13) 46.

Croatia had taken unilateral actions in relation to their disputed maritime area while holding negotiations, which amounted to a lack of good faith on Croatia's part.[777] A breaking down or postponement of negotiations would not absolve States from acting in accordance with the two obligations contained in Articles 74(3) and 83(3) LOSC.

On a broad interpretation of the phrase of 'pending agreement', the application of paragraph 3 is appropriately extended in two ways. First, it includes the period when the dispute is under consideration by an international court or tribunal, up to having handed down its final judgment. And, second, independent thereof, to the period that lies before an agreement on a delimitation of the maritime boundary, based on international law and providing an equitable solution, in the sense of paragraph 1, has not become binding on the States concerned.[778] Also, after a State has proposed to submit the delimitation to arbitration or a different form of judicial proceedings, or to conciliation pursuant to Annex V, section 2 – subject to any interim measures that may be indicated by an international court or tribunal – both the positive and the negative obligation in Articles 74(3) and 83(3) LOSC would be incumbent on claimant States.[779]

A further implication of the inclusion of the opening phrase of Articles 74(3) and 83(3) LOSC, that the States concerned must seek provisional arrangements 'pending agreement', is that, unless there is an intention to the contrary, the arrangement will continue to be relevant until reaching delimitation. The phrase that refers to the conclusion of a future delimitation agreement must be interpreted not only in light of paragraph 1, but also equally in light of paragraph 2 contained in the same provisions.[780] Paragraph 2 provides that after a 'reasonable amount of time' elapses, wherein States are unable to come to a delimitation agreement, they 'shall' submit the maritime boundary dispute to the procedures set out in Part XV LOSC. But when has a reasonable amount of time passed, thereby obliging States to submit their maritime boundary dispute to one of the procedures pursuant to Part XV? It is difficult to ascertain when a 'reasonable period of time' has expired, constituting the period within which claimants must have attained delimitation.[781] Case law addressing its meaning is limited to just one case: *Barbados* v. *Trinidad and Tobago*. In considering whether a 'reasonable period of time' had passed

777 Letter of the Permanent Mission of Montenegro to the United Nations addressed to the Secretary-General, 18 May 2015, available at www.un.org/depts/los/LEGISLATIONAND TREATIES/PDFFILES/communications/MNG_note20150619en.pdf.

778 Mensah (n. 69) 150.

779 Anderson and Van Logchem (n. 18) 210.

780 Nandan and Rosenne (n. 551) 815.

781 Anderson and Van Logchem (n. 18) 208–209.

between the parties to the dispute,[782] the Tribunal held as follows: holding nine rounds of talks over a time-span of three and a half years surpassed 'a reasonable period of time'.[783] Although the impression is created under Articles 74(2) and 83(2) LOSC that, after the breaking down of negotiations, States must submit their dispute to adjudication in accordance with Part XV, there is no way of compelling States to do this. Furthermore, this latter possibility is dependent on the States concerned having not declared any maritime boundary disputes in the sense of Articles 15, 74, and 83 LOSC being excluded from compulsory dispute settlement, by having made a declaration pursuant to Article 298 LOSC.

5.3.2.2 During This Transitional Period

The second temporal element, which is similarly contained in the first sentence of Articles 74(3) and 83(3) LOSC, is 'during this transitional period' (French text: 'pour ne pas compromettre ou entraver pendant cette période de transition'). The composition of the sentence, in that the phrase 'during this transitional period' is followed by States having an obligation to eschew certain types of unilateral actions, directly links the earlier-mentioned phrase to this part of paragraph 3.

It is not readily apparent what constitutes the 'transitional period' as mentioned in the second limb of the sentence of Articles 74(3) and 83(3) LOSC. The ordinary meaning of the word 'transitional' can be defined as relating to a movement or change in a situation, one being anticipated, or having been set in motion, but has not yet been completed. Implicit in the use of the word 'transitional', and when read together with 'period', is thus that the period alluded to here is meant to be exchanged for a different one at a certain point in time.

Due to this part of the sentence of Articles 74(3) and 83(3) LOSC being awkwardly drafted, the phrase 'transitional period' can be read in two different ways. One line of argument is that the words 'transitional period' refer back to the phrase 'pending agreement' at the beginning of the sentence. Interpreted in this way, the phrase 'during this transitional period' is tied to reaching an agreement on delimitation in the sense of paragraph 1. But the problem with this interpretation is laid bare by the fact that no qualifications would be made to what is already encompassed under the phrase 'pending agreement'.[784]

[782] *Barbados* v. *Trinidad and Tobago* (n. 582) 204 [195].

[783] Ibid. 204–205 [194]–[200].

[784] BIICL Report (n. 141) 31.

Another unconvincing interpretation is as follows: the condition activating the second limb of the sentence of Articles 74(3) and 83(3) LOSC, which begins 'during this transitional period' and whereby the obligation not to hamper or jeopardise is imposed on the coastal States concerned, is the successful conclusion of a provisional arrangement.[785]

Alternatively, 'during this transitional period' has to be interpreted as making clear that States are not only under the obligation to seek provisional arrangements, but in addition have a parallel obligation not to hamper or jeopardise; these obligations will both apply prior to delimitation. According to this interpretation, the transitional period contemplated under Articles 74(3) and 83(3) LOSC refers to the same period as pending agreement, with the variation that there is a second obligation incumbent on States, which is imposed to the end of not hampering or jeopardising delimitation.

Provisional arrangements, and making attempts at their conclusion, are part of a transition from States making EEZ/continental shelf claims, which subsequently overlap, to coming to a future delimitation. In this broader interpretation, the 'transitional period' is extended to the period during which the provisional arrangements are in place; when they are being negotiated; and, in certain situations, when it becomes clear that there is a disputed continental shelf area, or if there are overlapping claims as far as the same EEZ area is concerned.[786]

5.3.2.3 The States Concerned

As is clear from its language, the addressees of Articles 74(3) and 83(3) LOSC are the 'States concerned'. These are those States whose EEZ and continental shelf claims overlap, but which have been unsuccessful in delimiting their boundary, either in full or in part. Third States (i.e. States lacking entitlements or related rights to an EEZ or continental shelf in the same area),[787] or their nationals, are omitted from this category. This is irrespective of whether a third State, or its nationals, may have an interest in the fact that the continental shelf/EEZ boundary is delimited. For instance, if a petroleum company based in a third State has secured exploratory rights in relation to the disputed area. The act of a private actor obtaining exploratory rights cannot be attributed to the third State of which this private actor is a national.[788]

785 D Dzidzornu and SB Kaye, 'Conflicts over Maritime Boundaries: The 1982 Convention Provisions and Peaceful Settlement' in EM Borgese et al. (eds.), *Ocean Yearbook*, Vol. 16 (Brill, 2002) 541, 598.

786 Anderson and Van Logchem (n. 18) 209.

787 Van Logchem (n. 244) 108, 114–115.

788 Chapter 2, Section 2.4 above.

A different scenario is where a direct link exists between the act of a national of a third State and coastal State A – for example, if an act undertaken in a disputed area, prompting coastal State B to respond, has been explicitly licensed by State A. This act of licensing is attributable to claimant A and, in turn, can be assessed in light of the requirements of Articles 74(3) and 83(3) LOSC to determine its lawfulness.[789] Hence, licensing fishermen to fish or authorising a petroleum company to start exploratory drilling in a disputed area, even though the actual activity is often undertaken by a national of or a private entity incorporated in a third State, must be attributed – by virtue of international law – to the 'State concerned' that has paved the way for the activity to begin.

5.3.2.4 In a Spirit of Understanding and Cooperation

Under the first sentence of Articles 74(3) and 83(3) LOSC, States are required to show a certain attitude; they must conduct themselves 'in a spirit of understanding and cooperation'. There is no elaboration on what is meant by the fact that a spirit of understanding and cooperation must be observed, which was not clarified during the drafting history either, raising the question of what purpose lies behind its inclusion; if any, as one author considered this phrase to be a 'clause de style'.[790] The use of language along the lines that States must operate with a spirit of cooperation and understanding was first introduced during UNCLOS III in a draft article by India, Iraq, and Morocco.[791] Importantly, this proposal only referred to 'cooperation', not understanding, and was tailored to be applied exclusively in the context of the obligation to seek provisional arrangements.[792]

Prior to the entry into force of the LOSC, the meaning of the phrase a 'spirit of cooperation and understanding' was construed by the ICJ, in *North Sea Continental Shelf*, in the following way: there must be a certain receptivity on the part of the States concerned for the other State's position, and for compromise or revising a State's own position, in order to arrive at an agreement.[793]

The phrase that coastal States must act in accordance with a 'spirit' that is characterised by 'cooperation and understanding' has its most meaningful impact in the context of negotiating on provisional arrangements within the

[789] Van Logchem (n. 244) 116–117.
[790] Caflisch (n. 587) 495.
[791] Section 5.3.1 above; Platzöder (n. 559) 433–434 (NG7/26, Article 83(3), India, Iraq and Morocco).
[792] Ibid.
[793] Chapter 3, Section 3.6 above.

meaning of Articles 74(3) and 83(3) LOSC. 'In a spirit of understanding and cooperation' can be interpreted as reflecting the intention of the drafters of the LOSC to have claimants negotiate in good faith, as applied to negotiations on provisional arrangements.[794] During all rounds of talks, good faith efforts are required to be made by the States concerned in seeking provisional arrangements.[795] Here, sometimes the attitude of claimants may need to be softened at the beginning of talks. Certainly, the phrase is not a condition that must be satisfied before the States concerned can start negotiating. Even when States are negotiating on delimiting a maritime boundary, instead of cooperative arrangements, a spirit of cooperation and understanding on the part of the States concerned does not necessarily accompany this.[796] Hence, the phrase 'in a spirit of understanding and cooperation' must be read as being exhortatory in nature, being a specification of what the broader and rather abstract obligation to act in good faith requires of these States while negotiating,[797] and its outcome is still awaited. The phrase aims to tone down confrontational arguments between States whose EEZ or continental shelf claims overlap; create an atmosphere enhancing the chances of successfully reaching a delimitation agreement; aid States in finding acceptable provisional arrangements; encourage States to agree on what can and cannot be done while talks are in motion between them; or, at the very minimum, to have States enunciate some ground rules for conducting talks.[798]

At first glance, States needing to observe a certain spirit of understanding and cooperation seems less apt in the context of the obligation not to hamper or jeopardise.[799] An interpretation that is more in line with the gist of this obligation is that States must operate in relation to a disputed EEZ and continental shelf area with a measure of 'understanding'. This can be understood as the States concerned needing to take into consideration each other's respective entitlements and related sovereign rights and jurisdiction over their disputed area; for example, before they act in relation thereto.

However, the way in which the first sentence of paragraph 3 of Articles 74 and 83 LOSC is construed suggests something different, namely 'that States in a spirit of understanding and cooperation ... are not to jeopardize or hamper the reaching of the final agreement'. It is not easily established what the

794 CM Flynn, 'A Broad Framework for the Exploration of South China Sea Hydrocarbons Deposits in the Context of the Trans-ASEAN Gas Pipeline' (2004) 5(1) *MJIL* 66, 80.

795 *Guyana* v. *Suriname* (n. 7) 130–131 [461].

796 Anderson and Van Logchem (n. 18) 206.

797 Wang (n. 324) 537.

798 DH Anderson, 'Negotiating Maritime Boundary Agreements' in R Lagoni and D Vignes (eds.), *Maritime Delimitation* (Martinus Nijhoff, 2006) 121, 128–129.

799 Anderson and Van Logchem (n. 18) 208.

implications are of claimants 'in a spirit of understanding and cooperation' not hampering or jeopardising the reaching of a delimitation agreement. In its maritime boundary dispute with Ghana, Côte d'Ivoire understood it as follows: if a claimant is aware of the existence of a maritime boundary dispute but nonetheless decides to commence with, and intensifies, activities relating to the exploration and exploitation of mineral resources in their disputed area, that State breaches the spirit it must observe pursuant to Article 83(3) LOSC.[800] The Tribunal in its award in *Guyana* v. *Suriname* connected the phrase of 'in a spirit of understanding and cooperation' to the good faith principle, when interpreting whether there was a breach of the obligation not to hamper or jeopardise.[801] A lack of appreciation for this spirit that a State is required to show pursuant to Article 83(3) LOSC was visible, according to the Tribunal, in Suriname's response to the drilling rig, which was licensed by Guyana and removed from their disputed area by Suriname under the threat to use force.[802]

5.3.2.5 Shall Make Every Effort

An aspect that stands out in the second part of the sentence in Articles 74(3) and 83(3) LOSC is the phrase 'shall make every effort'. One reading is that this phrase only applies to the positive obligation, because of the gist of the obligation not to hamper or jeopardise being more similar to a prohibition. Under this view, calling on claimant States to make 'every effort' to avoid acting in a way that results in complicating EEZ/continental shelf delimitation is deemed inappropriate in light of the nature of the obligation not to hamper or jeopardise.[803]

An argument perhaps supporting the interpretation that the words 'make every effort' are reserved for the positive obligation is that the sentence may be read as being split up into two separate parts: the word 'and' denotes the start of the second limb of the sentence, containing the obligation not to hamper or jeopardise, and hence would be separate from the preceding part of the sentence. So construed, the nature of the latter obligation is altered into an obligation of conduct, providing as follows: 'pending agreement as provided for in paragraph 1, the States concerned' are 'during this transitional period, not to jeopardize or hamper the reaching of the final agreement'. But the main problem with this interpretation is laid bare by the fact that, if 'shall make

800 *Ghana/Côte d'Ivoire (Judgment)* (n. 46) Côte d'Ivoire's Counter-Memorial 239 [9.50].
801 *Guyana* v. *Suriname* (n. 7) 130 [460].
802 Ibid. 135 [476].
803 Anderson and Van Logchem (n. 18) 206.

every effort' is not linked to the second limb, the sentence would be incomplete, or grammatically incorrect;[804] as shown earlier, some tinkering with the text would be required, that is adding the word 'are' is necessary to make the sentence work grammatically. Therefore, as a matter of English syntax, the phrase 'make every effort' must apply to both the negative (i.e. to refrain from jeopardising or hampering) and the positive elements (i.e. seeking to reach provisional arrangements) contained in paragraph 3 of Articles 74 and 83 LOSC. This is arguably even clearer in the French version, reading: 'les Etats concernés … font tout leur possible pour conclure des arrangements provisoires de caractère pratique et pour ne pas compromettre ou entraver pendant cette période de transition la conclusion de l'accord définitif'.[805] The implication of adding the wording 'make every effort' is that it formulates an obligation of conduct,[806] which the Seabed Disputes Chamber of ITLOS characterised as States having 'to deploy adequate means, to exercise best possible efforts, to do the utmost' to achieve the aim sought by a provision.[807]

5.3.3 *Interpreting the Obligation to Seek Provisional Arrangements*

It is difficult to disentangle the obligation to seek provisional arrangements from the obligation not to hamper or jeopardise, because the sentence containing these two obligations is rather convoluted. The content of the obligation that States must seek provisional arrangements can be couched in the following terms: 'Pending agreement as provided for in paragraph 1, the States concerned, in a spirit of understanding and co-operation, shall make every effort to enter into provisional arrangements of a practical nature. … Such arrangements shall be without prejudice to the final delimitation.'

Pursuant to the first obligation encountered under Articles 74(3) and 83(3) LOSC, the States concerned are required to exert certain efforts to try to conclude provisional arrangements in relation to a disputed EEZ or continental shelf area.[808] International courts and tribunals have actively promoted the conclusion of provisional arrangements as an appropriate means for

804 Van Logchem (n. 245) 138.
805 Anderson and Van Logchem (n. 18) 206.
806 C Redgwell, 'International Regulation of Energy Activities' in MM Roggenkamp et al. (eds.), *Energy Law in Europe: National, EU and International Regulation* (Oxford University Press, 2016) 13, 61.
807 *Responsibilities and Obligations of States with Respect to Activities in the Area* (Advisory Opinion) [2011] ITLOS Rep 10, 41 [110].
808 Kim (n. 287) 46; Valencia and Miyoshi (n. 120) 213.

coastal States to deal with a disputed area in the period preceding delimitation.[809] But questions arise over the precise extent to which States are required to make efforts towards reaching a provisional arrangement: is there an obligation of result, or will a sincere attempt to agree thereon suffice, irrespective of the eventual outcome?

No specification is given as to the setting in which States must make efforts to come to a provisional arrangement. This implies that such efforts can be made in direct face-to-face negotiations, or through diplomatic channels.[810] The term 'arrangements' suggests that these can take less formal forms, in that they do not have to be treaties.[811] When an agreed provisional arrangement is in the form of a treaty, it is meant to lay down legal obligations; however, less formal agreements, such as concluding a memorandum of understanding, 'may not be legally binding', although they can be.[812] Most significant in this regard is not the label affixed to the arrangement but the intention of the States underpinning its conclusion.[813] The same test can be applied to the extent to which States have meant to take on legally binding commitments pursuant to the conclusion of a provisional arrangement, in light of Article 2(1)(a) 1969 Vienna Convention on the Law of Treaties (VCLT),[814] what do the circumstances under which the provisional arrangement was concluded, and the wording contained in the arrangement, reveal as to what has been the intention of the drafters? Certain concluded provisional arrangements leave no doubt in this regard, invoking Articles 74(3) or 83(3) LOSC as forming the basis upon which they were agreed, whereas other examples refrain from making such an explicit reference.[815]

There is no further circumscription in Articles 74(3) and 83(3) LOSC relating to the design and contents of provisional arrangements; this is beyond that they must be of a 'practical nature'.[816] The ordinary meaning of the word 'practical' is that it must relate to an actual use, rather than being a mere

809 *Guyana* v. *Suriname* (n. 7) 131 [462]; *Conciliation Commission on the Continental Shelf area between Iceland and Jan Mayen: Report and Recommendations to the Governments of Iceland and Norway* [1981] XXVII ILM 1, 28, 32–33.

810 Anderson and Van Logchem (n. 18) 206.

811 BIICL Report (n. 141) 18.

812 Ibid.

813 But see You (n. 221) 492.

814 Vienna Convention on the Law of Treaties (23 May 1969), 155 UNTS 331.

815 Exchange of Notes dated 18 October 2001 and 31 October 2001 between the Government of Ireland and the Government of the United Kingdom of Great Britain and Northern Ireland Constituting an Agreement pursuant to Article 83 Paragraph 3 of the United Nations Convention on the Law of the Sea 1982 on the Provisional Delimitation of an Area of the Continental Shelf, 2309 UNTS 21.

816 Nandan and Rosenne (n. 551) 394.

theory, and that it is useful.[817] Hence, when a provisional arrangement has a tangible practical impact and a relevance in managing the disputed EEZ or continental shelf area, the requirement of a practical nature would be satisfied.[818] Due to this low threshold, provisional arrangements can take many forms, ranging from establishing active cooperation to complete abstention by introducing a moratorium.[819] This corresponds with the idea that, when an arrangement seeking to forestall all economic development would be more suitable for achieving delimitation down the road, rather than to allow for the converse (i.e. actual development), States are able to agree thereon as well. State practice reflects this. Here a wide variety of such arrangements exists, being geared towards different purposes (i.e. abstention, cooperation, or a combination of both), covering different activities, and bringing disputed maritime areas to varying extents within their range.[820]

The obligation that motivates States to seek provisional arrangements can be placed within the broader objective, as expressed in the preamble to the LOSC, of realising 'the equitable and efficient utilization' of offshore natural resources. Despite this link, and the fact that provisional arrangements do not necessarily have to relate to natural resources, the extent to which claimants are obligated to cooperate with each other has been circumscribed as follows: coastal States must engage in good faith negotiations on 'provisional arrangements of a practical nature'.[821] Logic dictates that conducting good faith negotiations does not connote an obligation to attain a certain result or end.[822]

Deducing a more extensive obligation from the text of Articles 74(3) and 83(3) LOSC,[823] by placing States under an obligation to agree on cooperative arrangements, forces an unnatural reading on this paragraph, however. Its text includes the phrase 'make every effort', whereby a lower standard is set. Emphasis is thus placed on making some efforts, rather than reaching a successful result being required pursuant to paragraph 3. Alternative language could have been easily employed during the drafting of the LOSC if the

817 Oxford English Dictionary and Merriam-Webster Dictionary, online versions consulted.

818 Miyoshi (n. 479) 15; Anderson and Van Logchem (n. 18) 206.

819 PD Cameron, 'The Rules of Engagement: Developing Cross-Border Petroleum Deposits in the North Sea and the Caribbean' (2005) 55(3) *ICLQ* 559, 566; Mensah (n. 69) 148; Anderson and Van Logchem (n. 18) 206.

820 Ibid. 212.

821 Lagoni (n. 243) 354; Valencia and Miyoshi (n. 120) 213.

822 *Cameroon* v. *Nigeria* (n. 454) 424 [244].

823 Dzidzornu and Kaye (n. 785) 598; W Zhao, 'Resolving Maritime Delimitation Disputes by Agreement: Practices Bordering the South China Sea and Their Implications for China' (2013) 17 *COLR* 156, 171.

intention of its drafters would indeed have been to introduce a more extensive obligation. However, suggestions by certain States at UNCLOS III to abandon the voluntary nature of establishing provisional arrangements were met with stern criticism from most of the delegations.[824]

Another question is whether States must make continuous attempts towards the successful creation of provisional arrangements in case a previous attempt thereto has failed. In *Southern Bluefin Tuna*, the ITLOS considered the obligation to negotiate to be fulfilled after parties to the dispute had 'prolonged, intense and serious' talks, during which they expressly relied in their argumentation on norms of the LOSC.[825] The critical aspect that drove this consideration were the subjective views of the States concerned: both of them agreed that the usefulness of negotiations had run its course.[826] Following this approach, the ITLOS in the case between Malaysia and Singapore echoed that there is no obligation to continuously make efforts at coming to agreement, upon it becoming clear that this is not a realistic prospect.[827] Based on this case law, there is thus no continuous obligation on neighbouring States to seek provisional arrangements whatever the circumstances. The obligation can be considered to cease to exist once the States concerned deem its use depleted, or when it has become apparent to them that no successful result will emerge.

Looking at the first part of the sentence in Articles 74(3) and 83(3) LOSC, an aspect that stands out is the use of the combination of the words 'provisional' and 'arrangement'. This implies that concluded arrangements are not meant to be in existence indefinitely; to the contrary, the word 'provisional' draws attention to their temporal nature. On an ordinary reading, the word 'provisional' must be understood as 'arranged for the present, possibly to be changed later',[828] or that it is intended to serve for the time being.[829] Those arrangements that have been concluded pursuant to Articles 74(3) and 83(3) LOSC are in principle meant to apply 'pending agreement' on delimitation. Hence, at the core of provisional arrangements lies the idea that these are temporary arrangements, which will cease to exist at some point in time.

824 Platzöder (n. 559) 428–430 (NG7/23, Articles 74(3)/83(3), Chairman NG7).

825 *Southern Bluefin Tuna Case between Australia and Japan and between New Zealand and Japan* (Award on Jurisdiction and Admissibility) [2000] XXIII RIAA 4 42–43 [55].

826 A Peters, 'International Dispute Settlement: A Network of Cooperational Duties' (2003) 14 *EJIL* 1, 13.

827 *Land Reclamation in and around the Straits of Johor (Malaysia* v. *Singapore)* (Provisional Measures) [2003] ITLOS Rep 10 20 [48].

828 Oxford English Dictionary, online version consulted.

829 Merriam-Webster Dictionary, online version consulted.

Generally, provisional arrangements will retain their relevance in the absence of a final delimitation agreement,[830] unless there is a contrary intention. However, this does not imply that a provisional arrangement must apply for the full duration of the period when the maritime boundary dispute remains unresolved. Rather, States have autonomy in deciding on the duration of a provisional arrangement. They may also choose to conclude different arrangements that apply at different stages of the delimitation process, during which some or no efforts are made to enter into a delimitation agreement, and have these temporary arrangements relate to different types of activities.

The duration of a provisional arrangement can be set in a variety of ways, ranging from connecting its relevance to how long the maritime boundary dispute endures to carrying the applicability of the cooperative regime over to a delimitation agreement, thereby having the interim regime and the final maritime boundary coexist.[831] Between these options lies explicitly defining the period during which the provisional arrangement is meant to be active in terms of time. If the States concerned have not themselves circumscribed the period during which a provisional arrangement is envisaged to be active, the way in which Articles 74(3) and 83(3) LOSC are arranged, together with paragraph 3 beginning with the phrase 'pending agreement', implies that the arrangement will end after a delimitation agreement has become binding.[832]

Another issue is whether agreed provisional arrangements affect the underlying claims of States. Some States fear that, if they were to enter into such arrangements, it would weaken their underlying claims over a maritime area. Provisional arrangements falling within the meaning of Articles 74(3) and 83 (3) LOSC have in common that they do not affect a State's underlying claims over a maritime area, nor do they predetermine the final settlement of a maritime boundary dispute in any way. They also create no acquired rights for States when delimitation negotiations are opened – in these negotiations, States can make claims that are different from what has been previously agreed upon, pursuant to a provisional arrangement.

If provisional arrangements are given a prejudicial effect, the incentive for States to conclude such arrangements would be removed.[833] Most

[830] Lagoni (n. 243) 356; Z Gao, 'Legal Aspects of Joint Development in International Law' in M Kusuma-Atmadja et al. (eds.), *Sustainable Development and Preservation of the Oceans: The Challenges of UNCLOS and Agenda 21* (LOSI, 1997) 629, 639.

[831] Miyoshi (n. 479) 15; Nandan and Rosenne (n. 551) 815.

[832] ILA, *Report of the Sixty-Third Conference, Warsaw, 1988* (1988) 545; Lagoni (n. 243) 358.

[833] BH Oxman, 'International Maritime Boundaries: Political, Strategic and Historical Considerations' (1994–1995) 26(2) *UMIALR* 243, 290.

provisional arrangements will contain an explicit provision, echoing a phrase to the effect that they are without prejudice to the final delimitation.[834] The final sentence of Articles 74(3) and 83(3) LOSC also reassures States that these arrangements are without prejudice to a delimitation of an EEZ or continental shelf area.[835] In the drafting of the LOSC, the view of the States involved was that the non-prejudicial character of provisional arrangements was of great importance in designing a provision to this end.[836] International courts and tribunals have interpreted 'no-prejudice clauses' when they have been inserted in provisional arrangements as to mean that a modus vivendi had developed between the States concerned. The *Fisheries Jurisdiction (United Kingdom* v. *Iceland)* case[837] illustrates that entering into a cooperative arrangement will have no detrimental effects on a State's bargaining position, or its claimed rights.[838] When discussing the question whether the conclusion of a provisional arrangement deprived the case of its objective,[839] the ICJ recognised the importance of these arrangements having a non-prejudicial character. Had it concluded differently, this would have discouraged coastal States from concluding these arrangements, which the ICJ found highly undesirable considering their inherent qualities of 'reducing friction and avoiding risk to peace and security'.[840]

5.3.4 *Interpreting the Obligation Not to Hamper or Jeopardise*

The second obligation of Articles 74(3) and 83(3) LOSC stipulates that States with disputed EEZ or continental shelf areas must make every effort to abstain from taking any unilateral act having the consequential effect of hampering or jeopardising a final delimitation. Acts undertaken by claimant States in such areas can be either unintended or predesigned.[841] Unintended acts are not undertaken to assert a coastal State's position or claimed rights. Rather, they are the result of, for instance, a State being oblivious to or showing a lack of

834 Agreement on Provisional Arrangements for the Delimitation of the Maritime Boundaries between the Republic of Tunisia and the People's Democratic Republic of Algeria, 2002, 2238 UNTS 197.

835 Anderson (n. 6) 495; Dang (n. 199) 78. But see Y Huang and PT Vuong, 'Fisheries Cooperation and Management Mechanisms in the South China Sea: Context, Limitations and Prospects for the Future' (2016) 4(1) *CJCL* 128, 133–134, 138.

836 Oxman (n. 833) 290.

837 *Fisheries Jurisdiction* (n. 459).

838 Ibid. 18 [37].

839 Ibid. [41].

840 Ibid.

841 Anderson and Van Logchem (n. 18) 215–216.

appreciation for the disputed area. An example is a State official failing to fully acknowledge the extent of the claim of the other State in issuing concessions, or when activating a concession extending into the disputed area. After the *Valentin Shashin*[842] drilled an exploratory well in a disputed part of the continental shelf of the Barents Sea in May 1983, which prompted Norway to protest, Russia claimed that this drilling was accidental.[843] Local fishermen may also wander off course and unknowingly fish in disputed EEZ areas, which can have a potential spill-over effect on bilateral relations, especially when arrests follow these intrusions.[844] More often, however, States undertaking acts within disputed areas is by design, rather than inadvertent. Importantly, the text of Articles 74(3) and 83(3) LOSC does not distinguish between unintended and predesigned acts; the emphasis is on the act and the effects that it exerts on reaching a delimitation agreement. In this light, a State may be accused of violating the obligation not to hamper or jeopardise if it acts unilaterally, by authorising or undertaking conduct being subject to coastal State jurisdiction, with regard to a disputed EEZ or continental shelf area. This may entail international responsibility: that is, when the breach of the obligation is attributable to that State.[845]

The obligation of not hampering or jeopardising lays down a de facto limitation on when rights may be exercised. But there is no de jure restriction imposed on the legal rights claimant States have with regard to a disputed EEZ or continental shelf area, as paragraph 3 of Articles 74 and 83 LOSC does not specify what rights States must refrain from exercising in relation to that area before it is delimited.[846] Rather, limitations are imposed on when, and to what extent, coastal States can put their rights into actual use. More broadly, a dual function can be ascribed to the obligation not to hamper or jeopardise, in that it seeks to avoid States acting in relation to a disputed EEZ or continental shelf area in two ways: first, it places limitations on the scope for coastal States to actively undertake acts falling under coastal State jurisdiction unilaterally; and, second, the obligation curtails the ways in which States can respond to such activities.[847]

842 SJ Rolston and TL McDorman, 'Maritime Boundary Making in the Arctic Region' in DM Johnston and PM Saunders (eds.), *Ocean Boundary Making: Regional Issues and Developments* (Croom Helm, 1983) 16, 44.
843 Churchill and Ulfstein (n. 407) 77.
844 Chapter 2, Section 2.3.3 above.
845 Chapter 3, Section 3.11 above.
846 ILA (n. 832) 547.
847 Van Logchem (n. 21) 195.

The underlying reason for restricting an exercise of rights by coastal States is that otherwise a negative effect would be exerted on the success of completing a delimitation agreement. Viewed in this light, the obligation to refrain from hampering or jeopardising can be read as a specification of what the principles of good faith and not to abuse rights actually requires (Article 300 LOSC), that is, an exercise of rights by a State assumed under the Convention may not lead to its abuse.[848] Connected to this is the consideration that a State, through the use of its rights, has to 'not unnecessarily or arbitrarily harm the rights of other States or the interests of the international community as a whole'.[849]

A good faith component underlies the obligation not to hamper or jeopardise, with the States concerned having to 'make every effort' to that end. As a result, the core requirement under the obligation is that States are exhorted to abjure from taking acts that are under coastal State jurisdiction unilaterally that have the effect of hampering or jeopardising. Hence, a different kind of obligation than if claimants are explicitly prohibited from engaging in particular unilateral conduct is imposed: by exhorting a State to abstain from certain conduct by having them making their best effort in this respect, an obligation of conduct, not one of result, is imposed.[850] Determining a breach of this obligation of conduct would then be entwined with whether a claimant, both prior to undertaking a certain activity and while acting, has made good-faith efforts to prevent hampering or jeopardising a final agreement.

Following this interpretation, the main tenet of the negative obligation, which at first glance resembles a prohibition,[851] would in fact be that genuine efforts must be made, through exercising restraint, so as not to adversely impact a delimitation, in that this prospect is pushed further out of reach. This means that the obligation could be breached if the result expected by one State (i.e. completing a delimitation exercise) has not been achieved, or is regarded to have been complicated by one State, due to unilateral acts having been authorised by another claimant in relation to their disputed EEZ or continental shelf area.

In interpreting the meaning of the negative obligation in Articles 74(3) and 83(3) LOSC, the terms 'hamper' and 'jeopardise' are essential. One key issue is whether two separate standards are involved, or whether they are synonymous. Two further questions arise: first, if the words 'hamper' or 'jeopardise' differ, to what extent is this the case; and, second, what types of activities are caught

848 Chapter 3, Section 3.6 above.
849 Nordquist et al. (n. 465) 150–151.
850 Tran (n. 287) 91.
851 Anderson and Van Logchem (n. 18) 206.

under these two terms? In *Guyana* v. *Suriname*, the Tribunal did not distinguish between hampering or jeopardising, treating them as interchangeable terms.[852] Contrary to this, and as a matter of textual interpretation, 'hamper' and 'jeopardise' cannot have identical meanings, however.[853] Rather, the insertion of the terms hampering and jeopardising in the same sentence injects a distinction into Articles 74(3) and 83(3) LOSC: unilateral acts having one of these effects must be abstained from prior to delimitation. This view is confirmed by the text of the paragraph using the disjunction 'or' to separate the words 'hampering' and 'jeopardising'. The ordinary meaning of the word 'or' is that it refers to alternatives. Logic thus dictates that these terms lay down different standards of conduct – but the question that follows is: how do they differ?

Within the framework of the LOSC, the term 'hampers', or a variation thereof, is encountered seven times – surfacing primarily in relation to the passage regimes of innocent and transit passage through, respectively, territorial seas and straits.[854] 'Hamper' is defined in the Oxford English Dictionary as 'hinder or impede the movement or progress of'.[855] In the Merriam-Webster Dictionary, the meaning attributed to the same word is 'interfering with'.[856] From these two definitions, and applying the meaning of the word 'hampering' to disputed maritime areas, it can be inferred that it means to prevent unilateral actions from occurring that hinder, impede, or interfere with States moving closer to delimitation.

'Jeopardise' is a descriptor being used in only one other occasion in the LOSC: that is, in paragraph 1(b) of Resolution III in the Final Act of the Third UN Conference on the Law of the Sea, which includes some declaratory language about the rights and interests of States in the context of non-self-governing territories.[857] The definition of the word given by the Merriam-Webster Dictionary is putting something at risk, being harmed, or lost.[858] Similarly, the Oxford English Dictionary defines jeopardise as placing something at risk of being harmed or lost.[859] When applied to areas of disputed EEZ/continental shelf, the subject of reference is delimitation, in that successfully completing this exercise is not made more difficult because

852 Chapter 6, Section 6.3 below.
853 Anderson and Van Logchem (n. 18) 209.
854 Articles 24, 42(2), 44, and 211(4) LOSC.
855 Online version consulted.
856 Online version consulted.
857 Chapter 7, Section 7.1 below.
858 Online version consulted.
859 Online version consulted.

of this prospect being put at risk, harmed, or lost altogether, through a State acting unilaterally by authorising or undertaking acts that are under coastal State jurisdiction.

Given that the terms 'hamper' and 'jeopardise' are substantively different, the fact that the terms are included in the same sentence, and without an attempt to distinguish between them, suggests that, if an act exceeds one of these thresholds, a breach of Articles 74(3) and 83(3) LOSC can be assumed. The existing connection between the two notions is that 'hampering' seems to connote a lower standard; reasoning *a contrario*, conduct that jeopardises the delimitation is automatically captured under the lower threshold of hampering. Viewed in this light, the high threshold set by the Tribunal in *Guyana* v. *Suriname*, in that the other State's rights must be threatened with irreparability, is difficult to reconcile with the actual test of 'hampering' under Articles 74(3) and 83(3) LOSC.[860] However, what types of acts are caught under the respective terms of hampering or jeopardising is difficult to pin down.

5.3.5 *The Relationship between the Two Obligations*

The two obligations in Articles 74(3) and 83(3) LOSC, despite having different purposes, are closely related, however. At the same time, must their relationship be understood as that they can be breached independently of each other? Or is one of the obligations only activated if the terms of the other are fulfilled?[861]

A hierarchical relationship between the obligations contained in Articles 74(3) and 83(3) LOSC has been derived from how its text is organised: the negative obligation not to hamper or jeopardise follows the positive obligation exhorting States to seek provisional arrangements.[862] On one interpretation of the wording 'during this transitional period', the obligation not to hamper or jeopardise, as contained in the second limb of the sentence, is only activated when a provisional arrangement has been concluded. By introducing a hierarchical ordering of the two obligations, the relevance of the obligation of not hampering or jeopardising becomes very similar to the principle contained in Article 18 VCLT:[863] States must abstain from conduct that defeats the object and purpose of a treaty that has yet to come into force but to which a State is a signatory, or has expressed its consent to be bound by the

860 Chapter 6, Section 6.8 below.

861 X Zhang, 'Why the 2008 Sino-Japanese Consensus on East China Sea Has Stalled: Good Faith hand Reciprocity Considerations in Interim Measures Pending a Maritime Boundary Delimitation' (2011) 41(1–2) *ODIL* 53, 58.

862 Vukas (n. 550) 103–104; Dzidzornu and Kaye (n. 785) 598.

863 Ibid.

terms agreed therein.[864] Establishing a hierarchical order to the two obligations contained in Articles 74(3) and 83(3) LOSC cannot be convincing if their language is more closely analysed, however.

Two arguments can be invoked against this interpretation. First, the two obligations in paragraph 3 are separated by the use of the word 'and', signifying that two obligations having a standing of their own were meant to be introduced.[865] And, second, the phrase 'during this transitional period' encompasses the period prior to EEZ/continental shelf delimitation in its entirety.[866] Construing the relationship between the two obligations under paragraph 3 as separate, in that they can be breached independently and conjointly through the other claimant acting unilaterally, by authorising or undertaking acts that are under coastal State jurisdiction, finds support in the case law. In its reasoning in *Suriname* v. *Guyana*, the Tribunal confirmed the existence of two types of obligations in Articles 74(3) and 83(3) LOSC, which apply simultaneously in the period before delimitation.[867] Two reasons were given by the Tribunal: first, the two obligations seek to fulfil different objectives of the LOSC; and, second, they are imposed with different aims. In terms of their objectives, whereas the obligation to seek provisional arrangements is tied to natural resources being utilised equally and effectively, the obligation not to hamper or jeopardise is a specification of the general principle of international law to settle disputes peacefully. Therefore, a coastal State could be accused of failing to make every effort not to hamper or jeopardise delimitation, conceivably combined with it failing to live up to the measure of making efforts in good faith that a State is required to exert under the obligation to seek provisional arrangements.

While two distinct rationales underlie the two obligations contained in Articles 74(3) and 83(3) LOSC,[868] they are interconnected in ways,[869] which raises the issue of the measures of interaction between them. A first measure of interaction is that the obligation not to hamper or jeopardise takes on a particular relevance when provisional arrangements pursuant to the positive obligation have not been agreed upon, or where they are not comprehensive in their scope, as is usually the case.[870]

One effect of the obligation calling on States to make provisional arrangements is that a failure to negotiate thereon in good faith constitutes a breach of

864 Ibid. 600.
865 Van Logchem (n. 21) 179.
866 Zhang (n. 861) 58; Anderson and Van Logchem (n. 18) 206.
867 *Guyana* v. *Suriname* (n. 7) 130 [459].
868 Fietta (n. 153) 127.
869 *Ghana/Côte d'Ivoire* (Judgment) (n. 46) 166–167, 172 [626] [629].
870 Ibid. 180 [5] (Separate Opinion of Judge Paik).

the obligation itself. But beyond that, and because there is no hierarchical order to the two obligations contained in Articles 74(3) and 83(3) LOSC, a failure to negotiate in good faith, or a refusal to open negotiations on provisional arrangements for example, can have the effect of making future maritime delimitation more difficult; this means that such a failure or refusal can be appraised equally in light of whether it hampers or jeopardises delimitation.

There is also a way in which the successful conclusion of a provisional arrangement can breach the obligation not to hamper or jeopardise: that is, when the provisional arrangement, applying only *inter partes*, will infringe upon the entitlements and related rights of a third claimant over the area, and when that area is brought under the reach of such an arrangement.[871] Then, the obligation not to hamper or jeopardise is breached by both coastal States having concluded a provisional arrangement, in relation with the other third claimant, whose rights are infringed upon because of its conclusion. Furthermore, if one of the States concerned fails to abide by the terms of an agreed provisional arrangement, this may result in complications being added to reaching a delimitation agreement. This, in turn, is difficult to reconcile with the obligation not to hamper or jeopardise that particular prospect.

Beyond the fact that the obligation to seek provisional arrangements calls on States to make some efforts in that respect in good faith, it has a further implication: in the absence of provisional arrangements, the States concerned must exercise some restraint so as not to impede the chances of coming to a cooperative arrangement in a future round of negotiations, which are opened for that aim to eventually succeed – this is in addition to delimitation. This is a view born out of the decision of the Tribunal in *Guyana* v. *Suriname*: the inclusion of the obligation to seek provisional arrangements implies that, when a claimant wants to undertake an activity under a coastal State's jurisdiction unilaterally in a disputed area, it has a duty to consult the other claimant.[872]

Closely connected to this issue is whether an unlawful act under the obligation not to hamper or jeopardise will become a lawful one, upon complying with certain cooperation-related requirements existing under the obligation to seek provisional arrangements. In this vein, a refusal to negotiate in good faith on provisional arrangements, after invitations thereto have been extended, has, according to Lagoni, the consequence that the act of the unilateral exploitation of mineral resources from a disputed continental

871 BIICL Report (n. 141) 106.
872 Beckman (n. 643) 255.

shelf area would lose its otherwise unlawful character.[873] On this interpretation, any breaches arising under the obligation not to hamper or jeopardise could be remedied by complying with certain cooperation-related demands flowing from the obligation to seek provisional arrangements. Such emphasis is misplaced in view of there being a parallel obligation included in Articles 74(3) and 83(3) LOSC, which can be breached separately and is imposed to forestall conduct from being undertaken that detrimentally effects delimitation – to assess whether there has been such a breach requires a different type of analysis than focusing merely on cooperative requirements having been met. For example, consequential to the test set out under the obligation not to hamper or jeopardise, unilateral drilling can be considered unlawful. A negative effect that independent of whether certain cooperative conditions have been fulfilled will result from unilateral drilling is that the chances of reaching delimitation are likely to be substantially lessened because of the conflict that is usually created in the wake of this unilateral act, and that the other State's sovereign rights will be irreparably prejudiced.

5.3.6 *Activation and the Ending of the Two Obligations*

Articles 74(3) and 83(3) LOSC pose two questions: first, when do the two obligations contained therein begin, either conjointly or separately; and, second, when do these obligations cease to have relevance? A principal requirement in determining when their two obligations commence is that there must be an overlap of claims falling within the terms of Articles 74(1) and 83(1) LOSC.[874] This requirement must be combined with a reading of paragraph 2 of the same provisions, specifying that delimitation must be effected 'within a reasonable time'.[875]

In terms of their activation, both obligations of Articles 74(3) and 83(3) LOSC start when there are overlapping claims by States; and they end with a delimitation agreement becoming binding on the States concerned. The period lying between the start and end of the two obligations is captured under the terms 'pending agreement' and the 'transitional period'.[876] The use of the words 'transitional period' also implies that the obligations of Articles 74(3) and 83(3) LOSC will be lifted from claimant States once there is a change in the situation: that is, if the dispute over the EEZ/continental shelf boundary is conclusively settled.

873 R Lagoni, 'Oil and Gas Deposits across National Frontiers' (1979) 73(2) *AJIL* 215, 238.
874 ILA (n. 832) 545; Anderson and Van Logchem (n. 18) 208.
875 Ibid. 209–210; Tanaka (n. 766) 316.
876 Gao (n. 830) 639.

Different points of activation exist for Articles 74(3) and 83(3) LOSC in relation to a disputed EEZ or continental shelf area. The recognition of a need for a continental shelf boundary is an aspect that is less important in pinpointing the moment when the obligations of Article 83(3) LOSC arise for coastal States. Due to the inherency of the rights that the coastal State has in respect of the continental shelf, having ab initio and ipso facto entitlements thereto, the moment of activating Article 83(3) LOSC must be placed at when it is apparent that there are overlapping entitlements of coastal States to the same continental shelf area. It follows that if the breadth between two States' coasts is less than 400 nm, or when they are adjacent, Article 83(3) LOSC will come to apply automatically.[877]

An entitlement to the EEZ does not automatically attach to the coastal State, however, meaning that an explicit claim seeking to establish an EEZ, which in turn overlaps with the other State's EEZ claim, is necessary to activate Article 74(3) LOSC.[878] This logically follows from an explicit claim to an EEZ by States being a *conditio sine qua non* for its existence. If one or more States refrain from claiming an EEZ, there is no actual overlap of their claims; this is even if a disputed EEZ area will inevitably arise if the States in question make such a claim.

For the obligation to seek provisional arrangements to become relevant, there needs to be a sense of acknowledgement on the part of the States concerned that they need to work towards a final delimitation in the sense of Articles 74(1) and 83(1) LOSC. After States exchange diplomatic communications or adopt legislation, making it clear that there is an overlap of their claims to the same EEZ or continental shelf area, and a disputed area is created, a need for its delimitation arises.[879] In its wake, the positive component in Articles 74(3) and 83(3) LOSC to seek provisional arrangements is activated.

When viewed from a practical angle, without recognition of the need for delimitation, there seems little reason to impose an obligation of an exhortatory type on coastal States. Two further situations can be recognised where it seems less apt to require States to seek provisional arrangements of a practical nature: first, if there are no (economic) activities currently taking place within a disputed area and they are not likely to take place in the near future; and, second, there would be little merit in seeking provisional arrangements for States if they are to delimit their boundary shortly after an overlap of their

877 AE Bastida et al., 'Cross-Border Unitisation and Joint Development Agreements: An International Law Perspective' (2006–2007) 29(2) *HJIL* 355, 367–378.

878 Anderson and Van Logchem (n. 18) 209.

879 Ibid.

claims has arisen. To account for this, the significance of the obligation has been delayed to the moment when it has become clear that no expedient solution is expected on maritime delimitation in the sense of Articles 74(1) and 83(1) LOSC.[880] But on an ordinary reading of the language of Articles 74(3) and 83(3) LOSC, delimitation talks must not have been initiated between the States concerned in order for the obligations under paragraph 3 to be activated. Critical in this regard is the reference to the period of 'pending agreement',[881] which encompasses a broader period, in that no delimitation agreement has become binding on the States concerned in the sense of Articles 74(1) and 83(1) LOSC.[882]

Another exception as to when the obligation to seek provisional arrangements will become practically relevant is if diplomatic relations between States have been broken off. Then, each government will usually appoint a Protecting Power in which the title over a territory is placed temporarily.[883] It goes beyond what can be reasonably expected of a Protecting Power to undertake what are often difficult and lengthy negotiations for provisional arrangements of a practical nature.

Three situations can be distinguished when the obligation not to hamper or jeopardise could become operational in a disputed EEZ or continental shelf area.[884] First, the start of this obligation can be linked to the fact that delimitation negotiations have been started between States. Second, the activation of the obligation not to hamper or jeopardise can be connected to negotiations on provisional arrangements having been initiated by the States concerned, whereby the 'transitional period' begins.[885] Both of these alternatives have the same effect: the reduction that this obligation imposes on the possibility of claimant States to exercise 'jurisdiction' over a disputed area is limited to when they are actually involved in negotiations.[886] As a result, if talks have been aborted, or interceded by lengthy intervals, during these intermissions, the obligation not to hamper or jeopardise would not be applicable.[887] However, requiring negotiations to have been set in motion between coastal States, in order for this obligation to become relevant, is problematic: that is, ample opportunity is offered to these States to take unilateral actions

880 BIICL Report (n. 141) 17.
881 Section 5.3.2.1 above.
882 Lagoni (n. 243) 357.
883 Anderson and Van Logchem (n. 18) 201–211.
884 Lagoni (n. 243) 364.
885 Kittichaisaree (n. 43) 103.
886 Anderson and Van Logchem (n. 18) 201–211.
887 Klein (n. 9) 426; Lagoni (n. 243) 346–347.

prejudging the outcome of the negotiations before they have even started.[888] A more convincing starting point for when the negative obligation under Articles 74(3) and 83(3) LOSC arises, which can be seen as the third alternative, is when it is apparent that there is an overlap of EEZ/continental shelf claims over the same area, subsequently giving rise to the need for delimitation.[889]

However, it varies whether a disputed EEZ or continental shelf area is involved as to when it can be considered apparent that there are overlapping claims which need to be delimited. The aspect of the States concerned recognising a need for a continental shelf boundary has little importance in determining the moment when the obligation not to hamper or jeopardise will arise. The relationship between land territory and the continental shelf can be construed as when a State has undisputed title over a territory, it is given an inherent right to a continental shelf area and the resources contained therein.[890] The lack of an inherent existence of rights by coastal States over the EEZ delays the activation of the obligation not to hamper or jeopardise to when an explicit EEZ claim is made by a coastal State, which subsequently overlaps with the EEZ claim of another coastal State, creating a disputed area.

Upon the severance or absence of diplomatic relations – or more rarely in the case of one State not recognising one of the other States involved – the obligation not to hamper or jeopardise will (continue to) apply, however. Another issue is the effect of a provisional arrangement on the negative obligation of Articles 74(3) and 83(3) LOSC. When States have entered into a provisional arrangement, they are not absolved from the obligation not to hamper or jeopardise.[891] However, there is the possibility of the latter obligation becoming redundant, at least in practical terms: that is, when a provisional arrangement encompasses within its scope all eventualities related to a disputed EEZ or continental shelf area.[892] Most such arrangements that are in place are not all-inclusive, however. In this light, the obligation may become partially redundant: this is, if a subject matter (e.g. mineral resources, fisheries or law enforcement) has been comprehensively brought within the reach of a provisional arrangement. However, this leaves untouched the fact that activities that are not brought under a provisional arrangement will continue to be governed by the obligation not to hamper or jeopardise.[893]

888 Ibid. 364.
889 Ibid.; Van Logchem (n. 21) 178.
890 *Libya/Malta* (n. 594) 33–34 [34]; *North Sea Continental Shelf* (n. 8) 22 [19].
891 Anderson and Van Logchem (n. 18) 208–210.
892 BIICL Report (n. 141) 32–33.
893 Ibid. 18.

Moreover, in legal terms, the obligation not to jeopardise or hamper would continue to apply irrespective of the degree of comprehensiveness of a provisional arrangement; this is because the language of paragraph 3 of Articles 74 and 83 LOSC refers to the obligations that apply 'pending agreement'. Also, if a State breaches the terms of an agreed provisional arrangement, a breach of the obligation not to hamper or jeopardise may be assumed; that is, if it would make delimitation more difficult.

Although it will thus vary with the circumstances involved whether both obligations of Articles 74(3) and 83(3) LOSC will apply within a given situation, there are cases where both will be active. This is, for example, when delimitation negotiations between States have been proposed, commenced, or have been held but thereafter adjourned or aborted without agreement.

Upon submitting the delimitation dispute to third-party procedures (e.g. arbitration) resulting in a binding decision or a non-binding decision (e.g. mediation), the obligations of Articles 74(3) and 83(3) LOSC are not rendered redundant. This is because 'agreement', as referred to at the beginning of the first sentence of paragraph 3, should not be solely understood in a way that States having a disputed EEZ or continental shelf area have agreed on a delimitation agreement through their own efforts.[894] Support for this position can be found in Articles 74(1) and 83(1) LOSC, to which paragraph 3 explicitly refers, stipulating that delimitation must be effected by agreement. States can reach an agreement on submitting their maritime boundary dispute to international adjudication. Nevertheless, the use of the word 'agreement' in paragraph 3 of Articles 74 and 83 LOSC can be read as extending beyond States having agreed to submit their delimitation dispute to third-party dispute settlement. This is because the period pending agreement needs to be connected to when a delimitation is effected by the international court or tribunal, and thus that the maritime boundary dispute has been settled.[895]

As a corollary, when States decide to have the boundary delimited by an international court or tribunal, the obligations of Articles 74(3) and 83(3) LOSC continue to apply up to when a final decision has been handed down. However, in practical terms, the relevance of these obligations will perceivably be reduced due to two aspects: first, through the possible indication of measures of interim protection by the international court or tribunal; and, second, States being placed under additional obligations derived from international law once the dispute has been submitted to

894 Ibid. 32.
895 Ibid.

international adjudication, including an obligation not to prejudge or anticipate the outcome of the proceedings.[896]

Articles 74(3) and 83(3) LOSC cease to apply once a final EEZ or continental shelf boundary agreement has become binding on the States concerned. Provisional arrangements that in terms of their applicability are tied directly to the moment when a binding agreement is reached on a boundary will, unless the States concerned have agreed otherwise, expire then as well.[897]

5.3.7 *Scope of Application*

Depending on how widely the terms of Articles 74(3) and 83(3) LOSC are interpreted, the geographic and material reach of this paragraph changes accordingly. The primary difficulty in setting its geographical scope of application is the result of the text being unclear as to what is the area where paragraph 3 is meant to exert its influence. There are a variety of ways in which its geographical scope can be defined. For instance, it can be applied to areas where States' entitlements overlap, the area where overlapping claims exists,[898] or disputed maritime areas.[899] Alternatively, the emphasis could be placed on the effects that a State's conduct exerts on the chances of reaching a delimitation agreement.[900] By following the approach that paragraph 3 of Articles 74 and 83 LOSC is applicable to the area where States' entitlements to maritime zones overlap,[901] very extensive areas where this paragraph would apply are regularly created. For example if States are opposite and their coasts are 350 nm removed from each other, the entire area can be considered to be the area of overlapping EEZ/continental shelf entitlements. There were States participating in UNCLOS III that had already anticipated issues to arise in relation to the spatial scope of application of an interim rule. In this vein, Ireland and Morocco unsuccessfully sought to introduce a standard that

896 Ibid.

897 Article 22 of the Timor Sea Treaty (signed 20 May 2002, entered into force 2 April 2003) 2258 UNTS 3.

898 Nandan and Rosenne (n. 551) 800; R Beckman, 'The South China Sea Disputes: How States Can Clarify Their Maritime Claims' (2012) *RSIS Commentaries* (S Rajaratnam School of International Studies, 31 July 2012) 1–2.

899 X Zhang, 'Notion of Dispute in the Contemporary International Legal Order' in CH Schofield et al. (eds.), *The Limits of Maritime Jurisdiction* (Martinus Nijhoff, 2014) 269, 269–270.

900 Van Logchem (n. 21) 179, 195–197.

901 Becker-Weinberg (n. 25) 96.

States' claims to maritime zones must be 'bona fide' in nature.[902] This failure to include the wording of bona fide has limited consequences, however, as claims lacking a prima facie basis are extensively covered by other rules of international law.[903]

In setting the scope of application of paragraph 3, it is critical to consider that this paragraph is a constituent part of the delimitation provisions of Articles 74 and 83 LOSC. Because a clear interlinkage is established with the issue of delimitation, it is prudent to follow pronunciations of international courts and tribunals over what conditions must be present in order for them to effect a delimitation,[904] and to then apply these by analogy in defining the geographical scope of application of paragraph 3.[905] Generally, States will express different positions in maritime boundary proceedings as to where, in their view, the boundary should come to lie. The international court or tribunal is likely to identify the area falling between these claimed lines as being the 'disputed area', which will need to be delimited.[906] Hence, a decisive role in activating the two obligations of Articles 74(3) and 83(3) LOSC must be attributed to what can be considered to be the disputed maritime area.

Determining its geographical scope might be difficult, however, whenever only one of the States concerned has made its view known on where the maritime boundary should come to lie, or when a claim is viewed as being excessive or baseless. One way to sidestep such difficulties is to take the position that there is no 'territorial scope' attached to the obligation of not hampering or jeopardising;[907] due to its different nature, this consideration will not enter into play concerning the obligation of seeking a provisional arrangement. The rationale underlying this approach is the following: also acts that do not necessarily bear a direct connection to the disputed area can have the effect of complicating reaching a boundary agreement – amongst others, 'the issuing of an arrest warrant for the Minister of Foreign Affairs of the neighbouring State'.[908]

902 A/CONF.62/C.2/L.43 (n. 665) (Ireland); Platzöder, Third United Nations Conference (n. 559) Vol. IX, 395 (Morocco).

903 Lagoni (n. 243) 357.

904 *Bangladesh/Myanmar* (n. 42) 105 [397]; *Barbados* v. *Trinidad and Tobago* (n. 582) 211 [224].

905 M Miyoshi, 'The Aegean Sea and the Aegean Islands in Historical Perspective', in B Öztürk (ed.), 2000 *Proceedings of the International Symposium, 'The Aegean Sea, 2000'* (Turkish Marine Research Foundation, 2000) 86, 88; Evans (n. 598) 508; Oude Elferink (n. 520) 178–180.

906 *Guyana* v. *Suriname* (n. 7) 130 [460].

907 BIICL Report (n. 141) 31.

908 Ibid. 29.

When the link with a geographically defined area is cut, central importance is given to the effects the conduct of States in the broadest sense may have on the chances of coming to delimitation; this is determined through the extent to which the relations of the States concerned have been detrimentally affected. As a corollary, the possible acts that could have an effect of hampering or jeopardising are numerous, however, rendering its scope extremely broad and highly unspecific. But this compels an unnatural reading of Articles 74(3) and 83(3) LOSC. Inevitably, there needs to be some spatial scope attached to paragraph 3 to define its scope of application – confirming this is that these provisions are part of a collection of provisions dealing with EEZ/continental shelf delimitation. Hence, in order for an act to fall within the reach of this paragraph, an act must have been committed which bears some direct relation to the disputed EEZ or continental shelf area as such, and which will have the subsequent effect of making it more difficult to successfully reach a delimitation agreement thereon. However, this act does not necessarily need to physically occur in the disputed EEZ/continental shelf area. Rather, what is critical is whether the act has a direct connection with the area, and can thus, inter alia, include making an excessive claim, or enlarging a previous claim to an EEZ or continental shelf. This approach recognises that claims made on paper which relate to a disputed EEZ or continental shelf area can be sufficient to give rise to tensions in bilateral relations. Also, in relation to areas where there are more than two States that have claims to the same EEZ or continental shelf area, for example, in the Eastern Mediterranean Sea, characteristic of which is its geographical congestion, and where several disputed areas can be identified where the claims of multiple States overlap, delimitation agreements that relate to areas to which a third State has a similar claim can produce an effect of hampering or jeopardising. Then, the obligation would be breached not in relation with whom the delimitation agreement was reached but the other State that lays claim to the same area as well. This may well have been the case after Cyprus and Israel concluded a boundary agreement on 17 December 2010 to delimit their disputed EEZ area, which was unlawful according to Lebanon, because it included areas that it also claims.[909]

The applicability of Articles 74(3) and 83(3) LOSC can be questioned in two different types of cases of overlapping claims creating disputed EEZ/continental shelf areas. First, those that are generated either exclusively or conjunctively by

909 'Cyprus-Lebanon, Cyprus-Israel Offshore Delimitation', available at www.mees.com/2012/9/28/op-ed-documents/cyprus-lebanon-cyprus-israel-offshore-delimitation/f994d750-6d1a-11e7-9675-d5a0b0510107.

claims to maritime zones that are measured from disputed mainland territory or high-tide features;[910] and, second, when there are issues surrounding the status of a high-tide feature – this latter aspect can render it doubtful that a need for delimitation will ever arise.

Uncertainty over having a need for an EEZ or continental shelf boundary may occur when this need is dependent on the future determination of the status of a high-tide feature, that is, whether it is a rock or a fully entitled island. Under this scenario, the need for a maritime boundary is tied to whether the high-tide feature constitutes a fully entitled island.[911] Only then would an overlap of EEZ or continental shelf claims arise between the entitlements claimed from a high-tide feature of State A with State B, because of the latter claiming entitlements from the base points of a different piece of land territory.

The State claiming that the high-tide feature is entitled to a full 200 nm maritime zone, because it is a fully entitled island, will similarly likely argue that Articles 74(3) and 83(3) LOSC are applicable. This is because, in that State's view, there is an overlap of its EEZ/continental shelf claims made from the high-tide feature with the claims of the other coastal State's island or mainland territory. The other State may be of the view that the feature is a rock (allowing the State only to make claims to a territorial sea and contiguous zone), or may regard it as a low-tide elevation (having no entitlements to maritime zones). Then, such a State is likely to argue that Articles 74(3) and 83(3) LOSC are not applicable, due to there being no actual need for an EEZ or continental shelf boundary between their coasts. A State claiming that there is no need for a boundary might take the following position: the issue of the status of the feature must first be directly settled under Article 121 LOSC.[912] While the status of a high-tide feature remains unsettled, the State contending that there is no maritime boundary has several obligations under Article 279 LOSC and the UN Charter, consisting, inter alia, of acting in good faith and peacefully settling its disputes. The importance of these obligations is echoed in Articles 300 and 301 LOSC, both calling on States to act in good faith, and which are a translation of the general principle of international law to use peaceful means in settling disputes in treaty form.[913]

Articles 74(3) and 83(3) LOSC may become relevant once the status of the feature has been determined to be a fully entitled island, thereby making it

910 Chapter 7 below.

911 Anderson and Van Logchem (n. 18) 211.

912 DH Anderson, 'Islands and Rocks in the Modern Law of the Sea' in MH Nordquist et al. (eds.), *The Law of the Sea Convention: US Accession and Globalization* (Brill, 2012) 307, 318.

913 Chapter 3, Section 3.6 above.

entitled to a 200 nm zone. This is when a disputed EEZ or continental shelf area between States is created, which would then be the result of overlapping claims generated by two land territories. As long as the issue of the status of a feature has not been settled, however, and the existence of overlapping claims to the same maritime space, and hence the need for delimitation, remain dependent on the status of the high-tide feature, this would render paragraph 3 inapplicable. This is different only if the status of a high-tide feature is but a single element in a wider maritime boundary dispute.[914]

Another example is the need for an EEZ or continental shelf boundary to remain unclear, due to a lack of specification of the extent of a claim to maritime areas by a State. For example, China has included maritime areas within its claim that Indonesia considers to be under its exclusive jurisdiction, because they lie outside the reach of any entitlements to maritime zones that China can claim from its land territories.[915] The fact that China considers this area to be under its jurisdiction is exemplified by its undertaking various acts in the waters concerned, including patrolling and conducting fishing activities.[916] After a period whereby Indonesia consistently denied the existence of an overlap of its claims with China, in late 2015 it requested China to clarify the meaning of its nine-dashed boundary claim.[917] In terms of the applicability of Articles 74(3) and 83(3) LOSC, they only apply to areas that can be plausibly claimed by the other State as being part of its EEZ or continental shelf.[918]

A different situation is where there is uncertainty over whether a boundary exists between States' respective EEZs/continental shelves, or its precise extent, pending the outcome of negotiations, litigation, or conciliation. More specifically, the existence of a maritime boundary between two States can be still unclear, for instance, when one of them has commenced a procedure for determining the boundary with another coastal State, and whose outcome has to be awaited. It would only then be possible to appraise the necessity for, or the extent of, a different EEZ or continental shelf boundary between other States' coasts. So, the outcome of these proceedings would make it clear whether delimiting a boundary with a neighbouring State, with whom an overlap of claims currently does not exist, is required.

914 Chapter 7, Section 7.2 below.

915 Forbes (n. 580) 90; S Wu and H Ren, 'Energy Security of China and Oil and Gas Development in Disputed Area of the South China Sea' (2005) 2 *COLR* 314, 320.

916 IMA Arsana, 'Is China a Neighbor to Indonesia?', *The Jakarta Post*, 8 August 2011.

917 S Schonhardt and B Otto, 'Indonesia Invokes International Tribunal in South China Sea Dispute', *Wall Street Journal*, 12 November 2015.

918 Murphy (n. 75) 185–186.

Such an ambiguous situation used to exist for India and Myanmar, where the extent of their maritime boundary was unclear prior to judicial proceedings between Bangladesh and India, and Bangladesh and Myanmar, having been concluded.

As long as the need for delimiting a maritime boundary remains uncertain, the obligations of Articles 73(3) and 83(3) LOSC will not arise. However, when it is clear that there is a need for an EEZ or continental shelf boundary, but its precise length is dependent on other States delimiting their boundary, the two obligations of paragraph 3 would apply to those parts of the disputed area where the need for a boundary exists independent of this delimitation.

5.3.8 *The Equidistance Boundary as an Interim Rule*

An interim rule based on the equidistance boundary prevents that overlapping entitlements and related rights of different States over the same EEZ or continental shelf area occur, although there needs to be agreement on the relevant base points. Then, prior to delimitation, this line signifies the outermost point up to where the coastal States concerned can exercise their sovereign rights and jurisdiction.[919] Although all direct reference to equidistance has been erased from the text of Articles 74(3) and 83(3) LOSC, which is in stark contrast to disputed territorial sea areas in the form of Article 15 LOSC,[920] this has not prevented arguments to the effect that the interim rule in relation to disputed EEZ or continental shelf areas is the equidistance boundary.[921] Looking at paragraph 3's drafting history, after exhausting almost all variants of a text wherein the equidistance boundary was included as an interim rule, an approach along the lines of the equidistance boundary was abandoned in connection with disputed EEZ and continental shelf areas by the Chairman of NG7 at UNCLOS III.[922]

Evidence of the use of the equidistance boundary as an interim rule is provided by State practice, where, usually, States in favour of the rule of equidistance in delimitation will enact national laws providing that they have an EEZ or continental shelf extending to a maximum of 200 nm,[923] subject to maritime boundaries having to be determined with neighbouring

919 Hayashi (n. 13) 39.
920 Chapter 4 above.
921 Tas (n. 600) 53
922 A/CONF.62/C.2/L.14 (n. 558) (the Netherlands).
923 Article 7(2) Belize Maritime Areas Act, 1992; Article 6(3) Fiji Marine Spaces Act, 1978.

States based on that very rule.[924] However, the informative value that national laws and regulations have is that they provide individual examples of State practice. The lawfulness of the equidistance boundary as an interim rule is supported, so it has been argued, by such provisions not drawing protests from other States when they are included in national legislation.[925] But it is questionable whether the lack of any protest from other States against such legislation can be invoked in support of the equidistance boundary as an interim rule for two reasons. First, it is debatable whether a protest would be at all called for; and, second, a neighbouring coastal State may have a different provision in its own national legislation applying to the same area that is at variance with the equidistance rule. National laws and regulations prescribing the use of an equidistance boundary as an interim rule are also not sufficiently widespread to successfully argue that there is an actual practice that is sufficient to represent customary international law, let alone an *opinio juris*.[926]

Other examples from State practice where the equidistance boundary has had some role to play in the period prior to delimitation exist. Japan has taken the position that the disputed areas in the East China Sea are divided by an equidistance boundary, forming the outer point up to which it is free to exercise its rights and jurisdiction.[927] However, the other claimant, that is China, has continuously disputed the validity of the equidistance boundary as an interim rule, arguing that its agreement is required in order for this limitation to be imposed on where it can exercise its rights and jurisdiction in the East China Sea.[928] While not born out of a legal obligation under international law, the United States will often refrain from claiming an entitlement to the full 200 nm whenever an overlap of its EEZ claim is perceived to occur with a neighbour.[929] Rather, as a matter of policy, the United States will usually declare that it has rights up to the equidistance boundary and committing itself not to cross it. Sometimes States will mutually decide to have the equidistance boundary form the outer limit up to which they will exercise acts prior to delimitation.[930] In this vein, China and North

924 Klein (n. 9) 444.

925 S Sakamoto, 'Japan-China Dispute Over Maritime Boundary Delimitation – From a Japanese Perspective' (2008) 51 *JYIL* 98, 101.

926 Van Logchem (n. 52) 47–48.

927 JW Donaldson and M Pratt, 'Boundary and Territorial Trends in 2004' (2005) 10(2) *Geopolitics* 398, 408.

928 J Gu, 'An Analysis on the Legal Effects of the Exclusion Declaration Issues by China in Accordance with Article 298 of the United Nations Convention on the Law of the Sea' (2007) *COLR* 303, 335.

929 BIICL Report (n. 141) 51–52.

930 Ibid. 43.

Korea have both conducted exploratory work for mineral resources in the disputed Korea Bay up to the equidistance boundary.[931]

Based on the language of Articles 74(3) and 83(3) LOSC, as further confirmed by their drafting history, the application of the equidistance boundary as an interim rule cannot be considered to be automatic. There is an exception: that is, where States having overlapping EEZ or continental shelf claims have agreed on the use of the equidistance boundary. Along these lines, in 2013, Costa Rica suggested to Nicaragua that the equidistance boundary should be employed as a provisional arrangement in the sense of Articles 74(3) and 83(3) LOSC; Nicaragua rejected going along this route, however.[932] Alternatively, it may be that States have indicated a preference for the equidistance boundary, as an interim rule, in their respective national laws. Or a State could test the proverbial waters by proclaiming an equidistance boundary and await the reaction of the neighbouring State, whereby it thus relies on acquiescence for the boundary to become final. But in neither of these situations does the use of the equidistance boundary constitute a true 'interim rule', central to which is that it is activated irrespective of the viewpoints of the States involved, rather being linked to the arising of overlapping EEZ and continental shelf claims. Against this background, the justification for the equidistance boundary as an interim rule ebbs away quickly once the other State protests against it. However, the situation in the territorial sea is different, as the application of the equidistance boundary line as an interim rule is primarily intertwined with there being no historic title or special circumstances.[933]

5.3.9 *A Moratorium as an Interim Rule*

The effect of a moratorium is that economic activities which are under the jurisdiction of the coastal State (e.g. energy and natural resources activity) cannot be undertaken or authorised prior to delimitation, unless this is with the prior consent of the other claimant. Its core objective as an interim rule is that a moratorium ensures that the exclusivity of a coastal State's rights are fully preserved and prevents unilateral actions relating to natural resources acting as catalysts for conflict between neighbouring coastal States.

A claimant State may find it desirable, either for environmental or strategic reasons, to impose a moratorium on a disputed EEZ/continental shelf area in

931 J Guoxing, 'Maritime Jurisdiction in the Three China Seas: Options for Equitable Settlement' (1995) 19 *IGCC Policy Paper* 7.

932 *Costa Rica* v. *Nicaragua* (n. 481) Costa Rica's Memorial 15 [2.29].

933 Chapter 4, Section 4.2 above.

respect of energy and natural resources. Its apparent simplicity, effectiveness, and comprehensiveness are some of the main positive aspects underlying the introduction of a moratorium.[934] Contrary to this, a moratorium has been regularly evaluated in negative terms.[935] One criticism is that, because disputed EEZ or continental shelf areas can persist for significant amounts of time, the possibility for coastal States to pluck the financial fruits of economic development has to be postponed until after delimitation.[936] Another line of criticism perceives the moratorium as an open invitation to States to maximise their claims over a maritime area.[937] Despite this criticism, one essential question is whether, except by reaching an agreement thereon, meaning that it cannot be considered as an interim rule, an alternative route exists whereby a moratorium can be imposed.

Sometimes a pattern has emerged in State practice where neighbouring coastal States, after previous unilateral acts have generated conflict between them, from then on abstained from awarding concessions to the petroleum industry or allowing other activities related to mineral resources to commence.[938] Although at first glance akin to a moratorium as an interim rule, put more accurately, these moratoria are being imposed *ex post facto*, their imposition is directly linked not to the fact that the area is disputed but to the fact that a State acting on its claimed rights previously created conflict between the States involved.

Guyana v. *Suriname* is regularly invoked as a repudiation of the moratorium approach. Here the Tribunal sought to more objectively assess what is lawful and what unlawful from the view of Articles 74(3) and 83(3) LOSC, rather than going along the lines of imposing a moratorium, which it found undesirable, including in light of paragraph 3's drafting history.[939] Certain States participating in UNCLOS III also looked unfavourably on the solution of the moratorium and tried their utmost to prevent this solution from finding its way into Articles 74(3) and 83(3) LOSC.[940] Yet, when looking at its language, with the emphasis being placed on reaching delimitation and not to take unilateral acts which aggravate reaching this end, or, alternatively, that of shelving the issue of delimitation by establishing provisional arrangements, what if one of the States concerned holds the view that reaching delimitation

934 W Yin, 'Moratorium in International Law' (2012) 11(2) *CJIL* 321, 340.

935 Kittichaisaree (n. 43) 109; Wang (n. 324) 537.

936 Van Logchem (n. 52) 48.

937 Dang (n. 199) 70.

938 'Cambodia Says No Plans to Grant Oil Concessions in Disputed Area', *Rigzone*, 5 August 2009.

939 Chapter 6, Section 6.3.1 below.

940 Platzöder (n. 559) 433–434 (NG7/26, Article 83(3), India, Iraq, and Morocco); A/CONF.62/SR.126 (n. 753) (Iran).

or cooperation is best served by the imposition of a moratorium on energy and natural resources activity in their disputed area?[941]

5.3.10 A *Reflection of Customary International Law?*

The fact that not all States faced with disputed EEZ and continental shelf areas have become a party to the LOSC, including Israel, Turkey, and Venezuela, alerts one to the need for appraising whether Articles 74(3) and 83(3) LOSC amount to a customary rule. Various views have been offered in literature on whether this paragraph 3 is a customary rule. One line of argument has focused on the LOSC as a whole, arguing that the provisions contained therein have assumed, without discrimination, the status of customary international law.[942] By extension, this would mean that paragraph 3 of Articles 74 and 83 LOSC has become a customary rule. Such sweeping assertions, that the LOSC *simpliciter* is customary, oversimplify the matter. Another view is mainly derived from delimitation cases where international courts and tribunals have determined in very broad strokes that Articles 74 and 83 LOSC have become customary law.[943] Other commentators have, however, confined themselves to the anodyne statement that paragraph 3 of Articles 74 and 83 LOSC has become a customary rule.[944] A general difficulty with these varied assumptions over the partial or full customary status of Articles 74(3) and 83(3) LOSC is that the reasons underpinning these positions are often not put on paper.

After reviewing the drafting history, Lagoni concluded that the 'concept of interim measures pending delimitation' emerged in treaty form for the first time in paragraph 3, but which, already at that time, was slowly becoming a customary rule.[945] With the entry into force of the Convention, and the widespread support it received from States, it is opportune to reassess the customary status of its Articles 74(3) and 83(3). Has paragraph 3 become a customary rule, or, alternatively, is its status as a customary rule still in a state of flux?

Complicating matters significantly is that, in their statements or otherwise, States themselves rarely invoke Articles 74(3) and 83(3) LOSC. Côte d'Ivoire in its maritime boundary dispute with Ghana reflected on the fact that this paragraph is rarely invoked in delimitation cases. It offered the following explanation for this: coastal States most often observe restraint in relation to

941 Section 5.3.12 below.
942 T Martin, 'Energy and International Boundaries' in K Talus (ed.), *Research Handbook on International Energy Law* (Edward Elgar, 2014) 181, 182.
943 *Qatar* v. *Bahrain* (n. 525) 91 [167].
944 Milano and Papanicolopulu (n. 80) 611.
945 Lagoni (n. 243) 349.

their disputed areas.[946] However, this is an explanation that is not supported by the relevant State practice, with there being many examples to the contrary.[947] Usually, States in their statements prefer to refer to other general rules of international law, which contain elements bearing on the obligations that claimants have under international law in disputed maritime areas, or they base their protests on perceived superior entitlements, exclusivity, or closeness to the coast.[948] As a result, significant difficulties remain in drawing any firm conclusions over whether Articles 74(3) and 83(3) LOSC have become a customary rule.[949]

However that may be, it is important to emphasise that the two obligations contained in paragraph 3 are closely connected to other general rules of international law.[950] A principle reflected in the obligation not to hamper or jeopardise delimitation is to abstain from aggravating or extending a dispute; the latter can be considered a general rule of international law in its own right.[951] Therefore, a perceivably more fruitful line of inquiry is not whether Articles 74(3) and 83(3) LOSC have developed into customary rules but whether the principles underpinning this paragraph 3 have obtained such a status.[952]

At its core, agreeing on a provisional arrangement is more closely connected with two other general principles of international law: good neighbourliness and cooperation.[953] The Tribunal in *Guyana* v. *Suriname* regarded the obligation to seek provisional arrangements as being part of the broader obligation resting on coastal States to come to an effective use of the seas and oceans, as the preamble to the LOSC requires.[954] It discerned a double aim in the obligation not to hamper or jeopardise: that is, strengthening the bilateral relations of States having a disputed EEZ or continental shelf area and ensuring that their maritime boundary dispute is peacefully settled. In its award, the Tribunal invoked by analogy, while clarifying the contents of the obligations of Articles 74(3) and 83(3) LOSC, the principle of not causing irreparable prejudice to rights.[955] Not threatening irreparable prejudice to rights is attributed a key

946 *Ghana/Côte d'Ivoire (Judgment)* (n. 46) Côte d'Ivoire's Rejoinder 165 [6.22].
947 Chapter 8 below.
948 'Vietnam East Sea Issue in Spotlight', *Thai Press Reports*, 28 April 2011.
949 Anderson and Van Logchem (n. 18) 208.
950 Van Logchem (n. 52) 60–62.
951 Klein (n. 9) 458; Churchill and Ulfstein (n. 407) 76.
952 Chapter 3 above.
953 Gao (n. 476) 114–115.
954 Mensah (n. 69) 150.
955 *Guyana* v. *Suriname* (n. 7) 133 [469].

role generally by international courts and tribunals when they are interpreting the lawfulness of a unilateral act in light of Articles 74(3) and 83(3) LOSC; this is despite the fact that paragraph 3 sets a lower threshold. Hence, avoiding irreparability concerning the rights of the other claimant also must be abstained from pursuant to the obligation not to hamper or jeopardise. Another link was recognised by the Tribunal between Articles 74(3) and 83(3) LOSC and the general principle that disputes must be peacefully settled: Suriname's reaction to the unilateral exploratory drilling was an unlawful threat to use force under international law, meaning that a breach of paragraph 3 could be *a fortiori* assumed.[956]

5.3.11 *How Useful Are Articles 74(3) and 83(3) LOSC?*

Most of the criticism that Articles 74(3) and 83(3) LOSC are of little importance predates the entry into force of this Convention.[957] Its usefulness was seen to be affected by the fact that, in order to appease the two doctrinally split delimitation groups at UNCLOS III (i.e. equidistance and equity), language had to be selected that was agreeable to both groups.[958] Taking this argument one step further is Caflisch, who contends that, in this search for acceptable wording, the language of paragraph 3 of Articles 74 and 83 LOSC lost all relevance.[959]

With the coming into force of the LOSC, these criticisms largely receded into the background, as the language contained in Articles 74(3) and 83(3) came to be valued more highly, and only more incidentally attracted criticism.[960] Nowadays, paragraph 3 also plays an enlarged role in the international legal sphere as in more recent pleadings by States before international courts and tribunals, in which unilateral acts were undertaken or approved by another claimant in relation to a disputed area, have been condemned on the basis of Articles 74(3) and 83(3) LOSC. For instance, in the maritime boundary dispute submitted to the ICJ by Somalia, both Somalia and Kenya already invoked the paragraph during the earliest stages of the proceedings.[961]

956 Ibid. 131–132 [465].
957 Caflisch (n. 587) 495; Brown (n. 555) 159.
958 Oxman (n. 655) 23–24; S Fietta and R Cleverly, *A Practitioner's Guide to Maritime Boundary Delimitation* (Oxford University Press, 2016) 25.
959 Caflisch (n. 587) 495.
960 I Townsend-Gault, 'Zones of Cooperation in the Oceans – Legal Rationales and Imperatives' in MH Nordquist and JN Moore (eds.), *Maritime Border Diplomacy* (Martinus Nijhoff, 2012) 109, 113.
961 Chapter 6, Section 6.5 below.

Those authors highly critical of paragraph 3 of Articles 74 and 83 LOSC nonetheless admitted that it had some residual importance, by imposing a minimum requirement on claimant States: they must make sure that delimitation is not made more difficult, through unilateral acts falling under coastal State jurisdiction being undertaken in relation to a disputed EEZ or continental shelf area.[962] Coincidentally, subsequent interpretations have moved away from viewing the main import of paragraph 3 through the lens of avoiding unilateral conduct within such areas. Rather, a contrary trend can be detected, mainly set in motion by the Tribunal's award in *Guyana* v. -*Suriname*,[963] where the main emphasis of paragraph 3 is construed along the lines of cooperation, in that States should seek provisional arrangements allowing for the economic development of a disputed maritime area.[964]

The obligation to seek provisional arrangements is in the nature of a *pactum de negotiando* or an *obligation de s'efforcer*, but does that render it a toothless obligation? If a State fails to make the required effort as is contemplated under this obligation (e.g. if entering into negotiations towards coming to provisional arrangements are mere ploys to achieve something else), it can be accused of having failed to make every effort to enter into a provisional arrangement.[965] A final determination as to whether claimant States have lived up to the necessary effort that is required to be made under this obligation lies with an international court or tribunal, which can pronounce itself on efforts falling short thereof.[966] A State acting in good faith means that it cannot merely go through the motions of negotiating without an accompanying intention to come to a successful result.[967] It also presupposes sincerity on the part of States in the negotiations which have been commenced; this will be present if the States concerned show a willingness to compromise and modify their original position.[968] Thus, although it is of an exhortatory nature, the obligation to seek provisional arrangements does not entirely lack teeth. This obligation has had a positive practical impact as well. In some cases where there has been an urgent need to clarify the issue of jurisdiction, States have established provisional boundaries where this obligation has been a useful driving force behind their conclusion. A good example is the provisional delimitation of the continental shelf in the Irish Sea,

962 Caflisch (n. 587) 495.
963 *Guyana* v. *Suriname* (n. 7) 130 [460].
964 Van Logchem (n. 21) 191–192.
965 Lagoni (n. 243) 354; Wang (n. 324) 538.
966 *Application of the International Convention on the Elimination of All Forms of Racial Discrimination (Georgia* v. *Russian Federation)* (Preliminary Objections) [2011] ICJ Rep 70, 135–136 [169]–[170].
967 Chapter 3, Section 3.6 above.
968 Lagoni (n. 243) 356.

which was made explicitly pursuant to Article 83(3) LOSC.[969] France and Tuvalu decided to determine where their provisional boundary lies due to a lack of accurate charts as a result of Articles 74(3) and 83(3) LOSC.[970] Also, claimant States have created provisional arrangements for the purposes of fishing or mineral resources.[971] For example, the provisional arrangements concluded between Malaysia and Thailand, agreeing to jointly administer a zone thought to be rich in mineral resources, was inspired by Articles 74(3) and 83(3) LOSC.[972]

Determining the usefulness of the obligation not to hamper or jeopardise is far more difficult, however. State practice is rather diverse in two respects: first, in terms of the extent to which unilateral acts that are under coastal State jurisdiction are undertaken in disputed EEZ or continental shelf areas; and, second, whether such a unilateral act has prompted the other State into responding through, for example, a protest or law enforcement.[973] Some claimant States have limited their level of activity to varying degrees in relation to such areas; this restraint can possibly be traced back to the obligation not to hamper or jeopardise. However, this will often remain a matter of speculation – that is, unless the States concerned will identify the source from which this restraint is derived as being the obligation not to hamper or jeopardise contained in Articles 74(3) and 83(3) LOSC, but this will rarely be the case. Other States seem to regularly disregard the main thrust of this obligation by undertaking acts falling under the jurisdiction of a coastal State unilaterally, thereby often prompting the other claimant into responding, with the result that the possibility of reaching a delimitation of a disputed EEZ or continental shelf area is reduced in the process.[974]

5.3.12 *Recalibrating the Importance of Articles 74(3) and 83(3) LOSC*

In some interpretations of Articles 74(3) and 83(3) LOSC, an element that is regularly lost sight of, with emphasis often being placed on the cooperative

969 DH Anderson, 'Report No 9–5(3)' in C. Lathrop (ed.), *International Maritime Boundaries*, Vol. VII (Martinus Nijhoff, 2012) 1767–1780.

970 TL McDorman and CH Schofield, 'Report No 5–29' in DA Colson and RW Smith (eds.), *International Maritime Boundaries*, Vol. VI (Martinus Nijhoff, 2011) 4330.

971 Kim (n. 287) 94–149; Milligan (n. 586) 23–24.

972 Memorandum of Understanding between the Kingdom of Thailand and Malaysia on the Delimitation of the Establishment of a Joint Authority for the Exploitation of the Resources of the Sea-bed in a Defined Area of the Continental Shelf of the Two Countries in the Gulf of Thailand (24 October 1979), 1291 UNTS 245; Agreement between the Government of Malaysia and the Government of the Kingdom of Thailand on the Constitution and Other Matters Relating to the Establishment of the Malaysia-Thailand Joint Authority, 13 May 1990.

973 Chapter 8 below.

974 Chapter 9, Section 9.5 below.

aspect included therein,[975] is that the background to their introduction is the prospect of EEZ/continental shelf delimitation.[976] Given that paragraph 3 is an integral part of the delimitation provisions of Articles 74 and 83, it needs to be read in a way that seeks to somehow facilitate a delimitation, however. Hence, the *raison d'être* of its paragraph 3 must be seen through the lens of a delimitation not 'being extended', or made more complicated through acts being undertaken in relation to a disputed EEZ or continental shelf area, whereby the maritime boundary dispute is aggravated.[977]

Although the States concerned may shelve the issue of delimitation for the time being, by concluding provisional arrangements to manage a disputed EEZ or continental shelf area, their conclusion may function as an interlude between leaving such a disputed area completely ungoverned by provisional arrangements and delimitation being attained thereafter. Further, it will avoid that, in relation to those types of activities falling within the jurisdiction of coastal States that have been brought under the reach of a provisional arrangement, and assuming they are conducted in accordance therewith, conflict will not emerge between the States concerned because of these activities being undertaken unilaterally; this might facilitate a future delimitation of the disputed EEZ/continental shelf area in question.

Another significant aspect is that the two obligations in Articles 74(3) and 83(3) LOSC are tailored to be applied in the period preceding delimitation. This is brought out in the make-up of the text of paragraph 3: the two obligations are imposed with a view to ensuring that 'the reaching of the final agreement' will not be negatively impacted. To the contrary, continuously authorising or undertaking acts that are under coastal State jurisdiction unilaterally would exert an opposite effect: reaching a delimitation agreement will become more complex, and prolonging the required time to reach that result. The relevance of this aspect was recognised by Ghana in rebutting Côte d'Ivoire's claim that there had been a breach of Article 83(3) LOSC: in assessing whether the obligation not to hamper or jeopardise had been breached, Ghana did not deem it essential whether certain 'physical effects' had been exerted as a result of a unilateral act being undertaken, but rather how the unilateral act impeded 'on the process of reaching a final agreement'.[978]

975 R Beckman et al., 'Moving Forward on Joint Development in the South China Sea' in R Beckman et al. (eds.), *Beyond Territorial Disputes in the South China Sea: Legal Frameworks for the Joint Development of Hydrocarbon Resources* (Edward Elgar, 2013) 312–331.

976 Van Logchem (n. 21) 191–192.

977 Van Logchem (n. 52) 48–49.

978 *Ghana/Côte d'Ivoire* (Judgment) (n. 46) Ghana's Reply 151–152 [5.38].

A subjective component has been injected into Articles 74(3) and 83(3) LOSC because of the link of the two obligations contained therein to the issue of delimitation. This link is evident in the obligation that encourages States to seek provisional arrangements, being closely connected to the subjective views of the claimants concerned. This is because an absence of a willingness on the part of the States involved to establish any provisional arrangements will have the effect that no talks to that end will begin, nor are they obligated by international law to start such negotiations; this is unless one of the States concerned extends an invitation to that end.

Similarly, a subjective element is also in play when interpreting the range of unilateral conduct that is caught under the obligation not to hamper or jeopardise. Churchill and Lowe underline this subjective aspect when stating that States must refrain from taking actions that 'might be regarded as prejudicial' by the other claimant.[979] Cast in these terms, a key role is attributed to the individual position of the States concerned as to what activities have a prejudicial effect on the chances of coming to a delimitation agreement. As a corollary to this, the weight of the assessment as to whether Articles 74(3) and 83(3) LOSC have been breached comes to lie with the States concerned, which are ultimately the ones that have to complete the delimitation of maritime boundaries.[980]

Despite this underlying subjective component, international courts and tribunals will likely convert this subjective test into a more objective one, when faced with a claimed breach of Articles 74(3) and 83(3) LOSC.[981] Confirmation of this is found in *Guyana* v. *Suriname*, where the Tribunal in its award similarly construed a more objective test to determine whether a breach of the obligation not to hamper or jeopardise had occurred.[982] An explanation for the fact that international courts and tribunals will usually seek to evaluate the content of this obligation, as well as infringements thereon, through a more objective lens is as follows: a delimitation of the disputed EEZ or continental shelf area will be effected once the court or tribunal has handed down its final ruling – effectively removing any future role for Articles 74(3) and 83(3) LOSC. However, in light of the connection that the obligation not to hamper or jeopardise has with the issue of delimitation, combined with it being concerned with the period before delimitation, a seemingly more appropriate question that should rather be asked by an international court or tribunal in determining whether

979 Churchill and Lowe (n. 1) 192.
980 Van Logchem (n. 52) 48–49.
981 BIICL Report (n. 141) 25.
982 Chapter 6, Section 6.8 below.

this obligation has been breached is as follows: at the time when the unilateral act falling under coastal State jurisdiction was undertaken, was effecting EEZ or continental shelf delimitation complicated as a result?

5.4 CONCLUDING REMARKS

Worldwide, there are many disputed EEZ and continental shelf areas. When considering the inherency of a coastal State's rights in disputed continental shelf areas, this implies that these are to be exclusively exercised by the relevant coastal State, which might evoke claims to the exclusive use thereof by all of the States concerned. However, the coexistence of entitlements and related ipso facto and ab initio rights of coastal States over the same continental shelf area has the effect that any such exclusivity remains illusory up to when the continental shelf boundary has been determined, and the geographical extent of a coastal State's rights has become clear. Although the inherency aspect is absent concerning a coastal State's sovereign rights in the EEZ, this does not mean that, if a State has made a claim to one, the related rights are fictitious.

Article 6 1958 CSC is the forerunner to the provision dealing with continental shelf delimitation in the LOSC (i.e. Article 83). It is developed along the lines of equidistance: States are not entitled to extend their continental shelf beyond the equidistance boundary – that is, subject to the condition that there are no special circumstances.[983] Critical in the development of Article 6 1958 CSC was the ILC's 1956 Draft Articles on the Law of the Sea. When looking at what transpired in the debates within the ILC, combined with the language of Article 6 CSC, the conclusion emerges that this provision does not seek to deal with the period preceding continental shelf delimitation by providing an interim rule, however.

The identically phrased paragraph 3 of Articles 74 and 83 LOSC is particularly relevant to measure the extent to which neighbouring coastal States can act on their rights in disputed EEZ and continental shelf areas. At UNCLOS III, the different negotiation texts changed regularly on the point of an interim rule. When UNCLOS III was convened, a significant number of coastal States were already familiar with conflict that resulted from the lack of maritime delimitation.[984] The two obligations contained in paragraph 3 of Articles 74 and 83 LOSC reflect the recognition of the drafters of the LOSC[985] that rules

983 Section 5.2 above.
984 Nandan and Rosenne (n. 551) 492–493.
985 Lagoni (n. 243) 349.

had to be developed for States being faced with disputed EEZ and continental shelf areas. As part of the broader package of delimitation provisions, on which only in the very final stages of the negotiations an agreement was reached at UNCLOS III,[986] a compromise is clearly present in Articles 74(3) and 83(3) LOSC.[987] Its current tone represents a compromise between two positions of States at UNCLOS III: first, there were shared concerns amongst States over the negative effects of when acts falling under coastal State jurisdiction are unilaterally undertaken or authorised; and, second, that claimants had to find cooperative arrangements, otherwise a moratorium on economic conduct would be introduced. Mainly through the efforts of States unaligned to either the 'equidistance' or 'equitable principles' groups a compromise on a text containing an interim rule was ultimately reached.[988]

Articles 74(3) and 83(3) LOSC seek to prevent conflicts between claimant States prior to a delimitation in the sense of their paragraph 1; were such conflicts to happen, the prospect of delimitation would be pushed further out of sight. This is prevented by imposing two obligations, which apply simultaneously in the period before delimitation: first, by calling on States to seek provisional arrangements, whereby the delimitation issue is shelved; and, second, acts having a hampering or jeopardising effect must be abstained from pending delimitation. These two obligations will arise conjointly in some, but not all, situations where there is an overlap of EEZ and continental shelf claims. In terms of the scope of application, the obligation of not hampering or jeopardising applies in a broader range of situations than the obligation to seek provisional arrangements, as, amongst others, its activation is not entwined with States having friendly relations, or the States concerned recognising the need for delimiting their boundary.

Concluding a provisional arrangement in the sense of Articles 74(3) and 83(3) LOSC[989] is a useful way for States to manage a disputed EEZ or continental shelf area prior to its delimitation. However, no obligation rests on States to conclude a provisional arrangement. The States concerned must make good faith efforts in seeking a provisional arrangement, but the final result is irrelevant. In case they fail to agree thereon, this will not mean that no unilateral activities that are within coastal State jurisdiction will be authorised or undertaken in relation to a disputed EEZ/continental shelf area. In this scenario, the obligation not to hamper or jeopardise exerts much of its relevance.[990]

986 *Eritrea* v. *Yemen (Second Phase)* (n. 656) 362 [116].
987 Becker-Weinberg (n. 25) 94.
988 Fietta and Cleverly (n. 958) 84–85.
989 Mensah (n. 69) 149; Zou (n. 168) 106.
990 Van Logchem (n. 21) 178.

A dual function lies at the heart of the obligation not to hamper or jeopardise: first, it limits when rights can be exercised in the period preceding delimitation; and, second, it reduces the ways in which States can respond to activities falling under coastal State jurisdiction that are undertaken unilaterally. Due to this dual scope, the obligation not to hamper or jeopardise ensures a large sphere of application. It is also significant that a good faith component underlies this obligation; the States concerned 'shall make every effort' thereto.[991] Considering that the States concerned must 'make every effort' not to hamper or jeopardise a final agreement, a broader range of unilateral conduct can be brought within its reach. However, the main difficulty lies with determining the precise extent to which rights can be actively exercised in a disputed EEZ or continental shelf area, and in what way a State can respond when being faced with unilaterally undertaken conduct that is under the jurisdiction of the coastal State.

On an abstract level the answer seems obvious: the type of conduct that is meant to be captured under Articles 74(3) and 83(3) LOSC is circumscribed with reference to the fact that an act may not have an effect of 'hampering' or 'jeopardising'. At their core, these two terms seek something similar: restraint on the part of the States concerned.[992] If the effects generated by a unilateral act surpass the thresholds of hampering or jeopardising, a breach of paragraph 3 of Articles 74 and 83 LOSC can be assumed.

Judicial pronouncements have interpreted the language of not jeopardising or hampering as not implying that all economic unilateral conduct violates this obligation. But there has been little progress in this case law in disentangling the meaning and peculiarities of the obligations contained in Articles 74(3) and 83(3) LOSC from standards developed in the context of interim measures procedures.[993] Also, the test as to whether the obligation not to hamper or jeopardise was breached has often been converted in the case law into an objective one.[994] Following the approach of international courts and tribunals, the argument has been made that one simply needs to fall back on this case law and the standards developed thereunder to gauge the (un)lawfulness of a particular activity. But a shift in emphasis is warranted, however, considering the language of Articles 74(3) and 83(3) LOSC. The subjective assessments of the States concerned should be put more at the heart

991 BIICL Report (n. 141) 21–22; Van Logchem (n. 245) 138.
992 Van Logchem (n. 21) 178.
993 Chapter 6, Section 6.3.1 below.
994 BIICL report (n. 141) 25.

of the determination whether a unilateral act has hampered or jeopardised a final agreement.[995]

In interpreting a treaty provision, according to Article 31 VCLT, an ordinary reading of paragraph 3 of Articles 74 and 83 LOSC reveals that, in the period before delimitation is reached, in order not to complicate this aim of delimitation, States are under its two obligations. By placing the emphasis on the positions of the States concerned, it is recognised that States themselves must delimit the maritime boundary by agreement. It also makes the individual assessment of a claimant as to what types of unilateral activity negatively impact on reaching delimitation an integral part in identifying which unilateral acts can have an effect of hampering or jeopardising.[996] The difficulty with accepting this argument is that it introduces the possibility of a moratorium on economic activities being imposed on the suggestion of one of the claimant States concerned. Especially influential in shaping the view that a moratorium pursuant to Articles 74(3) and 83(3) LOSC is not justified is the drafting history,[997] but the insight drawn therefrom as to what is envisaged by certain States participating in UNCLOS III is valuable, but is not necessarily determinative.

Because certain States having disputed EEZ/continental shelf areas are not a party to the LOSC, the issue of whether Articles 74(3) and 83(3) reflect customary international law takes on particular urgency. However, it remains difficult to establish whether paragraph 3 can be considered to be a customary rule, as State practice is highly varied, and States themselves rarely invoke this paragraph to condemn acts of unilateralism by other States in disputed EEZ or continental shelf areas.[998] Nonetheless, several obligations exist under general international law to which Articles 74(3) and 83(3) LOSC are closely related, both in terms of substance and aim, and these will apply irrespective of a State being a party to the LOSC: that is, inter alia, the basic principle not to aggravate or extend a dispute, not to cause irreparable prejudice to the rights of the other State, to have due regard to the rights and interests of the other State, and not to abuse one's rights.[999]

995 Van Logchem (n. 245) 138–139.
996 Van Logchem (n. 21) 186.
997 Section 5.3.1 above.
998 Anderson and Van Logchem (n. 18) 208.
999 Chapter 3, Sections 3.4–3.5, 3.7 above.

6

Case Law Involving the Rights and Obligations of States in Disputed Maritime Areas

Conflicts had already arisen between coastal States, because of unilateral conduct in relation to disputed continental shelf areas, prior to the entry into force of the LOSC. Case law that emerged at this time was not extensive, however, and those disputes that did arise, and were brought before an international court or tribunal, were requests for measures of interim protection. The leading example is the *Aegean Sea Continental Shelf* (Interim Measures) case.[1000] At the centre of the dispute between Greece and Turkey in the Aegean Sea was a division over to what extent the two States can act unilaterally in relation to their disputed continental shelf area. Is a moratorium on activities which fall under coastal State jurisdiction imposed within the disputed area by international law, as suggested by Greece? Or is it rather that some room remains for unilateralism within the disputed area prior to final delimitation, as is argued by Turkey?

In the award of the Tribunal in *Guyana* v. *Suriname*, the merits and content of Articles 74(3) and 83(3) LOSC were dealt with, for the first time, in some depth.[1001] The Tribunal, inter alia, considered whether exploratory drilling by Guyana could be lawfully authorised unilaterally, and, second, whether Suriname's response to the drilling in their disputed area was in conformity with Articles 74(3) and 83(3) LOSC. In more recent cases, the parties to the dispute in *Ghana/Côte d'Ivoire* and *Somalia* v. *Kenya*[1002] also called into question the lawfulness of a plethora of unilaterally undertaken acts, which are all under a coastal State's jurisdiction, within their disputed areas.

At the core of this chapter is the international case law and the light that it shines on two issues: when and what rights can be exercised by States in the

[1000] *Aegean Sea Continental Shelf* (Interim Measures) (n. 41).
[1001] *Guyana* v. *Suriname* (n. 7).
[1002] *Ghana/Côte d'Ivoire* (Judgment) (n. 46); *Somalia* v. *Kenya* (n. 47).

period preceding delimitation, and the (extent of the) obligations States have under international law in relation to their disputed maritime areas. Sections 6.1 and 6.2 will identify the relevant case law that has been rendered prior to the entry into force of the LOSC, being *Aegean Sea Continental Shelf* (Interim Measures) and *Guinea-Bissau* v. *Senegal* (Provisional Measures).[1003] Thereafter, the emphasis of the analysis will shift to the developments which have taken place after the LOSC became binding on the States parties thereto. It starts in Section 6.3 with *Guyana* v. *Suriname*, where the contents of Articles 74(3) and 83(3) LOSC were fleshed out to some extent by an international tribunal. The Tribunal's ruling has given rise to a train of thought that, in finding an answer to whether a coastal State would be allowed to exercise its rights in a disputed EEZ or continental shelf area, one simply needs to revert to this case law and the standards developed thereunder. There are several difficulties with this approach, however,[1004] as is addressed in Section 6.8. Prior thereto, Sections 6.4 and 6.5 discuss two cases that are more recent: that is, *Ghana/Côte d'Ivoire* and *Somalia* v. *Kenya*, where the States concerned faced a number of difficulties because of activities falling under coastal State jurisdiction having been undertaken unilaterally within their disputed EEZ or continental shelf areas. Section 6.6 considers the fact that the case law on interim measures has been at the heart of much of the attempts to provide Articles 74(3) and 83(3) LOSC with content, an approach that is particularly visible in *Guyana* v. *Suriname*. Here the question arises whether applying standards developed in an interim measures case by analogy to determining what the rights and obligations of States are in disputed EEZ/continental shelf areas is appropriate.[1005] A communality can be seen across the case law: determining to what extent coastal States can act upon claimed rights in disputed maritime areas is tied to whether the consequential infringement could be financially compensated, raising the issue of whether this has not become the de facto paramount criterion. Section 6.7 addresses whether this does not overemphasise the aspect of repairing damage through financial means, neglecting, amongst others, the conflict that is often prompted by a State acting unilaterally by authorising or undertaking acts that are under a coastal State's jurisdiction? Section 6.9 places the Tribunal's condemnation of Suriname's response to an oil rig operating under a licence of Guyana in a broader light, focusing on how this may impact the ways in which a claimant

1003 *Guinea-Bissau* v. *Senegal* (Provisional Measures) (n. 11); *Aegean Sea Continental Shelf* (Interim Measures) (n. 41).

1004 Van Logchem (n. 21) 183–192.

1005 Lagoni (n. 243) 365–366; Ong (n. 771) 798–799; Kim (n. 287) 57–58.

State can respond to a unilateral activity falling under the jurisdiction of the coastal State within a disputed maritime area. The chapter is rounded off by a reflection on what can be learned from this international case law in terms of what the obligations and rights are of States in disputed maritime areas.

6.1 *AEGEAN SEA CONTINENTAL SHELF* (INTERIM MEASURES)

Two Turkish actions taking place in 1974 lay behind the Greek request for interim protection from the ICJ. The first incident revolved around a hydrographic vessel (the *Candarli*), flying the flag of Turkey, which, according to information provided by Greece, conducted a magnetometric survey in the north-eastern and central part of their disputed area,[1006] during which it was escorted by thirty-two Turkish warships. Initially, Greece protested through diplomatic channels, arguing that its consent was necessary before such an activity could be lawfully undertaken.[1007] Turkey contested this position, contending that the vessel was researching the Turkish continental shelf as permitted under international law. After diplomatic initiatives failed to resolve the dispute, Greece responded in two ways: first, by sending its naval vessels to the area concerned; and, second, by filing another official protest with the Turkish government.[1008]

Not long thereafter, on 2 July 1974, Turkey started to increase the number of concessions awarded to its national oil company; this was combined with more extensive parts of the disputed area being opened for seismic work. Following this, the *Sismik I* conducted a seismic survey of the disputed continental shelf area for a number of days in order to obtain some more precise estimates of its potential for mineral resources.[1009] Greece protested that in the course of its work, the *Sismik I* had unlawfully operated in areas that were clearly under Greek sovereignty and jurisdiction.[1010]

6.1.1 *Turkey's Unilateral Seismic Work*

Greece's overall strategy in convincing the ICJ of the necessity to indicate interim measures of protection was built on two pillars. The first pillar was that

1006 Rozakis (n. 624) 94.

1007 Y Acer, *The Aegean Maritime Disputes and International Law* (Ashgate, 2003) 37.

1008 *Aegean Sea Continental Shelf* (Interim Measures) (n. 41) Greece's Oral Pleadings 101.

1009 H Dipla, 'The Greek-Turkish Dispute over the Aegean Sea Continental Shelf: Attempts of Resolution' in TC Kariotis (ed.), *Greece and the Law of the Sea* (Martinus Nijhoff, 1997) 153, 166.

1010 *Aegean Sea Continental Shelf* (Interim Measures) (n. 41) Greece's Oral Pleadings 141.

unilateral exploratory work for mineral resources would merit the Court indicating measures of interim protection for two reasons: first, Greece's sovereign rights over the continental shelf area had been irreparably harmed; and, second, the activities invariably further aggravated and extended the underlying maritime boundary dispute.[1011] The second pillar was that disputes must be settled by invoking peaceful means, requiring the States concerned to abstain from taking measures that would contravene this basic requirement of international law.

At the stage of the oral proceedings, Greece argued that, in light of both unilateral seismic work and scientific research being prejudicial to the outcome of the dispute,[1012] the ICJ had to order the parties involved to abstain from undertaking acts that are under coastal State jurisdiction in relation to the disputed continental shelf area until after delimitation.[1013] In support of this position, Greece fell back on customary international law, arguing that a customary rule exists that States must abstain from exercising unilateral competence over a disputed continental shelf area.[1014]

Greece's position was that both the licensing and the subsequent activation of awarded concessions, enabling seismic work to be undertaken in a disputed area, violated Greece's rights over its continental shelf in a way that could not be remedied *ex post facto*.[1015] Because of this effect, Greece premised the conducting of these activities on the fact that the ICJ had handed down the final ruling on delimitation.[1016] Support for this position was derived by Greece from Article 2 of the 1958 CSC, pursuant to which a coastal State enjoys exclusive sovereign rights to explore and exploit the natural resources of its continental shelf. Falling within the scope of exclusivity offered by these sovereign rights is that acts relating to the 'acquisition and retention of knowledge about the seabed and subsoil' can only be undertaken after the geographical extent of a coastal State's sovereign rights has been made clear.[1017] Through unilateral seismic work by Turkey, which was intended to provide information on the disputed seabed area as to its mineral resource potential, Greece's rights had been irreparably prejudiced, leading to a loss of its exclusive knowledge of the continental shelf in its role as a coastal State.[1018]

1011 Ibid. Order 4–5 [2].
1012 Ibid. Greece's Oral Pleadings 108–109.
1013 Ibid. Order 4–5 [2].
1014 Ibid. Greece's Oral Pleadings 129.
1015 Ibid. 141.
1016 Ibid. Order 4–5 [2].
1017 Ibid. Greece's Oral Pleadings 107.
1018 Ibid.

A vital element in Greece establishing the perceived nexus between seismic work and its sovereign rights becoming threatened with irreparability was that it is an inherent prerogative of the coastal State to shape its energy policy as it sees fit. This is because a close-knit relation exists between the information collected concerning a continental shelf area, illuminating the actual quantities of mineral resources contained therein, and the ultimate formulation of a State's energy policy. Greece's formulation thereof had, however, been predetermined for it, because of Turkey's unilateral acts in the following ways: first, it was no longer able to decide on whether any information on the continental shelf area should have been made public; second, it was unable to select the specific areas of the continental shelf that would be opened for exploration; third, it could not decide on who could gather this information by being awarded a concession to that end; fourth, it was unable to freely decide on the appropriate time as to when information on the continental shelf area was to be obtained and revealed; and, fifth, the State that has not collected a particular piece of information on the seabed would be put in a visibly worse bargaining position when dealing with members of the petroleum industry. A parallel can be drawn with the general secrecy that is employed by a concessionaire holding a licence, which is often a foreign company. It will only share the information on the amount of mineral resources of a commercially viable nature being contained in a continental shelf area with the State that has licensed the activity.

A central argument by Greece was that consequential to a piece of information being collected by the other claimant State is the loss of control over to what use it will be put, whereby the information will take on a life of its own once it is out in the open, one that cannot be controlled or influenced by a coastal State that has not obtained that piece of information itself. A metaphor used by Greece in the phase of the oral pleadings perfectly captured the essence of this argument: information is like a genie, which, once it leaves the confines of its bottle, cannot be put back whatever one's intent.[1019] Once a piece of information has been collected, its subsequent use is placed at the mercy of the other State, which is in a position to use the information to its advantage by withholding relevant data if it so pleases, also to the detriment of the other coastal State. If the Turkish information would show that the area of continental shelf contains no or only marginal amounts of mineral resources in situ, thereby being of no commercial interest, petroleum companies would have no incentive to respond to a new tender issued by Greece for exploring the same continental shelf area; to open such a tender in

[1019] Ibid. 79, 108.

this situation would appear very similar to proverbially selling 'old wine in new bottles'. A loss of revenue will result for the State that has not licensed the petroleum industry to undertake such work.

Due to their comparable characteristics,[1020] unilaterally authorised scientific research, similar to seismic work, would result in irreparable prejudice, and hence provide sufficient reason for the ICJ to issue measures of interim protection, according to Greece. This similarity is brought about by the fact that scientific research and seismic work are undertaken with a comparable aim: that is, collecting information whereby a State's knowledge of the continental shelf is enhanced. Greece's further narrowing of the types of unilateral activity falling under the jurisdiction of the coastal State that could be lawfully undertaken seemed to have been partly instigated by Turkey's argument that the *Sismik I* was lawfully researching the continental shelf, being actually licensed to that purpose. However, Greece pointed out that the distinction made by Turkey between scientific research and seismic work had no bearing on the Greek request for interim protection: both activities infringe on the 'exclusivity of knowledge' that a coastal State has over its continental shelf.[1021]

Interim measures of protection could, in the view of Greece, even be indicated when there is an isolated danger of a dispute becoming aggravated or extended; this is without there being a possibility of rights becoming irreparably prejudiced. More specifically, Greece argued that it lay within the Court's discretion to offer interim measures of protection, on the basis of the 'general consideration' of seeking to forestall 'any step' being taken by a State that leads to aggravating or extending a dispute.[1022] To support this argument, Greece built on a finding of the PCIJ in the *Electricity Company of Sofia and Bulgaria* case of 1939, where a principle of international law requiring States not to take steps of any kind so as to aggravate or extend a dispute was recognised to exist.[1023]

According to Greece, inherent in the word 'prejudice' are two aspects: first, avoiding causing irreparable damage to a State's rights; and, second, not aggravating or extending a dispute.[1024] A further justification for considering both of these aspects to be included within the notion of 'prejudice' is that they are both geared towards the common aim of not prejudicing the future decision of an international court or tribunal.[1025] Therefore, there must be

1020 Ibid. 109.
1021 Ibid. 108.
1022 Ibid. 100.
1023 *Electricity Company of Sofia and Bulgaria* (n. 434) 199.
1024 *Aegean Sea Continental Shelf* (Interim Measures) (n. 41) Greece's Oral Pleadings 100–101.
1025 Ibid.

an inherent authority for the Court to prevent parties to a dispute from taking any steps which have the effect of either prejudicing, aggravating, or extending the dispute before it has handed down a ruling on the merits.[1026]

In another contention of Greece, it elaborated on the nexus that exists between undertaking seismic work and the emergence of a situation that compels the other claimant to react. This reaction might conceivably involve the use of force or the threat thereof, thereby setting in motion a spiral of action and reaction between the States concerned, which would ultimately threaten international peace and security.[1027] In view of this linkage, Greece argued, the ICJ, being firmly enshrined in the UN Charter, should seek to avoid such a threat from manifesting.

As to the magnitude of the threat caused by Turkey's exploratory work, Greece, in its oral pleadings before the ICJ, went to great pains to distinguish it from the threat that had emerged in *South-Eastern Greenland*, which was decided by the PCIJ in 1932. Greece rejected that the PCIJ's finding, that acts aimed at seeking to change the legal status of a territory are not irreparable or without legal remedy *ex post facto*, should be applied by analogy to the facts that existed between itself and Turkey.[1028] The reasoning behind this was that the threat that had emerged in *South-Eastern Greenland* between Denmark and Norway was incomparable.[1029] By way of contrast, to allow Turkey to continuously take unilateral actions that are under coastal State jurisdiction in relation to the disputed continental shelf area would give rise to a high level of threat: the dispute would be escalated up to a point where the very high threshold of endangering international peace and security would be exceeded.[1030]

Although choosing not to appear in the proceedings,[1031] Turkey communicated some observations on the dispute to the ICJ. Turkey presented its unilateral actions in a positive light: through conducting seismic work, the Court's task of delimiting the continental shelf boundary had been made easier.[1032] Article 48 of the ICJ Statute prescribes that the ICJ must make arrangements for the collection of evidence that is relevant to giving a final

1026 Ibid. 101.

1027 Chapter 3, Section 3.1.1 above.

1028 *Legal Status of Eastern Greenland (Denmark* v. *Norway)* (Request for the Indication of Interim Measures of Protection) [1933] PCIJ Rep. Series A/B No. 55, 157, 268.

1029 *Aegean Sea Continental Shelf* (Interim Measures) (n. 41) Greece's Oral Pleadings 105.

1030 Ibid.

1031 DHN Johnson, 'The International Court of Justice Declines Jurisdiction Again (the Aegean Sea Continental Shelf Case)' (1976–1977) 7 *AusYIL* 309, 310–311.

1032 *Aegean Sea Continental Shelf* (Interim Measures) (n. 41) Observations of the Government of Turkey on the Request by the Government of Greece for Provisional Measures of Protection (16 August 1976) 75 [21] (Turkey's Observations).

ruling. Information on the composition of the disputed seabed area would be the kind of evidence referred to in this provision, according to Turkey.

One reason offered by Turkey why the ICJ should not indicate interim measures of protection focused on the fact that the request of Greece sought the enforcement of the very rights it purported to place in dispute in its application brought to the Court.[1033] More specifically, the aspect of the exclusivity of the rights Greece claimed to have, and which were argued to have been irreparably prejudiced by the Turkish actions, would only exist after the final delimitation; but prior thereto, these rights could not be exclusively exercised by Greece in the continental shelf area. Turkey contended that, if in the final ruling the area in question would be considered to be on Greece's own side of the boundary, then any detrimental effects caused to its rights prior to delimitation could be repaired *ex post facto* by financial means.[1034] Further, by referring to itself as the 'relevant coastal State', being the State whose prior consent would be required, Greece actively took steps to anticipate the outcome of the delimitation judgment of the Court.

Critical to the success of the Greek request for interim protection was whether the Turkish actions had irreparably prejudiced a right of Greece, or, more generally, prejudged the outcome of the final decision of the ICJ. In order to determine this, the ICJ considered whether there was an exclusive right for Greece to obtain information on the natural resources contained in the disputed continental shelf area.

The Court began by acknowledging that unilateral exploratory work invariably raised the question of an infringement on a coastal State's sovereign rights over its continental shelf.[1035] It found that whether a particular unilateral act results in a breach of a State's sovereign rights can only be appraised once the Court has decided on the merits and it cannot be decided *ex hypothesi*.[1036] Further, this assessment was intertwined with the maritime area where the seismic work took place being considered to be on Greece's side of the boundary in a final ruling.

The ICJ took issue with the portrayal of Greece as the 'relevant coastal State'.[1037] As long as the area was disputed, no single coastal State had exclusive jurisdiction over the continental shelf area. Therefore, Greece should have deferred referring to itself as being the relevant coastal State until when it

1033 Ibid. 73–74 [19].
1034 Ibid. 73 [18].
1035 Ibid. Order 10–11 [31].
1036 Ibid.
1037 Ibid. 10 [28].

had been established where the boundary lay between the coasts of Greece and Turkey.

Collecting information on the seabed by Turkey would not, according to the ICJ, irrevocably deprive Greece of a right to acquire knowledge of the composition of the continental shelf area.[1038] Two aspects were central to this conclusion: first, the character of the activity – that is, whether it was of a transitory character; and, second, the type of damage that it would engender – that is, whether it would be irreparable. After applying these two aspects to seismic work and scientific research, the Court concluded that the damage incurred by Greece, as a result of such acts being undertaken without its consent, could be remedied by the 'appropriate means' *ex post facto*.[1039] Although it was not clarified what means of reparation could remedy such a breach,[1040] it may be reasonably inferred that the ICJ meant monetary means, which would be able to provide at least some redress in the given situation.

Central to the conclusion of the ICJ that seismic work did not have to be abjured pending delimitation because of the damage it causes not being irreparable was its inherently 'transitory character'. The seismic vessel was traversing 'the high seas', during which only small explosions were set off and sound waves were aimed at the seafloor. The Court observed that Greece of its own accord did not designate the method of prospecting, whereby small explosions echo off the seabed, as carrying the risk of causing physical damage to the seabed, subsoil, or the natural resources of the continental shelf.[1041] Nonetheless, the ICJ considered that these explosions would have had a more minor impact, whereby no risk of causing 'physical damage to the seabed or soil' arose.

After concluding that the damage caused by seismic work could be remedied *ex post facto*, the Court went on to observe that this conclusion could not be applied to the full range of unilateral acts falling under coastal State jurisdiction. Three categories of unilateral activity were identified by the Court through which, when undertaken in relation to a disputed continental shelf area, the threshold of effecting irrevocable and irremediable change was surpassed, and hence would have warranted the indication of interim measures of protection. It concerned the following activities: first, erecting installations on or above the seabed; second, exploiting or appropriating the natural

1038 Ibid. 11 [33].
1039 Ibid.
1040 Ibid.
1041 Ibid. 10 [30].

resources of the area of the continental shelf; and, third, activities causing physical damage to the seabed or subsoil or to any of the natural resources contained therein.[1042]

Given that the unilateral act complained of by Greece did not involve an installation being attached to the seabed, or had not caused irrevocable damage thereto, nor involved the actual taking of resources from within the continental shelf area, the ICJ concluded in its order that no measures of interim protection could be indicated.

In his concurring opinion, Judge Elias challenged two findings of the Court relating to the lawfulness of Turkey conducting unilateral seismic work: first, that this type of activity threatens no irreparable harm to the rights of Greece; and, second, the assumed possibility to redress any harm caused by the seismic work *ex post facto*. He argued that in the majority's finding excessive reliance was placed on the reparability argument. Monetary means can remedy some of the damage done but threatens to obscure another aspect: the intrinsic value of an act and the effects it engenders on the maritime boundary dispute. By elevating the importance of the element of reparability, the lawfulness of a unilateral act falling under a coastal State's jurisdiction is completely measured through the spectre of possible financial reparation *ex post facto*.[1043] It also gives a State carte blanche to act unilaterally, as long as it does not surpasses this threshold of financial reparation, and assuming it is willing to compensate the harm it may have caused. Pursuant to the approach adopted by the ICJ, Judge Elias felt that insufficient attention was paid to the detrimental effects that the Turkish unilateral acts exerted on the maritime boundary dispute as a whole.[1044] Determining the lawfulness of the decision by Turkey to conduct unilateral seismic work after the activity had come to an end, and upon it being clear where the continental shelf boundary lies, neglected the extent to which the dispute between the two States was aggravated and extended as a result.

But the ICJ's decision was not unanimous; Judge ad hoc Stassinopoulos, who was added to the bench by Greece, dissented from the majority ruling that Turkey could not be prohibited from undertaking seismic work pending delimitation. In his view, the ICJ's refusal to indicate interim protection constituted a clean break with its previous rulings.[1045] Here, measures of

[1042] Ibid.

[1043] Ibid. 28, 30 (Separate Opinion of Judge Elias).

[1044] Ibid. 30.

[1045] Ibid. 37 (Dissenting Opinion of Judge Stassinopoulos).

interim protection were indicated whenever the sovereign rights of a State are jeopardised. According to Judge Stassinopoulos, the gathering of information relating to mineral resources by Turkey had caused 'grave and irreparable prejudice' to the exclusive sovereign rights that Greece has over its continental shelf. This was because the exclusivity that a coastal State has over its continental shelf includes the right to know whether any mineral resources are embedded therein, as well as the extent to which these resources are present, and whether they can be commercially exploited. The dispersing of this information publicly would also cause an effect of irreparability, which would create 'an insurmountable obstacle' for Greece to exploit its continental shelf resources in a manner of its own choosing; this was due to Greece's loss of full autonomy in shaping its energy policy.[1046] Further, in exploring the continental shelf area, Turkey had used explosives, thereby irreparably damaging the seabed and the marine environment, which led to an aggravation of the dispute, according to Judge Stassinopoulos.

6.2 *GUINEA-BISSAU* V. *SENEGAL* (PROVISIONAL MEASURES)

In Guinea-Bissau's request for interim protection, a strong connection was assumed to exist between 'acts of sovereignty' undertaken unilaterally by Senegal in their disputed area, and the consequential prejudging of the ICJ's judgment on the merits.[1047] Protests were made by both States against the issuing of concessions allowing for explorations for mineral resources, their activation, as well as fishery activities on a variety of occasions.[1048] During the 1970s and 1980s, Senegal also authorised several drilling platforms to be erected in a disputed area, prompting a protest by Guinea-Bissau after it had learned of this.[1049]

Fishing vessels that were licensed by Guinea-Bissau to fish in the disputed area have been boarded, arrested, and brought to port for prosecution by Senegal. Two negative effects followed from this, according to Guinea-Bissau: first, taking these enforcement measures were at the detriment of maintaining the integrity of the disputed area pending a final settlement; and, second, they prejudiced the delimitation that the Court had been called upon to effect.

[1046] Ibid.

[1047] *Guinea-Bissau* v. *Senegal* (Provisional Measures) (n. 11) 67–68 [15].

[1048] Ibid.

[1049] Ibid. Annex to the Application Instituting Proceedings by the Government of the Republic of Guinea-Bissau (23 August 1989) 21–22 [25].

According to Senegal, the terms of a 1960 boundary agreement clearly brought the area in dispute under its exclusive jurisdiction. This entitled Senegal to take enforcement measures against fishing vessels licensed only by Guinea-Bissau and that were operating in contravention of Senegal's proclaimed laws and regulations.[1050]

Two incidents motivated Guinea-Bissau to request interim protection from the ICJ. On 9 October 1989, a Japanese vessel (*Hoyo Maru No. 8*), fishing in the disputed area, under a licence from Guinea-Bissau, was boarded and taken into port for prosecution. After having been processed, the vessel was found to have acted in breach of the fisheries laws and regulations of Senegal – it was released upon the payment of 90 million African Communauté Financière Africaine (CFA) francs.[1051] A second incident involved a Chinese vessel (*Yan Yu 625*), having received a licence from Guinea-Bissau, that was boarded on 9 November 1989 by Senegal for fisheries offences that had been committed within the disputed EEZ area. Thereafter, legal proceedings were instituted by Senegal and the vessel was released once a fee of 50 million CFA francs was deposited.[1052] Upon concluding the stage of the oral pleadings before the ICJ, two more fishing vessels licensed by Guinea-Bissau were arrested by Senegal for fishing in their disputed area.[1053] Conversely, on four occasions Guinea-Bissau had arrested fishing vessels flying the Senegalese flag for similar offences,[1054] which were subsequently escorted to port for further processing. The arrested fishermen testified to the effect that they were actively encouraged by the Senegalese government to fish in the disputed EEZ area.[1055] Senegal giving this encouragement may have been motivated by an attempt to fortify its EEZ claim.[1056]

The ICJ concluded that the measures sought by Guinea-Bissau, with the aim of putting a halt to unilateral acts falling under coastal State jurisdiction carried out by Senegal in their disputed area, could not be indicated as they were related to a subsidiary issue.[1057] In its application, Guinea-Bissau made no mention of the fact that the ICJ was being requested to pass judgment on what the rights and obligations of the States concerned were in the disputed

1050 Ibid. 20–21 [24].
1051 Ibid. Order 67–68 [15].
1052 Ibid.
1053 Ibid. 68 [17].
1054 Ibid. [18].
1055 Ibid.
1056 Chapter 2, Section 2.3.6 above.
1057 *Guinea-Bissau* v. *Senegal* (Provisional Measures) (n. 11) 69–70 [25].

maritime area; rather, the validity of the 1989 Arbitral Award had been placed at the heart of the dispute.[1058]

In his separate opinion, Judge Evensen considered that, because Guinea-Bissau and Senegal had both signed and ratified the LOSC,[1059] some inspiration could already be drawn from its provisions that were tailored to apply to disputed EEZ areas. It is particularly Article 74(1)(3) LOSC that contained some informative value with regard to whether the continuation of Senegal's law enforcement, which was argued by Guinea-Bissau to have upset the integrity of the disputed maritime area, was lawful. According to Judge Evensen, their relevance lies in that these two provisions formulated some 'guidelines' as to how coastal States needed to act in connection with their disputed EEZ area.[1060] He considered paragraphs 1 and 3 of Article 74 LOSC to be applications of the same principle of international law: that is, coastal States should seek to conclude cooperative agreements in relation to fishing activities in a disputed EEZ area, to which end the parties to the dispute could have been called upon by the ICJ to make active attempts. On the question of whether interim measures could be indicated, Judge Evensen agreed with the majority: Guinea-Bissau's request aimed at ensuring that the disputed maritime area would remain intact *pendente litis* was cast in terms that went clearly beyond the parameters of the subject matter in dispute.[1061]

In his dissenting opinion, Judge ad hoc Thierry argued that interim protection should have been indicated for a dual purpose. First, the States concerned should have been encouraged to enter into negotiations. And, second, limitations had to be put on the range of unilateral acts falling under coastal State jurisdiction that could be undertaken in relation to the disputed area, in order to prevent new incidents whereby a serious aggravation of their dispute would invariably occur and that 'neighbourly relations' between Guinea-Bissau and Senegal would be jeopardised as a result.[1062] Although international peace and security would not be endangered through unilateral acts, that are under coastal State jurisdiction, being undertaken in the disputed EEZ area,[1063] a particular cause of concern for Judge Thierry was the fact that, because of taking law enforcement measures, a fairly serious conflict had already arisen between the States concerned. By then, a clear pattern had emerged in the

[1058] Ibid. 70 [26].
[1059] Ibid. 72–73 (Separate Opinion of Judge Evensen).
[1060] Ibid. 73.
[1061] Ibid.
[1062] Ibid.
[1063] Ibid. 81 (Dissenting Opinion of Judge Thierry).

dispute between Guinea-Bissau and Senegal: after one of the States concerned enforced its rights against the other, a conflict had arisen between them. If law enforcement was to continue in the disputed area, resulting in the other claimant's claimed rights being infringed, this would invariably elicit a retaliatory response from the other claimant, leading to their dispute being aggravated incrementally. Acts, in the view of Judge Thierry, exceeding the threshold of irreparable damage being caused to a State's rights were the boarding, arresting of, and taking the vessels licensed by Guinea-Bissau to a foreign port. Hence, the indication of interim protection by the ICJ would have been warranted to avoid the risk of irreparability materialising.

Judge Thierry introduced a theory in which the size of a coastal State and the subsequent importance of offshore natural resources to that State interact with when a danger of causing irreparability to rights can be assumed to exist. His theory ran as follows: the precise importance of natural resources in disputed areas, which are of limited availability, is intertwined with the size of the coastal State concerned. This importance increases if it concerns a small State, and reduces gradually the larger the State is in terms of its size, wealth, and power. Depriving small States of access to the natural resources contained in their disputed maritime area, being closely connected to their interests, means that the threshold of a State's sovereign rights having been irreparably prejudiced is more easily surpassed. After applying this theory to the case at hand, Judge Thierry concluded that Guinea-Bissau's rights and interests as a small State would have been irreparably damaged if actions associated with natural resources were undertaken unilaterally by Senegal in the disputed area.[1064]

However, Judge Thierry agreed that the request of Guinea-Bissau, seeking a comprehensive prohibition on unilateral actions that are under coastal State jurisdiction pending settlement, was too broadly formulated, being particularly excessive in view of the length of time that a maritime boundary dispute often persists.[1065] However, this posed no insurmountable obstacle to the fact that interim measures of protection should have been indicated which prohibited Guinea-Bissau and Senegal from taking certain unilateral acts to avoid the dispute from aggravating any further and prejudicing its final settlement.[1066]

1064 Ibid. 82.
1065 Ibid. 84.
1066 Ibid.

6.3 *GUYANA V. SURINAME*

An incident involving an oil rig that was being operated by a company incorporated in a third State, and which was only licensed by Guyana to conduct exploratory drilling in a disputed EEZ and continental shelf area, brought the dispute between Guyana and Suriname to a new phase: on 24 February 2004, Guyana initiated ad hoc proceedings under Annex VII LOSC.[1067]

After the operator of the rig had been given an explicit warning by Suriname's navy officers to leave the disputed area or to suffer unspecified consequences,[1068] Suriname succeeded in its aim of removing the oil rig from the disputed area. Shortly thereafter, negotiations began on reaching a negotiated settlement, which took place over more than three years, before their boundary dispute was submitted to arbitral proceedings.[1069]

At the centre of their dispute was the issue of where the maritime boundary for the territorial sea, the EEZ, and the continental shelf should lie.[1070] Hence, Guyana's submission that Suriname had breached both obligations under Articles 74(3) and 83(3) LOSC was considered to be a subsidiary issue by the Tribunal; and the same applied to Suriname's own submissions on this point. As a result, the Tribunal's findings as to whether exploratory drilling in a disputed maritime area, and Suriname's way of responding thereto, were lawful from the perspective of international law formed a relatively small part of the award. However, the reasoning of the Tribunal offers some indication as to what is required of States pending the delimitation of their disputed EEZ and continental shelf areas.

The novelty of the award in *Guyana* v. *Suriname* lies in the fact that an international court or tribunal decided, for the first time, on the meaning and effect of Articles 74(3) and 83(3) LOSC. The Tribunal had been requested by the parties to the dispute to interpret two aspects related to paragraph 3. First, how paragraph 3 has to be understood in its entirety, as well as to define how the different components of its language interact. Second, the Tribunal had been called upon to pronounce on the contents and meaning of each of the two obligations in paragraph 3, as both parties to the dispute argued that they had been breached.

But to first set the scene, the incident involving the CGX oil rig was preceded by a history in which both Guyana and Suriname unilaterally licensed concessionaires and authorised seismic work to search for mineral

1067 *Guyana* v. *Suriname* (n. 7) 37 [156].
1068 Ibid. 121 [433].
1069 Fietta (n. 153) 120.
1070 *Guyana* v. *Suriname* (n. 7) 114 [410].

resources in their disputed area. This history is important as it informed the outcome of certain aspects of the final decision of the Tribunal, being especially visible in relation to whether Articles 74(3) and 83(3) LOSC had been breached. Since colonial times, the petroleum industry has been showing an interest in exploring the disputed area.[1071] In 1958, British Guiana (now Guyana) authorised California Oil Company to operate on the western side of a provisional equidistance boundary.[1072] In 1965, British Guiana licensed Guyana Shell limited. It subsequently activated this licence, enabling the petroleum company to start with exploratory work for mineral resources in the disputed area.[1073] Both this exploration work and the separate act of granting these concessions prompted a protest from the Netherlands at the time. After Guyana and Suriname became independent States, petroleum companies showed an unabated interest in obtaining concessions located in the disputed continental shelf area. At the time, both sides accepted some of these requests for obtaining exploratory rights.[1074]

Guyana continued the licensing practice of the United Kingdom by using the boundary which was 'equidistant' from the coasts of Guyana and Suriname.[1075] In 1998, CGX conducted a seismic survey after obtaining two concessions from Guyana.[1076] Because the vessel had to tow the instruments required for prospecting, thereby significantly increasing its length, it was forced to turn on the other side of the putative equidistance boundary in order to be able to prospect the entirety of the area covered by the awarded concessions. During these crossings into the 'Surinamese side' of the N34E line, the instruments aboard this vessel were seemingly not switched off, whereby information could be obtained with regard to mineral resources located on the eastern (Surinamese) side of the N34E line. If the survey vessel licensed by Guyana had to move beyond this line, it approached the Surinamese Harbour Master for permission, which, on every occasion, was granted without protest.[1077] Guyana argued that Suriname's silence was part of a broader and consistent pattern: during the second half of the twentieth century, Suriname had been generally inactive when it came to undertaking acts in relation to mineral resources on its own side of the N34E line, let alone by crossing it.[1078] Combining the law

1071 Ibid. Guyana's Memorial 23 [3.25].
1072 Ibid.
1073 Ibid. 32 [3.44].
1074 Ibid.
1075 Ibid. 48–49 [4.25]–[4.26] [4.29]–[4.30] [4.32] [4.38]–[4.39] [4.41].
1076 Ibid. 57–58 [4.41].
1077 Ibid. 63, 129 [5.2] [10.13].
1078 Ibid. 55 [4.36]–[4.37].

enforcement measures taken concerning fisheries[1079] with the actions it took in relation to mineral resources, Guyana claimed that there was overwhelming evidence of Suriname having acquiesced in the equidistance boundary.

Suriname claimed that its observance of this de facto boundary solely emanated from Guyana's imagination.[1080] On the contrary, it undertook several actions in connection with mineral resources, consisting of auctioning concessions, entertaining applications from the petroleum industry, and awarding concessions that were wholly or partly located in the disputed area, but which extended beyond the N34E line.[1081] Over time, however, the exact extent of the overlaps created by the awarded concessions varied, as the areas included under these concessions did not remain static, with some of them being modified, (partially) relinquished, or abandoned. In substantiating this claim, Suriname observed that both parties to the dispute started to open tracts located in their disputed area for mineral resource exploration around the same time.[1082] A map introduced by Suriname showed that, in the period from 1965 to 2000, it had conducted exploratory work beyond the N34E line on a number of occasions.[1083] In fact, this practice dated back to the 1950s, when Suriname gave its first concession.[1084] The reach of the concessions that were awarded by Guyana and Suriname continued to overlap ever since. After Suriname authorised Gulf to undertake exploratory work on the Guyanese side of an equidistance boundary,[1085] Guyana protested. According to Suriname, the licence against which Guyana protested was no longer valid, and would not be renewed. In a further example, Suriname International Petroleum Exploration Ltd (IPEL) wanted to start exploratory work in an area that was on the western side of the equidistance boundary, which likewise prompted a protest from Guyana; Suriname denied, however, that there was a concession agreement with IPEL.

On the whole, some differences are visible when the levels of activity of the two States in respect of their disputed area are compared. Suriname was less active on two fronts: first, in protesting against Guyana's unilateral activities, failing to do so consistently; and, second, it undertook less actual work of its own, pursuant to concessions that it had awarded to the petroleum industry,

1079 Ibid. 59–61 [4.44]–[4.49].
1080 Ibid. Suriname's Counter-Memorial 64 [5.4].
1081 Ibid. 67 [5.9].
1082 Ibid. 64.
1083 Ibid.
1084 Ibid. 65.
1085 Ibid. Award 34–35 [141].

than Guyana had done.[1086] The fact that Suriname exhibited more restraint was interpreted by Guyana as adding credence to its contention that the reason for Suriname showing restraint was that it recognised the validity of a de facto boundary. Suriname contended that its restraint was born out of its doing its utmost to act in accordance with international law.[1087] By that token, Guyana had breached international law by failing to be similarly restrained, through authorising unilateral drilling in their disputed area. In contesting that it had acquiesced in Guyana's claim, Suriname pointed out that the only expectation created by it was that unilateral seismic work could be lawfully undertaken by Guyana in the disputed area, being inherently of a non-harmful nature to a claimant's position and rights. However, no pattern of acceptance had been developed with respect to exploratory drilling,[1088] carrying with it a host of effects placing it in the prohibited category of unilateral activity, in the view of Suriname.

6.3.1 *Guyana's Authorisation to Allow Unilateral Drilling*

Suriname began its argumentation by emphasising that the Tribunal could only consider violations of Articles 74(3) and 83(3) LOSC that had taken place after 8 August 1998, as alleged by both claimants; this was the moment when the LOSC had entered into force for both States.[1089] It framed the gist of the obligation not to hamper or jeopardise as follows: claimants must exercise some measure of restraint in relation to their disputed EEZ/continental shelf area.[1090] In circumscribing the required restraint, Suriname drew the line at whether a unilateral act would threaten the other State's position or rights with irrevocable prejudice, and whereby reaching a delimitation agreement was made more difficult. Acts meeting this threshold, and thus had to be abjured, were the awarding and activation of drilling concessions and actual drilling.[1091]

Suriname observed that the two obligations of Articles 74(3) and 83(3) LOSC not only possess different legal characteristics, which merited their separate treatment, but also that the standards to assume a breach thereof likewise vary.[1092] Because of its more concrete nature, only the obligation not to hamper or jeopardise was suitable for full judicial application in that the Tribunal would be able to exchange the subjective views of the parties to the

1086 Ibid. Suriname's Rejoinder 84 [3.128].
1087 Ibid. Suriname's Counter-Memorial 88–89.
1088 Ibid. Suriname's Rejoinder 129 [4.18].
1089 Ibid. 48 [2.117].
1090 Ibid.
1091 Ibid. Suriname's Counter-Memorial 88–89.
1092 Ibid. Suriname's Rejoinder 48 [2.117].

dispute for an objective one as to whether a unilateral activity would hamper or jeopardise delimitation.[1093] In light of the obligation to seek provisional arrangements not laying down an obligation of result, the weight of the assessment as to whether this obligation had been breached is transferred to the States concerned in that deference must largely be given to their held positions, according to Suriname.[1094] As a corollary to its weak character,[1095] all that the Tribunal could decide upon was whether negotiations on such arrangements had been conducted in a meaningful way.

As aforementioned, the types of activities falling under the obligation not to hamper or jeopardise in Articles 74(3) and 83(3) LOSC were circumscribed by Suriname as those acts having the effect of violating or prejudicing the other State's rights or position. Acknowledging that a wide range of unilateral acts falling under coastal State jurisdiction could potentially generate such an effect, Suriname went on to add qualifications as to when acts would be prohibited by the obligation not to hamper or jeopardise, indicating that the prospect of delimitation must be 'radically affected' through them being undertaken unilaterally.[1096]

On the matter of converting a disputed area into a 'no-activity zone', Suriname observed that ensuring the strict observance thereof would prove nigh impossible.[1097] Rather, a dichotomy was made between 'permissible' and 'impermissible' unilateral acts, at the heart of which lies the notion of the status quo, against which the lawfulness of an act should be evaluated for the change that it would engender thereto.[1098]

Suriname sought to demonstrate that the current state of international law concerning seismic work is thus that it may be lawfully undertaken; however, drilling, exerting more detrimental effects, is placed in the category of activities falling under coastal State jurisdiction that cannot proceed unilaterally in a disputed area. Seismic work was observed to be a normal phenomenon within disputed areas; this was confirmed by the fact that coastal States frequently undertake seismic work themselves, or will license the petroleum industry to engage therein.[1099] The 'harmlessness' of both seismic work and licensing was, according to Suriname, supported in international case law.[1100] Following the

1093 Ibid.
1094 Ibid. 149 [5.11].
1095 Ibid. 48 [2.117].
1096 Ibid. 127 [4.14].
1097 Ibid. Suriname's Counter-Memorial 117 [7.42].
1098 Chapter 3, Section 3.8 above.
1099 Ibid. Suriname's Counter-Memorial 88.
1100 Ibid. 117–118 [7.43]–[7.44].

ICJ's decision in the *Aegean Sea Continental Shelf* (Interim Measures) case, where it recognised the transitory nature of seismic work, Suriname argued that such acts do not risk prejudicing the rights of the other coastal State.[1101] It also stated in broad terms that, through taking unilateral actions of a transitory nature, no 'new' rights are created for the acting State under international law.

Based on the same decision of the ICJ,[1102] Suriname concluded that drilling and paving the way for such an activity to begin by awarding a concession could not be considered transitory in nature, as a claimant's rights would be radically affected, and thus had to be fully eschewed pending delimitation.[1103] Two further considerations that demonstrated the unlawfulness thereof were: first, because of drilling, serious difficulties would arise in negotiating a final boundary agreement or, alternatively, a provisional arrangement; and, second, the maritime boundary dispute between Guyana and Suriname would be aggravated as a consequence.[1104]

Suriname argued that the guiding motivation for Guyana to start drilling was that it sought to present Suriname with a fait accompli – the modalities of which significantly benefited Guyana, and through which it sought to acquire a permanent right. Through occupying the seabed, by moving an oil rig into position to start drilling into the continental shelf, Guyana would gain privileged information as to the oil-bearing strata contained therein; this information would be exclusively available to the petroleum company, and therewith (often) to the licensing State.[1105] Suriname construed this as an active attempt to bring about a radical change to the status quo, in that it was aimed at creating a knowledge gap with Suriname, and beyond that Guyana sought 'to prejudice the outcome of a final settlement' through the drilling.[1106] Through drilling, 'extensive environmental damage' would be caused to the resources of the seabed and the subsoil thereof – for example, because a drilling rig must physically lock onto the seafloor in order to be able to start work, damage of a nature was caused that could not be appropriately compensated either in fact or in law *ex post facto*.[1107] Collecting information on the geography of the disputed continental shelf area likewise impedes the inherent autonomy of the coastal State to freely shape its energy policy, whose formulation is entwined with what is known by that State on the composition of the continental shelf

1101 Ibid.
1102 Ibid. Suriname's Rejoinder 128 [4.15].
1103 Ibid. 127, 148 [4.14] [5.7].
1104 Ibid. 128 [4.16].
1105 Ibid.
1106 Ibid. [4.15]–[4.16].
1107 Ibid. [4.16].

area and the extent of in situ mineral resources. Another possible effect is that unilateral drilling might lead to the acting State acquiring certain rights, whereby the other State may be 'bound to respect the long-term rights of the concession holder with respect to the area'.[1108] Along these lines, in implementing the decision of the ICJ in *North Sea Continental Shelf*, Denmark and Germany agreed to adjust the continental shelf boundary, to ensure that Danish concessionaires could continue operating on the continental shelf of Denmark.[1109] And, lastly, Suriname contended that natural resources are inevitably appropriated when an exploratory well is drilled in a disputed continental shelf area, causing irreparable damage to the other State's rights.

Guyana strongly disputed Suriname's contention that the act of drilling would 'threaten it with imminent injury of an irreparable nature'. In fact, according to Guyana's contention, modelling its argument on the ICJ's ruling in the *Aegean Sea Continental Shelf* (Interim Measures) case, drilling within the disputed area was within the parameters set by international law;[1110] it lacked the overall measure of permanency that was required in order to be placed in the category of prohibited unilateral activity. It appraised the aspect of permanency by looking exclusively at how long (i.e. in terms of time) the activity would last in the disputed area. In this light, Guyana claimed that there are no discernible differences between vessels engaged in drilling or seismic work. Their similarity lies in that in conducting a seismic survey, or when a well is drilled, the vessels concerned will only be in the disputed area for a short time in order to perform this work to then promptly leave.[1111] Another contention of Guyana was that no permanent damage was caused to the seabed or subsoil by the drilling rig because of its modus operandi,[1112] using only one leg to attach itself to the seabed.[1113]

Now, to turn to the Tribunal's findings concerning Guyana's authorisation of drilling in light of the standards laid down under paragraph 3 of Articles 74 and 83 LOSC, with both States alleging breaches of this paragraph. After comparing the thrusts of the two obligations contained therein, the Tribunal concluded that a certain tension is built into the provision; while it seeks to avoid certain actions from occurring, at the same time, some room must remain for conducting activities which are placed under coastal State jurisdiction in a disputed maritime area unilaterally. Further complicating matters is

1108 Ibid.
1109 Oxman (n. 833) 292.
1110 *Guyana* v. *Suriname*, Guyana's Reply 143 [8.14].
1111 Ibid.
1112 Ibid.
1113 Ibid. 144 [8.18].

that there is also the aspect of the related promotion of activities within a disputed EEZ or continental shelf area, by exhorting States to seek provisional arrangements, and how this obligation interacts with the obligation not to hamper or jeopardise. Given that these obligations are contained within the same treaty provision, the Tribunal needed to somehow unite their respective aims in its decision.

Mutual accusations were made by the parties to the dispute that the other State never exhibited a genuine intention to agree on provisional arrangements pursuant to Articles 74(3) and 83(3) LOSC; that is, either before or after the occurrence of the incident with the oil rig.[1114] Behaviour identified by Suriname as breaching this obligation to seek provisional arrangements were the recurrent demands of Guyana that the CGX oil rig should be allowed to resume drilling in their disputed area.[1115] A breach of the same obligation resulted from Guyana repeatedly trying to persuade Suriname to recognise the lawfulness of the concessions it had already granted in the area.[1116]

The Tribunal stated that, if the circumstances between the claimants so allow, provisional arrangements enabling the actual development of the disputed area should be sought by the States concerned.[1117] There were three principal aspects underlying this emphasis: (1) previous case law, in which a particular value was attached to States establishing means of cooperation; (2) the emphasis being placed by the preamble of the LOSC on the effective and equal distribution of natural resources amongst States; and (3) State practice, which was increasingly found to reflect this preference, but which the Tribunal refrained from actually analysing. In gauging whether the parties to the dispute had breached the obligation to seek provisional arrangements, the Tribunal relied heavily on a finding by the ICJ in its judgment in *North Sea Continental Shelf* where it considered the meaning of negotiating in good faith.[1118] Here the ICJ concluded that negotiations, irrespective of being geared towards either delimiting a disputed area or to conclude provisional arrangements, need to take place with an actual view to successfully arriving at an agreement;[1119] this needs to be supplemented by a genuine willingness to compromise and revise or moderate a previously held position by the States concerned.[1120] A key component to this obligation, as is borne out by the case

1114 Ibid. 153 [10.1]; Award 133–137 [471]–[478].
1115 Ibid. 133 [471].
1116 Ibid.
1117 Ibid. 130 [460].
1118 Ibid. 131 [463].
1119 *North Sea Continental Shelf* (n. 8) 46–47 [85].
1120 Ibid.

law, is that an obligation of result is not implied.[1121] Therefore, a failure to come to a provisional arrangement cannot be considered to be a breach of international law; that is, as long as the attempts had been genuine efforts.

In assessing the behaviour of both Guyana and Suriname in the light of the modalities of the obligation to seek cooperative arrangements, the Tribunal distinguished between two types of behaviour: first, acts that would result in a direct breach of this obligation; and, second, acts which may but would not necessarily result in a breach thereof. Conduct that directly breached the standard of behaviour that is required were: (1) not responding to an invitation from the other State to commence negotiations; (2) failing to send a representative upon having accepted an invitation to negotiate;[1122] and (3) not informing the other claimant of intended drilling in a disputed area prior to commencing therewith.[1123] Informing the other State would also have to go beyond announcing plans to begin drilling in a more obscure local newspaper, as Guyana had done.[1124] Particularly in light of the fact that Guyana had engaged in lengthy preparations, it had ample time and opportunity to properly inform Suriname,[1125] and to make more active attempts to enter into negotiations over the planned drilling in their disputed area.[1126]

Five steps were identified by the Tribunal that Guyana should have taken in the circumstances of the case pursuant to the obligation to seek provisional arrangements in order to have acted in compliance therewith.[1127] First, Suriname should have been given notice, through diplomatic channels, of Guyana's plans to drill in their disputed area. Second, the possibility of joint exploration should have been discussed with Suriname. Third, Suriname should have been given the option of observing the drilling when it took place. Fourth, an offer should have been made for Suriname to share ex ante in the results gathered through drilling. Fifth, Guyana should have offered to divide the financial benefits that would be gained from drilling between itself and Suriname. In light of the aforementioned required steps, Suriname would have acted in compliance with the obligation to seek provisional arrangements contained in Articles 74(3) and 83(3) LOSC if it had inter alia accepted the invitation of Guyana of 2 June 2000 to enter into negotiations to settle their

1121 Ibid. 47–48 [87]; *Railway Traffic between Lithuania and Poland* (Advisory Opinion) [1931] PCIJ Series A/B No. 42, 108, 115.
1122 *Guyana* v. *Suriname* (n. 7) 134 [473].
1123 Ibid. 136 [477].
1124 Ibid.
1125 Ibid.
1126 Ibid.
1127 Ibid.

dispute. By declining this invitation, both obligations under Articles 74(3) and 83(3) LOSC had been breached in the view of the Tribunal.[1128] Following the incident with the rig, both parties to the dispute did then adopt the proper mindset that is contemplated under the obligation to seek provisional arrangements, according to the Tribunal.[1129]

Both parties to the dispute were at one in claiming that the other party had undertaken actions which breached the obligation not to hamper or jeopardise, including the licensing of a concessionaire by Guyana, the drilling undertaken on that basis, and the response of Suriname to the drilling rig. In dealing with these contentions, the Tribunal designed a standard whereby a dichotomy was produced between lawful and unlawful acts in a disputed EEZ/continental shelf area. After reviewing the drafting history of Articles 74(3) and 83(3) LOSC,[1130] the Tribunal concluded that the lawfulness of a category of unilateral activities must be assessed from two perspectives: first, the impact on the marine environment; and, second, the extent of the damage that would be caused to the other State's rights. More specifically, activities falling under the jurisdiction of the coastal State that cannot be authorised unilaterally are those bringing about a permanent change in the rights of the other coastal State, or that permanently damage the marine environment,[1131] concerning which the prior consent of all the claimants involved is necessary, according to the Tribunal.[1132] Mineral resource exploitation forms an illustration of an activity that leads to the marine environment being permanently physically changed as a result thereof.[1133] The licensing of a concessionaire to drill in an area known to be in dispute *simpliciter* provides an insufficient reason for assuming a breach of the obligation not to hamper or jeopardise; however, acting upon such a concession had to be treated differently.[1134]

The Tribunal, in addressing whether exploratory drilling and seismic work fell within the ambit of unlawful activities, observed that there are substantive legal differences between them.[1135] As to how they differ, exploratory drilling caused permanent physical damage to the marine environment, resulting in a 'perceived change to the status quo'.[1136] Seismic work, due to its different

1128 Ibid. 135 [476].
1129 Ibid. 136–137 [478].
1130 Chapter 5, Section 5.3.1 above.
1131 *Guyana* v. *Suriname* (n. 7) 133 [470].
1132 Ibid.
1133 Ibid. 132 [467].
1134 Ibid. 137 [479].
1135 Ibid.
1136 Ibid. 137 [480]–[481].

characteristics, posed no irreversible threat of damage to the marine environment, or to the other State's rights.[1137] This line of argument can be traced back to the ICJ's decision in the *Aegean Sea Continental Shelf* (Interim Measures) case, on which the Tribunal heavily relied in framing its own judgment on the lawfulness of seismic work. Despite this being an interim measures procedure,[1138] the Tribunal applied the standards developed therein by analogy in interpreting the content of Articles 74(3) and 83(3) LOSC. It regarded such a *mutatis mutandis* application to be justified as what was held in this interim measures procedure was fully compatible with the content of paragraph 3, as well as other relevant rules of international law.[1139] This was even though the Tribunal recognised that the threshold to assume a breach of Articles 74(3) and 83(3) LOSC was lower as the standard that would enable an international court or tribunal to accede to a request for interim protection.[1140]

6.3.2 *Suriname's Response to the Rig*

The Tribunal was also confronted with the issue of whether Suriname's response to the oil rig was law enforcement or a threat to use force that was in breach of Article 2(4) UN Charter, the LOSC, and general international law, and thus *mutatis mutandis* of Articles 74(3) and 83(3) LOSC.[1141] Suriname's use of its coastguard vessels, from which the officers involved in the removal of the oil rig had uttered certain language, was argued by Guyana to have breached this assortment of rules of international law. Despite the alleged absence of weaponry with which the vessels were equipped,[1142] the crew working on board the rig felt threatened, believing that non-compliance with the order given by the Surinamese coastguard officers could have been met with a violent reaction.

A central contention by Guyana was that Suriname had refrained from pursuing any peaceful alternatives to settle their dispute over the drilling, including those laid down in Article 279 LOSC, cross-referencing Article 33(1) UN Charter. A response along these lines would have completely removed the need for Suriname to respond to the oil rig through the unlawful use of force.[1143] Guyana interpreted the argument of Suriname, whereby it

1137 Ibid. 132, 137 [467] [479]–[481].
1138 Section 6.6 below.
1139 *Guyana* v. *Suriname* (n. 7) 133 [469].
1140 Ibid.
1141 Ibid. 126, 137 [445] [476].
1142 Ibid. Suriname's Rejoinder 138 [4.52].
1143 Ibid. Guyana's Reply 139, 142 [8.3] [8.12].

sought to argue the lawfulness of its response to the oil rig based on the fact that it operated within its sovereign waters, as follows: 'a territorial dispute *ipso facto* justifies recourse to force, even against peaceful action by a neighbouring State in a disputed area'.[1144] Strongly disputing the claim of Suriname that the act of drilling would 'threaten it with imminent injury of an irreparable nature that required an immediate military response',[1145] Guyana contended that there was a continued obligation for Suriname to use peaceful means, which encompassed an obligation to abstain from the use of forceful measures.[1146]

Guyana argued that in its long history of authorising unilateral actions that are placed under the jurisdiction of a coastal State in the disputed area, also in close vicinity to where the GCX rig was operating, Suriname had never protested. Because of this, the ways in which Suriname could respond to the rig were likewise affected, as it had recognised the general lawfulness of drilling in the disputed area.[1147] In view of Suriname's previous silence, the expectation had been created, according to Guyana, that it would similarly refrain from responding to the drilling on this occasion.

Contrary to Guyana's claim that its territorial integrity had been violated through Suriname's reaction,[1148] Suriname contended that it enjoyed the right to physically remove the rig from a disputed maritime area[1149] and that its response fell within the accepted international legal parameters on law enforcement.[1150] A decisive consideration for Suriname to take enforcement measures against the drilling rig was the fact that through unilateral drilling the status quo which existed between the two States had been fundamentally and irrevocably upset.[1151] It turned the claim that its response to the drilling rig licensed by Guyana resulted in a breach of Articles 74(3) and 83(3) LOSC on its head, blaming Guyana instead. It was Guyana that undertook the act that lay at the root of the conflict that had arisen between the two States, and creating a need for Suriname to respond; everything would have remained calm had Guyana not sent the oil rig to their disputed area. Guyana, by permitting this drilling to take place, and thereby exacerbating their underlying maritime boundary dispute, forced Suriname into a position where it

1144 Ibid. 139 [8.2].
1145 Ibid. 143 [8.14].
1146 Ibid. 141 [8.10].
1147 Ibid. 139–141 [8.5]–[8.6].
1148 Ibid. Guyana's Memorial 1–2 [1.4].
1149 Ibid. Award 72–73 [268].
1150 Ibid. Suriname's Counter-Memorial 109–110 [7.12].
1151 Ibid. Suriname's Rejoinder 128–129, 132 [4.21] [4.32].

needed to formulate a physical response by dispatching some of its coastguard vessels to the area concerned in order to put a stop to this unlawful activity.[1152] A secondary contention by Suriname was that, if its reaction was judged not to be in the nature of law enforcement, it constituted a lawful countermeasure to put a halt to the international wrongful act committed by Guyana, being exploratory drilling in a disputed area.[1153]

In considering Suriname's response, the Tribunal started by recognising that under international law the use of force may be allowed in law enforcement activities: its use must be necessary, unavoidable and proportional. However, the Tribunal found that Suriname's response to the drilling was not a measure of law enforcement.[1154] On the matter of whether Suriname had lawfully resorted to a countermeasure, the Tribunal recognised that countermeasures may be lawfully taken by a State when faced with a breach of a rule of international law; that is, if certain conditions are met.[1155] However, Suriname's response did not meet these conditions: to use force disguised as a countermeasure was not recognised under international law as a means for Suriname to address the alleged breach by Guyana when it authorised the drilling activity.

As to how Suriname's response was related to the obligation not to hamper or jeopardise under Articles 74(3) and 83(3) LOSC, the Tribunal began by stating that its aim is to contribute to disputes being settled peacefully and the cementing of bilateral relations. Suriname's response had the opposite effect, according to the Tribunal: it seriously exacerbated the maritime boundary dispute, leading to a consequential decrease in the chances of successfully reaching a negotiated settlement with Guyana. Alternatively, Suriname could have chosen several other strategies as recognised under Section 2 of Part VX LOSC to challenge Guyana's unilateral act peacefully.[1156] The Tribunal concluded that Suriname's response to the oil rig amounted to a threat to use force,[1157] thereby breaching Article 2(4) UN Charter and general international law,[1158] which made its reaction *mutatis mutandis* inconsistent with Articles 74(3) and 83(3) LOSC.[1159] In arriving at this conclusion, the Tribunal found that it was not to Suriname's advantage that it had issued an ultimatum

[1152] Ibid. 148 [5.7]; Suriname's Counter-Memorial 109–110 [7.12].
[1153] Ibid. Award 124, 126–127 [441] [446].
[1154] Ibid. 126 [445].
[1155] Ibid. 126–127 [446].
[1156] Ibid.
[1157] Ibid. 126 [445].
[1158] Ibid. 126, 135 [445] [476].
[1159] Ibid. 126 [445].

to the individuals on the oil rig, along the lines of that the rig would need to 'leave the area at once, or the consequences will be yours'.[1160]

6.4 GHANA/CÔTE D'IVOIRE

When Ghana and Côte d'Ivoire agreed to submit their maritime boundary dispute to adjudication in December 2014, their forum of choice was a novelty: a Special Chamber of ITLOS. One of the issues the Special Chamber was called upon to address was Côte d'Ivoire's contention that Ghana had committed several breaches of international law, including violations of Article 83(3) LOSC, by undertaking acts unilaterally in relation to mineral resources within the disputed continental shelf area. By opening and creating exploration and exploitation blocks, as well as through authorising exploratory and exploitation work to be undertaken in their disputed area, Côte d'Ivoire argued that international responsibility had been incurred by Ghana as result of it.

6.4.1 *The Interim Measures Phase*

On 27 February 2015, Côte d'Ivoire requested interim protection from the Special Chamber,[1161] arguing that, without it, its rights would become threatened with irreparability and significant harm to the marine environment would ensue.[1162] A central theme in Côte d'Ivoire's contentions was that Ghana's unilateral activity in their disputed area was unlawful. One aspect to this claim was that, as a result, the exclusive nature of the sovereign rights that Côte d'Ivoire enjoys under, inter alia, Articles 2(2), 56(1), and 77(1) LOSC had been infringed upon.[1163] Acts of an economic nature in relation to a disputed continental shelf area had to be fully abstained from prior to delimitation, as they would inevitably jeopardise this aspect of exclusivity, according to Côte d'Ivoire. One logic underlying this position was that, through the inclusion of the obligation to seek provisional arrangements in paragraph 3 of Article 83 LOSC, unilateral conduct within a disputed area would automatically result in a breach thereof.[1164] However, Côte d'Ivoire's argumentation was

1160 Ibid. 121–123 [435]–[436] [438]–[439].

1161 *Ghana/Côte d'Ivoire* (Provisional Measures) (n. 42) Côte d'Ivoire's Request for the Prescription of Provisional Measures Submitted by the Republic of Côte d'Ivoire under Article 190, Paragraph 1, of the United Nations Convention on the Law of the Sea, 27 February 2015 (Request for Provisional Measures).

1162 Ibid. 2 [3].

1163 Ibid. 10–11 [15].

1164 *Ghana/Côte d'Ivoire* (Judgment) (n. 46) Côte d'Ivoire's Counter-Memorial 241–242 [9.56].

not consistent on this point. In the interim measures phase, it suggested that the *travaux préparatoires* suggest that the intention behind the introduction of paragraph 3 of Article 83 LOSC was not to introduce a moratorium.[1165] Of key importance was rather to draw a division, similar to the Tribunal in *Guyana v. Suriname*, between acts surpassing the threshold of hampering or jeopardising, which must be abstained from, and those acts falling under coastal State jurisdiction that could be lawfully undertaken. However, in the remainder of its argumentation Côte d'Ivoire tried to show the opposite: exercising complete restraint by the States concerned in relation to a disputed continental shelf area was dictated by international law.[1166]

Côte d'Ivoire argued that the way in which Ghana treated the disputed maritime area was as if it belonged to it exclusively,[1167] with the result that Côte d'Ivoire would be faced with a fait accompli if Ghana were to be allowed to continue exploring and exploiting the disputed seabed area.[1168] To prevent this, Côte d'Ivoire sought interim measures of protection with a dual effect: first, that Ghana had to abstain from undertaking unilateral acts carrying the risk of prejudicing its claimed rights; and, second, it had to refrain from those unilateral acts having an aggravating effect on their maritime boundary dispute.[1169]

Playing a vital role in Côte d'Ivoire's argumentation was the notion of restraint, which it argued that the LOSC as a whole encourages States to observe in relation to a disputed continental shelf area. Côte d'Ivoire bolstered this argument by invoking Article 83(3) LOSC, which it deemed to reflect the broad intention of the Convention to instil restraint in States, and to preserve the exclusivity of a coastal State's rights.[1170] Activities falling under coastal State jurisdiction that were identified as a breach of Article 83(3) LOSC were the following: concluding contracts with the petroleum industry, approving seismic work, drilling, or exploitation, and undertaking such acts, including placing installations, in the disputed area.[1171] Conducting activities within the framework of MSR, which results in the acquisition of information related to the disputed continental shelf area, made it, according to Côte d'Ivoire, an activity that should be deferred to when there is clarity over the geographical extent of a coastal State's sovereign rights.[1172] In the same vein, Côte d'Ivoire

1165 *Ghana/Côte d'Ivoire* (Provisional Measures) (n. 42) Oral Proceedings (ITLOS/PV.15/C23/1/Corr.1) 16–17.

1166 *Ghana/Côte d'Ivoire* (Judgment) (n. 46) Côte d'Ivoire's Counter-Memorial 237 [9.45].

1167 *Ghana/Côte d'Ivoire* (Provisional Measures) (n. 42) Côte d'Ivoire's Request 8 [9]–[10].

1168 Ibid. Oral Proceedings (ITLOS/PV.15/C23/1/Corr.1) 15–16.

1169 Ibid. Order 152–153 [25].

1170 Ibid. Oral Proceedings (ITLOS/PV.15/C23/1/Corr.1) 16.

1171 Ibid. Côte d'Ivoire's Request 8 [10].

1172 Ibid. 17 [30]–[31].

requested the Special Chamber to order the cessation of all ongoing and future 'exploration and exploitation operations', so that the disputed maritime area would be 'preserved' prior to delimitation.[1173]

Under the umbrella of the collection of information pertaining to mineral resources, several acts were encompassed by a coastal State's sovereign rights, all entailing exclusivity:[1174] knowing the amount of mineral resources present, the place where they are located, and whether these resources are suitable for commercial exploitation. Irreparable prejudice to the rights of Côte d'Ivoire was argued to be caused by Ghana possessing any such information related to mineral resources, when in the final ruling the area in question would be determined by the Special Chamber to be on Côte d'Ivoire's side of the boundary. Two detrimental effects would follow for Côte d'Ivoire if it did not have the same information as Ghana. First, the information gathered by Ghana would deprive Côte d'Ivoire of the possibility to capitalise on information relating to the continental shelf area; and, second, due to Côte d'Ivoire losing control over a piece of information that was already out in the open, its negotiating position would be weakened in talks with Ghana or the petroleum industry.[1175] Therefore, the data previously gathered by Ghana, or would be gathered on future occasions, should not be allowed to be used in a way that was detrimental to Côte d'Ivoire's rights and interests.[1176]

Côte d'Ivoire also highlighted the intensification of work by Ghana in relation to mineral resources within the disputed area, despite having received Côte d'Ivoire's protests, in the light of the requirements of Article 83(3) LOSC. Although this paragraph requires States, in the words of Côte d'Ivoire, to 'negotiate in good faith and to refrain from any unilateral activity likely to jeopardise or hamper the reaching of a final agreement on the delimitation of the boundary',[1177] Ghana started to conclude more concession contracts with the petroleum industry relating to the disputed continental shelf area. These concessions were subsequently activated, paving the way for seismic work, drilling, and exploitation to be undertaken unilaterally, with the result that the obligation not to hamper or jeopardise was being frequently breached.

Underlying much of Ghana's argumentation was that Côte d'Ivoire had acquiesced in Ghana's conduct by not protesting. Silence on the part of Côte d'Ivoire had manifested itself in a variety of different forms, including that its own licensing practice of not crossing the equidistance boundary was mirrored

1173 Ibid. Order 152–153 [25].
1174 Ibid. Côte d'Ivoire's Request 17 [30].
1175 Ibid. 18 [34]–[35].
1176 Ibid. Order 152–153 [25].
1177 Ibid. Côte d'Ivoire's Request 8 [10].

by the practice of Côte d'Ivoire.[1178] Were the Special Chamber to accede to Côte d'Ivoire's request to put a stop to all mineral resource activity in the disputed area, far-reaching financial implications were to follow for Ghana. Aside from Ghana's petroleum industry receiving 'a crippling blow',[1179] Ghana's economy would regress to the lowest point in decades as well.[1180] Investors would inevitably pull out from earlier commitments, which would lead to the abandonment of all development of mineral resources in the near future, and also leaving the equipment already moved into place to deteriorate up to a point where it could no longer properly function.[1181]

In order for the Special Chamber to be able to indicate measures of interim protection, there had to be an 'urgent necessity', which, according to Ghana, was lacking here. Illustrating this lack of urgency was that Ghana was able to progress to the development of mineral resources from the disputed continental shelf area.[1182] The damage complained of by Côte d'Ivoire also lacked the element of irreparability, as such damage could be remedied through the awarding of compensation *ex post facto*.[1183]

Another argument invoked by Ghana against the indication of measures of interim protection by the Special Chamber was Côte d'Ivoire's lack of intention to keep the disputed maritime area in an intact condition. Had the situation been reversed, in that the oil and gas fields were found in 'the territory of Côte d'Ivoire',[1184] the latter would have pursued these activities with the same enthusiasm, so it was argued by Ghana. In light of this, Ghana construed that, in the main, the dispute between the two States was about Côte d'Ivoire feeling entitled to a share of the proceeds derived from the development started lawfully by Ghana.[1185] Considering that their dispute was not divided along the lines of where State A sought to keep the disputed area in pristine condition, whereas State B sought its development,[1186] a parallel could not be drawn with *Guyana* v. *Suriname* or *Aegean Sea Continental Shelf* (Interim Measures). Here, in stark contrast, the State that objected to an act of unilateralism sought not to engage in similar conduct in the disputed area itself until after delimitation.

1178 Ibid. Ghana's Written Statement 128–143 [17]–[37].
1179 Ibid. 150 [48].
1180 Ibid. 150, 152–154 [48] [52]–[57].
1181 Ibid. 151–152 [51]–[52].
1182 Ibid. 169–170 [91]–[93].
1183 Ibid. 170–171 [94] [96].
1184 Ibid. 173 [104].
1185 Ibid. 173–174 [104]–[105].
1186 Ibid. [104].

The Special Chamber delivered its ruling on whether interim measures of protection could be indicated on 15 April 2015. In its considerations, the Chamber made no mention of Article 83(3) LOSC, however, which may be considered rather puzzling, as Côte d'Ivoire relied quite heavily on Article 83(3), and also Ghana payed some lip service to this paragraph. It seemed that the Special Chamber operated with the notion that Article 83(3) LOSC carries no relevance in an interim measures procedure.[1187]

Two requirements needed to be present in order for the Chamber to be able to accede to a request for the indication of measures of interim protection: first, a recognised urgency; and, second, a real and imminent threat of causing irreparable prejudice to rights.[1188] It acknowledged a risk of causing irreversible prejudice to claimed rights being present in this case because of the gathering of information on the continental shelf area unilaterally, and through other unilateral exploration and exploitation activities.[1189] The risk would materialise once the area was considered to be, in full or in part, under the exclusive jurisdiction of Côte d'Ivoire after delimitation.[1190] Importantly, this consideration suggests that the irreparability test can be satisfied even if a unilateral act does not cause physical damage to the marine environment; collecting information, by definition, lacks a physical element in that no permanent damage to the disputed area will be caused.[1191] Somewhat confusingly, in an earlier passage, the Special Chamber tied the chances of the risk of irreparable prejudice emerging to those acts leading to the 'significant and permanent modification of the physical character of the area in dispute'.[1192] The causing of such prejudice could not be repaired through compensation,[1193] as, after a significant and permanent modification of the continental shelf, it would be impossible to restore the shelf to its original physical characteristics.

While recognising the existence of a risk of causing irreparability, its materialisation – and thus whether the required urgency was present – was, according to the Chamber, dependent on two factors: first, the handing down of the final ruling by the Chamber on where the maritime boundary lies; and, second, the Chamber attributing 'rights in all or any part of the disputed

1187 BIICL Report (n. 141) 26.
1188 *Ghana/Côte d'Ivoire* (Provisional Measures) (n. 42) 156 [42].
1189 Ibid. 164 [94]–[96].
1190 Ibid. [94]–[95].
1191 Van Logchem (n. 245) 171.
1192 *Ghana/Côte d'Ivoire* (Provisional Measures) (n. 42) 163 [89].
1193 Ibid. [90].

area' to Côte d'Ivoire.[1194] Consequently, the Chamber saw the need to address this issue to be tied to on whose side of the boundary the area was ultimately going to fall. Therefore, Côte d'Ivoire's request that all of Ghana's activities had to be suspended was deprived of the necessary urgency.

A particular concern for the Special Chamber was the degradation of the equipment used in exploring and exploiting mineral resources that had already been moved into the disputed area. Leaving these infrastructures unused for the duration of the time that the case was being dealt with would risk seriously harming the marine environment.[1195] And, in addition, large financial losses were liable to be suffered by Ghana if it were to be ordered to halt its activities.[1196] Ultimately, it came down to the Chamber weighing the different considerations at stake for Ghana and Côte d'Ivoire. In striking a balance, the Special Chamber felt that the rights of both Ghana and Côte d'Ivoire would be preserved by prohibiting new drilling (which favoured Côte d'Ivoire), but at the same time allowing the previously initiated development of mineral resources to continue (which favoured Ghana).

6.4.2 *The Special Chamber's Decision on the Merits*

During the merits phase, Ghana repeated much of its earlier presented arguments requesting the Chamber to confirm the existence of a de facto maritime boundary.[1197] Because of Côte d'Ivoire's acquiescence, Ghana argued that it had not acted unilaterally within a disputed area.[1198] Despite this emphasis on acquiescence,[1199] Ghana entertained the arguments of Côte d'Ivoire that the activities undertaken by Ghana in relation to the disputed continental shelf area violated the former's sovereign rights and also breached Article 83(3) LOSC. In regard of the latter, it was highly critical of Côte d'Ivoire's reading of this provision as imposing a blanket ban on economic conduct in their disputed area.[1200]

Two considerations underlie Ghana's criticism: first, paragraph 3 of Article 83 LOSC does not lay down an obligation to conclude provisional arrangements; and, second, its negotiating history revealed that a failure to agree thereon would not automatically result in the imposition of a moratorium. Particularly

1194 Ibid. 163–164 [91] [95].
1195 Ibid. 164 [99].
1196 Ibid. [99]–[100].
1197 *Ghana/Côte d'Ivoire* (Judgment) (n. 46) Ghana's Reply 1285, 1441–1442 [1.10] [5.2]–[5.3].
1198 Ibid. 1441 [5.2].
1199 Ibid. 1443 [5.7].
1200 Ibid. 1454–1457 [5.36]–[5.40].

unconvincing, according to Ghana, was that Côte d'Ivoire in bolstering its moratorium argument relied on the award in *Guyana* v. *Suriname*, where, in one of its considerations, the Tribunal stated that activities included within the reach of a provisional arrangement may be undertaken pending delimitation.[1201] Only when isolated from its context can the award in *Guyana* v. *Suriname* support this argument. Contrary to this, the Tribunal underscored, in various other findings, the importance of leaving some room for unilateral economic conduct in relation to a disputed area, and that it went on to draw a distinction between permissible and impermissible unilateral acts.[1202]

In rebutting Côte d'Ivoire's claim that the unwillingness of Ghana to accede to a moratorium breached the spirit it was required to show under Article 83(3) LOSC,[1203] particularly pursuant to the obligation to seek provisional arrangements, Ghana invoked two arguments: first, a moratorium could not be perceived as a provisional arrangement in the sense of Article 83(3); and, second, there is no requirement for a claimant to amend a reasonably held position in the face of the other State's request to abandon it.[1204] In this light, not acceding to the other claimant's demands to suspend lawfully commenced activities could not, in the view of Ghana, be reasonably framed as an infringement of Article 83(3) LOSC.[1205]

Côte d'Ivoire reinforced its argument, previously advanced in the interim measures phase, around the claimed existence of an interim rule in relation to a disputed continental shelf area that obliges the coastal States concerned to refrain from undertaking economic conduct unilaterally – in French, 'les activités économiques unilatérales sont prohibées dans une zone litigieuse'.[1206] The various unilateral acts undertaken by Ghana in relation to the disputed continental shelf area were argued by Côte d'Ivoire to have infringed its sovereign rights, thereby engaging, in addition, Ghana's international responsibility. After drawing a parallel with the sovereignty that a coastal State has in the territorial sea, implying exclusivity, Côte d'Ivoire argued that its sovereign rights over the continental shelf area were underpinned by a similar exclusivity, as is reaffirmed in Articles 77 and 81 LOSC.[1207] A judgment on delimitation by the Chamber must be declaratory of these pre-existing sovereign rights rather than constitutive, according to Côte

1201 *Guyana* v. *Suriname* (n. 7) 131–132 [465]–[466].
1202 *Ghana/Côte d'Ivoire* (Judgment) (n. 46) Ghana's Reply 1455–1456 [5.38].
1203 Ibid. 1458–1459 [5.42].
1204 Ibid. 1459 [5.43].
1205 Ibid.
1206 *Ghana/Côte d'Ivoire* (Judgment) (n. 46) Côte d'Ivoire's Counter-Memorial 237 [9.45].
1207 Ibid. 221–222 [9.4]–[9.6].

d'Ivoire.[1208] To argue that the nature of delimitation is declaratory was irreconcilable with the fact that entitlements and related rights to a continental shelf exist ab initio and ipso facto for the coastal State.[1209]

Being of an all-embracing nature, the sovereign rights of the coastal State over the continental shelf area were being threatened with irreparability through the unilateral acts of Ghana, entailing that all exploration and exploitation activities within the disputed area had to be abstained from pending delimitation.[1210] According to Côte d'Ivoire, the need to draw any distinction between exploratory and exploitation activities, and to gauge the particular effects caused by a category of unilateral activity, would only arise when the issue of quantifying the extent of any resulting damage from Ghana's unilateral acts entered into the picture.[1211]

In its analysis of Article 83 LOSC, Côte d'Ivoire began by pointing out that Ghana's unilateral conduct breached this provision on two counts: first, the obligation underlying Article 83(1) to negotiate in good faith;[1212] and, second, Article 83(3) and its obligations to seek provisional arrangements and not to hamper or jeopardise.

Although acknowledging that the Tribunal in its award in *Guyana v. Suriname* placed seismic work in the category of permissible conduct in disputed areas, Côte d'Ivoire turned to State practice to prove the contrary position: all economic conduct, including seismic work, in relation to mineral resources had to be postponed until after delimitation.[1213] Two detrimental effects were identified by Côte d'Ivoire that underpinned this position. First, unilateral seismic work is a 'source of serious tension' between the States concerned; and, second, vital information on the in situ resources of the seabed area will be provided and placed at the disposal of that State, offering it considerable advantages in negotiations.[1214]

Côte d'Ivoire went on to claim that Ghana's unwillingness to stop with unilaterally conducting activities, falling under coastal State jurisdiction in the disputed area, after receiving several protests constituted a clean break with previous delimitation cases, where a consistent pattern was revealed:[1215] whenever 'invasive activities' undertaken in a disputed area have been protested

[1208] Ibid. 222 [9.8].
[1209] Ibid. 222–223 [9.9]–[9.10].
[1210] Ibid. 226 [9.18].
[1211] Ibid. 227 [9.20].
[1212] Ibid. 235 [9.40].
[1213] Ibid. 237 [9.46].
[1214] Ibid.
[1215] Ibid. 238–239 [9.47]–[9.48].

against by the other claimant, in the wake of this protest future acts of this type have not been pursued.[1216] In addition, the extent to which Ghana had acted unilaterally, by authorising or undertaking conduct that is under coastal State jurisdiction, within the disputed area was seen as making it markedly more difficult to delimit the maritime boundary,[1217] resulting in a breach of Article 83(3) LOSC.

The Special Chamber did not accept Ghana's claim that a de facto maritime boundary had developed through acquiescence by Côte d'Ivoire.[1218] The implication thereof is that the judgment can be considered through the spectre of what rights and obligations neighbouring States have in relation to a disputed continental shelf area.[1219] But the final judgment of the Special Chamber shines minimal light on the matter, also on how to interpret the obligation not to hamper or jeopardise.[1220] In defining its underlying nature, the Chamber held that there is a good faith component attached to this obligation that transforms it into an obligation of conduct, and which is as follows: the States concerned 'shall make every effort' not to hamper or jeopardise. In considering the submission of Côte d'Ivoire that Ghana's conduct in the disputed maritime area resulted in a breach of Article 83(3) LOSC,[1221] the Special Chamber emphasised that to assume that a breach of the obligation not to hamper or jeopardise existed, the area must be considered as having been in dispute between the States involved.[1222] After ruling that this was the case, the Chamber expressed it had particular difficulty with how Côte d'Ivoire had framed its submission, requesting the Chamber to adjudge that Ghana's unilateral acts were undertaken 'in the Ivorian maritime areas'. In light of the Chamber's earlier consideration that the areas were under the exclusive jurisdiction of Ghana, as they fell on its own side of the boundary, the conduct complained of by Côte d'Ivoire was not undertaken in an area that could be considered as being Ivorian.[1223] Therefore, no breach of Article 83(3) LOSC could have occurred. This finding of the Chamber, and endorsed by Judges Mensah and Paik in their separate opinions,[1224] is

1216 *Ghana/Côte d'Ivoire* (Provisional Measures) (n. 42) Oral Proceedings (ITLOS/PV.15/C23/1/Corr.1) 17–18.

1217 *Ghana/Côte d'Ivoire* (Judgment) (n. 46) Côte d'Ivoire's Counter-Memorial 241–242 [9.56].

1218 Ibid. 40–43 [104]–[105] [113] [116] [124]–[136].

1219 Van Logchem (n. 245) 170–171

1220 *Ghana/Côte d'Ivoire* (Judgment) (n. 46) 167–168 [629]–[630].

1221 Ibid. 162 [606].

1222 Ibid. 158 [588].

1223 Ibid. 185 [1] (Separate Opinion of Judge Ad Hoc Mensah); 178 [1] (Separate Opinion of Judge Paik).

1224 Ibid. Judgment 175–176 [660].

problematic because of the following: whether acts that are under the jurisdiction of the coastal State, when they are undertaken unilaterally by a coastal State within a disputed continental shelf area, breach the obligation not to hamper or jeopardise, need to be seen in the context of that time. And a breach thereof still exists even if, after delimitation, the area is located on that State's own side of the boundary. Admittedly, the phrasing by Côte d'Ivoire's submission that Ghana's unilateral acts occurred in the 'Ivorian maritime area' was unfortunate. However, considering that Côte d'Ivoire's submission was concerned with a larger area than the area up to the equidistance boundary as determined by the Chamber, the Chamber's dismissal of this submission on this ground cannot be completely convincing.

However that may be, the Chamber, in rejecting this submission, had failed, according to Judge Paik, to highlight the importance and positive aspects of the obligation not to hamper or jeopardise, for it being 'a fundamental duty of restraint',[1225] having significant 'weight as a fundamental norm'.[1226] Its practical weight was illustrated by the large number of disputed continental shelf areas that currently remain outstanding. Because the content of the obligation not to hamper or jeopardise remains somewhat unclear, Judge Paik felt that the Chamber had missed an opportunity to clarify its meaning.[1227] He agreed with the Chamber's characterisation of this obligation as being an obligation of conduct.[1228]

Judge Paik, however, questioned the Chamber's finding that Ghana's unilateral acts in the disputed area were lawful from the perspective of this obligation.[1229] Because it is not specified what conduct hampers or jeopardises, a breach thereof must in his view be determined by relying on an alternative set of standards. As the negotiating history demonstrates, the thought underlying the inclusion of this obligation in Article 83(3) LOSC was not the imposition of a moratorium on economic conduct.[1230] Rather, the relevant standard against which to determine the compatibility of unilateral conduct with the obligation not to hamper or jeopardise is the impact it has on reaching a delimitation agreement.[1231] Due to the link established with delimitation, the automatic effect is that a breach of the obligation not to hamper or jeopardise will become fully intertwined with the circumstances at hand.[1232]

1225 Ibid. 179 [3] (Separate Opinion of Judge Paik).
1226 Ibid.
1227 Ibid.
1228 Ibid. 179 [4].
1229 Ibid. 178 [1].
1230 Ibid. 180 [5].
1231 For an earlier version of this argument, see Van Logchem (n. 21) 185–186.
1232 *Ghana/Côte d'Ivoire* (Judgment) (n. 46) 180 [6] (Separate Opinion of Judge Paik).

Borrowing heavily from *Guyana* v. *Suriname*, Judge Paik stated that unilateral acts which are likely to have the result of prejudicing a delimitation are those that the Tribunal identified in its award as having the effect of causing 'a permanent physical change to the marine environment'. However, in light of that less intrusive unilateral conduct, which does not cause permanent physical change, can still have the effect of hampering or jeopardising, it must be seen as one 'relevant factor' amongst 'several'.[1233] Other relevant factors such as 'type, nature, location, and time', which can be combined with the 'manner in which' an act falling under coastal State jurisdiction is conducted unilaterally,[1234] together inform the assessment as to whether such a unilateral act is (un)lawful.[1235]

Judge Paik found that the obligation not to hamper or jeopardise had been breached in a second way by Ghana by its stepping up the frequency with which it undertook unilateral conduct in the disputed area; this was despite its having received a protest from Côte d'Ivoire. Here Judge Paik acknowledged that Ghana's unilateral acts having occurred in areas that were considered *ex post facto* to have taken place on its own side of the boundary are not transformed from an unlawful act if it is undertaken prior to delimitation into a lawful act after delimitation.[1236] Considering that Article 83(3) LOSC exerts its influence in the period before delimitation, and to prevent devaluing its importance, the lawfulness of undertaking a unilateral act that is under the jurisdiction of the coastal State within a disputed continental shelf area must be judged on its merits and in the context of the time when it was undertaken.[1237]

6.5 *SOMALIA* V. *KENYA*

After initiating proceedings before the ICJ in 2015, Somalia indicated in its memorial that the motivating factor behind the unilateral submission of the maritime boundary dispute with Kenya to the Court were the concessions that had been unilaterally awarded by Kenya and which encroached on their disputed area.[1238] On the basis of these concessions,[1239] Kenya had begun with the exploitation of both living and non-living resources within the disputed continental shelf area over which Somalia claimed sovereign rights

1233 Ibid. 180 [6]–[7].
1234 Ibid. 181 [10].
1235 Ibid. 180 [7].
1236 Ibid. 183–184 [17].
1237 Ibid.
1238 *Somalia* v. *Kenya* (n. 47) Somalia's Memorial 3 [1.8].
1239 Ibid. 127 [8.1]; Somalia's Application Instituting Proceedings 8 [25].

but 'possibly' also extended into disputed territorial sea areas, thereby breaching the sovereignty it has there.[1240] Somalia claimed that those concessions, whose reach extended beyond the equidistance boundary, were unlawful from the view of international law.[1241]

According to Somalia, up to the twenty-first century, Kenya had respected the equidistance boundary by not extending the reach of its concessions beyond that point.[1242] Thereafter, Kenya changed its position in relation to the disputed continental shelf area and started to offer several blocks to petroleum companies crossing the equidistance boundary line, also authorising exploratory activities there. For instance, in 2014, Kenya authorised seismic surveys within the disputed area and allowed drilling to proceed.[1243] Several tenders for conducting seismic surveys within the disputed area, with a view to issuing future licences, were also unlawfully opened by Kenya after Somalia had initiated proceedings before the ICJ.[1244]

For Somalia, it was a matter of logic to extend the exclusivity that a coastal State has over its natural resources, pursuant to the sovereignty, sovereign rights, and jurisdiction it enjoys over maritime zones under international law, also to disputed maritime areas.[1245] Gathering data from the disputed area in connection with natural resources,[1246] because Somalia has an 'exclusive right of exploration',[1247] thus resulted in State responsibility for an international wrongful act committed by Kenya. Issues of international responsibility would inevitably arise, in the view of Somalia, especially in light of the reasoning of both the ICJ in its decision in *Aegean Sea Continental Shelf* (Interim Measures) and the Chamber's interim measures order in *Ghana/Côte d'Ivoire*. In the latter decision, it was held that gathering information on a disputed continental shelf area through seismic work created a risk of irreparable prejudice. By analogy, these findings were applied by Somalia to the situation at hand, with Kenya similarly gathering information unilaterally. Authorising a petroleum company to conduct a survey or to drill in the disputed area were other examples of wrongful acts that had to cease, according to Somalia.[1248] In the view of Somalia, it was insufficient to put a stop to the

1240 Ibid. Somalia's Memorial 3, 5, 141 [1.8] [1.15] [8.28].
1241 Ibid. 35 [3.20].
1242 Ibid. 35–36 [3.20]–[3.22].
1243 Ibid. Oral Proceedings (CR 2016/13) 33–34, 41.
1244 Ibid. 41.
1245 Ibid. Somalia's Memorial 3, 131–132 [1.8] [8.11].
1246 Ibid. 132 [8.12].
1247 Ibid. 141 [8.28].
1248 Ibid. 141–142 [8.29].

collection of new data by Kenya in their disputed area prior to the ICJ handing down its final ruling. Also, the previously gathered data on parts of the disputed area, which in the final apportionment could be determined by the ICJ to be located on Somalia's side of the boundary, already had to be handed over to it.[1249]

Kenya rejected the claim of having entered the stage of exploiting mineral resources within the disputed area, pointing to its previous exploration efforts having failed to locate commercially interesting quantities of such resources.[1250] Beyond that, Kenya, by building on the decision in the *Aegean Sea Continental Shelf* (Interim Measures) case, claimed that its exploratory work was lawful under international law, having no risk of causing irreparable prejudice because of it being of a transitory nature.[1251]

6.6 THE RELEVANCE OF INTERIM MEASURES PROCEDURES FOR DETERMINING THE RIGHTS AND OBLIGATIONS OF STATES IN DISPUTED AREAS

A sufficient degree of similarity has been assumed to exist between the decisions on interim protection and paragraph 3 of Articles 74 and 83 LOSC,[1252] as this paragraph's content has been regularly defined in deference to this case law.[1253] Along these lines, Suriname in its pleadings in *Suriname* v. *Guyana* applied by analogy the ICJ's finding in *Aegean Sea Continental Shelf* (Interim Measures) that unilateral seismic work does not risk causing irreparability to rights, to conclude that it is fully in compliance with the content of Articles 74(3) and 83(3) LOSC as well.[1254]

At first glance, the *mutatis mutandis* application of standards developed in cases involving interim protection to interpreting whether a breach of paragraph 3 has occurred seems difficult to justify, as they are separate systems which operate according to their own rules. The main rationale underlying the indication of measures of interim protection is as follows: while a dispute is under the consideration of an international court or tribunal, the States

1249 Ibid. 142 [8.30].
1250 Ibid. Oral Proceedings (CR 2016/10) 27–28.
1251 Ibid.
1252 Anderson and Van Logchem (n. 18) 220.
1253 Lagoni (n. 243) 365–366; Kim (n. 287) 59; K Hossain, 'United Nations Convention on the Law of the Sea and Provisional Arrangements Relating to Activities in Disputed Maritime Areas' in L del Castillo (ed.), *Law of the Sea: From Grotius to the International Tribunal for the Law of the Sea: Liber Amicorum Judge Hugo Caminos* (Brill, 2015) 674, 678.
1254 *Guyana* v. *Suriname* (n. 7) Suriname's Rejoinder 128 [4.15].

concerned will be prevented from taking any actions that frustrate the execution of a ruling, devalue a final arbitral or judicial decision, or make the passing of the judgment totally superfluous.[1255] In short, the situation envisaged in Articles 74(3) and 83(3) LOSC is to prevent the overarching aim of reaching a delimitation agreement from being unnecessarily frustrated.[1256]

Two requirements exist in the context of requests for the indication of measures of interim protection, which have a direct application in the context of disputed maritime areas:[1257] first, avoiding the rights of the other State being endangered with irreparability; and, second, States having to refrain from acting in a way that would result in aggravating or extending their dispute. These requirements have some similarity with the negative obligation in Articles 74(3) and 83(3) LOSC, although the language of not hampering or jeopardising is different from the standard wording found in many interim measures orders, with the latter calling upon States to take no steps leading to an aggravation or extension of their dispute.[1258] An explanation for this difference in wording is that the obligation not to hamper or jeopardise and not to aggravate or extend a dispute are included in these respective instruments for different reasons and to achieve and facilitate, to a certain extent, different aims.[1259] The setting against which the general rule not to aggravate or extend a dispute operates is different, in that in the background of a request for interim measures of protection there is an underlying dispute being brought to international adjudication for a final settlement. In the drafting phase of Articles 74(3) and 83(3) LOSC, there were States seeking to replicate the phrase not to 'aggravate' a dispute in a provision providing an interim rule; however, as talks at UNCLOS III progressed, this word was replaced with hampering.[1260]

The similarity between hampering or jeopardising and the indication of measures of interim protection lies in the fact that either is tied to the application of the same principle: States need to exercise restraint to ensure that their dispute is settled. Understood in this sense, although the regime that is applicable to interim protection may be different when compared to Articles 74(3) and 83(3) LOSC, especially on the point of circumscription, underlying them is the common thought of preventing a certain prospect from being

1255 *Aegean Sea Continental Shelf* (Interim Measures) (n. 41) 16 (Separate Opinion of President Jiménez de Aréchaga).
1256 Chapter 5, Section 5.3 above.
1257 Chapter 3, Sections 3.4 and 3.5 above.
1258 Van Logchem (n. 52) 60–62.
1259 Anderson and Van Logchem (n. 18) 207–208.
1260 Platzöder (n. 559) 461 (NG7/39, Chairman NG7).

negatively affected by acts of unilateralism. However, this is probably also where the real similarities end, giving rise to the question of what value does the category of decisions on interim measures of protection have in assessing the rights and obligations of States in disputed maritime areas.

Importantly, the legal tests under Articles 74(3) and 83(3) LOSC and the provisions relating to interim measures are different: the threshold for the latter is significantly more demanding than for the former. Logic dictates that, due to the lower standard included in paragraph 3, a violation of this paragraph *simpliciter* would not give an international court or tribunal, when faced with a request for the indication of interim measures of protection, sufficient reason to allow such a request.

The Tribunal in *Suriname* v. *Guyana* was, for the most part, aware of the fact that interim measures procedures have a special character, designating the power to prescribe interim protection as an extraordinary one.[1261] After juxtaposing the legal regimes that are applicable to interim measures and to 'activities in disputed waters', the Tribunal stated that the regime for indicating 'interim measures is far more circumscribed'.[1262] The relationship between the case law on interim measures and the obligation not to hamper or jeopardise under Articles 74(3) and 83(3) LOSC was couched by the Tribunal in the following terms: despite the fact that the threshold for the indication of interim protection is set significantly higher in the case law,[1263] standards developed therein 'are informative', and have particular prominence in relation to defining the permissibility of unilateral activities that fall under the jurisdiction of a coastal State within a disputed maritime area.[1264] This introduced an *a contrario* reasoning into the Tribunal's award, in that all other acts, falling short of exerting a particular effect, would be permissible without the prior consent of the other coastal State.

It makes perfect sense to argue that activities that have been conducted within disputed maritime areas unilaterally, and whose effects warrant the indication of interim protection, would in the same vein breach the obligations under Articles 74(3) and 83(3) LOSC.[1265] Contrary to what the Tribunal asserted, however, the legal value that cases concerning interim measures have in interpreting paragraph 3 is that they shine some light on what types of activities that are under the jurisdiction of the coastal State are in fact

1261 *Guyana* v. *Suriname* (n. 7) 133 [469].
1262 Ibid.
1263 Beckman (n. 643) 255–256.
1264 Ibid.
1265 Van Logchem (n. 21) 186–191.

prohibited to be authorised or undertaken unilaterally.[1266] Acts causing irreparability a fortiori more easily breach the standard of not hampering or jeopardising as formulated in Articles 74(3) and 83(3) LOSC, but an *a contrario* conclusion that 'what is not forbidden is allowed' cannot be automatically derived from this.

While recognising that a lower standard is appropriate to determine whether the obligation not to hamper or jeopardise had been breached, the standard that the Tribunal used to determine a breach thereof is one that is sufficient for the indication of interim measures of protection. Applying by analogy 'those criteria used by international courts and tribunals in assessing a request for interim measures'[1267] to its own interpretation of paragraph 3 of Articles 74 and 83 LOSC, the Tribunal indicated that the criterion of 'the risk of physical damage to the seabed or subsoil'[1268] marks the dividing line between which are lawful unilateral acts in a disputed maritime area and which are not. By treating these two regimes as being fully compatible with each other, the extent to which the obligation not to hamper or jeopardise diverges from criteria developed in the context of the indication of interim measures of protection was not considered by the Tribunal, blurring the lines between the two in a way that is difficult to reconcile with Articles 74(3) and 83(3) LOSC setting a lower threshold.

6.7 FINANCIAL REPARABILITY: THE DE FACTO PARAMOUNT CRITERION?

International courts and tribunals, whenever they have been faced with issues involving unilateral conduct in disputed maritime areas, have struck a balance between two elements: first, the possibility for certain acts that are under coastal State jurisdiction to be undertaken unilaterally; and, second, not allowing the other coastal State's sovereign rights to be excessively infringed upon. Financial considerations figured heavily in the Judges' minds in the relevant case law when determining to what extent coastal States can act upon claimed rights in disputed maritime areas, giving rise to the suggestion that the key determinant for a unilateral act falling under coastal State jurisdiction being lawful is its financial reparability.

In its decision in the *Aegean Sea Continental Shelf* (Interim Measures) case, the ICJ considered the lawfulness of unilateral acts which are under the

1266 Ibid. 187.
1267 *Guyana* v. *Suriname* (n. 7) 133 [469].
1268 Ibid.

jurisdiction of the coastal State mainly through the lens of compensation, presumably financial, *ex post facto*. A Special Chamber of the ITLOS equally looked at the financial reparability aspect of unilateral acts undertaken by Ghana, and whose lawfulness was being challenged by Côte d'Ivoire because of these falling under coastal State jurisdiction, thus following up the line of thinking that began with the ICJ in its ruling in *Aegean Sea Continental Shelf* (Interim Measures) and that was repeated, to a certain degree, in the award of the Tribunal in *Guyana* v. *Suriname*. Although the Chamber in its order considered that Ghana's unilateral drilling threatened the rights of Côte d'Ivoire with irreparability, thus in a way that could not be financially compensated *ex post facto*,[1269] it refrained from ordering Ghana to put a stop to the drilling which had been earlier authorised.[1270]

Yet, an issue remains which international courts and tribunals have not addressed: how to calculate the amount of the damage caused by unilateral seismic work, or other unilateral acts which fall under coastal State jurisdiction, when they are undertaken in relation to a disputed continental shelf area? Calculating the amount of damage resulting from these types of unilateral activity might be a far from straightforward exercise. For instance, calculating the losses suffered through unilateral seismic work seems to be problematic; how can obtaining an advantage by one claimant over the other claimant, in terms of the information it possesses concerning the disputed continental shelf area as a result of conducting seismic work, be compensated? However, Ghana in its maritime boundary dispute with Côte d'Ivoire perceived no such difficulties to arise, suggesting that the damage caused by seismic work, drilling, or exploitation could all be compensated after delimitation with the same ease,[1271] although it failed to specify how.

One of the main problems with the lawfulness of a unilateral act being dependent on the consideration whether financial compensation *ex post facto* can undo any wrongs is as follows: it renders preserving the exclusivity of these sovereign rights subsidiary to the accompanying consideration to act upon these rights. It also suggests that, despite the continental shelf rights of States being inherent, and presupposing exclusivity, there is no obligation for States under international law to avoid infringing these rights. Rather, what is critical is that such conduct will not surpass a particular threshold: that is, financial reparability.

1269 *Ghana/Côte d'Ivoire* (Provisional Measures) (n. 42) 163 [88]–[91].

1270 Section 6.4.1 above.

1271 *Ghana/Côte d'Ivoire* (Provisional Measures) (n. 42) Ghana's Written Statement 170–171 [94]–[96].

Another difficulty of using reparability as the main measure against which to determine the lawfulness of a unilateral act which falls under coastal State jurisdiction is that it does not sufficiently consider the effects on bilateral relations and, a fortiori, on the chances of reaching a final delimitation or agreeing on cooperative arrangements. Judge Elias echoed this criticism of placing the notion of irreparable prejudice on a pedestal in determining the (un)lawfulness of such an act in his separate opinion in the *Aegean Sea Continental Shelf* (Interim Measures) case. Once the ultimate foundation of the lawfulness of a unilateral act falling under coastal State jurisdiction rests on its financial reparability, it becomes an appraisal that is largely separate from the broader negative effects it will bring about, including in bilateral relations and on the chances of reaching a final delimitation.[1272] It is specifically to avoid such effects from materialising that the obligation not to hamper or jeopardise is imposed on States having disputed EEZ or continental shelf areas.

6.8 CAN THE STANDARDS DEVELOPED IN CASE LAW BE GENERALISED?

An argument based on *Guyana* v. *Suriname* is that the ruling of the Tribunal defines, *in abstracto*, the scope for unilateralism in disputed maritime areas.[1273] This generalisation is as follows: the appraisal whether a coastal State can undertake a particular act falling under coastal State jurisdiction unilaterally, or, rather, that the other claimant's prior consent must be sought, is fully entwined with whether that act causes 'a physical change to the marine environment'.[1274] However, various arguments mitigate against generalising the standards, as first set out in the ICJ's decision in *Aegean Sea Continental Shelf* (Interim Measures), and which the Tribunal emulated in its award in *Guyana* v. *Suriname*, as defining the scope for unilateralism in disputed EEZ and continental shelf areas generally.[1275]

First, the reasoning of the Tribunal in its award in *Guyana* v. *Suriname* is not always easy to construe, sometimes confusing and gives rise to entirely new sets of questions, which it refrains from answering.[1276] An illustration hereof is that

1272 *Aegean Sea Continental Shelf* (Interim Measures) (n. 41) 30 (Separate Opinion of Judge Elias).

1273 D Roughton, 'The Rights (and Wrongs) of Capture: International Law and the Implications of the *Guyana/Suriname* Arbitration' (2008) 26 *JENRL* 374, 398; Sakamoto (n. 925) 101.

1274 Fietta (n. 153) 120.

1275 Van Logchem (n. 21) 183–192.

1276 Ibid. 183–184.

before the Tribunal laid down the ultimate standard against which to measure the lawfulness of unilateral acts falling within coastal State jurisdiction – that is, those that 'do not cause a physical change to the marine environment' – it employed five other standards, thereby sowing the seeds of uncertainty as to which unilateral acts can be considered to be (un)lawful.[1277] As a corollary, the Tribunal introduced a variable into what scope remains for unilateralism in disputed EEZ or continental shelf areas, as the lawfulness of a unilateral act that is under the jurisdiction of the coastal State changes depending on the criterion against which this is determined, with the threshold that needs to be met in order for such a unilateral act to be lawful or unlawful showing some variation from one criterion to another. To illustrate this point, consider the scope of activities that can be covered by the phrase 'physical change to the marine environment', which is larger than 'permanent physical change to the marine environment'. Logic dictates that, through the addition of the word 'permanent', all types of damage not surpassing this threshold would be excluded. Applied to seismic work, which involves firing sound waves at the seafloor, difficulties emerge in bringing this activity under the standard of permanent damage being done to the marine environment. Setting off explosives of a certain magnitude in conducting a seismic survey, resulting in damaging the marine environment, warrants reaching a different conclusion, however. At the same time, seismic work can, without difficulty, be brought under the standard of effecting a 'physical change' to the marine environment – alterations to the marine environment take place at all stages connected to mineral resource development. Releases of acoustic energy through seismic work have also been observed to have detrimental impacts on the marine environment, fisheries,[1278] and marine mammals.[1279]

Second, the language used by the Tribunal at certain places in its award is more in the nature of *de lege ferenda*.[1280] Particularly telling in this regard is the use of various normative and prescriptive phrases, such as that acts undertaken 'ought to be' allowed, or that the States concerned 'ought to do' something in relation to their disputed maritime area.[1281] An example is the Tribunal's holding that disputed maritime areas should not be turned into 'no-activity zones'.[1282] Because of this selection of words, an obligation of result that applies in all

[1277] *Guyana* v. *Suriname* (n. 7) 132 [466]–[468].

[1278] R McCauley et al., 'Marine Seismic Surveys – A Study of Environmental Implications' (2000) 40(1) *The APPEA Journal* 692–708; JR Skalski et al., 'Effects of Sounds from a Geophysical Survey Device on Catch-Per-Unit-Effort' (1992) 49(7) *Canadian Journal of Fisheries and Aquatic Sciences* 1357–1365.

[1279] D Malakoff, 'A Roaring Debate Over Ocean Noise' (2001) 291 *Science* 576, 576–578.

[1280] *Guyana* v. *Suriname* (n. 7) 133 [469]–[470].

[1281] Ibid. 137 [480]–[481].

[1282] Ibid. 133 [470].

circumstances is not connoted, although a failure to do something one 'ought' to do may still be construed as breaching a rule of international law in a given context. A prescriptive use of language by the Tribunal in that States ought to do something is mostly found in relation to its interpretation of the obligation to seek provisional arrangements, being a *pactum de negotiando*.[1283]

Partly overlapping with this second line of criticism is another third one, directed at the language employed by the Tribunal in dealing with the claims of both Guyana and Suriname that the obligation not to hamper or jeopardise was breached. The Tribunal's conclusions suggest that they do not reflect the state of international law that is applicable in disputed maritime areas in a general sense, but rather that its conclusions were tailored specifically to the circumstances that existed between Guyana and Suriname. In particular, the conclusion reached in relation to the lawfulness of unilateral seismic work seemed to be informed by the specifics of the case. In light of the Tribunal's finding that Guyana and Suriname both undertook 'seismic testing in disputed waters, and these activities did not give rise to objections from either side',[1284] in fact they explicitly recognised its lawfulness, meant that coming to a different conclusion with regard to seismic work would be irreconcilable with the positions of the States concerned on this issue. Nonetheless, the Tribunal decided to address the status of conducting seismic work in a disputed area by means of an *obiter dictum*. Furthermore, if the intention of the Tribunal was to designate seismic work as a permissible use of disputed areas in a general sense, it would have been a more appropriate approach to begin by assessing the characteristics of the unilateral act undertaken in the area disputed between Guyana and Suriname, and then to ascertain whether the act in question can be defined as seismic work. A further difficulty is that the Tribunal in its argumentation gave short thrift to the fact that unilateral seismic work regularly creates conflict in State practice; this was to a lesser extent the case when the ICJ was dealing with Greece's request for the indication of interim protection in the 1970s. Admittedly, local variations exist in State practice: in a given locality the conducting of seismic work may not give rise to conflict by prompting the other State into responding through a protest or law enforcement, as was the case between Guyana and Suriname, whereas in another it may be highly problematic. In those localities where seismic work does generate conflict, the difficulties with generalising the Tribunal's view in relation thereto come into focus. All this implies that the finding that unilateral seismic work was lawful cannot be a fortiori applied

1283 Ibid. 136 [477].
1284 Ibid. 137 [481].

to disputed maritime areas generally, which is a conclusion reinforced by the Tribunal's normative use of language. Two opinions of the Tribunal attest to this: namely, that seismic work, when conducted unilaterally in a disputed maritime area, is generally lawful, and, combined therewith, that unilaterally undertaken seismic work 'should be permissible'.[1285]

Fourth, the Tribunal's heavy reliance on the ICJ's decision in the *Aegean Sea Continental Shelf* (Interim Measures) case, sometimes to a point where little distinction between the two cases is discernible, puts into question whether the Tribunal fully appreciated that this concerned an interim measures procedure, which it recognised as setting a higher threshold than is perceived under Articles 74(3) and 83(3) LOSC.[1286]

Fifth, in striking a balance between the two obligations found in paragraph 3, which are based on different rationales – that is, cooperation and abstention – the Tribunal seems to have placed the primary accent on the economic development of the disputed area, rather than avoiding acts that are prejudicial to delimitation that the other obligation seeks to prevent.[1287]

A sixth difficulty that arises can be retraced to the standards laid down by the Tribunal being tailored to be applied to activities related to mineral resources.[1288] This raises the issue whether these can be applied *mutatis mutandis* to other activities falling under the jurisdiction of a coastal State, including fishing activities.[1289]

6.9 THE FAILURE OF SURINAME TO RESPOND TO THE DRILLING IN A LAWFUL MANNER

Wider conclusions have been drawn from the Tribunal's condemnation of the Surinamese response to the drilling. At one extreme of the spectrum there is the view that taking enforcement measures in response to a unilateral act undertaken within a disputed maritime area invariably constitutes an unlawful use of force.[1290] Others have criticised this aspect of the award for setting the threshold quite low as to when such a threat can be assumed.[1291]

1285 Ibid. (emphasis added).
1286 Ibid. 133 [469].
1287 Van Logchem (n. 21) 192.
1288 *Guyana* v. *Suriname* (n. 7) 133 [470].
1289 Chapter 9, Section 9.3.3.2 below.
1290 A Elias-Roberts, 'Legal Reflections on the Guyana-Venezuela Maritime Issue' (2014) 2(1) *Caribbean Journal of International Relations & Diplomacy* 13, 17.
1291 Papanicolopulu (n. 248) 4; Van Logchem (n. 21) 193–195; DH Anderson, 'Some Aspects of the Use of Force in Maritime Law Enforcement' in N Boschiero et al. (eds.), *International Courts and the Development of International Law* (Springer, 2013) 233; Phan (n. 641) 497.

However, the argument that law enforcement in a disputed maritime area is unlawful per se runs into significant difficulties. Threatening a non-national installation and the crew on board the oil rig licensed by Guyana was in the given circumstances found to be in violation of the prohibition on threatening the use of force[1292] – however, the Tribunal did not determine that the use of some measure of force in law enforcement *in abstracto* is unlawful.[1293] This is when its use is necessary, unavoidable, and proportional,[1294] but this did not apply to Suriname's reaction, which, according to the Tribunal, was not in the nature of law enforcement. Rather, the main impact of the Tribunal's condemnation of the Surinamese response to the drilling lies in the possibilities that are available to a claimant State when it is faced with unilateral conduct that is perceived as infringing on its rights, and to which it seeks to formulate a response.[1295] By placing emphasis on the availability of other options to Suriname to put the lawfulness of the unilateral drilling into question under Section 2 of Part VX LOSC, which were unanimously favoured by the Tribunal, it can be seen to have restricted the range of situations wherein a State would be allowed to take enforcement measures against the other claimant who has unilaterally authorised or undertaken conduct falling within coastal State jurisdiction in a disputed maritime area.[1296] In terms of effectiveness, there is an important difference between the recognised 'lower intensity' responses, which were unanimously preferred by the Tribunal, when these are contrasted with taking enforcement measures. Negotiating, asking for the indication of interim protection, or submitting the dispute to adjudication do not provide instantaneous results. This is an aspect that questions whether these can be considered to be true alternatives to law enforcement in all cases.[1297]

It also raises the question whether the reasoning of the Tribunal impairs the autonomy of States to dispose of a dispute via their preferred route? If, for whatever reason, negotiations were to be unsuccessful, the only means remaining for a claimant to challenge the lawfulness of a particular unilateral act would be to request the indication of interim protection, or to submit the dispute to adjudication. In order for a State to be able to request interim measures it must have submitted a dispute to proceedings before the ICJ, ITLOS, or an Arbitral Tribunal to which the parties have access according to

1292 Van Logchem (n. 21) 193.
1293 *Guyana* v. *Suriname* (n. 7) 126 [445].
1294 Ibid.
1295 Fietta (n. 153) 120.
1296 RP Barnidge, Jr, 'The International Law of Negotiation as a Means of Dispute Settlement' (2013) 36(3) *FILJ* 545, 561–569.
1297 Papanicolopulu (n. 248) 4.

Article 287 LOSC under Part XV. Pursuant to Article 290(1) LOSC, the *condiciones sine quibus non* for requesting interim measures of protection are, first, that 'a dispute has been duly submitted' to an international court or tribunal, over which it, second, has established to have prima facie jurisdiction. When a dispute is submitted to a compulsory proceeding resulting in a binding decision, each of the parties to the dispute may request interim protection from the international court or tribunal seized of the dispute. The aforementioned effectively means that a de facto obligation is imposed on States to resort to a particular means of dispute settlement, which seems difficult to reconcile with States being autonomous in deciding on the specific manner in which their dispute is to be settled.[1298] Submitting a dispute to adjudication to merely request interim measures of protection also seems to be an ineffective, time-consuming, and costly process,[1299] particularly when a State has no intention of having the underlying maritime delimitation dispute adjudicated.

A final issue is the situation in which one of the States concerned has declared any maritime boundary disputes in the sense of Articles 15, 74, and 83 LOSC to be excluded from compulsory dispute settlement, by having made a declaration pursuant to Article 298 LOSC. Would this exclusion also extend to the two obligations contained in Articles 74(3) and 83(3) LOSC?[1300] If such a declaration would encompass these paragraphs as well, this would mean that this route might be closed off to a State that wants to respond to a unilateral activity. However, if a State has made a declaration under Article 298(1)(a)(i) LOSC, it must accept compulsory conciliation if another State makes an unilateral application to that end, and if a reasonable amount of time has expired in which the States concerned were not able to resolve the dispute themselves.[1301]

Central to the issue of how extensively an Article 298 declaration needs to be interpreted is how to understand the wording of 'disputes concerning the interpretation or application of articles 15, 74 and 83 relating to sea boundary delimitations'.[1302] The use of the word 'relating' could perhaps be interpreted as to also exclude matters that do not involve the maritime boundary delimitation per se, but are somehow related thereto, and which could encompass

1298 Van Logchem (n. 21) 193–195.

1299 Ibid. 194.

1300 Ibid. 195; Klein (n. 431) 124–126.

1301 *Timor-Leste* v. *Australia Conciliation*, Decision on Australia's Objections to Competence (19 September 2016) 17, 26 [68] [95], available at https://pcacases.com/web/sendAttach/10052.

1302 Van Logchem (n. 21) 194–195; K Nishimoto, 'The Obligation of Self-Restraint in Undelimited Maritime Areas' (2019) 3(1) *Japan Review* 28, 36–37.

questions around Articles 74(3) and 83(3) LOSC as well. No international court or tribunal has yet dealt with a jurisdictional objection from a State having made an Article 298(1)(a)(i) declaration while it was asked to hear a question related to Articles 74(3) and 83(3).[1303] However, the Conciliation Commission, in the compulsory conciliation proceedings between Timor-Leste and Australia, held in its decision that it was competent to address the issue of 'transitional arrangements' pending a final delimitation, which involves an interpretation of Article 83(3) LOSC.[1304] This was despite Australia having made a declaration under Article 298(1)(a)(i) LOSC. The question arises whether an international court or tribunal would reach the same conclusion, however.[1305] Based on the Conciliation Commission's decision, the argument has been made that issues related to Articles 74(3) and 83(3) LOSC could be addressed in compulsory conciliation, but this would conversely not be possible for an international court and tribunal, where such issues would be covered by a declaration made under Article 298(1)(a)(i) LOSC.[1306] Considering that conciliation is vastly different from international adjudication, in terms of procedure and aim,[1307] caution is warranted in generalising the Conciliation Commission's finding – both in the sense that it would apply *mutatis mutandis* to international adjudication, and drawing the *a contrario* inference that this would mean that issues related to Articles 74(3) and 83(3) would be excluded from consideration before an arbitral tribunal or international court when a State to the dispute has made a declaration pursuant to Article 298(1)(a)(i) LOSC.

Disputes that have arisen because of a State having acted unilaterally, by authorising or undertaking conduct falling under coastal State jurisdiction, in a disputed EEZ area may also be excluded from compulsory dispute settlement under Article 297 LOSC. This will be mainly the case for those disputes that arise in relation to a claimant State's exercise of sovereign rights or jurisdiction within a disputed EEZ area, which would possibly extend to disputes created by the unilateral undertaking or authorising of fishing activities or MSR projects.

1303 S de Herdt, 'Meaningful Responses to Unilateralism in Undelimited Maritime Areas' (2019) 6(2) *Journal of Territorial and Maritime Studies* 5, 10–12.

1304 *Timor-Leste* v. *Australia Conciliation* (n. 1301) 26 [93]–[94].

1305 Nishimoto (n. 1302) 36–37.

1306 X Zhang, 'Jurisdictional and Substantive Aspects in the Application of UNCLOS Article 83(3) in Recent International Decisions' in MH Nordquist et al. (eds.), *Cooperation and Engagement in the Asia-Pacific Region* (Brill, 2020) 99, 108–109.

1307 N Klein 'The *Timor Sea Conciliation* and Lessons for Northeast Asia in Resolving Maritime Boundary Disputes' (2019) 6(1) *JTMS* 30, 34–35.

6.10 CONCLUDING REMARKS

Judicial clarification of what the rights and obligations are of States in a disputed maritime area was first offered by the ICJ in its decision in the *Aegean Sea Continental Shelf* (Interim Measures) case. Here Greece failed to convince the ICJ to indicate measures of interim protection. Greece contended that, through Turkey's gathering of knowledge on the disputed continental shelf area, the risk of causing irreparability was created, as the resulting prejudice would not be reparable *ex post facto*. It perceived that a further nexus existed between undertaking seismic exploration – which would invariably be followed by making a threat to use force against the acting State – and the ensuing of military conflict, creating a threat to international peace and security in its wake.[1308] While the ICJ recognised that Greece's rights over the disputed continental shelf area were infringed upon, the actual measure thereof fell short of being irreparable, which was the threshold that needed to be exceeded in order for the ICJ to indicate interim measures of protection.[1309] One of the most influential elements of the ICJ's decision in the *Aegean Sea Continental Shelf* (Interim Measures) case that remains relevant today has been the identification of three types of unilateral activity that would require the indication of measures of interim protection, as these activities threaten to make the other State's rights irreparable. This concerned authorising the emplacement or the actual placing of an installation on or above the seabed; appropriating or exploiting the natural resources of the continental shelf area; and causing physical damage to the seabed or subsoil or any of its natural resources, including drilling in a disputed continental shelf area.[1310]

The continued relevance of *Aegean Sea Continental Shelf* (Interim Measures) is demonstrated in the award of the Tribunal in *Guyana* v. *Suriname*, which contains the most elaborate judicial pronouncement on the application of Articles 74(3) and 83(3) LOSC.[1311] Here the Tribunal, in addressing *obiter dictum* whether unilateral seismic work in a disputed EEZ or continental shelf area is (un)lawful, patterned its reasoning after that of the ICJ in the *Aegean Sea Continental Shelf* (Interim Measures) case concluding that it is a lawful unilateral activity. More invasive activities, including drilling and placing installations within a disputed area, as Guyana had done, breached the obligation not to hamper or jeopardise in Articles 74(3) and 83(3) LOSC.

[1308] Chapter 3, Section 3.1.1 above.
[1309] *Aegean Sea Continental Shelf* (Interim Measures) (n. 41) 10 [30].
[1310] Ibid.; Section 6.1.1 above.
[1311] *Guyana* v. *Suriname* (n. 7); Section 6.3 above.

Although the Tribunal's award has been hailed with enthusiasm, because it would clearly indicate what is required of States pursuant to paragraph 3,[1312] this overstates its importance as it merely provides a partial expression of the implications and content of Articles 74(3) and 83(3) LOSC.[1313] Despite having several flaws, the Tribunal's ruling does have relevance, however, in that it fleshes out some of the constitutive elements of paragraph 3 of Articles 74 and 83 LOSC.

Somewhat ironically, reducing the relevance of the Tribunal's award is that it largely replicates the reasoning of the ICJ in the *Aegean Sea Continental Shelf* (Interim Measures) case. This reliance was deemed appropriate by the Tribunal in light of the close-knit relationship between Articles 74(3) and 83(3) LOSC and the case law on measures of interim protection.[1314] Although the Tribunal spoke in the plural, the only interim measures case that perceivably has relevance is the aforementioned *Aegean Sea Continental Shelf* (Interim Measures) case. By relying heavily on this case, the Tribunal implicitly rejected that a new standard had to be developed in order to determine a breach of paragraph 3 of Articles 74 and 83 LOSC.[1315] However, what is puzzling is that the Tribunal acknowledged that the underlying standards are substantively different, with the standards set under Articles 74(3) and 83(3) LOSC being lower, to subsequently deal with them as if they were virtually identical.[1316] Taking this argument a step further, the Tribunal could even be accused of blurring the lines between the standards that are necessary to indicate interim measures of protection and to assume a breach of the negative obligation of Articles 74(3) and 83(3) LOSC, which sets the different and significantly lower threshold of hampering or jeopardising.[1317] As a result, the guidance provided by the Tribunal's award as to how States must conduct themselves prior to delimitation is as follows: unilateral acts that are sufficiently serious to merit the prescribing of interim protection have an equal effect of hampering or jeopardising the final delimitation.[1318]

Ghana/Côte d'Ivoire is an anomaly in all this, constituting a clean break with previous rulings. Here, for the first time, an international court was asked to pass judgment on the lawfulness of a claimant coming close to unilaterally taking drilled oil wells to the production stage in a disputed maritime area. At

1312 Fietta (n. 153) 127; Hossain (n. 1253) 674–675, 684; J Gao, 'Comments on Guyana v. Suriname' (2009) 8(1) *CJIL* 191, 199–200.
1313 Van Logchem (n. 21) 196–197.
1314 *Guyana* v. *Suriname* (n. 7) 133 [469].
1315 Ibid. [470].
1316 Van Logchem (n. 21) 187–188.
1317 Ibid.
1318 Ibid. 196.

first glance, the most logical lines of argument for the Special Chamber to follow, given their similarity with the facts faced in the maritime boundary dispute between Ghana and Côte d'Ivoire, were those developed in *Aegean Sea Continental Shelf* (Interim Measures) and *Guyana* v. *Suriname*. A similarity with the ICJ's decision in the *Aegean Sea Continental Shelf* (Interim Measures) case is the way in which the Special Chamber construed its analysis, and its identification of two respective stages, that is, before and after delimitation. Another similarity is that exploration activities within a disputed continental shelf area were found to carry the inherent possibility of causing imminent prejudice;[1319] that is, if the area falls on the side of the non-acting State after delimitation. But that is probably also where the similarities end.

By way of contrast, the Special Chamber decided in its interim measures order not to order Ghana to put a stop to the already commenced drilling *pendente litis*. Somewhat paradoxically, in order to protect the marine environment, the conduct had to proceed rather than being aborted, according to the Chamber: ordering a halt to exploitation would have put the marine environment in serious danger, as installations that were already in place and unused would start to deteriorate. However, an aspect that was not really addressed by the Special Chamber was why the degradation caused to the marine environment by aborting exploration and exploitation would be more extensive than the damage that was caused through drilling? In addition, in shaping the outcome of the decision of the Special Chamber on this point, the dislocating effects that would be produced for Ghana's economy played a critical role.

In its decision on the merits, the Special Chamber found that the areas where the mineral resources-related activities had begun were located on Ghana's side of the boundary, and that, as a result, the obligation not to hamper or jeopardise had not been breached. Especially problematic in this regard was, according to the Special Chamber, that in the formulation of its submission Côte d'Ivoire referred to the area in question as being 'Ivorian'.[1320] Nevertheless, caution has been urged in attributing too much relevance to *Ghana/Côte d'Ivoire* when it comes to interpreting Article 83(3) LOSC, also given that in the interim measures procedure this paragraph was not interpreted directly.[1321] Although the latter is true, this argument is not completely convincing. For example, the ICJ's decision in *Aegean Sea Continental Shelf* (Interim Measures), also being an interim measures procedure, figured heavily in *Guyana* v. *Suriname*, in which the Tribunal was called upon to interpret Articles 74(3) and 83(3) LOSC directly.

1319 *Ghana/Côte d'Ivoire* (Provisional Measures) (n. 42) 164 [95]–[96].
1320 Van Logchem (n. 245) 163.
1321 BIICL Report (n. 141) 26.

Another conclusion that has been drawn from the order of the Special Chamber is that 'pure economic loss' did not constitute irreparable harm.[1322] This is debatable, as the Chamber established the following relationship hitherto not explicitly recognised to exist in the case law: gathering information on a disputed continental shelf area, and putting it to use, although constituting an act that does not alter the geography of the continental shelf, may possibly lead to irreparability being caused to another State's rights.[1323]

Importantly, the Chamber's finding that the area where Ghana started its work was after delimitation located on the other claimant's side of the boundary, transformed the question around international responsibility: can this be engaged when unilateral acts which are under coastal State jurisdiction have been 'carried out in a part of the area attributed by the judgment to the other State'?[1324] The Chamber answered this question in the negative: although the activities had been undertaken unilaterally in what could be considered, at the time, a disputed maritime area,[1325] there was no breach of Côte d'Ivoire's sovereign rights. Central to this conclusion is that, if the unilateral conduct occurs in a part of the disputed maritime area that is claimed in good faith by that State, then the act would not breach a rule of international law, meaning that no international responsibility would be incurred.[1326] This is a meagre threshold, however, putting few constraints on unilateral conduct falling under coastal State jurisdiction being undertaken in disputed areas, regardless of the conflict that would be engendered between claimant States as a result. It also provides a State seeking to act unilaterally within a disputed maritime area with judicial authority to do so.[1327]

Only in *Guyana* v. *Suriname*, an international tribunal determined whether a response of a State when faced with an act that is under coastal State jurisdiction was in conformity with international law. The Tribunal concluded that the Surinamese response was not law enforcement or a lawful countermeasure.[1328] Less intrusive ways were available for Suriname to question the lawfulness of the unilateral drilling, according to the Tribunal.[1329] It

1322 PE Dupont and A Solomou, 'Provisional Measures in Maritime Delimitation Cases' in J Crawford et al. (eds.), *The International Legal Order: Current Needs and Possible Responses: Essays in Honour of Djamchid Momtaz* (Brill, 2017) 312, 333.

1323 *Ghana/Côte d'Ivoire* (Provisional Measures) (n. 42) 164 [95]–[96].

1324 *Ghana/Côte d'Ivoire* (Judgment) (n. 46) 158 [589].

1325 Ibid. [588].

1326 Chapter 3, Section 3.11 above.

1327 Van Logchem (n. 245) 176.

1328 *Guyana* v. *Suriname* (n. 7) 124, 126–127 [441] [445]–[446].

1329 Ibid.

took particular offence at the use of dubious language by the Surinamese navy officers in the attempt to remove the rig from the disputed area: 'leave the area at once, or the consequences will be yours'.[1330] Setting dubious language being uttered as the applicable standard, which can be interpreted in a variety of ways, introduces a low threshold for when a threat of use of force can be inferred, however.[1331] But, at the same time, less ambiguous wording could have been used by the Surinamese officers. Nonetheless, if the position of the Tribunal is generalised, law enforcement seems to be placed largely beyond the scope of appropriate responses under international law when a claimant State is faced with a unilateral act, falling under the jurisdiction of the coastal State, by another State in a disputed maritime area. However, the argument that the Tribunal's ruling in *Guyana* v. *Suriname* shows that law enforcement in disputed maritime areas is *simpliciter* unlawful oversimplifies the matter.[1332]

A consistent pattern can be detected in the case law: restraint needs to be observed by neighbouring coastal States in relation to their disputed maritime area. As to the extent to which claimants can exercise their sovereign rights in disputed EEZ or continental shelf areas, or the extent to which they must exercise restraint, the line is usually drawn at seismic work, with drilling and exploitation being considered unlawful. This has led to the unconvincing argument that, by falling back on the international case law and the standards developed thereunder, the answer could be found to whether a coastal State would be allowed to exercise its rights or jurisdiction in a disputed EEZ/continental shelf area unilaterally. Contrary to this, the scope for undertaking acts which fall under coastal State jurisdiction may be more strictly circumscribed in certain disputed areas; this is perhaps even to the extent that a moratorium is introduced. The key to this interpretation regarding disputed EEZ and continental shelf areas lies in the language of Articles 74(3) and 83(3) LOSC.[1333]

1330 Ibid. 126 [445].
1331 Van Logchem (n. 21) 193–195; Anderson (n. 1291) 233.
1332 Chapter 9, Section 9.3.3.4 below.
1333 Van Logchem (n. 245) 138–139; Chapter 9, Section 9.3.2 below.

7

Disputed Waters Generated by Claims Made from Disputed Land Territory: What Are the Rights and Obligations of States?

Disputes where title over high-tide features or mainland territory is contested between States are not uncommon in the international legal landscape. They have been estimated to exceed thirty, some of which originate from disputes over land boundaries and/or their terminus, and other disputes centre on high-tide features.[1334] Disputes where issues of who has title to territory and the associated disputed waters are conjointly in play are imbued with difficulties, making them rather difficult to resolve.[1335] Despite their complexity, this has not led States with competing claims to title over a land territory to adopt greater restraint in relation to disputed waters located off disputed mainland territory or high-tide features,[1336] with the result that conflict frequently emerges between them. Along these lines, conflict in the Red Sea has emerged between its bordering countries (Egypt, Sudan, Eritrea, and Saudi Arabia) that have awarded overlapping concessions for mineral resource activities within disputed waters located off their disputed land territories. Another example is a conflict that emerged in November 2008, after Cyprus authorised two vessels to conduct seismic surveying within an area that Turkey also claims. Upon being detected, a Turkish naval vessel was dispatched to the area requesting that these activities be halted and that the vessels would evict the area.[1337] This request went unheeded, as the two seismic vessels later moved to a different part of the disputed area, in order to engage in similar activities there. Turkey, in a more visible show of strength, dispatched a research vessel of its own,

1334 Van Dyke (n. 628) 39.

1335 I Buga, 'Territorial Sovereignty Issues in Maritime Disputes: A Jurisdictional Dilemma for Law of the Sea Tribunals' (2012) 27(1) *IJMCL* 59, 62.

1336 PM Blyschak, 'Offshore Oil and Gas Projects amid Maritime Border Disputes: Applicable Law' (2013) 6(3) *JWELB* 210, 225–226.

1337 A/63/574-S/2008/741 (n. 353) 3.

which was accompanied by several warships, to the disputed waters off Cyprus.[1338]

Generally speaking, it is essential to make a distinction between when a State has undisputed title over land territory, which is used to claim maritime zones from its base points, and where an underlying land territory is involved over which title is disputed. This is because the applicable legal regime may be different for these two situations.[1339] Any such differences are considered in this chapter. Its central question is that, when the issues of competing claims to title over the same land territory and States claiming sovereignty, sovereign rights, and/or jurisdiction over its related maritime spaces are combined (i.e. when there is a mixed dispute), what is the applicable international law with regard to the disputed waters created more or less automatically as a result, and prior to resolving the dispute on title to territory? Section 7.1 starts with establishing what implications follow from the fact that there is a combination of the elements of who has title to territory and the claiming of maritime zones from the same basepoints of a disputed land territory for identifying the applicable international legal framework in the disputed waters that will be created. Attention will be paid in Section 7.2 towards whether the applicability of Articles 74(3) and 83(3) LOSC in cases where disputed waters are generated either exclusively or conjunctively by claims to maritime zones that are measured from disputed mainland territory or high-tide features is in the nature of *de lege lata* or *de lege ferenda*? Section 7.3 concludes by reviewing the main elements of the international legal framework that shine light on what rights and obligations States have in disputed waters located off land territory over which title is disputed.

7.1 THE APPLICABLE LEGAL REGIME

Entitlements to maritime zones can be claimed both from mainland territory and high-tide features.[1340] From 'fully entitled islands' as defined by the LOSC in Article 121(2), the following maritime zones can be claimed: a territorial sea, a contiguous zone, an EEZ, and a continental shelf; possibly, they may also have an entitlement to the extended continental shelf, if the requirements thereto are met (Article 76 LOSC). 'Rocks' form the exception: that is, high-tide features falling under Article 121(3) LOSC. A rock, as a maximum, is

1338 II Kouskouvelis, '"Smart" Leadership in a Small State: the Case of Cyprus' in SN Litsas and A Tziampiris (eds.), *The Eastern Mediterranean in Transition, Multipolarity, Politics and Power* (Ashgate, 2015) 93, 98.

1339 Kittichaisaree (n. 43) 140.

1340 *Qatar* v. *Bahrain* (n. 525) 97 [185]; *Nicaragua* v. *Honduras* (n. 413) 751 [302].

entitled to a territorial sea not going beyond the maximum limit of 12 nm and a contiguous zone that may not extend further than 12 nm from the outer limit of the territorial sea – that is, if a State opts for a 12 nm territorial sea. States claiming maritime zones from high-tide features, which are subject to a title dispute or where clear title is held by one State, have contributed significantly to the overall number of disputed maritime areas,[1341] which are regularly of great complexity. Once the dispute over title has been settled, high-tide features will be entitled to their own maritime zones; also, a rock is entitled to its own zones, even though not an EEZ or continental shelf. High-tide features also may be relevant in determining where the maritime boundary comes to lie.

The interconnection between the issues of dispute over title and disputed maritime zones can be constructed in the following way: when competing claims to title are made over the same piece of land territory, and presuming it has a coastline, a dispute with respect to the maritime areas to which this territory is entitled logically follows. Maritime boundary disputes have been equated, concerning their characteristics, with their counterparts on land;[1342] for example, at UNCLOS III, Israel argued that they exhibit 'no inherent differences'.[1343] But does this also apply to the applicable international legal regime?

Disputes over title to land territory are governed by customary international law.[1344] Central to the issue of deciding which State has title is, in the absence of a relevant treaty, the question of who has a stronger title over a land territory. An international court or tribunal will likely decide this issue by weighing and comparing the acts of peaceful administration that have been taken by States claiming title over the same piece of territory.[1345] If it concerns a small island, little may be required in terms of occupation and activities of peaceful administration in order to trump a rival State's claim to title that may, for instance, rest on discovery, the placing of a flag, or the geographical proximity of the feature to its coast.[1346] In principle, a State – generally the one that is in control of the disputed high-tide feature or mainland territory – may seek to fortify its claim to title over territory through peaceful means. This is unless the

1341 Prescott and Schofield (n. 55) 246.

1342 YK Kim, 'Maritime Boundary Issues and Island Disputes in Northeast Asia' (1997) 25(1) *KJILCL* 49.

1343 A/CONF.62/C.2/SR.57 (n. 740) 60 [49].

1344 Nasu and Rothwell (n. 85) 55–79.

1345 *Legal Status of Eastern Greenland (Denmark* v. *Norway)* (Judgment) [1933] PCIJ Rep. Series A/B No. 53, 39, 45–46; *Islands of Palmas case (the Netherlands/United States)* [1928] 2 RIAA 831, 840.

1346 MM Garcia, 'Boundary Delimitation and Hydrocarbon Resources' in G Picton-Turbervill (ed.), *Oil and Gas: A Practical Handbook* (Globe Business Publishing Ltd., 2014) 39, 43–44.

critical date has passed,[1347] with the effect that further activities do not strengthen a claim of title to territory.

Difficulties may, however, arise with regard to distinguishing between acts that have been conducted in waters located off disputed mainland territory or high-tide features, that is with a view towards enhancing a title claim and acts that are undertaken to assert a claim to a maritime area.[1348] One way of avoiding this problem, so it has been suggested, is to deduce the intention behind the conduct, which would be indicative of its effects.[1349] Complicating matters in trying to infer the true intention behind a unilateral act is that States are rarely specific as to what has motivated them to undertake a particular act in disputed waters.

When the issues of competing claims to title being made by States over the same land territory and then claiming sovereignty, sovereign rights, and/or jurisdiction over its related maritime spaces are combined, would the LOSC be applicable with regard to the disputed waters that are created thereby, and prior to settling the dispute on title to territory? Considering that most parts of the LOSC are built on the assumption that one State has uncontested title to a territory,[1350] and thus that clarity exists as to where the authority of the coastal State geographically extends, its overall use and application may be reduced in these mixed disputes. At UNCLOS III, the issue of the applicability of the LOSC to mixed disputes was not explicitly addressed. This is aside from the incidental mention of not including territorial sovereignty issues in the category of disputes that are subject to compulsory third-party settlement,[1351] which was based on the view that Part XV is concerned with disputes over the interpretation and application of the LOSC and not with disputes on title to territory.[1352]

However, States at UNCLOS III did more intensively debate the highly politicized and controversial issue of territorial sovereignty and disputed waters, in the specific context of non-self-governing territories. Kenya, being the first to design a provision with respect to the waters located off non-self-governing territories, suggested that these territories are not entitled to an EEZ

1347 R Beckman, 'ASEAN and the South China Sea Dispute' in P Chachavalpongpun (ed.), *Entering Uncharted Waters: ASEAN and the South China Sea* (ISAS, 2014) 15, 19.

1348 BIICL Report (n. 141) 34.

1349 Ibid.

1350 Anderson and Van Logchem (n. 18) 222.

1351 Doc. A/CONF.62/SR.62 (7 April 1976), Official Records of the United Nations Conference on the Law of the Sea, Vol. V, 42 [78] (Venezuela).

1352 RW Smith, 'The Effect of Extended Maritime Jurisdiction' in AW Koers and BH Oxman (eds.), *The 1982 Convention on the Law of the Sea: Proceedings, LOSI Seventeenth Annual Conference* (University of Hawaii Press, 1984) 336, 343.

while they are under foreign occupation.[1353] This point was repeated in proposals that were subsequently introduced by States at UNCLOS III.[1354] Here the subject under debate was not one involving the law of the sea, but more aptly framed concerning the international law of territory.[1355] However that may be, Article 136(2), despite not being concerned with a law of the sea related issue, was included in the ISNT. Its main thrust is that a foreign power, during its occupation, could not make a claim from an occupied territory to the maritime zones it would become entitled to under the (future) convention; thus, preventing it from plucking the fruits of economic development offshore. The ability of a State to claim maritime zones was made conditional upon the territory becoming self-governing.[1356]

Due to its controversial nature,[1357] a provision to this end was removed from the official negotiating text.[1358] Eventually, some declaratory language in relation to the rights and interests of non-self-governing territories under the LOSC was included in Resolution III, in the Final Act of UNCLOS III. Paragraph 1(b) of Resolution III pertains explicitly to disputed waters located off the coast of non-self-governing territories that are subject to competing claims to title of States, reading as follows: 'That States concerned shall make every effort to enter into provisional arrangements of a practical nature and shall not jeopardise or hamper the reaching of a final settlement of the dispute.' In terms of its substance, this paragraph closely resembles Articles 74(3) and 83(3) LOSC. There is, however, an important difference between them and that is that paragraph 1(b) of Resolution III is tailored to be applied in a very different setting, namely disputed waters adjacent to non-self-governing territories. Yet, as a result, some mixed disputes can be included within the reach of paragraph 1(b). For instance, at the initiative of the United Kingdom, the Falklands were placed on the list of non-self-governing territories, pursuant to Chapter XI UN Charter.[1359] Although Argentina protested against this

1353 Ibid. 346.

1354 Doc. A/AC.138/SC.II/L.40, Draft Articles on Exclusive Economic Zone, Article XI, Sea-bed Committee, Sub-Committee II Summary Records, reproduced in Report of the Committee on the Peaceful Uses of the Sea-bed and the Ocean Floor beyond the Limits of National Jurisdiction, Doc. A/9021, Vol. III (supplement) (1 January 1973) 87, 89 [29] (Algeria et al.).

1355 Nordquist et al. (n. 465) 480.

1356 RD Hodgson and RW Smith, 'The Informal Single Negotiating Text (Committee II): A Geographical Perspective' (1976) 3(3) *ODIL* 225, 233.

1357 Doc. A/CONF.62/L.86 (26 March 1982), Official Records of the United Nations Conference on the Law of the Sea, Vol. XVI, 199 [19] (Report of the President on the Question of Participation in the Convention).

1358 A/CONF.62/WP.8/Part II (n. 677) Article 136.

1359 F Toase, 'The United Nations Security Resolution 502' in S Badsey et al. (eds.), *The Falklands Conflict Twenty Years on: Lessons for the Future* (Frank Cass, 2005) 147, 147–148.

decision, the Falklands having been placed on this list has enabled the possibility of viewing the lawfulness of the unilateral acts falling under the authority of the coastal State, taken in relation to the surrounding disputed waters, through the lens of the requirement of not jeopardising or hampering.[1360]

7.2 APPLYING ARTICLES 74(3) AND 83(3) LOSC: *DE LEGE LATA* OR *DE LEGE FERENDA*?

The potential relevance of Articles 74(3) and 83(3) LOSC for disputes underpinned by issues of who has title over mainland territory or high-tide features is illustrated by the fact that the States concerned, most often the States that are in factual control of the land territory or feature, do take certain actions in relation to the adjacent disputed waters. This will often provoke a protest from the other claimant. There are views that include the broad range of situations involving disputed waters created by mainland territory and high-tide features that are subject to competing claims to title within the scope of application of Articles 74(3) and 83(3) LOSC.[1361] But these views are more in the nature of *de lege ferenda* in two situations.[1362] First, where the way in which a dispute on title to territory is resolved is decisive for whether an overlap of claims to maritime zones will arise between the State to which title over the disputed land territory is attributed and the claims of a third coastal State. This, for example, refers to a scenario where State A and State B both claim ownership of a high-tide feature, and that the outcome of this dispute as to who has title over the land territory is decisive for the arising of an overlap of respective claims to the same EEZ or continental shelf area with State C. Second, if an overlap of claims to waters located off a disputed mainland territory or high-tide feature is the result of States using the same base points of that disputed land territory as the main source for their claims to the adjacent maritime zones.

There are intermediate cases of disputed maritime areas where disputes over land territory or high-tide features (be it disputes over title to them or disputes over the status of a feature) figure in some way, but in relation to which Articles 74(3) and 83(3) LOSC would, due to the specifics of the situation, nonetheless apply. These can be referred to as 'maritime areas subject to a dual overlap of claims', the main characteristic of which is that

1360 Van Logchem (n. 52) 57–60.
1361 Lagoni (n. 243) 354; Papanicolopulu (n. 248) 3.
1362 Anderson and Van Logchem (n. 18) 222.

the creation of a disputed maritime area is not the mere result of claims having been measured by States from the base points of the same disputed land territory. Rather, under this scenario, there must already be a clear need for delimitation independent of how the underlying issue of competing claims of title to territory is resolved, or that the use of the same base points of a disputed land territory are the sole reason underlying that a disputed maritime area is created.[1363] A different scenario in which Articles 74(3) and 83(3) LOSC would be similarly applicable is if the source of creating an overlap of claims over the same maritime area is not only a high-tide feature over which States have differing views as to its status; that is, whether it is a fully entitled island or a rock.[1364]

Under either of these scenarios, the role of a high-tide feature is that it is an element in a wider maritime boundary dispute, in the sense that maritime boundaries cannot be conclusively drawn until title over a high-tide feature, and/or its status, has been determined.[1365] However, due to the peculiarities involved, there will be an additional layer of overlapping claims by States that activates Articles 74(3) and 83(3) LOSC. An example are the disputed waters surrounding the Senkaku Islands, in relation to which China and Japan face the difficult problem of which State has title over these high-tide features and rights and jurisdiction over the adjacent disputed waters.[1366] Independent of this underlying issue on title, and this is the aspect that activates Articles 74(3) and 83(3) LOSC, the two States have overlapping claims to an EEZ and continental shelf between their mainland coasts, which are separated roughly 360 nm from each other.[1367]

When reasoned through, the application of Articles 74(3) and 83(3) LOSC to, for example, the broader South China Sea is more difficult to justify. Certainly, paragraph 3 cannot be applied to the disputed waters in their entirety, as the general range separating the coasts of States of the South China Sea is somewhere between 600 and 700 nm.[1368] Certain parts of the

1363 AG Oude Elferink, 'Clarifying Article 121(3) of the Law of the Sea Convention: The Limits Set by Nature of International Legal Processes' (1998) *IBRU Boundary and Security Bulletin* 62.

1364 Chapter 6, Section 6.3.7 above.

1365 Anderson and Van Logchem (n. 18) 211.

1366 J Pan, 'Way Out: The Possibility of a Third-Party Settlement for the Sino-Japanese Maritime Boundary Dispute in the East China Sea' (2008) 6(2) *CIJ* 187, 189.

1367 K Zou, 'China and Maritime Boundary Delimitation: Past, Present and Future' in R Amer and K Zou (eds.), *Conflict Management and Dispute Settlement in East Asia* (Ashgate, 2011) 149, 150.

1368 S Bateman, 'Maritime Boundary Delimitation, Excessive Claims and Effective Regime Building in the South China Sea' in Y Song and K Zou (eds.), *Major Law and Policy Issues in the South China Sea: European and American Perspectives* (Ashgate, 2014) 119, 123.

South China Sea do, however, fall within the category of situations where mainland coasts over which undisputed title is held are *simpliciter* sufficiently close to each other for claims to maritime zones to overlap; for example, in the northern part of the South China Sea between China and the Philippines, and between Indonesia and Malaysia,[1369] as well as off the mainland coasts of Brunei and Malaysia.[1370] Similarly, the Paracel Islands that are disputed between China and Vietnam constitute an element in a wider maritime boundary dispute. Here, irrespective of the question of who has title over the Paracel Islands, the distance between the mainland coasts of the two States is close enough to create an overlap of their claims to the same EEZ/continental shelf area. Then, Articles 74(3) and 83(3) LOSC would apply to those areas where the claims to an EEZ or continental shelf overlap.

An example in which Articles 74(3) and 83(3) LOSC are not directly applicable is the Falklands (Islas Malvinas) dispute. The current overlap to the adjacent waters off the coast of the Falklands is created by Argentina and the United Kingdom, both claiming title over the islands, combined with making claims to maritime zones from their baselines. With the most nearby other territory of the United Kingdom being too far removed to create any sort of alternative overlap of claims to maritime zones with Argentina, this example cannot be placed in the category of disputes where the States concerned clearly have a need for an EEZ/continental shelf boundary, irrespective of to which State title over the disputed islands will be attributed.[1371] Therefore, the applicable framework to conducting unilateral acts that are under the authority of the coastal State in the waters adjacent to the disputed territory will be composed of general rules of international law,[1372] with the addition of Paragraph 1(b) of Resolution III in the Final Act of UNCLOS III, containing some declaratory language bearing on the Falklands, as a consequence of the unilateral designation by the United Kingdom of this being a non-self-governing territory.

[1369] S Bateman, 'Sovereignty as an Obstacle to Effective Oceans Governance and Maritime Boundary Making – The Case of the South China Sea' in CH Schofield et al. (eds.), *The Limits of Maritime Jurisdiction* (Martinus Nijhoff, 2014) 201, 209.

[1370] 'Brunei: Early Solution to Dispute Says Abdullah', *Borneo Bulletin*, 9 July 2003; 'Malaysian Foreign Minister to Address Maritime Dispute with Brunei', *World Markets Analysis*, 7 July 2003.

[1371] Van Logchem (n. 52) 30.

[1372] Chapter 9, Section 9.2 below.

7.3 CONCLUDING REMARKS

States claiming title over a high-tide feature or land territory will almost invariably also make claims to the maritime zones that these territories are entitled to, thereby creating two layers of overlapping claims: one set that pertains to having title over the land territory as such, and the other to the maritime zones it is entitled to. These mixed disputes consist of two exercises that are separate but at the same time interlinked from the view of the international law of the sea.[1373] At their core, mixed disputes are primarily about territory, which is, broadly formulated, about how territory is acquired. Yet, the international law of the sea is relevant in the following sense: the content of the rights in the maritime zones of the disputed land territory will depend on the law of the sea. However, in the context of effecting a delimitation, there is a hierarchical ordering between the two issues: delimiting a disputed maritime area is subordinate to having an exclusive title over the land territory concerned.[1374]

Issues over title to land territory are regularly combined with conflicts created by the States concerned acting in relation to the adjacent disputed waters, usually being the State in control of the disputed territory,[1375] inter alia, because of conducting mineral resource or fishing activities. The LOSC does not contain a provision that is specifically designed with this type of situation in mind. This is aside from Paragraph 1(b) of Resolution III, included in the Final Act of UNCLOS III, which deals with a special category of mixed disputes: that is, non-self-governing territories, and that States occupying these are not entitled to the rights and privileges attributed to the coastal State under the LOSC, in relation to the waters lying off the coast of such a territory.[1376]

The absence of conventional law in the LOSC being geared specifically to mixed disputes does not imply, however, that there is an absence of international law rules governing those disputed waters that are created by States claiming maritime zones from the base points of the same land territory. Varying with the specifics involved, there are limitations, flowing from other provisions in the LOSC or general international law, or a combination of the two, imposed on the range of acts that fall under the authority of the coastal State which can be undertaken unilaterally within disputed waters located off

1373 R Beckman and CH Schofield, 'Defining EEZ Claims from Islands: A Potential South China Sea Change' (2014) 29(2) *IJMCL* 193, 195.

1374 Van Logchem (n. 52) 34–36.

1375 N Klein, 'Resolving Disputes under UNCLOS when the Coastal and User States are Disputed' in N Hong and G Houlden (eds.), *Maritime Order and the Law in East Asia* (Routledge, 2018) 253, 254.

1376 Section 7.1 above.

land territories over which title is disputed. Amongst others, the UN Charter principles on the peaceful settlement of disputes and not to threaten the use or actual use of force, having received a further elaboration in the Friendly Relations Declaration are applicable in disputed waters *simpliciter*. The fourth paragraph of the Friendly Relations Declaration reiterates that the principle of the prohibition on using force in bilateral relations also applies to situations where competing claims to title are made over the same territory.[1377] It declares it unlawful for a State to use force as a means of settling such a dispute. Due to the close link between competing claims to title over a land territory being made, and the disputed waters that invariably will arise as a result thereof, this requirement emanating, amongst others, from the Friendly Relations Declaration extends to the disputed waters as well. An additional requirement, being a specific application of the principle of States having to settle their disputes peacefully, is to abstain from taking actions that would aggravate or extend the dispute.[1378] Furthermore, pending the settlement of their mixed dispute, States must avoid acts that result in the rights of the other State being prejudiced in such a way that remedial means no longer exist.[1379]

The two obligations contained in Articles 74(3) and 83(3) LOSC might be applicable in certain situations where a dispute on title to territory underlies the creation of disputed waters. However, if these disputed water are the direct result of entitlements to maritime zones being claimed from the same base points of a land territory over which title is disputed, these are excluded from its reach. But this is different if the issue of title is part of a broader maritime boundary dispute in that, irrespective of how the dispute on title to territory is resolved, there are other land territories over which undisputed title is held and from which claims to maritime zones are made, and due to the distance separating them, an overlap of States' EEZ/continental shelf claims is created. Then, Articles 74(3) and 83(3) LOSC would be applicable to those areas where the EEZ or continental shelf claims of States overlap. This is with the exception of territorial sea areas, extending to, at a maximum, the 12 nm limit, which similarly includes those waters directly adjacent to high-tide features whose status is in dispute, and that would be entitled to a territorial sea irrespective of it having the status of a fully entitled island or a rock under Article 121 LOSC.

1377 Chapter 3, Section 3.2 above.
1378 Ibid. Section 3.5.
1379 Ibid. Section 3.4.

8

Acts of Unilateralism in Disputed Maritime Areas: A Survey of State Practice

Various conflicts have arisen between neighbouring States because of activities that are under the authority of the coastal State having been authorised or undertaken unilaterally in disputed areas. These conflicts are not exclusively concentrated in disputed maritime areas located in certain parts of the world. Nonetheless, there are geographic variations as to the extent to which acts falling under coastal State authority are undertaken unilaterally in disputed areas. For instance, West African States have been argued to be particularly willing to award and activate mineral resource concessions located in disputed areas.[1380]

The main aim of this chapter is to bring together relevant examples of State practice where a claimant, or a national of a third State, has undertaken conduct that falls within the authority of the coastal State in a disputed maritime area, which has prompted the other claimant into responding – be it through taking subsequent action by sending naval vessels, seeking to bring such a unilateral activity to an end; diplomatic protests; or taking other enforcement measures against the perceived transgressor. To provide the most complete picture of acts undertaken unilaterally in disputed waters, examples are collected from both where disputes over title to territory underlie the disputed maritime area, and where overlapping claims to maritime zones *simpliciter* exist.

Each section of this chapter will focus on a different category of unilateral activity that falls under the authority of the coastal State having been authorised or undertaken within a disputed maritime area, and conflicts that have arisen in State practice in relation thereto. It will also look at, when faced with such a unilateral act by the other State, what are the types of reactions that States have devised in response. Section 8.1 begins with examples from State practice with regard to unilateral conduct relating to mineral resources in

1380 'Protracted Boundary' (n. 50) 1.

disputed maritime areas by coastal State A, and which have provoked a reaction from coastal State B. Next, in Section 8.2, disputes in relation to fisheries will be examined. This is followed, in Section 8.3, by looking at the broader category of 'collecting information' about the marine environment of disputed maritime areas, and any conflicts that have arisen in this regard. Then, Section 8.4 will assess whether State practice and international judicial practice are aligned, in the sense that the line drawn in the case law that it is lawful to undertake unilateral seismic work in a disputed maritime area, as it does not threaten irreparability, whereas drilling and exploitation activities because they exceed this threshold are unlawful, is reflected in State practice as well. Section 8.5 concludes by making some general observations as to what can be learned from the practice of States as to the (un)lawfulness of activities in disputed maritime areas.

8.1 MINERAL RESOURCES

There is often a repeated pattern in the practice of States whenever acts related to mineral resources begin in disputed maritime areas with the authorisation of one claimant State: they provide a recurring source of conflict between the States concerned, regularly amongst others prompting protests.[1381] Beyond protesting, different types of responses will be employed in reaction to when mineral resource activities are undertaken unilaterally, including States intensifying their patrols of a disputed maritime area or taking law enforcement measures.

8.1.1 *Adriatic Sea*

Croatia opened a tender process for several blocks located in an area that Montenegro also claims in April 2013. Montenegro protested, indicating that its rights over the disputed area would be 'irreparably prejudiced'.[1382] Then, in the same protest, Montenegro softened this claim, by adding a caveat: the prejudice to its rights was 'possibly irreparably'.[1383] Also, Croatia's authorisation of two petroleum companies – one for conducting a 'seismic survey' and the other for conducting 'hydrocarbon exploration and exploitation' – was protested by Montenegro for encroaching on maritime areas that are under its exclusive jurisdiction.[1384] Despite the

1381 Chapter 2, Section 2.3.6 above.
1382 Letter from Montenegro (n. 777).
1383 Ibid.
1384 Ibid.

protest of Montenegro, Croatia conducted its planned seismic survey between September 2013 and January 2014.[1385] Montenegro learned of this after the work licensed by Croatia had been completed. The data gathered as a result was subsequently used by Croatia to seek further bids from the petroleum industry for conducting additional work within the disputed area. Montenegro claimed that this unilateral seismic work had breached international law, requiring its prior consent because of it being an activity under its jurisdiction, and it requested that it be provided with the results that had been gathered in the process.[1386]

In 2015, Croatia decided to open another tender, inviting the petroleum industry to put in bids for the development of blocks in a disputed part of the Adriatic Sea, located south of azimuth 231°. Again, Montenegro protested, stating that these areas could not be opened for consideration by Croatia, because they were located within their disputed territorial sea area.[1387] Croatia applied, by analogy, its preference for equidistance as a delimitation rule[1388] to the period prior to territorial sea delimitation in the form of an interim rule: both States were 'obligated to refrain from exercising any type of jurisdiction beyond the line of equidistance'.[1389]

8.1.2 *Atlantic Ocean*

A maritime boundary agreement concluded between Venezuela and Trinidad and Tobago, delimiting their disputed territorial sea, EEZ, and continental shelf areas was unlawful, according to Guyana, because it included areas that it also claims.[1390] Based on this agreement, both Venezuela and Trinidad and Tobago have welcomed the petroleum industry to put in bids to obtain exploratory rights on their own side of the boundary line; this was protested by Guyana on the ground of its rights over the area being infringed upon. Although the lease sale generated some initial interest, petroleum companies

1385 Communication from the Government of Montenegro to the United Nations, dated 1 December 2014, concerning the Exploration and Exploitation of Resources in the Adriatic Sea by the Republic of Croatia; Note from the Ministry of Foreign Affairs and European Integration to the Ministry of Foreign Affairs and European Affairs of the Republic of Croatia, 19 November 2014, available at www.un.org/depts/los/LEGISLATIONANDTREATIES/PDFFILES/communications/MNG_note20150619en.pdf, 11 and 14.

1386 Ibid.

1387 Ibid.

1388 Klemenčić and Gosar (n. 522) 132.

1389 Arnaut (n. 522) 434.

1390 BIICL Report (n. 141) 61.

withdrew after gaining knowledge of Guyana's position and the protests it had made.[1391]

Several incidents arose between France and Canada off the coast of the French overseas territory of St. Pierre and Miquelon in the period between 1966 and 1993, because of unilateral conduct undertaken concerning mineral resources in relation to their disputed continental shelf area.[1392] For example, in 1983, a seismic vessel being authorised by France to conduct a seismic survey of the disputed area was forced to abandon its intentions after a protest by Canada.[1393] Against the background of an increasing interest in the offshore development of mineral resources in the 1960s, augmented by the conclusion of the 1958 CSC giving coastal States sovereign rights over the seabed, both Canada and France started issuing licences and enacted legislation allowing the disputed continental shelf area to be explored for mineral resources.[1394] In 1967, the two States tacitly agreed not to allow any subsequent acts on the basis of earlier issued concessions to proceed unilaterally.[1395] When the Arbitral Tribunal dealt with the underlying maritime boundary dispute, it appraised the behaviour of the two States as follows: 'no drilling was undertaken' in their disputed area, as a result of their protests and counter-protests.[1396] Similar restraint was not shown by France with regard to seismic work. Illustrating this was that a French concessionaire (Elf-Aquitaine) was authorised to undertake a seismic survey at a point that was removed some 60 km southeast off the coast of St. Pierre.[1397] However, although Canada has consistently refrained from activating previously awarded exploration concessions, it continued to

[1391] O Ismael, *The Trail of Diplomacy: a Documentary History of the Guyana-Venezuela Border Issue* (Xlibris, 2013), available at www.guyana.org/features/trail_diplomacy_pt9.html #chap48.

[1392] 'Falklands Impasse Jarring to French on Isles in Disputed Area Off Canada', *The New York Times*, 20 May 1982.

[1393] LS Parsons, *Management of Marine Fisheries in Canada* (NRCCDFO, 1993) 313.

[1394] D Day, 'The St. Pierre and Miquelon Maritime Boundary Case: Origin, Issues, Implications' in C Grundy-Warr (ed.), *International Boundaries and Conflict Resolution: 1989 Conference Proceedings* (IBRU, 1990) 151, 154, 158–159; BG Buzan and DD Middlemis, 'Canadian Foreign Policy and Exploitation of the Seabed' in B Johnson and MW Zacher (eds.), *Canadian Foreign Policy and the Law of the Sea* (University of British Columbia Press, 1977) 1, 37–38.

[1395] TL McDorman, 'The Search for Resolution of the Canada–France Ocean Dispute Adjacent to St. Pierre and Miquelon' (1994) 17(1) *DLJ* 35, 39.

[1396] *Delimitation of Maritime Areas between Canada and France* [1992] XXI RIAA 265, 275–276, 295–296 [8] [89].

[1397] Day (n. 1394) 158.

award new ones – this was a practice that was mirrored by France, which granted two more licences in 1987.[1398]

8.1.3 *Bay of Bengal*

Deposits of mineral resources in the Bay of Bengal are rumoured to be vast and commercially viable.[1399] All of its coastal States (i.e. Bangladesh, India, and Myanmar) have attempted, on several occasions, to assess the mineral resource potential of disputed parts of the Bay of Bengal, as a result of which various conflicts have occurred between them. In this vein, both India and Myanmar have undertaken unilateral acts concerning mineral resources within their disputed areas, including seismic work, leading to protests from the other claimants. Bangladesh's position has been that mineral resources activities had to be postponed until after delimitation.[1400] However, Bangladesh did open concession areas in disputed parts of the Bay of Bengal, and invited bids from the petroleum industry, but decided to put its plan on ice after India and Myanmar protested.

Reports emerged in 2008 that Myanmar had given assurances to Bangladesh that it would abstain from mineral resource activity within their disputed area.[1401] However, on a routine patrol, a Bangladeshi naval vessel encountered four vessels – some of which flew Myanmar's flag, others operating under the latter's licence – that were prospecting some 50 nm off the coast of St Martin's Island.[1402] A number of Myanmar warships accompanied these four vessels,[1403] one of which was dispatched to the disputed maritime area to begin drilling.[1404]

Bangladesh's protest took two forms. First, it protested against Myanmar's unilateral actions via diplomatic channels, in which it ordered Myanmar's vessels to leave the disputed area at once.[1405] Second, Bangladesh responded

1398 Ibid. 158–159.

1399 M Shah Alam and A Al Faruque, 'The Problem of Delimitation of Bangladesh's Maritime Boundaries with India and Myanmar: Prospects for a Solution' (2010) 25(3) *IJMCL* 405, 405–406.

1400 'Bangladesh, Burma Dispute Oil Exploration in Bay of Bengal', *Voice of America News*, 4 November 2008.

1401 Bissinger (n. 24) 109.

1402 Shah Alam and Al Faruque (n. 1399) 405–406.

1403 'Bangladesh and Burma Send Warships into Bay of Bengal', *The Guardian*, 4 November 2008.

1404 'Myanmar Warships Withdraw from Disputed Waters in Bay of Bengal', *OneIndia*, 9 November 2008.

1405 'Myanmar Brings Warships to Explore Bangladesh Waters', *The Daily Star*, 3 November 2008.

through deploying three of its naval vessels to the area concerned to put an end to Myanmar's activities.[1406] However, upon arriving at the drilling location, there was a stand-off with the vessels from Myanmar that lasted no less than a week.[1407] After extensive diplomatic efforts were made by the two States, all vessels withdrew from the disputed maritime area.

Following this incident, and while the underlying maritime boundary dispute was being considered by the ITLOS, both States refrained from exploratory conduct in their disputed area. However, in 2009, ConocoPhillips put in a bid with Bangladesh to develop certain blocks located in the disputed maritime area,[1408] prompting a protest from both Myanmar and India.[1409]

In 1974, a dispute arose between Bangladesh and India, at the heart of which were two aspects: first, that Bangladesh had started to entertain bids from the petroleum industry for conducting exploratory work in their disputed area; and, second, that Bangladesh had awarded concessions to six different petroleum companies, with a view to authorising them to start work in relation to the disputed continental shelf area.[1410]

In 1981, an Indian vessel equipped with instruments to conduct a survey of the seabed started operating near the disputed South Talpatty/New Moore Island. After learning of this, Bangladesh dispatched its naval vessels to the area in question, to put a halt to India's unilateral conduct.[1411]

Another incident occurred between Bangladesh and India in 2008. Then, the CGG *Symphony* was licensed by India to survey the disputed area, giving rise to protests by both Bangladesh and Myanmar.[1412] Bangladesh protested via diplomatic channels and by sending two of its warships to the area, reiterating its position that acts concerning mineral resources within a disputed maritime area had to be refrained from prior to its delimitation.[1413]

At the end of 2008, a new conflict arose between Bangladesh and India, after three vessels were authorised by India to conduct seismic work in their

1406 'Bangladesh Protests "Trespassing" of Myanmar Oil and Gas Ships in Bay of Bengal', *Global Insight*, 3 November 2008.
1407 RA Balaram, 'Case Study: The Myanmar and Bangladesh Maritime Boundary Dispute in the Bay of Bengal and Its Implications for South China Sea Claims' (2012) 31(3) *JCSAA* 85, 88.
1408 'Signing Agreement with IOCs for Gas Block Seems Unlikely Before UNCLOS Settlement', *United News of Bangladesh*, 28 March 2011.
1409 Bissinger (n. 24) 136.
1410 Habibur Rahman (n. 137) 1308.
1411 Prescott and Schofield (n. 55) 282.
1412 'Indian Ships Leave' (n. 24).
1413 'Bangladesh, Burma' (n. 1400).

disputed area; they were accompanied by various other vessels, including an Indian coastguard vessel.[1414] Bangladesh lodged a protest with India, accusing the latter of intruding into its waters, and unlawfully conducting a seismic survey. As a further response, Bangladesh dispatched two of its 'warships' to the area where the seismic work was to begin.[1415] Initially, the Indian vessels showed a willingness to clear the area and, in fact, did so. However, as the Bangladeshi naval vessels continued to maintain a presence in the disputed maritime area, the seismic vessels licensed by India later rethought their position, returned to the area that they had earlier left, and refused to leave, now arguing that it belonged exclusively to India.

8.1.4 *Barents Sea*

Prior to the entry into force of the LOSC, Norway and the Union of Soviet Socialist Republics (USSR) had both authorised seismic work in a disputed part of the Barents Sea, which has now been delimited. Before long, a consistent pattern could be detected in that whenever one of the States concerned decided to act without the other State's consent in relation to the mineral resources located in the disputed continental shelf area, these acts were met with protests from the other claimant.[1416]

After successfully striking mineral resources in the eastern part of the Barents Sea, Norway was reportedly provided with the impetus to explore more parts of the disputed continental shelf area.[1417] Reflecting on its outstanding maritime boundary dispute with Russia, the Norwegian Minister for Oil and Energy made a statement in Parliament in 1982 that international law obligates claimant States to exercise restraint, and to refrain from undertaking conduct that makes reaching a delimitation agreement more difficult.[1418]

A year later, in May 1983, a Russian drilling vessel (*Valentin Shashin*) drilled an oil well approximately 1.5 nm west of an area located on the Norwegian side of a hypothetical equidistance boundary. Russia initially denied that drilling had taken place,[1419] but later admitted to its occurrence, although pointing to the act being accidental rather than predesigned. Norway

1414 'Bangladesh Summons Indian Envoy over "Intrusion" in Bay Waters', *The Press Trust of India*, 27 December 2008.

1415 Ibid.

1416 Churchill and Ulfstein (n. 407) 89.

1417 Ibid. 85.

1418 Ibid. 87.

1419 Ibid. 77.

framed its protest in mild terms: given that an equidistance boundary ran through the disputed maritime area, Russia had encroached on the side where Norway could exercise exclusive jurisdiction. Because the drilling took place quite close to the putative boundary, falling within the fault margin calculated by Norway, the severity of the infraction, and the extent to which Norway's interests had been infringed upon, were considered to be rather marginal.[1420] Norway indicated, however, that, had the drilling been undertaken in a location placed further on its side of the equidistance boundary, the protest would have been worded more strongly.[1421] Not long thereafter, in 1984, the two States came to an agreement, both pledging not to undertake any exploratory activities in relation to mineral resources pending delimitation of the continental shelf area boundary.

8.1.5 *Beaufort Sea*

Attempts at exploration or exploitation of the Beaufort Sea have been made by both Canada and the United States, but these have been complicated by two factors: the overlapping claims of the two States and the sometimes harsh environmental conditions in the area.[1422] Conflict has been prevented from arising between the States concerned largely as a result of no work being authorised in areas of the disputed Beaufort Sea on the basis of previously awarded concessions.[1423]

Yet, over the years, Canada and the United States have developed a mutual licensing practice for exploration in parts of the disputed Beaufort Sea to determine its oil and gas potential. Canada's practice of concessioning the petroleum industry goes back to the beginning of 1965. A licence awarded by Canada in 1973 stipulated, however, that drilling had to be postponed until 1976.[1424] That same year, the United States issued a protest challenging the lawfulness of Canada issuing licences for exploratory work and drilling that extended into disputed parts 'of the continental shelf that are or may be subject to the jurisdiction of the US'.[1425]

1420 Rolston and McDorman (n. 842) 44.

1421 RR Churchill, 'Maritime Boundary Problems in the Barents Sea' in G Blake (ed.), *Maritime Boundaries and Ocean Resources* (Croom Helm, 1987) 147, 157.

1422 L Rey, 'Resource Development in the Arctic' in DG Dallmeyer and L DeVorsey Jr (eds.), *Rights to Oceanic Resources* (Martinus Nijhoff, 1989) 167, 170–171.

1423 Byers (n. 304) 73; D Gray, 'Canada's Unresolved Maritime Boundaries' *IBRU Boundary and Security Bulletin*, 63.

1424 LJ Carter, 'Oil Drilling in the Beaufort Sea: Leaving It to Luck and Technology' (1976) 191 (4230) *Science* 929, 929–931.

1425 Byers (n. 304) 75.

Canada, undeterred by the United States protest, granted exploratory rights to two petroleum companies in 1986 and 1987 for blocks located in their disputed area[1426] – however, these concessions were not activated. The 141st meridian of west longitude was used by Canada as forming the point up to which it could freely award concessions pending delimitation of the continental shelf boundary.[1427] After the United States included disputed parts of the continental shelf area within prior lease sales, and issued some concessions to the petroleum industry, these concessions were not subsequently activated either.[1428]

8.1.6 *Celebes Sea*

The mutual licensing practice of Malaysia and Indonesia in relation to the disputed western part of the Celebes Sea has regularly led to tensions between them.[1429] In 2005, Malaysia allowed one of its concessionaires to make a start with unilateral seismic work in the disputed area located between Ambalat and Batuan Unrarang off the coast of Borneo. Then, Indonesia, on at least three separate occasions, protested against this seismic work authorised by Malaysia.[1430]

Indonesia's protest centred on the fact that conducting seismic work would breach the sovereignty it enjoyed over the disputed continental shelf area.[1431] Malaysia denied ever receiving a protest from Indonesia, however,[1432] and decided to survey the disputed area. It took the position that the area in question was under its exclusive jurisdiction, thereby allowing Malaysia to authorise seismic work.[1433] After a series of protests and counter-protests, both Indonesia and Malaysia decided to dispatch their navy and coastguard vessels to the disputed waters surrounding Ambalat, becoming embroiled in a stand-off shortly thereafter.

8.1.7 *East China Sea*

As the States of the East China Sea started to claim more extensive continental shelf entitlements in the 1960s, they also started to enter into exploration

1426 Northern Oil and Gas Annual Report 2005, 16 and the enclosed map.

1427 B Baker, 'Filling an Arctic Gap: Legal and Regulatory Possibilities for Canadian–U.S. Cooperation in the Beaufort Sea' (2009) 34(1) *VLR* 57, 69.

1428 Ibid. 70, 99.

1429 CH Schofield and IMA Arsana, 'Ambalat Revised: The Way Forward?', *The Jakarta Post*, 9 June 2005; 'Indonesia to Fight Malaysia's Ambalat Oil Claims', *Jakarta Globe*, 22 October 2009.

1430 'Areas in Sulawesi Sea within Malaysia's Borders', *Malaysia Star*, 2 March 2005.

1431 'Indonesia Protests Malaysia's Oil Pacts', *Associated Press*, 25 February 2005.

1432 Areej et al. (n. 412) 181.

1433 Forbes (n. 580) 69.

contracts with the petroleum industry at a rapid pace. The areas of continental shelf covered under these contracts overlapped, to varying extents, with the claims and concessions of other claimant States of the East China Sea.[1434] Complicating matters further was that sometime later China also claimed sovereign rights over several already disputed continental shelf areas and, in addition, claimed to have title over the Senkaku/Diaoyu Islands.[1435]

In 1970, the Japanese Ryukyu government had already received several bids from the petroleum industry for obtaining drilling rights in relation to the disputed waters located off the Senkaku/Diaoyu Islands.[1436] However, Japan refused to consider these bids, because it did not want to provoke China.[1437]

Because of China's announcement that it had claims as well, exploration activities that were already in progress by other claimant States in disputed parts of the East China Sea largely came to a halt by the middle of 1971.[1438] Thereafter, in March 1973, after a US-incorporated oil vessel moved into a disputed area of the East China Sea, China protested.[1439] After China began to claim parts of the East China Sea, the United States had warned its petroleum companies deciding to conduct work under contracts entered into with other claimants that they would no longer enjoy its protection.[1440]

Areas in relation to which Japan and South Korea successfully concluded a provisional arrangement to share the mineral resources in 1974 were included within the reach of the Chinese claim.[1441] Although China protested,[1442] Japan and South Korea explored the disputed continental shelf area between 1980 and 1986, but no commercially viable deposits of mineral resources were struck.[1443]

1434 CH Park, 'Joint Development of Mineral Resources in Disputed Waters: The Case of Japan and South Korea in the East China Sea' (1981) 6(11) *Energy* 1335.

1435 VH Li, 'China and Off-Shore Oil: The Tiao-yu Tai Dispute' (1975) 10 *SJILS* 143, 147.

1436 Ibid. 145–146.

1437 R Drifte, 'From "Sea of Confrontation" to "Sea of Peace Cooperation and Friendship"? – Japan Facing China in the East China Sea' (2008) 3 *Japan Aktuell* 27, 35–37.

1438 KF Royer, 'Japan's East China Sea Ocean Boundaries: What Solutions Can a Confused Environment Provide in a Complex Boundary Dispute?' (1989) 22(3) *VJTL* 581, 618; PC Yuan, 'Disputes over Marine Resources in East Asia: Conflict Ahead' (1986) 1(4) *IJECL* 391, 394–395.

1439 Ibid. 395.

1440 Park (n. 1434) 1337.

1441 Agreement between Japan and the Republic of Korea concerning the Establishment of a Boundary in the Northern Part of the Continental Shelf Adjacent to the Two Countries (with Map and Agreed Minutes) (signed 30 January 1974, entered into force 22 June 1978) 1225 UNTS 103.

1442 Zou (n. 1367) 159; Van Dyke (n. 628) 57.

1443 Drifte (n. 1437) 32.

In June 1992, China welcomed bids from foreign petroleum companies for exploratory rights in parts of the East China Sea that were also claimed by South Korea; the latter protested after learning about this.[1444]

In the 1990s, problems in China's relations with Japan started to mount when China started exploitation of gas fields in the East China Sea in areas located approximately 5 nm on the 'Chinese side' of the provisional equidistance boundary.[1445] After learning thereof, Japan protested: the exploitation of mineral resources on the Chinese side of the provisional boundary, due to their fugacious properties, has led to those resources, which are placed on the Japanese side, being extracted to its detriment.[1446] China has argued that, due to the gas fields being located in areas that fall on its own side of the equidistance boundary, it is allowed to commence exploitation.[1447]

After reports emerged that China sought to drill in increasingly closer proximity to the provisional equidistance boundary,[1448] Japan protested on 8 June 2004.[1449] Upon learning of this protest, the concessionaires backed out of earlier commitments in relation to the development of mineral resources located within the disputed area.[1450] In the wake thereof, Japan abandoned its previous self-restraint by granting a drilling concession for an area next to where China wanted to undertake gas exploitation activities.[1451] China protested against the granting of this concession.[1452] Despite the Chinese protest, Teikoku Oil Company, after initially stating it would postpone drilling for safety reasons,[1453] indicated that, if Japan was able to give assurances that drilling could be undertaken without Chinese interference, it was willing to make use of its concession.[1454]

In 2005, after learning that China was planning to drill in one of the gas fields (i.e. Chunxiao), Japan 'regretted' this unilateral move by

1444 JH Paik, 'The United Nations Convention on the Law of the Sea and Northeast Asian Maritime Practice' (1994) 22 *KJILCL* 107, 117–118.

1445 Tan (n. 399) 141; Zhang (n. 54) 315.

1446 'Joint Press Conference by Minister for Foreign Affairs Masahiko Koumura and Minister of Economy, Trade and Industry Akira Amari (Regarding Cooperation between Japan and China in the East China Sea)', 18 June 2008, available at www.mofa.go.jp/announce/fm_press/2008/6/0618.html.

1447 Gao (n. 261) 294.

1448 'Japan Moves to Drill in East China Sea', *The Japan Times*, 17 January 2005; 'Japanese Firms' Answer to Undersea Rivalry: Share', *The Associated Press*, 21 April 2005.

1449 Donaldson and Pratt (n. 927) 418.

1450 SK Kim, 'China and Japan Maritime Disputes in the East China Sea: A Note on Recent Developments' (2012) 43(3) *ODIL* 296.

1451 'LDP Eyes Law to Protect Gas-Drilling Ships', *The Japan Times*, 9 June 2005; 'Teikoku Oil to Get Test-Drilling Rights', *The Japan Times*, 1 July 2005.

1452 'Defending Rightful Sea Territory', *China Daily*, 28 July 2005.

1453 'Teikoku Oil Seeks Rights to Test-Drill in Disputed Areas', *The Japan Times*, 29 April 2005.

1454 'Teikoku to Drill Despite Risk of China Action', *The Japan Times*, 27 August 2005.

China.[1455] A year later, in 2006, Japan protested when China intended to take the Bajiaoting field into production, which is similarly located on the Chinese side of a provisional equidistance boundary.[1456] In that same year, and after China had started exploitation in the Pinghu field, Japan requested China to delay production up until their maritime boundary dispute was settled.[1457] Due to Japan's protests, China pledged to abandon its intention to develop the Chunxiao field unilaterally.[1458] Thereafter, there were Japanese sightings of 'mystery equipment' moving into the disputed area.[1459] Evidence compiled by Japan demonstrated that China had proceeded to develop disputed fields located in parts of the East China Sea.[1460] It was reported by the Chief Cabinet Secretary of Japan that, in 2015, China had increased the number of installations present in the disputed area by twelve, bringing the total amount of installations having been placed on the Chinese side of the equidistance boundary line to sixteen.[1461] After receiving another protest from Japan, China replied by stating that the waters in question were without doubt under China's exclusive jurisdiction, meaning that it enjoys the sovereign right to exploit the available mineral resources from its continental shelf in any way it chooses.[1462]

8.1.8 *Eastern Atlantic Ocean*

Several conflicts have arisen between Barbados and Trinidad and Tobago because of unilateral conduct being undertaken in connection with mineral resources, and prior to Barbados submitting their maritime boundary dispute to an Arbitral Tribunal constituted in accordance with Part XV LOSC.

Barbados began with licensing in 1979, in November of that year issuing its first concession and later another one in 1996,[1463] both of which extended up to the

1455 'Japan "Regrets" China Drilling', *The Japan Times*, 1 September 2005.

1456 'Protest over China Move to Develop New Gas Field', *The Asahi Shimbun*, 30 August 2006.

1457 'Japan Protests China Gas Drill in Dispute Field, Shiozaki Says', *Bloomberg*, 8 November 2006.

1458 Japan–China Joint Press Statement of 18 June 2008, 'Cooperation between Japan and China in the East China Sea' and two accompanying Understandings', Website of MOFA, Japan, available at www.mofa.go.jp/files/000091726.pdf (in English).

1459 'Mystery Equipment Spotted at Disputed Gas Field', *The Japan Times*, 18 September 2010.

1460 'The Current Status of China's Unilateral Development of Natural Resources in the East China Sea', Website of the Japanese Ministry of Foreign Affairs, 31 March 2021, available at www.mofa.go.jp/a_o/c_m1/page3e_000356.html.

1461 Ibid.

1462 'China's Oil and Gas Exploration in the East China Sea Is Rightful and Legitimate', Website of the Ministry of Foreign Affairs of the PRC, 24 July 2015, available at www.fmprc.gov.cn/mfa_eng/wjdt_665385/2649_665393/t1285037.shtml (in English).

1463 *Barbados* v. *Trinidad and Tobago* (n. 582) Barbados's Memorial 33 [74].

equidistance boundary lying between the coasts of Barbados and Trinidad and Tobago. On both occasions, Barbados contended that Trinidad and Tobago did not protest upon the receipt of its notifications.[1464] A similar silence was maintained, according to Barbados, when two petroleum oil companies conducted exploratory work within the disputed area on the basis of earlier-issued concessions.[1465]

Trinidad and Tobago tendered two opened blocks located in the disputed area in 1996 and 2001, which prompted protests from Barbados. On receiving these protests, Trinidad and Tobago withdrew these blocks from sale.[1466] Similarly, when Trinidad and Tobago was considering authorising a seismic survey of the disputed area in 2001, Barbados, upon learning of this, informed the petroleum industry that such an act would provoke a response from it.[1467] Trinidad and Tobago construed this as constituting interference, by Barbados, with what would be a lawful activity in a disputed maritime area.[1468] In 2003, Trinidad and Tobago opened another tender process, which was once again protested against by Barbados.[1469]

After initiating proceedings before an Arbitral Tribunal in 2004, Barbados claimed that it had protested consistently against acts undertaken concerning mineral resources unilaterally by the former in their disputed area. In rebutting this claim, Trinidad and Tobago indicated that, although it had received protests from Barbados, it successfully organised bidding rounds inviting the petroleum industry to bid for exploration rights and authorised seismic work in their disputed area.[1470] In its award, the Tribunal confirmed that both States had given concessions in relation to their disputed maritime area and, on this basis, allowed seismic work to be undertaken.[1471]

8.1.9 *Gulf of Guinea*

Cameroon and Nigeria both unilaterally authorised the mapping of the mineral resources potential of their disputed maritime area located off the disputed Bakassi Peninsula.[1472] According to Nigeria, 'a lot of oil activities have been carried out in the boundary between Nigeria and Cameroon within the

1464 Ibid. 34 [75].
1465 Ibid.
1466 Ibid. 40 [89].
1467 Ibid. 40 [90].
1468 Ibid. Trinidad and Tobago's Counter-Memorial 3–4 [10].
1469 Ibid. Barbados's Memorial 40–41 [91].
1470 Ibid. Trinidad and Tobago's Counter-Memorial 14–15 [38]–[41].
1471 Ibid. Award 108 [363].
1472 *Cameroon* v. *Nigeria* (n. 454) Nigeria's Rejoinder Part I Chapter 3 [3.267].

continental shelf area',[1473] including concessioning, seismic work, and drilling.[1474] For instance, Elf-Aquitaine had surveyed the disputed continental shelf area pursuant to a licence granted by Cameroon.[1475] Nigeria started drilling in the disputed area in 1961. Drilling by Cameroon in the same area went back to 1967,[1476] and it reportedly started seismic work in 1964.[1477]

Cameroon claimed to have issued several concessions located in the disputed continental shelf area, without receiving a protest from Nigeria.[1478] Nigeria did not contest this claim,[1479] but it construed their history as that Cameroon also remained silent in relation to similar acts undertaken by Nigeria in the same area.[1480] An arrangement concluded earlier with Nigeria would have required Cameroon to observe this silence, so the latter argued.[1481]

In November 1989, a Nigerian army helicopter detected an oil rig that was being brought into position by Elf-Serepca, which had been authorised by Cameroon to conduct drilling activities. While circling over the rig, the army personnel in the helicopter ordered the oil rig to leave the disputed area.[1482]

Equatorial Guinea also granted concessions for blocks located in the same disputed area; these conflicted with concessions awarded by both Cameroon and Nigeria.[1483] After gaining independence from Spain, Equatorial Guinea, in 1982, started to alter the scope of the concessions that had been granted earlier by Spain, resulting in them overlapping with concessions previously awarded by Nigeria.[1484] Unilateral activities in relation to mineral resources had been undertaken by both Equatorial Guinea and Nigeria, leading inter alia to the discovery of the oil-rich Zakiro field.[1485] However, Equatorial Guinea protested against the drilling licensed by Nigeria.[1486]

1473 Ibid. [3.270].
1474 Ibid. [3.291].
1475 DJ Young, 'Energy Developments and Maritime Boundary Disputes: Two West African Examples' (1984) 19(2) *TILJ* 435, 443.
1476 BIICL Report (n. 141) 89.
1477 *Cameroon* v. *Nigeria* (n. 454) Nigeria's Rejoinder Part I Chapter 3 [5.15].
1478 Ibid. Cameroon's Reply 244–245 [5.14]–[5.16].
1479 Ibid. Nigeria's Rejoinder Part I Chapter 3 [3.278].
1480 Ibid. Cameroon's Reply 439–440 [9.114]–[9.115].
1481 Ibid.
1482 Ibid. Nigeria's Rejoinder Part I Chapter 3 [5.15].
1483 Ibid. Part I Chapter 10 [10.31].
1484 Ibid. [10.30].
1485 Ibid.
1486 Ibid. [10.30]–[10.31].

8.1.10 *Gulf of Maine*

Starting in 1964,[1487] both Canada and the United States had extended invitations to the petroleum industry to bid for blocks located in their disputed area, and subsequently they granted exploratory licences to various petroleum companies. The licences granted by Canada used a strict equidistance boundary line, which in its view depicted the putative maritime boundary between the two States' coasts prior to delimitation.[1488]

In 1968, the United States suggested to Canada that it should abstain from all mineral resource-related activities within their disputed area pending its delimitation.[1489] Accompanying this suggestion was that, at a minimum, drilling should be eschewed in the disputed area. However, Canada opposed the banning of all such conduct in the area; a moratorium on the 'exploitation' of mineral resources was as far as it was willing to go.[1490] While the ICJ was considering the maritime boundary dispute, no drilling was undertaken in the disputed continental shelf area;[1491] it appears that none of the parties to the dispute wanted to make the delimitation negotiations that were being held in parallel more difficult.[1492]

8.1.11 *Gulf of Thailand*

Beginning in the second half of the twentieth century, Vietnam, Kampuchea (now Cambodia), and Thailand awarded several overlapping concessions in relation to disputed parts of the Gulf of Thailand. However, after Thailand sought to renew some of these concessions in the 1960s, Vietnam cautioned Thailand not to allow mineral resource-related work to be undertaken in areas to which it claimed to have rights as well – due to this protest, the concessions awarded by Thailand remained inactive.[1493] Furthermore, in 1983, Vietnam warned Thailand not to proceed with its intentions to grant concessions and to start exploring their disputed maritime area.[1494]

1487 *Delimitation of the Maritime Boundary in the Gulf of Maine Area (Canada/United States of America)* [1984] ICJ Rep 246, 279 [61].
1488 Ibid.
1489 Ibid. United States Memorial 355 Annex 55.
1490 Ibid. 356 Annex 56.
1491 McDorman (n. 1395) 35.
1492 *Canada/United States of America* (n. 1487) 282 [67]; United States Memorial 55–56 [154].
1493 Valencia and Miyoshi (n. 120) 226.
1494 Fox et al. (n. 113) 163.

The shared position of Cambodia and Thailand was that no mineral resource exploration activities could be undertaken unilaterally pending the delimitation of their disputed area.[1495] On the eve of discussions between Cambodia and Thailand on the issue, reports emerged that Cambodia was planning to grant an exploration concession to a petroleum company;[1496] Cambodia refuted these reports, however.[1497]

In the mid-1980s, Malaysia decided to authorise drilling in relation to a maritime area disputed between itself and Vietnam.[1498] In its wake, Vietnam issued a formal protest to the Malaysian government, framing its objections in terms of the drilling being irreconcilable with the 'friendly and cooperative spirit' defining their bilateral relations.[1499]

8.1.12 *Kattegat*

Shortly after negotiations over delimiting the continental shelf boundary in the Kattegat strait between Denmark and Sweden were aborted, Denmark decided to activate the licence of one of its concessionaires, allowing an exploratory well to be drilled in the disputed continental shelf area.[1500] However, Sweden had previously expressed the view that, prior to delimitation, the gathering of information on the disputed continental shelf area could not be undertaken without its prior consent.[1501] Once Sweden learned of the drilling, it protested.[1502]

8.1.13 *Mediterranean Sea*

In terms of its characteristics, the Mediterranean Sea can be qualified as a semi-enclosed sea in the sense of Article 122 LOSC.[1503] Many of its coastal States have not proclaimed an EEZ[1504] – were they to claim one, the

1495 'Oil Sidelined in Thailand-Cambodia Dispute', *Platts Oilgram News*, 18 May 2011; Schofield and Tan-Mullins (n. 186) 78.

1496 'Cambodia Says' (n. 938).

1497 'Talks Urged for Disputed Zone', *Bangkok Post*, 25 August 2011; 'Thailand/Cambodia Wikileaks Reveals Thai–Cambodia Relations Before Thaksin's Ouster', *Thai Press Reports*, 26 July 2011.

1498 Thao (n. 159) 81.

1499 Ibid.

1500 Lagoni (n. 243) 364.

1501 Churchill and Ulfstein (n. 407) 87.

1502 Lagoni (n. 243) 364.

1503 Chapter 2, Section 2.2 above.

1504 Vukas (n. 550) 150.

remaining sea areas would be turned into disputed EEZ areas. Complicating the maritime boundary disputes in the Mediterranean Sea is the political landscape;[1505] a notable example of this is the absence of diplomatic relations between Israel and Lebanon.[1506]

Since the 1970s, petroleum companies have been attempting unsuccessfully to obtain exploratory rights from Lebanon in relation to a maritime area that is in dispute with Israel.[1507] Discoveries of significant amounts of mineral gas resources off their coasts in the eastern part of the Mediterranean Sea, particularly in the Levantine Basin, made under the sole licence of Israel have revamped the conflict between the two States at the beginning of the twenty-first century.[1508]

Various letters were sent by both Lebanon and Israel to the UN Secretary-General, in which they contested the lawfulness of each other's mineral resources activities that were undertaken in relation to their disputed area. In a letter from February 2017, Israel protested against Lebanon having opened a tender process for several blocks located in an area that Israel felt exclusively belonged to itself.[1509] In its response, dated a month later, Lebanon took a position along similar lines: it pointed to the exclusive usage it argued to have over the maritime area concerned, which allowed it to take steps to start developing the mineral resources contained therein.[1510] At the end of 2017, after the Lebanese government announced that it had accepted a bid from a consortium of petroleum companies and that it would grant a licence, Israel reiterated its earlier protest that these concessions encroached into its maritime areas.[1511] Lebanon's response centred around the position that the area in question is under its exclusive jurisdiction, which entitled it to give mineral resource concessions in respect thereto.[1512] Further, Lebanon took issue with Israel's commitment to protect its sovereign rights, which Lebanon perceived

[1505] T Scovazzi, 'Maritime Boundaries in the Eastern Mediterranean Sea' (2012) *Policy Brief* 1, 8–10, 11 June 2012, available at www.gmfus.org/publications/maritime-boundaries-eastern-mediterranean-sea.

[1506] Zhang and Zheng (n. 519) 117.

[1507] SR Langford, *Issues and Problems in Mediterranean Maritime Boundary Delimitation: A Geographical Analysis* (PhD Thesis, Durham University, 1993) 834.

[1508] Zhang and Zheng (n. 519) 117–121.

[1509] Letter of the Permanent Mission of Israel to the United Nations addressed to the Secretary-General, UN Doc. MI-SG-02022017, 2 February 2017.

[1510] Letter of the Permanent Mission of Lebanon to the United Nations addressed to the Secretary-General, UN Doc. 574/2017, 20 March 2017.

[1511] Letter of the Permanent Mission of Israel to the United Nations addressed to the Secretary-General, UN Doc. MI-SG-12212017, 21 December 2017.

[1512] Letter of the Permanent Mission of Lebanon to the United Nations addressed to the Secretary-General, UN Doc. 154/18, 26 January 2018.

to be a scarcely veiled threat, in effect meaning Israel would resort to an unlawful use of force. Beyond making clear that it would not hesitate to use force in self-defence, Lebanon in the same letter also indicated that, if Israel authorised one of its concessionaries to begin 'directional drilling' in blocks adjacent to those created by Lebanon and through which Lebanon's mineral resources would be siphoned off, it would take 'all appropriate measures' to prevent that. In November 2019, Lebanon complained to the UNSC after Israel authorised the *Med Survey* (a 'hydrographic survey vessel') to operate within their disputed EEZ area, at a point 18 nm removed from Lebanon's coast.[1513]

For Malta and Italy, the need for delimiting their overlapping EEZ/continental shelf claims in the Ionian Sea became clear after Italy announced that it was preparing to simplify its existing legislation relating to mineral resource development within these waters.[1514] Combined with this, Italy invited the petroleum industry to put in bids to obtain exploratory rights. Malta made a similar announcement, indicating that it was open to receive bids from the petroleum industry for disputed areas of continental shelf. Italy lodged a protest: Malta's intention to auction off concession rights located in a disputed area was contrary to international law, breaching the 'spirit and letter' of the LOSC.[1515] Furthermore, Italy invoked paragraph 1 of Articles 74 and 83 LOSC in its protest, claiming that Malta's auctioning of rights was in violation of what can be regarded as an 'equitable solution' pursuant to this paragraph.[1516]

During the 1970s, several incidents occurred between Libya and Tunisia because of unilateral conduct being undertaken in their disputed continental shelf area.[1517] After Libya awarded several concessions located in the disputed area in 1974, an overlap was created with concession areas opened prior thereto, in 1968 by Tunisia, and in relation to which it had issued exploration rights to the petroleum industry.[1518] In 1976, a Tunisian concessionaire struck oil in a part of the disputed area, being approximately 80 km removed off the coast of Tunisia in the Gulf of Gabes.[1519] A drilling vessel (*Scarabeo IV*) operated by Agip, a subsidiary of Total that was commissioned by Tunisia, was forced to leave the disputed area by Libya in early 1977.[1520] After the

1513 Identical letters dated 24 January 2020 from the Permanent Representative of Lebanon to the United Nations addressed to the Secretary-General and the President of the Security Council, UN Doc. A/74/665–S/2020/71, 27 January 2020.

1514 'Italy Joins Rush for Oil and Gas Rights', *Financial Times*, 10 October 2011.

1515 Ibid.

1516 Ibid.

1517 *Guyana* v. *Suriname* (n. 7) Suriname's Counter-Memorial 81.

1518 *Continental Shelf (Tunisia/Libyan Arab Jamahiriya)* (Judgment) [1982] ICJ Rep 18, 35 [21].

1519 Langford (n. 1507) 876.

1520 Ibid. 861.

removal of its rig, Total indicated that the resumption of all future work in the disputed maritime area was dependent on a delimitation agreement being reached. Not long thereafter, and while the underlying maritime boundary dispute was under the consideration of the ICJ, Siapem was commissioned by Libya to start exploratory drilling in a disputed part of the Gulf of Gabes. Tunisia protested and responded by sending a naval vessel to the location where the Libyan licensed rig (*J.W. Bates*) sought to drill. After the rig withdrew from the area, Libya exerted pressure on the operators of the rig to resume the drilling as agreed, on penalty of the petroleum company's interests being nationalised.[1521] Thereafter, in May 1977, Libya made a renewed attempt to move the *J.W. Bates* into the disputed area to start drilling.[1522]

Conflict has frequently arisen between Greece and Turkey when unilateral seismic work has been authorised to be undertaken in disputed areas of the Aegean Sea and the Eastern Mediterranean Sea. During the 1960s and up to at least 1972, Greece issued concessions for conducting exploratory work in disputed parts of the Aegean Sea.[1523] At the time, Turkey refrained from taking similar actions and neither did it protest against the granting of concessions by Greece.

However, Turkey changed its position in November 1973 when it published a decision in the Official Turkish Gazette that it was going to offer no less than twenty-seven concessions to its Turkish State Petroleum Company.[1524] Their scope of application was defined so as to encompass maritime areas directly adjacent to the 6 nm territorial sea limit.[1525] Faced with an accumulation of Turkish exploration activities in their disputed continental shelf area in the Aegean Sea in the mid-1970s, Greece challenged the lawfulness of Turkey's conduct by making a unilateral application to the ICJ and it requested the UNSC to intervene in the matter.[1526]

In 1981, after the Greek socialist party (PASOK) came into power, it wanted to abandon the previous government's policy of not unilaterally exploring the disputed parts of the Aegean Sea. In 1987, seeking to pave a new path for conducting exploratory work in these disputed areas,[1527] the Greek socialist

1521 Ibid. 860.
1522 Ibid.
1523 AF Koymen, 'The Aegean Sea Continental Shelf Problem: Presentation of the Turkish Case' (1978) 6 *International Business Lawyer* 479, 503.
1524 *Aegean Sea Continental Shelf* (Interim Measures) (n. 41) Greece's Application Instituting Proceedings 3.
1525 S/18759 (n. 341).
1526 Chapter 3, Section 3.1.1 above.
1527 D Salapatas, *Aegean Sea Dispute between Greece and Turkey* (AKAKIA Publications, 2014) 16.

government made the controversial decision to nationalise the North Aegean Petroleum Company.[1528]

Because of this, Turkey's concerns mounted that Greece would abandon its restraint and resume unilateral work to obtain some more precise estimates of the potential for mineral resources within disputed areas of the Aegean Sea.[1529] Not long thereafter, the Turkish Ambassador received a notice of Greece's plans to start exploratory drilling in the disputed continental shelf area.[1530] Turkey's subsequent protest was based on the terms of the 1976 Bern Agreement, making it clear that unilateral conduct seeking to clarify the potential of the mineral resources located in the disputed continental shelf area had to be eschewed prior to its delimitation.[1531] According to Greece, this agreement was no longer valid as it only applied while the two States were actively engaged in (delimitation) negotiations.[1532] In responding thereto, Turkey indicated that it would resort to any means necessary to bring the unlawful conduct to a halt, if Greece would begin drilling.[1533]

Turkey, attempting to protect its claim,[1534] decided to open up disputed areas of the Aegean Sea which it previously had excluded for consideration, and started preparations for conducting exploratory work there. After one of these concessions was activated, the *Sismik I*, provided with an escort from the Turkish Navy, was despatched to the disputed area to conduct mineral resource exploration.[1535] In response, Greece mobilised its naval fleet in a state of readiness. Turkey's decision to recall the *Sismik I* to port, before it started exploration within the disputed area, was critical in preventing a further exacerbation of the maritime boundary dispute.

When calm was re-established, and both Greece and Turkey vouched to put any intentions to start seismic work concerning the disputed continental shelf area in the Aegean Sea on hold, several rounds of (unsuccessful) delimitation negotiations were held. During these negotiations, Turkey proposed to make a joint statement indicating that, in moving forward, the two States would abstain from drilling beyond the 6 nm limit of the territorial sea. Greece responded

1528 A Phylactopoulos, 'Mediterranean Discord: Conflicting Greek-Turkish Claims on the Aegean Seabed' (1974) 8(3) *International Lawyer* 431.

1529 Bölükbaşi (n. 517) 287; Dipla (n. 1009) 164.

1530 Acer (n. 1007) 41.

1531 Dipla (n. 1009) 164.

1532 Acer (n. 1007) 41.

1533 Bölükbaşi (n. 517) 291.

1534 Ibid.

1535 DS Saltzman, 'A Legal Survey of the Aegean Issues of Dispute and Prospects for a Non-Judicial Multidisciplinary Solution' in B Öztürk (ed.), *2000 Proceedings of the International Symposium, 'The Aegean Sea, 2000'* (Turkish Marine Research Foundation, 2000) 179, 190.

unfavourably to this suggestion.[1536] In clarifying its position, Turkey stated that, pending delimitation of the continental shelf boundary, any unilateral mineral resource activities taken in relation thereto had to be abjured.[1537]

After averting a crisis in 1997, a period of relative calm followed. Some sixteen years later, tensions re-emerged between the two States. All this was set in motion by Greece in January 2013, when it resumed preparations for drilling operations in disputed parts of the Aegean Sea.[1538] Greece argued that such unilateral drilling was lawful mainly by limiting itself to replicating earlier explanations, the gist of which was that as the relevant coastal State, Greece has exclusive sovereign rights over the mineral resources contained in the continental shelf area allowing it to proceed with drilling in connection thereto.[1539] Turkey cautioned the Greek government, reminding Greece that ignoring its protests would prompt a new response.[1540]

After Greece and Egypt signed a boundary agreement delimiting their disputed EEZ area on 7 August 2020, Turkey condemned this agreement, because it included areas that it also claims. Tensions came to a head between Greece and Turkey, when the latter authorised the *Oruc Reis* to start seismic surveying in disputed parts of the Eastern Mediterranean located south off the Greek island Kastellorizo.[1541] Cyprus, Greece, and Egypt made a joint declaration in which they condemned the Turkish action as unlawful.[1542] Third States, including France, Germany, the United States, and also the EU, voiced their concerns.[1543]

8.1.14 *Natuna Sea*

There is a clear pattern of awarding overlapping exploration concessions to the petroleum industry by both Indonesia and Vietnam in the disputed Natuna Sea.[1544] Exploratory work authorised by Indonesia prompted Vietnam to protest.[1545] At the end of the 1970s, Indonesia assured that petroleum

[1536] Dipla (n. 1009) 164.
[1537] Acer (n. 1007) 42.
[1538] 'Turkish FM Warns Greece on Steps in Aegean', *Hurriyet Daily News*, 8 January 2013.
[1539] 'Samaras Wants to Resolve Aegean Sea Dispute with Turkey', *Bloomberg*, 20 February 2013.
[1540] 'Turkish FM' (n. 1538).
[1541] 'Turkey Ignores Greece's Dispute, Moves on with Mediterranean Seismic Surveys', *World Oil*, 22 July 2020.
[1542] 'Joint Declaration of the 8th Cyprus – Egypt – Greece Trilateral Summit', *In-Cyprus*, 21 October 2020.
[1543] 'U.S. Slams Turkey's Renewed Seismic Survey Push in Eastern Mediterranean', *Reuters*, 13 October 2020.
[1544] Valencia and Miyoshi (n. 120) 218–219, 231–232.
[1545] Ibid. 219.

companies operating under its licence in the disputed maritime area would receive aid from the Indonesian Navy in the case of a Vietnamese response.[1546]

In a communiqué protesting against Indonesia's activation of an exploration concession and it entertaining bids for the development of disputed blocks, Vietnam stated the following: without its prior consent 'conduct[ing] survey and exploration operations' could not be undertaken in the disputed area.[1547] This protest appeared to have been ignored as Indonesia allowed various petroleum companies to operate within the disputed maritime area not long thereafter.

China also believes that it is a player in the dispute over the Natuna Sea, claiming to be entitled to parts of this area as they fall 'within the dotted line of China'[1548] – activities undertaken there by Indonesia were considered encroachments into China's maritime areas.[1549]

8.1.15 *Pacific Ocean and Caribbean Sea*

Nicaragua published a map in 2002 showing that it had awarded several concessions in relation to maritime areas disputed with Costa Rica.[1550] After learning of the concessions granted, Costa Rica protested and extended an invitation to Nicaragua to open talks on delimiting their boundaries in the Pacific Ocean and the Caribbean Sea, which failed to produce any results, however.

In 2013, Costa Rica obtained promotional materials prepared by Nicaragua, inviting the petroleum industry to declare their interest in securing exploration rights for their disputed area.[1551] Once again, Costa Rica protested and urged Nicaragua to resume delimitation negotiations.[1552] In a position paper published before their dispute was submitted to the ICJ in 2014, Costa Rica made it clear that it would not allow mineral resources-related conduct by Nicaragua to be undertaken in the disputed areas, as it considered these to be under its exclusive jurisdiction.[1553]

1546 Ibid. 233.

1547 Ibid.

1548 Wu and Ren (n. 915) 320.

1549 K Zou, 'The Chinese Traditional Maritime Boundary Line in the South China Sea and Its Legal Consequences for the Resolution of the Dispute over the Spratly Islands' (1999) 14(1) *IJMCL* 27–55.

1550 *Maritime Delimitation in the Caribbean Sea and the Pacific Ocean (Costa Rica v. Nicaragua)* ICJ Rep 2018, Costa Rica's Memorial 15, 19–20 [2.21] [2.33].

1551 Ibid. 18–19 [2.30].

1552 Ibid.

1553 'Position of the Republic of Costa Rica on the Offering of Oil Blocks for Exploration by the Republic of Nicaragua', available at www.costarica-embassy.org/sites/default/files/Position%20of%20Costa%20Rica%20on%20the%20offering%20of%20blocks%20for%20oil%20explotation.pdf.

8.1.16 *South China Sea*

The disputes in the South China Sea area are of great legal and political complexity. A general complication in identifying some examples of incidents that have arisen as a consequence is determining the location where these incidents have occurred. Complicating matters further is that what constitutes the maritime area in dispute shifts according to the perspective of the individual coastal States of the South China Sea.[1554] Illustrative in this respect is China's commitment to the nine-dashed claim, whereby disputed maritime areas are being created with virtually all States of the South China Sea. Two other categories of areas of overlapping claims in the South China Sea can be identified irrespective of those created by the Chinese claim.[1555] First, overlaps that occur between the mainland coasts proper of the States concerned; and, second, disputed areas created by the claiming of (full) entitlements to maritime zones from high-tide features over which title is disputed.

The beginning of the 1990s is when the situation in the South China Sea was augmented in terms of complexity. Then, with increasing rapidity, as well as frequency, motivated by concerns over energy security and attempts at the diversification of energy supplies,[1556] the States concerned sought to unilaterally act in relation to mineral resources, putting these States increasingly on a collision course.[1557] Prior thereto, however, already in the late 1970s, Vietnam was increasingly put on edge by exploration concessions awarded by China in relation to disputed waters off Hainan Island.[1558] Drilling authorised by Vietnam in disputed maritime areas in the period prior to 1974 had already drawn protests from China.[1559] In the same vein, other claimants also protested against China's earliest unilateral drilling in disputed parts of the South China Sea.[1560]

As mineral resource activity increased, so did the number of conflicts between the States of the South China Sea.[1561] As time passed, spurred on by the unilateral tendencies by the claimants concerned, there is a long history of incidents over mineral resources activities.[1562] Despite this troubled history,

1554 BIICL Report (n. 141) 95–96.
1555 Ibid.
1556 CH Schofield et al., *From Disputed Waters to Seas of Opportunity: Overcoming Barriers to Maritime Cooperation in East and Southeast Asia* (NBR Special Report, 2011) 19.
1557 L Buszynski, 'The South China Sea: Oil, Maritime Claims, and U.S.–China Strategic Rivalry' (2012) 35(2) *The Washington Quarterly* 139.
1558 Park (n. 737) 309.
1559 Kamminga (n. 16) 553–554.
1560 Dzurek (n. 128) 262.
1561 Schofield and Townsend-Gault (n. 81) 664–665.
1562 Gao (n. 476) 107–108.

most of the coastal States of the South China Sea[1563] have continued their policies of granting concessions be it for seismic work or drilling located in disputed areas, and they continue to act upon them by authorising such activities, keeping the potential for future disputes alive.

Both Brunei and Malaysia have issued overlapping concessions for the exploration of mineral resources located in their disputed area, including in close vicinity to, and covering, the Kikeh field.[1564] Murphy Oil, being authorised by Malaysia to begin drilling in 2003, was upon moving into the disputed area expelled by a Brunei patrol vessel.[1565] In the wake of this incident, both States ceased all unilateral activity aimed at clarifying the true extent of mineral resources located in their disputed area.[1566]

Over the years, China and Vietnam have accumulated a long list of incidents because of their unilaterally undertaking acts in relation to mineral resources in their disputed maritime areas.[1567] For example, their granting of concessions located in disputed parts of the Gulf of Tonkin and Bohai Gulf has constantly prompted protests from each State.[1568] In this vein, after China had entered into joint ventures with the petroleum industry in 1979, with a view to start mapping out the resource potential of these disputed areas, Vietnam protested.[1569]

Diplomatic relations between China and Vietnam had been seriously affected by the skirmishes in 1974 and 1988 over the Paracel and Spratly Islands. In November 1991, their relations improved after the initiating of low-level contacts.[1570] However, the progress was short-lived as bilateral relations became strained due to activities being undertaken unilaterally in relation to mineral resources in their disputed maritime areas.[1571] Their dispute was reignited in 1992 when China signed a contract with Crestone Energy to undertake exploratory work in the disputed Vanguard Bank ('Tu Chinh' in Vietnamese) – the area in question lies within 200 nm from the Spratly

1563 International Crisis Group (n. 315) 25.

1564 'Brunei and Malaysia Bury Hatchet in South China Sea Dispute', *International Oil Daily*, 24 March 2009.

1565 'KL Plan to End Oilfield Row with Brunei', *The Straits Times*, 3 July 2003.

1566 MN Basiron, 'The Search for Sustainability and Security: Malaysia's Maritime Challenges and Priorities' in JH Ho and S Bateman (eds.), *Maritime Challenges and Priorities in Asia: Implications for Regional Security* (Routledge, 2012) 72, 78.

1567 Li and Amer (n. 774) 92–93.

1568 Z Gao, 'The South China Sea: From Conflict to Cooperation?' (1994) 25(3) *ODIL* 345, 349.

1569 Ibid.

1570 AC Guan, 'The South China Sea Dispute Revisited' (2000) 54(2) *AJIA* 201, 207.

1571 R Amer, 'Sino-Vietnamese Border Disputes' in B. Elleman et al. (eds.), *Beijing's Power and China's Borders: Twenty Neighbors in Asia* (ME Sharpe, 2013) 295, 296–297.

Islands. Vietnam's response was threefold.[1572] First, Vietnam protested on the ground that the exploration had occurred in an area that is located some 200 nm off its coast, which is under its exclusive jurisdiction. Second, the concession agreement concluded by China comprised areas that lie outside the reach of entitlements to maritime zones that could be claimed from the disputed Spratly Islands.[1573] Third, Vietnam, in response, authorised VietSovpetro to undertake exploratory drilling in the disputed area.[1574] As tensions grew, in 1994, a number of ASEAN member States called on China and Vietnam to exercise mutual restraint and to refrain from taking actions that would further exacerbate and deteriorate their dispute.[1575]

On 5 May 1992, China activated a concession in disputed waters off Vanguard Bank. Subsequently, a seismic vessel was dispatched to the area to conduct a seismic survey. According to a Chinese Foreign Ministry official, 'seismic operations ... are normal scientific exploration activities'.[1576] In 1994, two Vietnamese naval vessels sought to prevent a Chinese seismic vessel from surveying their disputed area.[1577] Around the same time, Vietnam started to make preparations for exploratory drilling in the same block that China had awarded to Crestone in 1992 (Wan-Bei 21).[1578] Tensions grew between Vietnam and China as a result. Vietnam also granted a concession to US Mobil Corp. in 1994 with a view to exploring for mineral resources in a disputed area located west of Wan-Bei 21; this act of concessioning was protested by China. On the basis of this concession, exploratory drilling was authorised by Vietnam,[1579] thus ignoring China's protest that the area is located within the maritime zones that the Spratly Islands are entitled to.[1580] In June 2017, Vietnam authorised another round of drilling in the same block.[1581] Repsol, the oil company whose concession had been activated by Vietnam, was ordered by China, after it successfully struck oil, to leave the disputed area.[1582]

1572 Zou (n. 168) 88–89.

1573 'Vietnam East Sea Issue' (n. 948).

1574 Buszynski and Sazlan (n. 127) 158.

1575 C Joyner, 'The Spratly Islands Dispute: Rethinking the Interplay of Law, Diplomacy, and Geo-politics in the South China Sea' (1998) 13(2) *IJMCL* 193, 207.

1576 Gao (n. 1568) 350.

1577 C Snyder, 'The Implications of Hydrocarbon Development in the South China Sea' (1996–1997) 52(1) *International Journal* 142, 146; Zou (n. 168) 88.

1578 'Oil Riches' (n. 313).

1579 BIICL Report (n. 141) 97.

1580 NH Thao, 'Vietnam's Position on the Sovereignty over the Paracels & the Spratlys: Its Maritime Claims' (2012) 5(1) *JEAIL* 165, 202.

1581 'Vietnam Drills for Oil in South China Sea', *BBC News*, 5 July 2017.

1582 'South China Sea: Vietnam Halts Drilling after "China Threats"', *BBC News*, 24 July 2017.

In May 2014, China allowed an oil rig (*Haiyang Shiyou 981*) to be deployed in a disputed area, located within 200 nm from the coast of Hainan Island, that is in addition claimed by Vietnam (i.e. from Triton Island in the Paracel Islands). Shortly thereafter, it started with exploratory drilling. Around the drilling site, several vessels belonging to the Maritime Safety Administration of China established a zone measuring 3 nm, to which only certain Chinese vessels had access.[1583] Vietnam, arguing that its EEZ and continental shelf rights had been infringed upon,[1584] protested by means of a diplomatic protest and by sending several vessels to the area concerned. Initially, twenty-five Chinese vessels accompanied the drilling rig, but their number grew to eighty as the incident progressed, amongst which were Chinese ships behaving aggressively towards Vietnamese ships.[1585] After a six-week stand-off, China abandoned the drilling operation one month early;[1586] the halting of the work was argued to have been born out of restraint.[1587] In the wake of the stand-off, China started to entertain bids in the same area as where Vietnam had earlier put up blocks for auction, and on which India's national oil company had successfully bid.[1588] Reflecting on the incident with the *Haiyang Shiyou 981* in one of its resolutions,[1589] the US Senate regarded the unilateral drilling by China to have breached international law, in that it changed the status quo 'by force'.[1590]

A short time later, China authorised another four drilling rigs to be positioned in different disputed parts of the South China Sea. One of these rigs was meant to start work off the coast of Hainan Island, precipitating a new round of protests and counter-protests between the two States.[1591] A similar sequence of events repeated itself a year later in 2015 when China decided to resume

1583 Senate Resolution (n. 493).
1584 'China's Illegal Placement of Haiyang Shiyou 981 Oil Rig in the Exclusive Economic Zone and Continental Shelf of Viet Nam, and the Sovereignty of Viet Nam over the Hoang Sa Archipelago', Bangkok, 4 July 2014, available at www.vietnamembassy-thailand.org/en/nr070521165843/nr070725012202/ns140704195817.
1585 CA Thayer, 'South China Sea Tensions: China, the Claimant States, ASEAN and the Major Powers' in TT Thuy and LT Trang (eds.), *Power, Law, and Maritime Order in the South China Sea* (Lexington Books, 2015) 3, 9.
1586 Ibid. 11.
1587 F Zhao, 'Between Assertiveness and Self-Restraint: Understanding China's South China Sea Policy' (2016) 92(4) *IA* 869, 871, 889.
1588 Wu (n. 189) 154.
1589 Senate Resolution (n. 493).
1590 Ibid.
1591 'China Sends Four Oil Rigs to South China Sea Amid Regional Tensions', *Reuters*, 21 June 2014.

drilling in waters in close proximity to the disputed Paracel Islands, thereby creating a new stream of protests between China and Vietnam.[1592]

8.1.17 *Timor Sea*

In 1974, Indonesia granted a concession for a disputed area of the Timor Sea, crossing a provisionally drawn equidistance continental shelf boundary, leading to Australia protesting.[1593] Australia operated on the belief that, on its own side of the equidistance boundary, it could exercise exclusive jurisdiction prior to delimitation. In its licensing practice, Australia consistently respected the equidistance boundary, as the reach of its awarded concessions did not cross the boundary.[1594] Australia has also actively discouraged its concessionaires from conducting work near this putative boundary.[1595]

8.1.18 *Yellow Sea*

Parts of the disputed continental shelf areas of the Yellow Sea have been depicted as favourable for exploiting mineral resources.[1596] But there is a paucity of information confirming this: if seismic surveys are authorised or conducted unilaterally, conflict inevitably arises between the claimant coastal States concerned. For example, attempts that had been made by South Korea to enter into concession agreements with petroleum companies incorporated in the United States to explore areas of disputed continental shelf were firmly condemned by China.[1597]

After South Korea opened a round of bidding in the late 1960s, Gulf Oil successfully obtained a concession located in an area also claimed by China.[1598] Another two companies also received licences from South Korea to explore the

1592 'China Deploys Drilling Platform to East Vietnam Sea Again for Oil Exploration', *Tuoi Tre News*, 26 June 2015.

1593 Valencia and Miyoshi (n. 120) 213.

1594 M Richardson, 'Drawing the Seabed Line' (1978) *FEER* 79, 79–81.

1595 Valencia and Miyoshi (n. 120) 213.

1596 KG Lee, 'Recent Developments of Maritime Delimitation in Northeast Asia from an International Law Perspective' in MH Nordquist and JN Moore (eds.), *Maritime Border Diplomacy* (Martinus Nijhoff, 2012) 135, 146–147; MJ Valencia, 'Northeast Asia: Petroleum Potential Jurisdictional Claims and International Relations' (1989) 20(1) *ODIL* 35, 42.

1597 DM Johnston and MJ Valencia, *Pacific Ocean Boundary Problems: Status and Solutions* (Martinus Nijhoff, 1991) 37.

1598 Z Hai Qi, 'Oil and Gas Exploration and Development in the Yellow Sea' in SS Harrison (ed.), *Northeast Asia: Conflict or Cooperation* (Woodrow Wilson International Center for Scholars: Asia Program, 2005) 49, 50.

disputed area at the beginning of the 1970s.[1599] The increasing pace at which South Korea started to award concessions located in the disputed area placed China on edge, dispatching, in 1971, 'lightly armed fishing vessels' to the area where the seismic work eventually began, cutting the cables which were being towed behind the survey vessels on a number of occasions.[1600]

In 1973, Gulf Oil drilled two exploratory wells pursuant to the licence granted by South Korea.[1601] China protested, accusing the petroleum company of robbing its mineral resources.[1602] Despite China's protests, South Korea was reportedly adamant that Gulf Oil would honour the terms of the concession and proceed with drilling, as was agreed.[1603]

After a hiatus of some two decades, in which there seems to have been relative calm in relation to the area claimed by both China and South Korea, in 2004 reports emerged that South Korea was about to resume exploration activities in the same part of the disputed area where in the 1970s several incidents had arisen with China.[1604] Once again, China protested, taking the position that conducting a seismic survey breached its sovereign rights over the disputed area. Faced with this protest, South Korea decided to put a stop to its mineral resources activities in the disputed area that apparently had begun in 2005.[1605] In 2006, the roles were reversed. Then, China's principal oil company (CNOOC) activated the licence of Devon Energy Cooperation, enabling it to conduct unilateral exploration within the disputed area – reportedly, five wells had previously been drilled there.[1606] South Korea protested against both China activating this licence and its drilling activities.

One incident was reported to have taken place between China and North Korea, when, in 2005, North Korea concessioned Petronas to explore for mineral resources in a disputed part of the Yellow Sea. China protested on the basis that the area covered under the concession is under its sovereignty – this led to North Korea backing out from the previously concluded contract with the petroleum company.[1607]

1599 Harrison (n. 262) 10.
1600 Ibid. 11.
1601 Lee (n. 1596) 148.
1602 Harrison (n. 262) 12.
1603 Ibid.
1604 Lee (n. 1596) 148.
1605 Ibid.
1606 Ibid.
1607 Harrison (n. 262) 13.

8.2 FISHERIES ACTIVITIES

The granting of licences for fishing activities in disputed EEZ areas, or undertaking fishing activities thereunder, does regularly create a conflict between claimants, but not invariably. Illustrating this is the United States practice of licensing fishermen to operate within an EEZ area also claimed by the Bahamas, which, reportedly, has not prompted the latter to protest.[1608] Underlying this lack of response was seemingly that the Bahamas has not attempted to exploit the living resources in the disputed area itself.[1609] Another example is Guyana regularly permitting vessels flying the flags of third States to fish in an area disputed with Suriname by granting licences which, so it was argued by Guyana, did not lead to a protest from Suriname.[1610] These examples seem to be more the exception than the rule, however, with State practice regularly showing positions being taken by coastal States that are at variance therewith.

Reflecting on the regularity with which claimant States take enforcement measures against vessels acting in contravention of their laws and regulations concerning fishing activities, Suriname claimed that States regularly turn to law enforcement when faced with a breach thereof.[1611] One example of this is both Norway and Denmark arresting each other's fishing vessels and crews for offences committed within their formerly disputed area located between Jan Mayen and Greenland, which led to mutual protests.[1612]

Furthermore, in the 1980s, a diplomatic conflict arose between Sweden and the (then) USSR after the latter stopped and inspected fishing vessels belonging to Sweden and third States in a disputed area of the Baltic Sea.[1613] After the United States and the (then) USSR both claimed 200 nm fisheries zones in the Bering Sea, these States clashed on several occasions over enforcement action taken against the other State's fishing vessels for operating unlawfully in their disputed area.[1614]

In 2004, Croatia protested, on at least two occasions, against Slovenia's eviction of fishing boats flying Croatia's flag from a disputed area located in the Bay of Piran.[1615]

1608 BIICL Report (n. 141) 65.
1609 Ibid.
1610 *Guyana* v. *Suriname* (n. 7) Guyana's Memorial 60 [4.46].
1611 Ibid. Suriname's Rejoinder 132–133 [4.33].
1612 *Maritime Delimitation in the Area between Greenland and Jan Mayen (Denmark* v. *Norway)* [1993] ICJ Rep 38, 54–55 [36].
1613 Oude Elferink (n. 53) 209–210.
1614 BIICL Report (n. 141) 46.
1615 Donaldson and Pratt (n. 927) 413–414.

In a disputed EEZ area located in the northern part of the Persian Gulf, Iraqi fishermen have been frequently arrested by the coastguard vessels of both Iran and Kuwait, as they both considered these fishing activities to be unlawful, having taken place within an area under their exclusive jurisdiction.[1616]

Trinidad and Tobago and Venezuela, prior to bringing the issue of fisheries in a disputed area under a cooperative arrangement,[1617] clashed frequently over unilateral fishing activities,[1618] repeatedly protesting against each other's actions in this regard.[1619] Strong warnings were issued by Barbados that, if Trinidad and Tobago decided to take law enforcement measures against Barbadian fishermen, Barbados would take whatever steps may be necessary to avoid their arrest. Arrests of Barbadian fishermen by Trinidad and Tobago did however occur in 1994, and continued up to 2004; in this period, a total of eighteen ships and their crews were arrested.[1620] Barbados consistently protested against these arrests.[1621]

Nicaragua and Honduras have a long history of granting fisheries licences to their own vessels, thereby creating several difficulties between the States concerned, particularly once they started to arrest each other's fishermen for fishing offences in their disputed area.[1622] These arrests resulted in the exchange of written protests between Honduras and Nicaragua, in which they reiterated their views that, because the disputed area was under their exclusive jurisdiction, prior permission to fish was required.[1623]

In 2000, Nicaragua urged both Colombia and Honduras to exercise caution in building up a naval presence similar to its own in a disputed part of the Caribbean Sea. Considering these waters to be part of its 'sovereign territory', Nicaragua felt exclusively entitled to maintain a naval presence there, with the purpose of regularly conducting patrols to combat illicit acts and to protect fish stocks from foreign exploitation.[1624]

On 27 September 2002, a Venezuelan naval vessel crossed a hypothetical equidistance boundary dividing a disputed area to compel Guyana's

1616 'Iraq: Faw Fishermen Trapped by Maritime Disputes', *Agence France Presse*, 22 June 2011.
1617 *Barbados* v. *Trinidad and Tobago* (n. 582) Barbados's Memorial 37 [82].
1618 KG Nweihed, 'Report Number 2–13(2): Trinidad and Tobago-Venezuela' in JI Charney and LM Alexander (eds.), *International Maritime Boundaries*, Vol. 1 (Martinus Nijhoff, 1993) 655, 656.
1619 'Trinidad Warns Barbados: Be Prepared for Retaliation in Fishing Dispute', *BBC Summary of World Broadcasts*, 21 February 2004.
1620 *Barbados* v. *Trinidad and Tobago* (n. 582) Barbados's Memorial 38–39 [86].
1621 Ibid.
1622 *Nicaragua* v. *Honduras* (n. 413) 678–679, 681, 700–701 [49] [52] [58] [131].
1623 Ibid. 682, 700–701 [64] [65] [131].
1624 'Nicaragua Warns Neighbors About Naval Presence', *United Press International*, 7 April 2000.

coastguard to release a fishing vessel flying the flag of Venezuela that had earlier been arrested.[1625] After arriving on the scene, the Venezuelan naval vessel was warned by Guyana's coastguard due to her having ventured into Guyana's territory, which led to the withdrawal of the Venezuelan naval vessel without achieving its intended purpose of retrieving the arrested fishermen and their ship.[1626]

Guyana and Suriname both have a history of fishing and law enforcement in their disputed area. Guyana, trying to prevent overfishing and the imminent collapse of fish stocks in waters adjacent to its coast, enacted the 1977 Maritime Boundaries Act.[1627] Its geographical scope of application was expanded to include all maritime areas up to the N34E line, thus including areas to which Suriname also laid claim.[1628] Under the Act, Guyana could deny or limit access to fishing vessels of third States to these areas – an enforcement mechanism was also provided in the case of a breach.[1629] Guyana arrested several vessels flying the flags of other States based on this Act, including those of Suriname and Venezuela, when they were caught fishing without Guyana's licence in the disputed area. In arguing its case before the Tribunal, Guyana identified as the common theme running throughout its history with Suriname that acts undertaken on Guyana's side of the N34E line, including fisheries activities and enforcement measures, did not prompt a single protest from Suriname.[1630] Suriname's version of events was at variance therewith, claiming that it frequently enforced its own laws relating to fisheries offences committed in the disputed area.[1631] During its regular patrols in the disputed area located between the 10° line of Suriname and the N34E line of Guyana, Suriname took enforcement measures against vessels, flying both the Surinamese flag as well as flags of other States, including Venezuelan vessels, suspected of carrying out illegal fishing activities in the disputed area.[1632] Two vessels flying the Guyanese flag were 'stopped and inspected' for illegally operating in the disputed area.[1633] After completing its inspections, Suriname decided not to arrest these vessels because they were operating at the outer edges of the area that were included in its claim. The key insight underlying this exercise of restraint was that Suriname thought it appropriate to build in

1625 Ismael (n. 1391).
1626 Ibid.
1627 *Guyana* v. *Suriname* (n. 7) Guyana's Memorial 59 [4.44].
1628 Ibid. Guyana's Reply 76 [4.46].
1629 Ibid.
1630 Ibid. Guyana's Memorial 61–62 [4.48]–[4.52].
1631 Ibid. Suriname's Counter-Memorial 91.
1632 Ibid.
1633 Ibid.

a reasonable margin of fault by not enforcing its laws and regulations at these marginal edges of the disputed area, which could fall on Guyana's side of the boundary after delimitation, whereby it would also avoid possible claims of having committed international wrongful acts.

8.2.1 *South China Sea*

Fish stocks living in the South China Sea are put in peril at an alarming rate.[1634] Two reasons for this are the frequent use of destructive methods in catching fish, and a lack of cooperation in the conservation and management of fisheries as required under Articles 61 and 62 LOSC.[1635]

Since 1995, the Chinese government has been enforcing an annual ban on fish catches, ostensibly aimed at replenishing fish species, within disputed parts of the South China Sea.[1636] Imposing the ban in the northern part of the South China Sea (i.e. north of 12°) has, however, proven to be particularly controversial, motivating other States of the South China Sea to protest frequently. Sightings of Chinese fishing vessels operating in the area when, at the same time, the moratorium is supposed to be active[1637] have raised questions around whether the genuine reason behind its introduction is indeed to allow fish stocks to recuperate.[1638] Its controversial nature is enhanced by China also enforcing this ban within disputed waters, as it possesses the naval capacity to take action against potential transgressors.[1639] The levying of fines, imprisoning the crews of captured fishing vessels, and the burning of arrested vessels were examples of specific actions taken by China against vessels flying the flags of other claimant States that flaunted the ban imposed by China.

China's yearly renewal of the ban has consistently given cause for concern that controversy between itself and other States of the South China Sea will re-emerge.[1640] Vietnam has declared that it will defy China's unilaterally imposed ban because it breaches the sovereignty and jurisdiction that Vietnam claims to have over some of the waters included within its scope,[1641] and that the

1634 Dang (n. 199) 66.
1635 Wu (n. 189) 164.
1636 Xue (n. 81) 320.
1637 'Chinese Fishing Boats Violate Vietnam Waters; Gov't Mulls Patrol Boats', *Thanh Nien News*, 29 May 2011.
1638 HS Tseng and CH Ou, 'On Taiwan and China: A Unique Fisheries Relationship' (2010) 34(6) *MP* 1156.
1639 Dupont and Baker (n. 219) 85.
1640 Song and Tonnesson (n. 601) 254.
1641 'Chinese Ship Violates Vietnam's Sovereignty', *Vietnam News Agency*, 13 May 2011; 'Vietnam Opposes China's Fishing Ban in East Sea', *Voice of Vietnam News*, 14 May 2011.

livelihood of its fishermen is detrimentally affected by this ban.[1642] In May 2012, after a stand-off emerged between China and the Philippines off Scarborough Shoal, one of China's fisheries administrations proclaimed a ban on fishing within these disputed waters.[1643]

After, in May 2012, China decided to dispatch one of the largest fish production vessels in the world (the *Hainan Baosha 001*) – having a total capacity to process some 2,100 tons of fish on a daily basis – as well as some vessels acting in support to disputed areas of the South China Sea,[1644] questions arose around how this can be reconciled with the obligations that China has under the LOSC, including Articles 61 and 74(3).[1645] Beyond taking enormous amounts of fish, raising concerns around over-exploitation, the dispatch of the *Hainan Baosha 001* provoked protests from other States of the South China Sea, because of their various maritime boundary disputes being exacerbated as a result.

In January 2014, the Chinese province of Hainan enacted legislation in which inter alia a prior consent requirement was set out for conducting 'fishery production or fishery resources surveys' in maritime areas that China believes to be under its exclusive jurisdiction.[1646] A failure to secure its prior consent would result in the penalty of these fishing vessels being removed from the area concerned, the confiscation of any catches that had already been made, as well as the vessels being fined. Concerns over fish stocks not being appropriately protected, and preserving their ability to rejuvenate, by the setting of catch limitations, are ostensibly the main motivation behind the enacting of this legislation by China. However, the legislation prompted protests from both Vietnam and the Philippines as they linked the proclaiming of this law to China's desire to expand its current policy of enforcing its own laws and regulations in the entire South China Sea. Concerns were also raised by the United States over enforcement actions by China both in the past and in the future – this practice could be interpreted by other States of the South China Sea as 'provocative and potentially dangerous'.[1647]

China and the Philippines have regularly taken enforcement measures, or have attempted to do so, against vessels flying their respective flags in disputed

1642 Buszynski (n. 1557) 143.
1643 'BFAR Declares Fishing Ban at Panatag Shoal', *Philippine Star*, 17 May 2012.
1644 Y Lyons and T Davenport, 'South China Sea: Limits to Commercial Fishing by Claimants' (2012) 113 *RSIS Commentaries* (S Rajaratnam School of International Studies, 3 July 2012).
1645 Ibid.
1646 MJ Valencia, 'Fishing Rules Row May Push China to Clarify Its South China Sea Claims', *South China Morning Post*, 14 January 2014.
1647 Ibid.

maritime areas. For example, in 2011, the Philippines decided to deploy a naval frigate to parts of the South China Sea up until the 200 nm limit measured from its coast, in order to enforce its own relevant laws and regulations.[1648] In a further example, after a Philippine warship sought to arrest Chinese fishing vessels and their crew for illegal poaching, which failed due to the intervention of two Chinese vessels,[1649] a stand-off emerged between China and the Philippines in April 2012.[1650] Once the Philippines withdrew its naval vessel from the area, China decided to henceforth patrol the area more actively.[1651] Faced with this, the Philippines made the decision to return its naval frigate to the disputed area as well; at some point, to avoid the conflict from escalating as the stand-off progressed, it was replaced with vessels owned by the coastguard and the Fisheries Bureau – in response, China dispatched the *Yuzheng 310*, an 'armed fisheries patrol and law enforcement' vessel.[1652]

In a disputed area located in the southern part of the South China Sea, a conflict arose between Indonesia and Malaysia over the mutual arrests of each State's nationals for fishing offences committed there, including in disputed territorial sea areas.[1653] After arresting several Malaysian fishermen for unlawful fishing and trying to take them into port, Malaysia arrested, as a counter-response, a number of the Indonesian enforcement officials for undertaking unlawful enforcement action within the disputed area.

8.3 MARINE DATA COLLECTION

Attempts at the gathering of data from disputed maritime areas have created conflicts between claimant States; one reason is that such activities are seen as fronts for acts undertaken in relation to mineral resources.[1654] An example is Japan, whose suspicions were raised because of various sightings of research vessels flying the Chinese flag off the coasts of the disputed Senkaku/Diayu Islands,[1655] which also drilled several experimental oil wells.[1656] Sightings of

1648 'Philippines Says Naval Ship to Enforce Maritime Law', *Agence France Presse*, 19 June 2011.
1649 'PH, Chinese Naval Vessels in Scarborough Shoal Standoff', *Philippine Daily Inquirer*, 11 April 2012.
1650 Bonnet (n. 79) 5.
1651 Dupont and Baker (n. 219) 85.
1652 Ibid.
1653 'Arrests at Sea' (n. 281).
1654 Chapter 2, Section 2.3.1 above.
1655 *East Asian Strategic Review 2000* (NIDS, 2000) 104; *East Asian Strategic Review 2001* (NIDS, 2001), 199.
1656 Ibid.

four Chinese vessels in 1999 that concentrated their research work in waters off the coast of the Amami Islands, being a part of the Ryukyu archipelago,[1657] also drew Japan's attention. Its Maritime Safety Agency, after learning of this, sought to put a stop to these activities but was unsuccessful, as the Chinese vessels refused the Japanese requests to leave the area. China's position was that conducting activities within the framework of MSR in the disputed EEZ area was lawful from the perspective of international law.[1658] China's position has not been entirely consistent on this point, as at variance therewith, in the context of the South China Sea, it has claimed that conducting activities in the framework of MSR cannot be undertaken without another claimant's prior consent.[1659]

Several incidents have occurred between Japan and Korea in relation to data gathering within their disputed maritime areas. In 2006, South Korea authorised activities within the framework of MSR in a disputed area of the East China Sea. Japan protested upon receiving notice of the planned activity, making it clear that this act could not be undertaken by South Korea without its prior consent – rather, in order for this act to proceed, it had to be embedded within the framework of a cooperative arrangement.[1660] Despite receiving various calls for the abandonment of this research activity, South Korea went ahead with its plans on 5 July 2006. Also, Japan and South Korea clashed over the unilateral gathering of information in the disputed waters surrounding Dokdo/Takeshima.[1661]

In May 2006, a marine survey by Japan in a disputed part of the Yellow Sea led to South Korea dispatching its coastguard vessels to the area in question.[1662] This sequence of events was set in motion when South Korea announced its intention to suggest a name change to the International Hydrographic Organization for a number of submerged features located in the disputed area.[1663] Faced with this announcement, Japan revealed its

1657 MJ Valencia, 'Maritime Confidence and Security Building in East Asia. Recent Progress and Problems' (2006) 3 *Ocean Policy Studies* 25, 31.

1658 *East Asian Strategic Review 2001* (n. 1655) 106–107.

1659 Chapter 2, Section 2.3.4 above.

1660 'Statement by the Press Secretary/Director-General for Press and Public Relations, Ministry of Foreign Affairs, on the Marine Scientific Research by the Government of the Republic of Korea in the Waters Where Claim of the Exclusive Economic Zones (EEZ) Overlap between Japan and the ROK and the Territorial Sea around Takeshima Islands', 3 July 2006, available at www.mofa.go.jp/announce/announce/2006/7/0703-2.html (in English).

1661 Kanehara (n. 255) 97–99; Emmers (n. 191) 27.

1662 SK Kim, 'Understanding Maritime Disputes in Northeast Asia: Issues and Nature' (2008) 23(2) *IJMCL* 213, 231.

1663 'Ban Warns Japan over Dokdo Survey', *The Korea Herald*, 17 April 2006.

intention to survey these same waters as well. South Korea protested in the following terms: it was only after their outstanding dispute on title over Dokdo/Takeshima and its related maritime zones had been settled that a hydrographic survey could be lawfully conducted.[1664] Otherwise, South Korea argued that it would be compelled to take coercive measures to put a halt thereto. Shortly thereafter, news reports emerged that Japan had already dispatched two research vessels to the disputed area. In reaction, Korea dispatched twenty warships to prevent the survey from being undertaken.[1665] One month later, on 3 June 2006, the roles were reversed. Then, South Korea announced its intention to conduct a survey of the marine currents in the same disputed part of the Yellow Sea, leading to Japan protesting.[1666] South Korea was unfazed by Japan's protest, starting with its planned survey on 5 July in the disputed waters off the coast of Dokdo/Takeshima. Japan protested for a second time, arguing that conducting a hydrographic survey in a disputed area was unlawful under international law.[1667] Allegedly, however, as of 2000, Korea has been conducting several similar surveys in the disputed area, which have been undertaken without prompting a reaction from Japan.[1668]

Another example is that China contested the lawfulness of South Korea placing a research installation in a disputed EEZ area, in order to be able to monitor weather conditions and to survey the waters surrounding Socotra Rock,[1669] which is 'permanently submerged'.[1670] China and South Korea have publicly denied that a title dispute exists over the insular feature,[1671] although sometimes the dispute has been framed in such terms.[1672] Rather, the disputed EEZ area has arisen because they are situated opposite each other and are separated by less than 400 nm.

Within the Aegean Sea, Greece's suspicions were raised when, in disputed parts thereof, the RSS *Shackleton*, flying the flag of the United Kingdom, conducted research in 1974, pursuant to a licence granted by Turkey alone.[1673]

1664 Kanehara (n. 255) 98.
1665 Emmers (n. 191) 27.
1666 'Tensions Rise in East Sea', *The Korea Herald*, 4 July 2006.
1667 K Zou, 'Disrupting or Maintaining the Marine Legal Order in East Asia' (2002) 1(2) *CJIL* 449, 485.
1668 'Tensions' (n. 1666).
1669 MJ Valencia, 'The East China Sea Dispute: Context, Claims and Possible Solutions' (2007) 31(1) *Asian perspective* 127, 134.
1670 Zou (n. 1367) 157–158.
1671 'Leodo Not Part of Territorial Dispute with China', *Seoul Korea Herald*, 13 March 2012; 'China Chafes at Korean Observatory on Reef Island', *Chosun Ilbo*, 14 September 2006.
1672 'Row over Reef', *Korea Times*, 10 August 2008.
1673 M Gorina-Ysern, *An International Regime for Marine Scientific Research* (Brill, 2004) 276.

After learning of this, Greece decided to wait before taking enforcement measures against the vessel – that is, until the vessel started operating in an area over which Greece enjoys exclusive sovereignty.[1674] Tensions resurfaced in June 2010, after Greece sighted a Turkish ship (the *TCG Cesme*) in a disputed area of the Aegean Sea, upon which Greece accused Turkey of having unilaterally approved research in relation to mineral resources.[1675] Turkey rebutted this accusation,[1676] indicating that the *TCG Cesme* was updating marine charts – an activity that Turkey routinely undertakes twice a year. In July 2010, another research vessel (*Piri Reis*) was making its way to a point near the same disputed area, raising Greece's suspicions anew. Subsequently, evidence emerged demonstrating that the vessel in question was researching earthquake activity.[1677] Reflecting on the unlawfulness of this activity, the then Greek Alternate Foreign Minister stated that Turkey sought to exacerbate their dispute by challenging Greece's sovereign rights over the continental shelf area, which would inevitably lead to conflict between them.[1678]

8.4 ARE STATE PRACTICE AND INTERNATIONAL JUDICIAL PRACTICE ALIGNED?

International courts and tribunals, while determining whether conduct falling within coastal State jurisdiction, and which was authorised or physically undertaken unilaterally in a disputed maritime area, was lawful from the view of international law, have placed emphasis on the standard of damage of an irreparable nature being caused to a neighbouring coastal State's rights or the marine environment. On this basis, seismic work and the act of licensing have been considered to be a lawful unilateral activity, whereas exploratory drilling and exploitation were placed within the impermissible category. But can States' views as to the (un)lawfulness of these activities be organised along identical lines as those of international courts and tribunals?

Paving the way for an act to be physically undertaken in a disputed maritime area in the future by a claimant State opening a tender for bids, inviting bids from the petroleum industry to obtain exploratory rights, as well as granting

1674 Ibid.

1675 International Crisis Group, *Turkey and Greece: Time to Settle the Aegean Dispute* (Europe Briefing, 2011) 4.

1676 'Press Release Regarding The Tcg Çeşme – Hydrographic Survey Activities', 1 July 2010, available at www.mfa.gov.tr/no_-148_-01-june-2010_-press-release-regarding-the-tcg-cesme–hydrographic-survey-activities.en.mfa.

1677 International Crisis Group (n. 1675) 4.

1678 Salapatas (n. 1527) 16–17.

concessions located within a disputed area, have not been considered by international courts and tribunals to be unlawful. On the whole, in delimitation cases, States have seldom contended that issuing licences/concessions for mineral resource activity in respect of defined areas that extend into the disputed area breach international law. However, Suriname, basing its argument on the premise that Guyana bore responsibility for causing their dispute by conducting unilateral drilling in their disputed area, argued unsuccessfully that such licensing had breached the obligation not to hamper or jeopardise under Articles 74(3) and 83(3) LOSC.[1679] As State practice further shows, the announcement of an intention by a coastal State to offer concessions located in a disputed maritime area can be sufficient to prompt a protest from the other coastal State.[1680] At the same time, concessions located in disputed maritime areas will be frequently awarded to the petroleum industry, often without prompting a protest.

While it has been asserted that drilling in disputed maritime areas would run into practical difficulties, due to the unwillingness of the petroleum industry to commit itself thereto,[1681] subsequent State practice has developed in a different direction, however, in that exploration drilling within disputed areas has been attempted fairly regularly. In reaction to a dispute that arose with Vietnam after China allowed an oil rig to be placed in a disputed area, China stated that this was completely normal and, moreover, was an example of a lawful unilateral activity.[1682] If the practice on which China bases this argument is more closely analysed, it is clear that the following element was omitted: unilateral drilling almost invariably prompts a protest from the other claimant; this, in turn, makes the argument that unilateral drilling is permitted under international law doubtful.[1683] For example, after Esso Exploration Company was authorised to drill by Burma (now Myanmar) in a disputed area of the Northern Andaman Sea, this was protested by India.[1684] Another example is that Bangladesh in responding to Myanmar having authorised an oil rig to be positioned in a disputed part of the Bay of Bengal stated that this and 'any unilateral action is seen to be unfriendly' if it extends into the disputed area.[1685] Case law has developed along similar lines, although arguably an anomaly is provided by the Special Chamber's judgment in *Ghana/*

[1679] *Guyana* v. *Suriname* (n. 7) Suriname's Rejoinder 152.
[1680] Chapter 2, Section 2.3.1 above.
[1681] WT Onorato, 'A Case Study in Joint Development: The Saudi Arabia-Kuwait Partitioned Neutral Zone' (1985) 10(3–4) *Energy* 539, 540.
[1682] 'China Sends' (n. 1591).
[1683] Section 8.1 above.
[1684] McDorman (n. 35) 217.
[1685] 'Bangladesh, Burma' (n. 1400).

Côte d'Ivoire, as both exploration and exploitation drilling have been included within the ambit of unilateral activities that would be caught by either the obligation not to hamper or jeopardise under Articles 74(3) or 83(3), or, prior to the LOSC entering into force, the obligation not to threaten rights with irreparability. In *Guyana* v. *Suriname*, Guyana was unsuccessful in convincing a Tribunal that drilling and seismic work are effectively two sides of the same coin, claiming that both are of an exploratory nature.[1686]

More pronounced are the differences between State practice and international judicial practice concerning the argument that it is lawful to authorise seismic work in a disputed maritime area unilaterally.[1687] A view that is rooted in the international case law is that seismic work is of an exploratory character, causing a limited degree of infringement, and because of this is an example of an act that may be undertaken unilaterally in disputed EEZ/continental shelf areas. The findings of the Tribunal in *Guyana* v. *Suriname* have had a crucial role in shaping this view. Discussing the issue of seismic work in a disputed continental shelf area in an *obiter dictum*, the Tribunal followed the line of argumentation set out by the ICJ in its decision in the *Aegean Sea Continental Shelf* (Interim Measures) case that this is an acceptable use thereof.[1688] In State practice, three ways can be identified as to how unilateral seismic work is perceived. First, there are States which undertake or authorise seismic work in disputed maritime areas unilaterally without any difficulties arising (e.g. between Suriname and Guyana). Second, there are other States which perceive seismic work to be their sole prerogative, thereby protesting against this type of conduct whenever it is undertaken without their prior consent by other States in disputed maritime areas, but at the same time undertaking it themselves with the result that conflict is created.[1689] For example, a recurrent pattern can be observed, for example, in the South China Sea and the Aegean Sea, where unilateral seismic work invariably leads to conflict between claimant States. A similar pattern is found in the Gulf of Tonkin, where granting concessions and approving seismic surveying by China, after being detected by Vietnam, were followed by a conflict between the States concerned.[1690] Also, Vietnam has regularly been at odds with Indonesia over the lawfulness of seismic work that was authorised by the latter in the disputed Natuna Sea.[1691] Third, other States will protest against

1686 *Guyana* v. *Suriname* (n. 7) Guyana's Reply 141–143 [8.10]–[8.14].
1687 Tas (n. 600) 59.
1688 *Guyana* v. *Suriname* (n. 7) 137 [480]–[481].
1689 Davenport (n. 320) 113.
1690 Dzurek (n. 142) 164.
1691 Valencia and Miyoshi (n. 120) 219.

seismic work whenever it is authorised without their prior consent and will refrain from undertaking it themselves, because they operate on the assumption that this is an activity that has to be abstained from until the geographical extent of a coastal State's rights or sovereignty is clear. In this vein, Bangladesh held the position that seismic work had to be postponed until an agreement was reached on delimiting the disputed Bay of Bengal.[1692] Similarly, Cambodia and Thailand both indicated that seismic work cannot be authorised by either State pending the delimitation of their disputed area in the Gulf of Thailand.[1693] During the 1990s, Vietnam similarly considered unilateral seismic work to be unlawful.[1694] In a similar vein, the unilateral authorisation of seismic work was argued, although unsuccessfully, by both Greece and Côte d'Ivoire – in separate cases – to fall within the category of activities that can only be conducted once the geographical extent of a coastal State's sovereign rights has been conclusively established.[1695]

8.5 CONCLUDING REMARKS

As is reflected in State practice, the inherent potential for disputed maritime areas to create conflicts in bilateral relations is regularly brought out into the open when activities that are under the authority of the coastal State are undertaken, or are planned to be undertaken, under the authorisation of one claimant State. Conflicts can be triggered by both States taking certain actions in disputed areas, or making certain announcements in relation thereto (e.g. announcing an intention to issue concessions for activities relating to mineral resources),[1696] although, comparatively, the former is usually more controversial than the latter.

The complete range of activities that are under the authority of the coastal State (e.g. with regard to energy resources, fisheries, and collecting data) can spark conflict between claimant States in disputed maritime areas. Variations in terms of the frequency with which conflict arises as well as their severity can be detected, however. Unilateral conduct in relation to mineral resources in a disputed area regularly proves to be a sensitive and contentious issue.

1692 'Bangladesh, Burma' (n. 1400).

1693 Schofield and Tan-Mullins (n. 186) 78.

1694 MJ Valencia and JM Van Dyke, 'Vietnam's National Interests and the Law of the Sea' (1994) 25(2) *ODIL* 217, 220.

1695 Chapter 6, Sections 6.1.1 and 6.3.1 above.

1696 TT Thuy, 'Code of Conduct and the Prevention and Management of Incidents in the South China Sea' in TT Thuy and LT Trang (eds.), *Power, Law, and Maritime Order in the South China Sea* (Lexington Books, 2015) 317, 326.

Concessioning, conducting a seismic survey, exploratory drilling, and exploitation are all activities which prompted conflict in State practice. Fishing activities in disputed maritime areas do also regularly create difficulties.[1697] In this vein, conflicts between the fishermen of the States that have overlapping claims over the same area might arise, which can spill over to the diplomatic level, thereby complicating reaching delimitation or cooperative arrangements. Particularly controversial is often the arresting of (fishing) vessels flying the flag, or operating under the licence, of another claimant State, whereby almost invariably the bilateral relations between the arresting State and licensing and/or flag State are detrimentally affected.

If State practice is contrasted with international judicial practice, where seismic work and licensing have been regarded as generally lawful, but exploratory and exploitation drilling as unlawful, both similarities and differences are laid bare. As regards drilling and exploitation activities, State practice and international judicial practice are largely aligned. Only more limited contrary State practice emerges, in that, if these activities do proceed without the prior consent of the neighbouring coastal State, this would not prompt a protest, or an enforcement response, from the latter. When looking at authorising seismic work, but also, to a certain extent, the preliminary stage of licensing, whereby the way is paved for an act to be physically undertaken in a disputed maritime area in the future, a less harmonious picture emerges. Here a discrepancy between international judicial practice and State practice is more clearly visible, in that both acts regularly create a conflict between States laying claim to the same maritime area.[1698]

1697 Anderson and Van Logchem (n. 18) 218–219.
1698 Section 8.4 above.

9

Are the Rights and Obligations of States in Disputed Maritime Areas Sufficiently Defined in International Law?

Certain questions became pressing once disputed maritime areas emerged in the international landscape.[1699] Two of these questions are: first, what forms the basis on which overlapping claims to maritime zones can be resolved; and, second, what are the rules and obligations of States, pending the delimitation of their disputed maritime area?[1700] One aspect of the second question lay at the heart of this book: that is, if a disputed maritime area is unregulated by provisional arrangements or a modus vivendi, what rights and obligations do States have with respect to such an area?

Disputed maritime areas regularly become a source of conflict between States. This is because such areas, in a way, appertain to all the coastal States involved that have entitlements and related rights to the area concerned.[1701] Yet, this leaves unresolved the extent to which an individual State is allowed to, or has to, act in connection with a disputed area that effectively 'belongs' to more than one coastal State pending delimitation.

If a provisional arrangement covers a disputed area, the activities brought within its reach must be conducted in accordance with what has been agreed by the States concerned. However, in terms of their scope, provisional arrangements are often not comprehensive, thereby keeping intact the possibility of conflicts arising in relation to those types of acts that are unregulated by these arrangements, whenever such acts are undertaken unilaterally in a disputed maritime area. In case provisional arrangements are absent, or partial in their scope, one of the principal challenges centres on what scope there is for a claimant State to act unilaterally, by authorising or undertaking conduct that is under coastal State authority, in relation to a disputed maritime area.

1699 BIICL Report (n. 141) 50.
1700 Gao (n. 476) 107.
1701 Milano and Papanicolopulu (n. 80) 590.

Conflict in bilateral relations and, as a result, an exacerbation of the underlying maritime boundary dispute may arise when an act that is under the authority of the coastal State in relation to a disputed area is authorised or undertaken unilaterally. A further relationship exists between unilateral acts causing conflict, and the chances of successfully delimiting a disputed maritime area: when a claimant State acts unilaterally, by authorising or undertaking an activity over which the coastal State has authority, and the other State protests, delimitation is often made more complicated as a result.[1702] If this effect has occurred, this points to a breach of international law having occurred. Ever since the LOSC came into effect, conflicts created by unilateral conduct in disputed areas have become an increasingly prominent issue because of two developments: first, the expansion of the limits of coastal State sovereignty and jurisdiction; and, second, the increased willingness of claimant States to assert their claims and rights with greater eagerness and frequency.

Once claimants actively oppose each other's claims to the area in question, a readiness often develops to protect their own claim, either verbally or through physical means, particularly when they are confronted with unilateral conduct that is under the authority of the coastal State within their disputed maritime areas. Avoiding a finding that a State's silence leads to acquiescence in the claim of the other coastal State is one of the key reasons underpinning the need that is felt for responding to the act.[1703] Regardless of the underlying motivation, an accompanying effect of such a response is that it can put a strain on bilateral relations that makes reaching a final or temporary solution to deal with a disputed maritime area significantly more complicated.

It is against this background that the book has identified the applicable international rights and obligations, and what their implications are, when applied to disputed maritime areas. Several questions have arisen in this context. First, does current international law clearly indicate to which extent claimant States may exercise sovereignty, sovereign rights, and/or jurisdiction in their disputed maritime areas? Second, does international law provide when States are obliged to exercise restraint and refrain from exercising their authority in such areas? Third, does international law provide for when and how another claimant State can respond against the other State, or the nationals it has authorised to undertake conduct unilaterally that falls under coastal State authority, within a disputed maritime area?[1704] And, fourth, what about any other obligations States may have in relation to disputed maritime areas?

1702 Chapter 8 above.
1703 Oxman and Murphy (n. 237) 3.
1704 Ibid.

This concluding chapter starts in Section 9.1 with an assessment of whether the conventional rules that are either specifically designed for dealing with disputed maritime areas, or those that are not but have a similar application in these areas, are sufficiently defined. In addition to these conventional rules, there is a range of general rules of international law that are relevant in such areas. These are assessed in a similar light in Section 9.2. Most often, these general rules of international law operate alongside provisions in the LOSC, but there are instances where this is not the case, for example due to the latter's limited sphere of operation.[1705] Only after combining both conventional and general rules of international law does the full picture of rights and obligations that States have in relation to disputed maritime areas emerge. Section 9.3 addresses the scope for unilateralism within a disputed area. It considers whether this can be set *in abstracto*, or that a differential is involved, in that the particular setting in which overlapping claims has arisen must be taken into account. Then, Section 9.4 focuses on third States and their nationals and the international law that is applicable to them when acting, or seeking to act, in disputed maritime areas. The concluding section considers State practice which shows that many conflicts have occurred in disputed maritime areas, because of States acting unilaterally, through authorising or undertaking conduct that is under coastal State authority, which gives rise to the question whether the States concerned, or the applicable legal framework, are to be blamed for this.

9.1 CONVENTIONAL RULES APPLICABLE TO DISPUTED MARITIME AREAS

While negotiations at UNCLOS III were in train, Oxman suggested framing an interim rule by making cross-references to other provisions in the (at the time, future) LOSC that laid down particular obligations, to emphasise their similar application to disputed maritime areas.[1706] Although not going along this route, the States at UNCLOS III were able to give some teeth to the rules that were explicitly created for disputed areas of the territorial sea, the EEZ, and the continental shelf, in Articles 15, 74(3), and 83(3) LOSC. This is different when States cannot agree on delimiting their overlapping contiguous zone claims, with Article 33 LOSC being silent on the issue of an interim rule.

The interim rules designed respectively for disputed territorial seas, and disputed EEZ or continental shelf areas, differ extensively in terms of content

[1705] Chapter 5, Section 5.3.7 above.
[1706] Oxman (n. 655) 23.

and applicability.[1707] None of these provisions makes explicit reference to other parts of the LOSC, but this does not mean that they do not apply with the same force in disputed maritime areas as they do in their undisputed counterparts.

Part XII of the LOSC, which imposes various obligations on States, including in connection with protecting the marine environment in Articles 192–195, applies irrespective of a maritime area being undisputed or disputed. As a result, coastal States have significant obligations in relation to protecting the marine environment of disputed maritime areas, and to actively taking measures to that end. Also, claimant States have legislative jurisdiction with regard to dumping and pollution caused by vessels.[1708] Obligations that are normally imposed on coastal States in connection with EEZ and continental shelf areas thus similarly apply to those areas where their claims to the same EEZ or continental shelf area overlap.[1709] In the context of fisheries in disputed EEZ areas, this means that the coastal States concerned have obligations of conservation and utilisation in relation thereto;[1710] particularly relevant are those obligations requiring the claimant States to cooperate. In addition, within disputed maritime areas located in a closed or semi-enclosed sea, the additional requirements of Article 123 LOSC come into play. Arguably, however, this provision does not add much to the obligations that already apply outside semi-enclosed seas, as it lays down an obligation to coordinate in certain matters.[1711]

Conventional international law is mainly found in the LOSC, notably laying down certain interim rules in Articles 15, 74(3), and 83(3).[1712] These provisions provide some guidance for the States concerned whenever they have disputed territorial sea, EEZ, or continental shelf areas. Article 15 LOSC is in principle applicable to disputed territorial sea areas, in relation to which claims of sovereignty by coastal States overlap. As a matter of English syntax, Article 15 LOSC provides the following interim rule: 'failing agreement between them to the contrary', and in the absence of special circumstances and a historic title, one coastal State is not allowed to extend its territorial sea beyond the equidistance boundary. The application of an equidistance boundary as an interim rule is thus conditional upon there being no historic title or special circumstances. If there is disagreement over the validity of any relevant baselines, this might complicate determining where the provisional

1707 Chapters 4 and 5 above.

1708 Articles 210 and 211 LOSC. Under paragraphs 5 and 6 of Article 211 LOSC, States are permitted to go beyond international standards in certain situations.

1709 Chapter 2, Section 2.3 above.

1710 Articles 61–63 LOSC.

1711 Chapter 2, Section 2.2 above.

1712 Chapters 4 and 5 above.

equidistance boundary lies. But otherwise, an equidistance boundary as an interim rule provides the States concerned with fairly straightforward guidance:[1713] this line forms the outer point up to where acts of sovereignty may be undertaken or authorised by a coastal State pending the delimitation of the territorial sea.[1714] Through creating this division of the disputed area, it is also clear for a third State, or its nationals, as to which coastal State to approach for a licence, if conducting an activity under the sovereignty of the coastal State in a disputed territorial sea area is envisaged.

Articles 74(3) and 83(3) LOSC are applicable to disputed EEZ and continental shelf areas and lay down two obligations. First, the neighbouring coastal States must make every effort to agree on cooperation in the form of a provisional arrangement in the sense of paragraph 3, with the objective of managing a disputed area pending delimitation. Its conclusion can have a soothing effect on bilateral relations, making it less likely that conflicts will emerge between coastal States. Beyond that, a provisional arrangement can function as a stepping-stone to a permanent solution to settle the maritime boundary dispute. In the second sentence of Articles 74(3) and 83(3) LOSC, the obligation not to hamper or jeopardise is laid down.[1715] This obligation is closely connected to other general rules of international law, including the obligation of non-aggravation or non-extension of a dispute or that a State may not assert rights in a way that amounts to an abuse of rights. The obligation not to hamper or jeopardise *stricto sensu* does not directly address certain types of activities, such as fisheries or mineral resources. Rather, in an indirect sense – and mediated by the fact that it seeks to avoid unilateral activities that fall under the jurisdiction of a coastal State from occurring, that hamper or jeopardise a final delimitation – acts exceeding one of these thresholds can be caught within its scope. There are two sides to this obligation, in that it has both a limiting effect on when a coastal State would be able to act on its sovereign and/or jurisdictional rights in a disputed EEZ or continental shelf area, and how it can react to an act that is only authorised by the other claimant State that infringes on these rights.

Articles 74(3) and 83(3) LOSC could, grammatically, have been clearer, however.[1716] Some of paragraph 3's opaqueness arises from the fact that it has been drafted in a convoluted way, which makes defining its precise meaning more difficult.[1717] Much of the interpretational difficulties of this paragraph 3

[1713] Caflisch (n. 587) 495.
[1714] Chapter 4, Section 4.2 above.
[1715] Van Logchem (n. 21) 176.
[1716] Chapter 5, Section 5.3.2 above.
[1717] Anderson and Van Logchem (n. 18) 205.

can be traced back to its language not reflecting a firm normative choice by the States at UNCLOS III to develop a solution along the lines suggested by one of the two delimitation groups: that is, to use an equidistance boundary to divide a disputed EEZ or continental shelf area, or to introduce a moratorium on natural resources located in such areas, which could be lifted if the coastal States were to agree on cooperative arrangements.[1718] One way in which paragraph 3 of Articles 74 and 83 LOSC as it currently stands would have been easier to understand is if the phrases 'in a spirit of understanding and cooperation' and 'in this transitional period' were removed from the text – in fact, the argument can be made that these two additions have more ornamental value than serving a genuine purpose. Also, the addition of the phrase 'in this transitional period' has given rise to the mistaken train of thought that paragraph 3 of Articles 74 and 83 LOSC does not contain two separate obligations which function independent of each other.[1719]

Despite being awkwardly drafted, the main aim underlying Articles 74(3) and 83(3) LOSC is more easily established: that is, to prevent conflicts between claimant States that might negatively affect their successful completion of a delimitation of the disputed EEZ or continental shelf area in the sense of paragraph 1 of Articles 74 and 83 LOSC. Therefore, States being placed under the dual obligation of seeking provisional arrangements and abstaining from acts that hamper or jeopardise delimitation must be interpreted through the prism of paragraph 1 of Articles 74 and 83 LOSC.[1720]

9.2 GENERAL TENETS OF INTERNATIONAL LAW APPLICABLE TO DISPUTED MARITIME AREAS

No matter the intricacies surrounding a particular disputed maritime area, which may even render the LOSC inapplicable, this does not mean that there is a lacuna in the international law. As discussed earlier, a variety of obligations of international law are applicable in disputed maritime areas in general, most of which can be considered customary rules, pursuant to which States are required to exercise restraint.[1721] First, based on general rules of international law, States must settle their disputes peacefully. In its award in *Guyana v. Suriname*, the Tribunal acknowledged that, once there is an unlawful (threat

[1718] Chapter 5, Section 5.3.1 above.
[1719] Ibid. Sections 5.3.2.2 and 5.3.5.
[1720] Ibid. Section 5.3.12.
[1721] Chapter 3, Section 3.3 above.

to) use of force, it follows *a fortiori* that there has been a breach of the obligation not to hamper or jeopardise under Articles 74(3) and 83(3) LOSC.[1722] Suriname's naval officers threatening a non-national oil rig (including its crew) with armed force had such an effect.[1723] Second, the States concerned must avoid acts that cause irreparability to each other's rights.[1724] Third, States must act in good faith, which encompasses the obligation that their actions may not amount to an abuse of rights; this is laid down in treaty form in Article 300 LOSC.[1725] Fourth, States must avoid aggravating or extending a dispute; this principle was first introduced in *Electricity Company of Sofia and Bulgaria*.[1726] Since then, it has been replicated in various interim protection orders of international courts and tribunals, and has formed an integral part of a number of UN Resolutions related to the peaceful settlement of disputes.[1727] In *Philippines* v. *China*, the Tribunal held that non-aggravation or non-extension of a dispute is a general rule of international law.[1728] Non-aggravation and non-extension bears a significant resemblance to the aim that is sought by the obligation not to hamper or jeopardise in Articles 74(3) and 83(3) LOSC. Their interrelationship can be framed in negative terms: those acts that aggravate a maritime boundary dispute, or lead to it being extended, will ipso facto hamper or jeopardise the reaching of a delimitation agreement.

There is also a category of unilateral activities in disputed maritime areas in relation to which there is significant evidence that these are prohibited from being undertaken, as a matter of customary law: that is, exploitation and exploratory drilling.[1729] Valencia and Miyoshi concluded in 1986 that a customary rule prohibiting the unilateral exploitation of mineral resources in a disputed area was in the process of being developed.[1730] When reassessing this conclusion, with the entry into force of the LOSC and the widespread support it has gained, creating State practice in its wake, it is opportune to consider this to have become a rule of customary international law.

However, Bundy argued more than two decades ago that, at the time, the guiding principle in 'the exploitation of international oil and gas deposits is . . . the rule of capture'.[1731] Later, this has been assumed to be the case particularly

1722 *Guyana* v. *Suriname* (n. 7) 126, 135 [445] [476].
1723 Ibid.
1724 Chapter 3, Section 3.4 above.
1725 Ibid. Section 3.6.
1726 *Electricity Company of Sofia and Bulgaria* (n. 434) 199.
1727 Chapter 3, Section 3.6 above.
1728 *Philippines* v. *China* (n. 448) 601 [1173].
1729 Churchill and Ulfstein (n. 407) 85.
1730 Valencia and Miyoshi (n. 120) 213.
1731 Bundy (n. 112) 24.

in 'enclosed or semi-enclosed seas',[1732] or has been framed as the guiding principle in the absence of cooperative arrangements.[1733] While these statements are not explicitly framed in terms of the existence of a customary rule, mention is made of a practice of States where they commonly start drilling and exploiting a deposit located in a disputed continental shelf area,[1734] which suggests that reference is made to this having become a customary rule.

Two detrimental legal effects ensue when a claimant State unilaterally exploits a disputed area, which questions its lawfulness:[1735] first, the inherent rights of the other coastal State over the continental shelf will be infringed upon irremediably;[1736] and, second, conflicts will more or less inevitably occur between the coastal States concerned.[1737] Prior to *Ghana/Côte d'Ivoire*, international courts and tribunals adopted a consistent line of thinking: that is, whenever they were faced with arguments by States contesting the lawfulness of unilateral exploitation in a disputed maritime area, the conclusion was reached that this act is indeed unlawful under international law. The position that international law prohibits the 'unilateral development' of mineral resources pending delimitation first emerged in the ICJ's decision in *Aegean Sea Continental Shelf* (Interim Measures) and was subsequently endorsed in *Guyana* v. *Suriname*, where the Tribunal framed its decision largely along identical lines, while placing greater emphasis on protecting the marine environment from harm.[1738]

However, the decision in *Ghana/Côte d'Ivoire* – where Ghana despite being on the verge of starting the production of mineral resources in a disputed area was not considered to have acted unlawfully, and despite there being no acquiescence by Côte d'Ivoire[1739] – does not help the argument that a rule of customary law prohibiting the unilateral exploitation of mineral resources in a disputed maritime area has fully crystallised. Irrespective of the existing judicial authority, it has been argued in this book that unilateral conduct that has the effect of causing

1732 MH Loja, 'Is the Rule of Capture Countenanced in the South China Sea? The Policy and Practice of China, the Philippines and Vietnam' (2014) 32(4) *JENRL* 483, 484.

1733 E Voyiakis, 'Shared Oil and Gas Resources: Does the Rule of Capture Reflect International Law?' in I Bantekas et al. (eds.), *Oil and Gas in Kazakhstan: National and International Perspectives* (Kluwer, 2004) 77.

1734 Ibid.

1735 Miyoshi (n. 479) 18; ILA (n. 832) 531.

1736 *North Sea Continental Shelf* (n. 8) 22 [19].

1737 Tas (n. 600) 59.

1738 Chapter 6, Section 6.3 above.

1739 Ibid. Section 6.2.

irreparability or that leads to an aggravation or extension of the maritime boundary dispute is generally prohibited in disputed maritime areas, as a matter of general international law.[1740]

Now, to turn to unilateral drilling activity, in relation to which there is some authority for arguing that a customary rule has come into being that prohibits this type of act in disputed maritime areas. Unilateral drilling has two detrimental effects: it leads to the rights of the other State being endangered with irreparability, and it might be caught under Articles 74(3) and 83(3) LOSC, for having the effect of hampering or jeopardising delimitation. In one of the earliest investigations into the subject, Churchill and Ulfstein concluded that there was no single answer to the question whether a customary rule existed which prohibited unilateral drilling in a disputed continental shelf area.[1741] In State practice, drilling has been undertaken in disputed areas fairly regularly, with the result that conflict almost invariably emerged in the bilateral relations of the States concerned.[1742] This, in turn, undermines the argument that unilateral drilling would be lawful under international law.[1743] Also, most case law has included drilling within the ambit of unilateral activities that are under coastal State jurisdiction, which would be caught by either the obligation not to hamper or jeopardise, or, prior to the LOSC entering into force, the general rule not to threaten rights with irreparability.[1744] Whereas prior to the coming into force of the LOSC doubts surrounded the status of unilateral drilling as a customary rule, thereafter, specifically after the Tribunal's ruling in *Guyana* v. *Suriname*, the pendulum has swung more towards a prohibition on unilateral drilling becoming a customary rule. The view that unilateral drilling is unlawful is reinforced by the relevant standard of 'irreparability' having been exchanged for 'hampering or jeopardising' under the LOSC in Articles 74(3) and 83(3), which lowers the bar.[1745] Hence, the Special Chamber's judgment in *Ghana/Côte d'Ivoire* should be treated as an anomaly, rather than a sign of a shift towards exploratory drilling being an acceptable unilateral use of a disputed maritime area.[1746]

1740 Chapter 3, Sections 3.4 and 3.5 above.
1741 Churchill and Ulfstein (n. 407) 89.
1742 Chapter 8, Section 8.5 above.
1743 Ibid. Sections 8.4 and 8.5.
1744 Chapter 6 above.
1745 Chapter 5, Section 5.3.4 above.
1746 Chapter 6, Section 6.4 above; Van Logchem (n. 245) 176–177.

9.3 THE SCOPE FOR UNILATERALISM IN DISPUTED MARITIME AREAS

A broad spectrum of approaches to manage a disputed maritime area can be identified. These range from being purely preventive, by employing an equidistance boundary, or the introduction of a moratorium on economic conduct that is under the authority of the coastal State, to claimants taking active steps to design cooperative arrangements. Distinguishing between different acts under the authority of the coastal State, and determining their respective validity from the perspective of international law if these are undertaken, or are planned to be undertaken, in a disputed maritime area, is an approach falling somewhere in between. This is the predominant approach adopted by international courts and tribunals, which has been subsequently endorsed in the literature by some authors and has given rise to the view that the scope for unilateralism in disputed maritime areas can be defined objectively.

Two potential 'dangers' can be identified in this approach, however. First, States could use the resulting 'list' as an excuse not to cooperate in relation to a disputed maritime area. Weakening this argument is the fact that States are not required under international law to successfully agree on a cooperative arrangement that covers their disputed areas, either implicitly or explicitly.[1747] A second 'danger' associated with definitively determining the scope for unilateralism in disputed maritime areas under international law might arise in the situation where a claimant State would want to undertake a certain act, for which legal or judicial authority exists that it would be lawful unilateral conduct, but against which the other claimant State is likely to protest. However, if the act goes ahead and the protest by the other claimant is ignored, this indicates a breach of the applicable international law in disputed maritime areas. This will be the case if, in short, as a result, it will be more difficult to settle the maritime boundary dispute, either temporarily or conclusively.[1748]

On the other hand, clarifying the status, under international law, of unilateral conduct that falls within the authority of the coastal State when it is undertaken, or planned to be undertaken, in disputed maritime areas is a meaningful exercise in practical terms: that is, in light of the actual amount of such unilateral conduct in disputed maritime areas and that it regularly leads to conflicts in bilateral relations.[1749] The usefulness of this exercise is

[1747] Chapter 5, Section 5.3.3 above.
[1748] Section 9.3.2 below.
[1749] Chapters 2 and 8 above.

enhanced by the fact that bringing the full range of disputed maritime areas under the reach of cooperative arrangements borders on the utopian.

Aside from any perceived dangers linked to appraising the scope for unilateralism *in abstracto*, which are more imaginary than real, other considerations are if and to what degree it can be considered a meaningful approach. A first issue stems from case law, providing that, in order to violate international law, at a minimum an act must have had a more severe impact on a State's rights than having been 'just' an infringement. But where does this leave the idea that sovereignty, sovereign rights, and/or jurisdiction are assumed to be exclusively exercised by a coastal State? Must such thinking be deferred to the period after delimitation, when there is clarity over the geographical extent of a coastal State's sovereignty, sovereign rights, and/or jurisdictional competences, or has it some role to play in the period prior thereto as well? A second issue is whether idiosyncrasies surrounding a maritime boundary dispute are a variable that shifts the extent to which States are allowed to act unilaterally, in that they would be allowed to authorise or undertake an act that is under coastal State authority, within a given context. Following from this, a third issue arises: what can be reasonably said on what scope remains for unilateralism in disputed maritime areas?

9.3.1 *The Exclusivity Approach*

In view of the character of the coastal State's rights over the continental shelf, and hence over the natural resources that are contained within it, States having entitlements to a continental shelf can be argued to possess a similar 'exclusive' right to engage in exploration and exploitation of its resources.[1750] The same argument can be upheld in connection with the EEZ, even though States do not have inherent rights in connection therewith, as one must be explicitly claimed. If a coastal State has claimed an EEZ in accordance with international law, and this claim overlaps with another State's EEZ claim, the claimed entitlement to one and the rights and obligations it carries with it do exist as well. This is irrespective of the fact that the geographical extent of the EEZ, and thus to which point the coastal State's sovereign rights and jurisdictional competences precisely extend, is unclear as long as the boundary has not been delimited.

As a corollary to when one of the States concerned acts on its claimed rights in a disputed EEZ or continental shelf area – or on the sovereignty that it has in a disputed territorial sea area, implying exclusivity as well – in turn, the

[1750] Article 77 LOSC.

other State's rights or sovereignty are deprived of their exclusivity aspect. But is there a legal basis in international law that supports the assumption that the exclusivity aspect of a State's rights or sovereignty must be kept intact?

In the past, international courts and tribunals have been confronted with States contending that having exclusivity over a disputed EEZ/continental shelf area means one of two things: either that a moratorium on economic acts that fall under coastal State jurisdiction is imposed or that one coastal State is exclusively entitled to conduct such acts in the disputed area, whereas another neighbouring coastal State would not be entitled to do the same. Both of these contentions have been consistently met with scepticism.[1751] For example, despite Côte d'Ivoire arguing that, also as a matter of customary law, 'les activités économiques unilatérales sont prohibées dans une zone litigieuse',[1752] the Special Chamber of the ITLOS in *Ghana/Côte d'Ivoire* went in a different direction.[1753] In its decision in the *Aegean Sea Continental Shelf* (Interim Measures) case, the ICJ made it clear that the exclusivity of a coastal State's rights over the continental shelf did not mean, as Greece contended,[1754] that gathering information thereon can only be lawfully undertaken once the geographical extent of a coastal State's rights is clear.[1755] Similarly, the Tribunal's overall methodology in *Guyana v. Suriname* was designed around interpreting both obligations under Articles 74(3) and 83(3) LOSC so to avoid a moratorium being imposed.[1756] On the whole, the line established in the case law suggests that, although the rights of States to the continental shelf are inherent and exclusive, certain acts by the other claimant, although infringing on these rights, may be lawfully undertaken; this is unless a particular threshold is exceeded.[1757]

State practice also seems to lend little support to the view that a complete abstention from economic conduct, that is subject to the authority of the coastal State, in disputed maritime areas is required under international law, in order to preserve the exclusive nature of a coastal State's rights or sovereignty. If a complete abstention is required, then many States seem to disregard international law at their peril by regularly authorising or undertaking conduct that is within the authority of the coastal State unilaterally within disputed maritime areas. Consequently, conflict regularly arises in bilateral

1751 Chapter 6 above.
1752 *Ghana/Côte d'Ivoire* (Judgment) (n. 46) Côte d'Ivoire's Counter-Memorial 237 [9.15].
1753 Chapter 6, Section 6.4 above.
1754 *Aegean Sea Continental Shelf* (Interim Measures) (n. 41) Greece's Oral Pleadings 119, 128–129.
1755 Ibid. Order 10 [30].
1756 *Guyana* v. *Suriname* (n. 7) 131–132 [465].
1757 Chapter 6, Section 6.7 above.

relations if unilateral conduct has been undertaken in connection with mineral resources, fisheries, or MSR, as these are all activities that are under the authority of a coastal State.[1758]

But how can this be explained, legally speaking, given that sovereignty, sovereign rights, and/or jurisdiction of a coastal State are meant to be exercised exclusively, and as regards the continental shelf its sovereign rights are even inherent? One explanation for this is that, because of there being two 'exclusive entitlements' for coastal States with regard to the same disputed maritime area, the exclusivity aspect is effectively invalidated prior to its delimitation.[1759] For example, while the exact point to where a coastal State's continental shelf and related sovereign rights and jurisdictional competences extend remains unclear, the exercise of these rights and competences is qualified, inter alia, by Article 83(3) LOSC. Pursuant to this provision, acting on these pre-existing sovereign rights and jurisdictional competences is premised on whether the particular threshold of hampering or jeopardising is not surpassed.

Yet, on an ordinary reading of the language used in Articles 74(3) and 83(3) LOSC, this paragraph can be interpreted as requiring a moratorium on economic conduct (e.g. energy and natural resources activity, and a MSR project that falls within the scope of Article 246(5) LOSC) in certain circumstances, through which the exclusivity of a State's sovereign rights would be preserved. On this interpretation, prevalence is given to the subjective element underpinning the obligation not to hamper or jeopardise: that is, the obligation is imposed on claimants, who might be of the view that the chances of reaching a final delimitation are best served by observing a moratorium on economic conduct prior to the delimitation of the EEZ/continental shelf boundary.[1760] Interpreted in this way, the exclusivity aspect of a State's sovereign rights and jurisdictional competences is kept intact.

9.3.2 *Circumstances as the Defining Variable*

No two disputed maritime areas are the same, either in terms of geography or their intricacies and surrounding dynamics. In some disputed maritime areas, calm prevails – in that no unilateral acts which fall under the authority of the coastal State are authorised or undertaken, or those that are authorised do not ignite a conflict – whereas other areas are constant venues for conflicts

[1758] Chapter 2, Section 2.3 above.
[1759] Chapter 5, Section 5.1 above.
[1760] Ibid. Section 5.3.12.

between claimant States. Given the specificities that are inherent to a disputed maritime area, the applicable international legal framework needs to be sufficiently flexible to accommodate this. Indeed, this is the case, as the rules and mutual restraint obligations that are applicable in disputed maritime areas (be it by virtue of conventional law or general rules of (customary) international law, including the obligation to exercise restraint by not threatening irreparability of the other State's rights) have a high degree of generality and are sufficiently malleable to account for any specificities.

In terms of conventional law, this is illustrated by Articles 74(3) and 83(3) LOSC, which are exclusively applicable in disputed EEZ or continental shelf areas and are open-ended in two ways: first, paragraph 3 does not identify particular acts that must be refrained from; and, second, it does not indicate the concrete acts that must be taken to comply with this obligation. This open-endedness should not be seen negatively; rather, the overall relevance of paragraph 3 is increased as a result. Essentially, the two obligations contained in Articles 74(3) and 83(3) LOSC work independently, and yet often in sync, similar to separate parts in a great machine – a machine that seeks to facilitate the delimitation of a disputed EEZ or continental shelf area, by taking its context into account. Therefore, the open-endedness of paragraph 3 caters for the fact that some interaction exists between unilateral conduct in relation to a disputed EEZ/continental shelf area and the chances that delimitation is hampered or jeopardised. To illustrate this, in certain disputed maritime areas, particular unilateral acts falling under coastal State jurisdiction will have an effect of hampering or jeopardising, or are at least claimed by one of the coastal States concerned to have such an effect, whereas in other areas the same act will not generate any conflict. Consequently, no exact lines can be drawn across the range of disputed EEZ or continental shelf areas, as to the extent to which the States concerned must exercise restraint, by abstaining from exercising their rights and jurisdictional competences pending delimitation. This is because the degree to which bilateral relations are influenced, or the extent to which a conflict is created, and thus whether the maritime boundary dispute is exacerbated, as a result of conduct which is under the jurisdiction of the coastal State and is authorised unilaterally, varies decisively according to the given circumstances.

Further, this introduces a variable into the assessment whether the primary obligations flowing from the LOSC, including Articles 74(3) and 83(3), have been breached through unilateral conduct within a disputed EEZ or continental shelf area.[1761] This paragraph 3 contains a subjective element that is inherent in the aim for which it was imposed, which inevitably enhances the

[1761] *Guyana* v. *Suriname* (n. 7) Suriname's Counter-Memorial 117 [7.42].

relevance of this aspect of the circumstances surrounding such a maritime boundary dispute in assessing a breach thereof: that is, achieving EEZ and continental shelf delimitation. Its primary goal is that it seeks to avoid 'the reaching of the final agreement' being negatively impacted.[1762] By its very nature, delimitation, and the reaching thereof, is linked to the willingness of the States involved. Like delimitation, which for its success is dependent upon the positions of the States concerned, the interpretation of which unilateral acts that are under coastal State jurisdiction breach Articles 74(3) and 83(3) LOSC becomes to an extent intertwined with the positions of the claimant States concerned. Giving a central role to the circumstances surrounding the maritime boundary dispute is not only in line with how to view the *raison d'être* of paragraph 3 more broadly, but also provides an approach that is tailor-made to deal with the exigencies of a disputed EEZ or continental shelf area. The language of Articles 74(3) and 83(3) LOSC also leaves room for this interpretation. Key to this interpretation is that the obligation not to hamper or jeopardise is underpinned by a good faith component, in that the States concerned must make every effort thereto. This widens the range of conduct that could breach this obligation, compared to if this composition of wording was not added. The implication of this is that one of the States concerned can claim that the other State shows a lack of such an effort concerning a broader range of unilateral activity, as a result of which the underlying maritime boundary dispute is exacerbated, whereby the obligation not to hamper or jeopardise is considered to be breached.[1763]

By way of example, if one of the claimant States views unilateral seismic work within a disputed EEZ or continental shelf area as a provocative act, authorising or undertaking such an act may impede the chances of successfully delimiting their maritime boundary. Currently, construing the relation between conducting seismic work and its lawfulness as interacting with the positions of the States concerned is not part of the general prevailing view that has been set out in the case law or in the relevant literature on this topic, however.[1764] Although perhaps somewhat unorthodox, this interpretation, as maintained in this book, is reconcilable with the language of Articles 74(3) and 83(3) LOSC, as well as its underlying aim – that is, successfully reaching delimitation – to which end the States concerned must make every effort.[1765]

1762 Van Logchem (n. 245) 138.
1763 Chapter 5, Section 5.3.12 above.
1764 Chapter 6, Section 6.8 above.
1765 Van Logchem (n. 245) 138; Anderson and Van Logchem (n. 18) 206.

Further, when acts that are under the jurisdiction of the coastal State are unilaterally authorised to be undertaken in a disputed EEZ or continental shelf area, even those which are generally considered to be largely benign, the chances of agreeing on a delimitation agreement can be detrimentally affected in two ways: first, an individual unilateral act may have the effect of hampering or jeopardising the possibility of a successful delimitation (e.g. this may be the case if bilateral relations are already strained); and, second, this may happen through an accumulation of more minor detrimental effects, eventually exerting a similar effect of hampering or jeopardising. In this light, it has been argued in this book that, for instance, collecting data within the framework of MSR or seismic work in the disputed EEZ or continental shelf area can be unlawful under certain circumstances.

Particularly relevant is the history between the claimants as to their disputed maritime area. This inevitably plays a role in determining the lawfulness of acts within coastal State jurisdiction that have been undertaken unilaterally. On balance, and to broaden the discussion to disputed maritime areas generally, the scope for a State to act in relation thereto may be either enhanced or reduced, for instance, according to the overall state of the bilateral relations between the States concerned. Several other relevant factors can be identified as interacting with the extent to which sovereignty, sovereign rights and/or jurisdictional competences may be acted upon, and obligations must be exercised by States *in concreto* within a disputed maritime area: political factors; geographical factors; historical factors; economic factors; (similar or identical) past conduct, particularly whether it prompted the other claimant into responding; and the primary obligations of international law that are incumbent on States.[1766]

However, when a claimant State has undertaken a unilateral activity in relation to which the coastal State has authority, for instance seismic work, and another claimant State would want to do the same, it is reasonable to assume that the act may be undertaken without prior consent: a State cannot blow hot and cold at the same time. The status quo concept provides an insight into what types of acts which fall under the authority of the coastal State do not have a detrimental effect on delimitation. In *Guyana* v. *Suriname*, Suriname elevated the status quo, consisting of 'transitory or tolerated occasional actions'[1767] to form the standard against which to measure the lawfulness of a unilateral act, which is under the authority of the coastal State, when it is authorised or undertaken in connection with the disputed area. In this light,

1766 Ibid.

1767 *Guyana* v. *Suriname* (n. 7) Suriname's Counter-Memorial 117 [7.42].

through Guyana's decision to authorise the CGX to drill, and prior thereto by giving a concession to that end, the status quo that existed between the two States in relation to their disputed area had been radically altered.[1768] This was not the case concerning seismic work, which was a constituent part of their status quo as both Guyana and Suriname acknowledged that this type of activity was lawful.

To the contrary, if a certain type of unilateral conduct that is under the authority of the coastal State has been undertaken previously within a disputed maritime area, which is followed by making a protest, and possibly a counter-protest, or that conflict has manifested itself differently between the claimant States concerned, the lawful range for similar unilateral conduct is reduced. Inherent in this is that the extent to which jurisdictional competences, sovereign rights, or sovereignty can be exercised by claimant States in their disputed maritime areas is intimately linked to the circumstances surrounding the maritime boundary dispute. The more complex or volatile such a dispute is, the more demanding the obligation to exercise restraint becomes for the claimants concerned, by which token a greater limitation is imposed on what scope there is for unilateral conduct that falls under the authority of the coastal State. Under this logic, the maritime boundary disputes in the Aegean Sea, the Mediterranean Sea, the South China Sea, and the East China Sea are examples of areas where the scope for unilateralism is argued to be reduced, because of their complexity and because, if the States concerned act unilaterally, by authorising or undertaking an act that is under the authority of a coastal State, conflict is almost invariably created between them.[1769] There is thus an important dialectical relationship between the disputed maritime area in question and the amount of restraint that must be observed by the States concerned in relation thereto. The more conflict that the disputed maritime area has historically created in bilateral relations, the more circumscribed the room for acting unilaterally there will be, in terms of authorising acts that fall within the authority of a coastal State. Thus, more restraint than would otherwise perhaps be necessary needs to be observed by claimants, if they have dug their heels in over the course of the maritime boundary and have a history of unilaterally undertaken acts that are subject to coastal State authority relating to a disputed area which have provoked subsequent protests or incidents.

[1768] Ibid. 109–110 [7.11]–[7.12]; Suriname's Rejoinder 128 [4.15].
[1769] Van Logchem (n. 245) 138–139; Davenport (n. 71) 311.

9.3.3 *'Determining' the Scope for Unilateralism*

Despite the fact that circumstances are a limiting factor in determining the scope for unilateral conduct that falls under the authority of the coastal State in relation to a disputed maritime area, an approximation thereof can be given. This is possible through assessing the current state of international law covering disputed maritime areas, and then applying the applicable law to the different categories of unilateral activity which are under the authority of the coastal State, to 'determine' their lawfulness. In what follows, this exercise will be conducted in relation to acts relating to mineral resources (Section 9.3.3.1), fisheries (Section 9.3.3.2), and the collection of data within the framework of MSR (Section 9.3.3.3).

9.3.3.1 Mineral Resources

Most State practice and interpretations by international courts and tribunals of the relevant international rules lend little support to the view that a complete abstention from concessioning in relation to a disputed continental shelf area is required under international law.[1770] Quite often, unilateral acts that exist solely on paper, which includes concessioning, have not been regarded as unlawful, being similarly excluded from the reach of Articles 74(3) and 83(3) LOSC.[1771]

By way of contrast, significant support exists for the position that unilateral exploratory and exploitation drilling are unlawful under international law, under both conventional law and customary international law.[1772] Less strong is the evidence that would underpin a similar conclusion with regard to conducting unilateral seismic work, however. A first difficulty is that there is some disconnection between judicial pronunciations and the actual practice of States, as the latter presents a highly diversified picture concerning when unilateral seismic work is undertaken in a disputed maritime area.[1773] A second difficulty is judicial pronouncements, where unilateral seismic work is generally seen as being relatively harmless, because of its minor impact on the marine environment. However, this position might become less tenable as our understanding of the impact of seismic work on the marine environment advances. Scientific reports have indicated that seismic work does produce certain negative effects to the marine environment.[1774] Various commentators

1770 Chapter 8, Section 8.4 above.
1771 Chapter 5, Section 5.3.7 above.
1772 Chapter 8, Section 8.4 above.
1773 Tanaka (n. 766) 316.
1774 Jahn et al. (n. 157) 28–33; C Yiallourides, 'Protecting and Preserving the Marine Environment in Disputed Areas: Seismic Noise and Provisional Measures of Protection' (2018) 36(2) *JENRL* 141, 144–150.

have concluded from *Guyana* v. *Suriname* that seismic work in a disputed maritime area is a type of activity that may be lawfully authorised unilaterally by a coastal State.[1775] But this position wrongly suggests that the context surrounding the disputed area does not matter.[1776] It also fails to take into account the specific aspects of the situation, to which the Tribunal in *Guyana* v. *Suriname* tailored its analysis accordingly, as both parties to the dispute recognised the lawfulness of unilateral seismic work within their disputed maritime area. More generally, the extent to which there might be certain circumstances when seismic work is prejudicial to delimitation cannot be defined *in abstracto*.[1777] This is because the kinds of issues that States may have to deal with in a disputed maritime area are unique and are effectively informed by its context and surrounding circumstances. As discussed earlier, this dynamic is also at work when determining whether a unilateral act that is under coastal State jurisdiction in a disputed EEZ or continental shelf area has violated the obligation not to jeopardise or hamper the reaching of a final delimitation agreement under Articles 74(3) and 83(3) LOSC.[1778] The judgment delivered by a Special Chamber of the ITLOS in *Ghana/Côte d'Ivoire* illustrates the point that this assessment is informed by the context and specific circumstances surrounding a maritime boundary dispute. Here the obligation not to hamper or jeopardise delimitation was not found to have been breached through unilateral exploratory drilling, seismic work, or being on the verge of mineral resource exploitation.[1779]

9.3.3.2 Fisheries

The significant obligations that coastal States have under the LOSC with regard to managing and conserving EEZ fisheries apply with equal force in disputed EEZ areas.[1780] A coastal State bringing fish stocks to a near collapse,[1781] or allowing them to be carried beyond that point, breaches inter alia the obligations that State has within its EEZ, including the obligation to prevent overfishing (Article 61(2) LOSC). Beyond that, such a State may also breach Article 74(3) LOSC when the underlying maritime boundary dispute

1775 Roughton (n. 1273) 398; Sakamoto (n. 925) 101.
1776 Van Logchem (n. 245) 138–139; Van Logchem (n. 21) 185–186.
1777 Section 9.3.2 above.
1778 Ibid.
1779 Chapter 6, Section 6.4 above.
1780 Chapter 2, Sections 2.3.3 and 2.3.4 above.
1781 DF Anwar, 'Resource Issues and Ocean Governance in Asia Pacific: An Indonesian Perspective' (2006) 28(3) CSA 466, 467–477.

is exacerbated by a fisheries-related act, making delimiting the disputed EEZ area more difficult.[1782]

No international court or tribunal has as yet considered the lawfulness of fishing activities, or the granting of fisheries licences, or taking enforcement action against fishermen of the other claimant State in a disputed maritime area.[1783] This is not because claimant States have never faced difficulties in connection thereto, but rather that States involved in international adjudication have rarely opted to present an argument that fishing activities within a disputed maritime area were unlawful. The exception is the Philippines, which made a claim of unlawful fishing by China in disputed areas of the South China Sea in *Philippines* v. *China*.[1784]

Broader implications may, however, follow from *Guyana* v. *Suriname*, in that the Tribunal held in its award that acts which permanently affect the marine environment cannot be undertaken unilaterally, as they breach Article 74(3) LOSC.[1785] When this standard is applied to fishing activities,[1786] the argument can be made that these would, to a certain extent, be permissible in a disputed EEZ area.[1787] This is in light of the renewable properties of fish stocks. But there is a converse side to applying, by analogy, the standard of permanently affecting the marine environment to fishing activities, in that it imposes certain limitations thereon. Differences that exist between acts related to fisheries and mineral resources in disputed maritime areas, especially in terms of their ability to recover, can, however, be more cosmetic than genuine. Fish stocks may equally become depleted, as their natural ability to reproduce can be affected by human interference, or by a combination of different factors.[1788] These can be so severe that, when fisheries are exploited in an unsustainable way, overfishing or the depletion of fish stocks will follow. Even if the damage caused is not irreparable, the effects on a fish stock may be long-lasting, with the time required to recuperate being extensive. Sometimes it will be difficult to predict whether a fish stock will recover at all, especially if no scientific studies have been done into its viability. Damaging effects caused to a fish stock may thus be of an irreparable nature: that is, when stocks fall to very low levels, and come near to extinction. Then, they are susceptible to several problems that may jeopardise their future, such as genetic problems,

1782 Chapter 5, Section 5.3.12 above.
1783 Van Logchem (n. 21) 185–186.
1784 *Philippines* v. *China* (n. 448) 443–453 [717]–[757].
1785 *Guyana* v. *Suriname* (n. 7) 133 [470].
1786 Chapter 6, Section 6.8 above.
1787 Anderson and Van Logchem (n. 18) 218–220.
1788 Ibid. 218–219.

inbreeding, and so forth. Nonetheless, because fisheries are by their nature of a renewable character, it will be less easily justified if a coastal State imposes a categorical ban on fishing activities in a disputed area. Yet, when a fish stock is overfished, and scientific data corroborates this decline, and this data is shared with the other State(s) claiming the same EEZ area, a moratorium on fishing for the fish stock at risk can be lawfully imposed. This justification would cease after the fish stock recovers, and this should be demonstrated, once again, by scientific evidence.[1789]

In an attempt to enlarge the protection of fish stocks and allow stocks to recuperate in a disputed maritime area, certain coastal States have adopted unilateral protective measures with regard to fisheries and the broader marine environment. Practise shows, however, that taking unilateral measures aimed at their protection can become a possible source of conflict in the bilateral relations of neighbouring coastal States. This happens when the other claimant's interests are believed to be affected, or when enforcement measures are taken to act against breaches by the other claimant State. The possibility of taking enforcement action is a separate matter, however. Because whether a claimant State is allowed to enforce its laws, if faced with a breach thereof by the other claimant, is a different issue from whether prescriptive jurisdiction exists for a coastal State to proclaim national legislation with the aim of protecting fish stocks and the marine environment of a disputed area.[1790]

Also, claimant States encouraging their national fishermen to conduct fishing activities in a disputed maritime area, if this leads to over-exploitation, or the arresting of each other's nationals which can seriously disrupt bilateral relations, breaches several rules of international law, including Articles 61(2) and 74(3) LOSC.[1791] Overfishing of fish stocks located in disputed maritime areas can further create conflicts between the fishermen of the States concerned, which can spill over to the diplomatic level, especially when enforcement action is taken against the other claimant's nationals.[1792]

9.3.3.3 Collecting Information through Activities Conducted in the Framework of MSR

Although generally seen as one of the less controversial categories of activity that is under the authority of a coastal State, authorising an MSR project

1789 Chapter 2, Section 2.3.3 above.
1790 Ibid. Sections 2.3.5 and 2.3.6.
1791 Ibid. Section 2.3.3.
1792 Ibid.

unilaterally in a disputed maritime area has given rise to conflict between neighbouring coastal States.[1793] Research institutions, or the nationals of a third State, may encounter difficulties in gaining access to disputed maritime areas. Although it may also be that whenever such areas are included within the scope of an MSR project, its scope will be changed prior to its occurring, or it will be abandoned altogether. Permission for the MSR project could be sought from all claimants, without informing either State that similar permission is being sought from the other claimant. However, this approach might run into difficulties when a claimant insists that it is exclusively approached for permission. An effect of a coastal State allowing an MSR project to commence within a disputed maritime area is that it accepts that the other coastal State's sovereignty or sovereign rights are infringed upon. But is this infringement unlawful from the perspective of international law?

With regard to disputed EEZ and continental shelf areas, it is critical to make a distinction as to whether the MSR project falls under either paragraph 3 or 5 of Article 246 LOSC. Article 246(3) LOSC stipulates that consent by 'the coastal State' for research that 'increases scientific knowledge of the marine environment for the benefit of all mankind' is normally given when a State is presented with a request from a third State to conduct such MSR. This is unless the type of research pursued would fall within one of the exceptions provided in Article 246(5) LOSC, which is the case if it is concerned with natural resources, or involves drilling into the continental shelf. Then, all coastal States must be approached for their prior consent. The consequence is that, if one of the claimant States approached decides to withhold its consent, the MSR project cannot be lawfully undertaken. However, if a research institution or national does decide to proceed with MSR in the disputed EEZ area, after receiving consent from one claimant State, an MSR project that falls under one of the categories identified in Article 246(5) – in relation to which a coastal State has discretion – runs the risk of prompting a response from the other claimant. Thus, if the MSR project falls within one of the exceptions identified in paragraph 5, then the prior consent of all of the coastal States concerned would be required. However, when the MSR project falls under Article 246(3) LOSC, it should be able to proceed in a disputed EEZ area with the consent of one claimant State. But there might be an obligation for that State to notify another claimant State of an approved MSR project, as in exercising its rights, due regard must be had for another State's rights. With regard to disputed territorial sea areas that are not governed by the interim rule provided in Article 15 LOSC or Article 12 1958 CTS,[1794] where there

1793 Chapter 8, Section 8.3 above.

1794 Chapter 4, Sections 4.1 and 4.2 above.

are competing sovereignties, a MSR project needs to be authorised by all of the claimant States concerned, however.

9.3.3.4 Lawful Responses

Coastal States regularly enact legislation that includes disputed maritime areas within its scope. This might *simpliciter* be sufficient to persuade another State to protest. But difficulties often intensify between States when activities that are under the authority of the coastal State are undertaken in disputed maritime areas without the other State's consent. Then, the other coastal State can feel compelled to respond somehow, if this conduct is seen as infringing upon its perceived sovereignty, sovereign rights, jurisdictional competences, or interests. This perceived need and whether it is lawful to respond varies with the type of conduct and the maritime zone concerned, as well as with the circumstances involved.

States regularly protest through diplomatic channels if they want to object to a particular action or reaction by another State in relation to a disputed maritime area.[1795] A protest is only problematic from the perspective of international law when it is made on the basis of excessive claims to maritime areas. States may respond to alleged unlawful activities by physically acting to assert their rights, as well, for example through an act of retorsion or law enforcement. Taking enforcement measures against the other claimant is viewed as highly sensitive by neighbouring coastal States, however, because it directly challenges their entitlement and authority over the maritime zone.[1796] Also, if a claimant takes enforcement measures against an act undertaken by another claimant, which more often concerns an activity licensed by it, this almost invariably creates a conflict between the States concerned.[1797]

Enforcement measures taken by a claimant against a third State, or its nationals, for undertaking an activity that is under the authority of the coastal State, and that has not been approved by any of the coastal States concerned, is a different matter, one which often proves to be far less contentious.[1798] This is perhaps unless a claimant operates on the assumption that the area belongs to it exclusively, making it generally wary of any activities that are undertaken in 'its' maritime zone by other States. For instance, if the nationals of a third State conduct fishing activities in a disputed EEZ area without having obtained

1795 Oxman and Murphy (n. 237) 1.
1796 Van Logchem (n. 21) 175.
1797 Chapter 2, Section 2.3.6 above.
1798 Milano and Papanicolopulu (n. 80) 623–624. But see BIICL Report (n. 141) 29.

a fishing licence, all claimants would be allowed to take enforcement measures against the vessel flying the flag of a third State, because their EEZ rights are being equally breached. More controversial is when enforcement action is taken against third States, or their nationals who have been licensed by a claimant State to undertake a particular activity that falls under the authority of the coastal State. Then, the licensing State is likely to feel similarly targeted through the enforcement action by the other claimant, as the former will view the act of licensing as a lawful exercise of its rights.

An argument according to which law enforcement cannot be considered lawful, whatever the effects of a unilateral act on the other claimant State's rights or position may be, is the following: law enforcement against the licensing State, most often its nationals who will mainly be the ones that conduct activities in a disputed maritime area, can be equated with threatening the licensing State's rights with irreparability, hence rendering it unlawful.[1799] An alternative line of argument is that law enforcement invariably aggravates the maritime boundary dispute and thereby, assuming it occurs within a disputed EEZ or continental shelf area, jeopardises or hampers reaching a final delimitation agreement, which Articles 74(3) and 83(3) LOSC seek to prevent. Judge Thierry recognised the existence of a correlation between law enforcement and rights being irreparably damaged in his dissenting opinion in *Guinea-Bissau* v. *Senegal* (Provisional Measures).[1800] The implication of this is not insignificant, particularly in light of the standard of irreparability being used by analogy by, for example, the Tribunal in *Guyana* v. *Suriname*, when clarifying the content of the obligation not to hamper or jeopardise in Articles 74(3) and 83(3) LOSC.[1801] Concluding that law enforcement cannot be considered lawful because it inevitably leads to irreparability, and thus breaches the obligation not to hamper or jeopardise, is, however, less convincing when applied to disputed maritime areas in a general sense.

Articles 74(3) and 83(3) LOSC limit the possibility for a claimant State to act against a breach of its national legislation in relation to a disputed EEZ and continental shelf area through law enforcement. Its limiting effect especially flows from the obligation not to hamper or jeopardise, which reduces both when, and the ways in which, coastal States can respond to unilateral conduct that is under the jurisdiction of the coastal State.[1802] The award of the Tribunal in *Guyana* v. *Suriname* serves as a cautionary tale in this regard: Suriname's

1799 Kim (n. 287) 58–59.

1800 *Guinea-Bissau* v. *Senegal* (Provisional Measures) (n. 11) 81 (Dissenting Opinion of Judge Thierry).

1801 *Guyana* v. *Suriname* (n. 7) 133 [469].

1802 Van Logchem (n. 21) 192, 195.

naval officers uttering certain words was not in the nature of law enforcement action, but, rather, a warning that force might be used if their directions were not complied with.[1803] A critical consideration for the Tribunal was the fact that Suriname could have sought interim measures of protection, submitted the (underlying maritime boundary) dispute to adjudication, or commenced with negotiations.[1804] However, weakening this argument is that inherent in these responses is that they do not produce instantaneous or guaranteed results – for instance, negotiations might well turn out to be fruitless.[1805] Restricting the possibilities for States to take law enforcement measures might have the following implication: a coastal State faced with an unlawful act may be without ways in which to immediately respond; this is also when this might be warranted in order to protect its rights over the disputed maritime area. Another aspect that remains unaddressed in case law is why for example unilateral exploratory or exploitation drilling, similarly resulting in the irreparability of rights, is accorded less weight than engaging in law enforcement, as both affect the other State's sovereign rights to a comparable extent. Also, to draw a parallel with undisputed waters in relation to which a coastal State has the right to proclaim its laws and regulations as part of its prescriptive jurisdiction, it automatically also has enforcement jurisdiction to act against any breaches thereof.[1806] By way of contrast, and if one would accept the view that taking law enforcement measures is removed from the arsenal of responses that are available to States, this would boil down to the fact that having rights over a disputed EEZ or continental shelf area would not bring along with it similar policing powers to act against an infringement thereof. Coastal States have extensive obligations with regard to fisheries and the protection of the marine environment, which equally apply in disputed maritime areas. But, if a claimant state were to be deprived of the option of enforcing the law in a disputed area, how would it be able to seriously fulfil the obligations it has concerning fisheries and the broader marine environment[1807] when faced with a breach of its adopted national environmental or fisheries legislation?

In view of the aforementioned competing considerations, to deny the existence of the option to engage in law enforcement in a disputed maritime area altogether for a claimant State seems to be, in the balance of things, a step

1803 *Guyana* v. *Suriname* (n. 7) 126 [445].
1804 Ibid. [446] 126–127.
1805 Van Logchem (n. 21) 193–194.
1806 J Crawford, *Brownlie's Principles of Public International Law* (Oxford University Press, 2012) 268.
1807 Chapter 2, Sections 2.3.3 and 2.3.5 above.

too far. Therefore, as to whether the possibility for taking law enforcement measures exists, it seems prudent to draw the line at when a State's rights are threatened with irreparability, which inter alia occurs if a State unilaterally attempts to drill or exploit mineral resources. Then, a gradual response, which could as an *ultima ratio* include law enforcement, can be envisaged as being lawful; this is assuming the enforcement action is conducted in conformity with the parameters set by international law. But there is a fine line to be walked here. Enforcement operations akin to those of Suriname, which it employed in its response to the rig licensed by Guyana, could lead to a finding by an international court or tribunal that the enforcing State has violated its obligations in relation to a disputed area, including, depending on the location, not to jeopardise or hamper the reaching of a final delimitation agreement as laid down in Articles 74(3) and 83(3) LOSC.

Although no State has followed this route as of yet, an alternative strategy that could be formulated to argue a violation of paragraph 3 of Articles 74 and 83 LOSC is to request interim measures of protection from an international court or tribunal. Such a request for interim protection could refer to a future violation of this paragraph, that is, when the requesting State is able to demonstrate that an act which is under the jurisdiction of the coastal State and that has been initiated, or is being planned, may result in a breach of Articles 74(3) and 83(3) LOSC. The international court or tribunal could then indicate measures of interim protection with the aim of that State ceasing a unilateral activity, or preventing it from being undertaken.

A potential difficulty is the effect a declaration made pursuant to Article 298(1)(a)(i) LOSC could have on Articles 74(3) and 83(3) LOSC, and the two obligations contained therein.[1808] Because when the State undertaking the activity has made a declaration pursuant to Article 298(1)(a)(i) LOSC and if such an Article 298 declaration would encompass these paragraphs as well, thereby preventing a court or tribunal from looking at Articles 74(3) and 83(3) LOSC, this would mean that this route might be closed off to a State that wants to put into question the lawfulness of a unilateral activity which is under the jurisdiction of the coastal State.[1809]

Alternatively, a claimant State that wants to respond to an act of unilateralism in a disputed maritime area but does not want to limit its response to a paper protest may do so in the form of a countermeasure.[1810] If a State decides to take a countermeasure, it will do so at its peril. There are no circumstances

1808 Van Logchem (n. 21) 195.
1809 Chapter 6, Section 6.9 above.
1810 Chapter 2, Section 2.3.6 above.

precluding wrongfulness that the State could invoke, that is, if the act against which the countermeasure was directed would be determined lawful by an international court or tribunal. Possibly that State also accepts the risk that, if, after delimitation, the act turns out to have taken place on the other State's side of the boundary, it has committed a breach of international law, giving rise to international responsibility.[1811] Another difficulty is that the effect a countermeasure generates might possibly aggravate or extend the dispute, and when it relates to an activity in a disputed EEZ/continental shelf area, it might hamper or jeopardise delimitation.[1812] Suriname, in *Guyana* v. *Suriname*, unsuccessfully contended that it resorted to a lawful countermeasure to put a halt to the international wrongful act of unilateral exploratory drilling authorised by Guyana in their disputed area.[1813] In its award, the Tribunal struck this line of argument down on the ground that a threat with the use of force cannot be considered a lawful countermeasure.[1814]

9.4 THIRD STATES AND THEIR NATIONALS

Rights and freedoms that are attributed to third States concerning navigation, collecting data, and the laying and maintaining of submarine cables and pipelines[1815] would be preserved in their original form, pending delimitation of a disputed maritime area.[1816] Certain claimant States do, however, sometimes seek to affect activities by third States, or their nationals, when the latter are exercising their rights and freedoms in disputed maritime areas, for example by closing off certain parts to navigation.[1817] With regard to disputed EEZ/continental shelf areas, the obligation not to hamper or jeopardise contained in Articles 74(3) and 83(3) LOSC is irrelevant when it comes to resolving disputes between a claimant and a third State that have been created when a third State exercises its rights and freedoms, which have been directly granted by international law (and not by a claimant coastal State), in such disputed areas. An intermediate approach based on the notion of due regard can address these clashes of sets of rights more successfully. To this end, several provisions are included in the LOSC, which apply with equal force in disputed EEZ or continental shelf areas, pursuant to which both groups of

[1811] Chapter 3, Section 3.11 above.
[1812] Chapter 2, Section 2.3.6 above.
[1813] *Guyana* v. *Suriname* (n. 7) 124, 126–127 [441] [446].
[1814] Chapter 6, Section 6.3.2 above.
[1815] Van Logchem (n. 244) 118.
[1816] Lagoni (n. 243) 365.
[1817] Chapter 2, Section 2.4 above.

States are under a similar duty of needing to have due regard to each other's rights (i.e. Articles 56(2), 58(3), and 79(5) LOSC).[1818] Furthermore, as a basic principle of international law thus operating more broadly with regard to disputed maritime areas, due regard must be had to the rights and interests of other States, which also extends to the scenario of a third State seeking to act on its rights and freedoms within such an area.[1819]

Difficulties can arise between private actors that are incorporated in third States, and that have only been licensed by one claimant State to undertake an act that falls under the authority of the coastal state, while the other claimant State that has not been approached for a licence objects to this. The other claimant is then likely to respond in some way, because it believes that its licence is also required for the activity to be lawfully undertaken in the disputed maritime area. The undertaking of an activity that falls under the authority of the coastal State by a national or private actor of a third State pursuant to a licence issued by one claimant State cannot be reasonably attributed to the third State as such; rather, it must be attributed to the claimant coastal State enabling the act to proceed. Practice shows that it can be risky for a national of a third State to undertake an act which is under the authority of a coastal State without obtaining a licence from all of the claimant coastal States concerned. As various private actors, particularly the petroleum industry, have discovered the hard way, the other claimant State might take measures to put a halt to any activity it views as infringing on its sovereignty, rights, and/or interests. Whether the neighbouring coastal State can respond against a unilateral act, which is subject to coastal State jurisdiction, with regard to a disputed EEZ or continental shelf area, and if so how, is inter alia determined by Articles 74(3) and 83(3) LOSC, particularly the obligation not to hamper or jeopardise.[1820]

9.5 WHERE DOES THE FAULT LIE?

Considerable doubts have been expressed as to whether international law in its current form is successful in managing maritime boundary disputes.[1821] The many conflicts that have occurred in disputed maritime areas in the past, due to unilateral conduct that is under coastal State authority being undertaken, is one aspect that lies behind this scepticism concerning the success of international law concerning such areas. In this vein, a number of disputed

1818 *Chagos Marine Protected Area Arbitration (Mauritius* v. *United Kingdom)*, Arbitral Award of 18 March 2015, 202 [519]; *Philippines* v. *China* (n. 448) 449–450, 608 [741]–[742] [744] [1197].

1819 Chapter 3, Section 3.7 above.

1820 Section 9.3 above.

1821 Song and Tonnesson (n. 601) 237.

maritime areas in the world can be identified where a general undercurrent of tension exists between the States concerned (e.g. in the East China Sea and Eastern Mediterranean Sea), which has already given rise to various incidents, and is likely to continue to create conflict.[1822] But can the 'fault' for conflicts that do arise in practice because of States acting unilaterally, by authorising or undertaking acts that are under coastal authority, be reasonably placed with the international legal framework?

The extent to which guidance can be gleaned from the LOSC as to how States need to act in relation to disputed maritime areas varies according to the maritime zone in question and the interim rule that is applicable thereto. Apart from disputed contiguous zone areas, the LOSC does address the situation prior to delimitation concerning disputed territorial sea, EEZ, and continental shelf areas, by providing States with standards of behaviour.

For those States that are not a party to the LOSC, but are a party to the CSC, the situation is more complicated with regard to disputed continental shelf areas, as the history of the development of Article 6 1958 CSC reveals that it is not meant to lay down an interim rule.[1823] However, the international legal framework that is applicable to disputed maritime areas not only consists of conventional law, but also includes general rules of international law. Combined, these form a template of rules and obligations that must be observed by States in relation to their disputed maritime areas. If both are analysed and combined, one cannot escape the conclusion that the rights and obligations that States have in disputed maritime areas are regulated rather extensively under international law. An obligation is placed on States to follow any international rules and obligations and, in case of a breach, international responsibility can be incurred.

Complicating matters is that only limited strides have been made in the international case law towards clarifying the rights and obligations of States in disputed maritime areas. Already in 1984, Lagoni concluded, on the basis of the ICJ's decision in the *Aegean Sea Continental Shelf* (Interim Measures) case, that acts causing irreparable prejudice 'would doubtless be prohibited under paragraph 3 of Articles 74/83'.[1824] Thereafter, there have been some relevant developments in this regard; particularly the ruling of the Tribunal in *Guyana* v. *Suriname*, but which due to its reliance on the notion of irreparability offered little additional clarification.[1825] After *Ghana/Côte d'Ivoire*, there has been

[1822] Chapter 8 above.
[1823] Chapter 5, Section 5.2 above.
[1824] Lagoni (n. 243) 366.
[1825] Chapter 6, Sections 6.7 and 6.8 above.

a proverbial muddying of the waters as to what rights and obligations States have in their disputed maritime areas. In his separate opinion, Judge Paik designated paragraph 3 of Article 83 LOSC as the 'only reliable legal device' presently available that seeks to govern the unilateral conduct of States in a disputed continental shelf area.[1826] However, the Special Chamber in its judgment in *Ghana/Côte d'Ivoire* construed Article 83(3) LOSC as a provision according to which the lawfulness of undertaking a unilateral act falling under coastal State jurisdiction pending delimitation can be determined with the knowledge of hindsight: that is, when it has become clear where the continental shelf boundary lies, and hence on whose side of the boundary the area where the unilateral activity was undertaken falls. In a way, the international case law finds itself at a crossroads. Will it continue to frame the content of the obligation not to hamper or jeopardise along the lines of the Special Chamber, which not only undercuts the purpose for which Articles 74(3) and 83(3) LOSC are imposed on claimant States (i.e. to apply pending delimitation), but also transforms the obligation not to hamper or jeopardise into an obligation that is deprived of much purpose?[1827] Or will the case law revert to the approach laid out by the Tribunal in *Guyana* v. *Suriname*, whereby the test as to whether an act hampers or jeopardises is converted into an objective one, which, although flawed, is preferable.

Along the entire breadth of activities that fall under the authority of the coastal State, varying extents of conflicts have been created when they were authorised or undertaken unilaterally in a disputed maritime area.[1828] But there is also an important differential at work in disputed maritime areas, which similarly renders devising closed categories of 'permissible' and 'impermissible' unilateral acts in disputed maritime areas a rather meaningless exercise:[1829] when an act under the authority of the coastal State is undertaken unilaterally, the response thereto by the other claimant State, if one is at all forthcoming, will vary in its intensity. Certain (types of) conduct under the authority of the coastal State will prove to be uncontroversial in one disputed maritime area if they proceed under the licence of one claimant State, while they may stir up significant conflict elsewhere. Two combined effects usually follow when a coastal State undertakes such acts unilaterally in a disputed area, through which a breach of international law can be assumed: which are, first, that unnecessary complexities to successfully completing delimitation

1826 *Ghana/Côte d'Ivoire* (Judgment) (n. 46) 184 [18] (Separate Opinion of Judge Paik).
1827 Van Logchem (n. 245) 170.
1828 Chapter 8 above.
1829 Section 9.3.2 above.

are added; and that, second, thereby the maritime boundary dispute is prolonged.

Ultimately, however, whether the potential for conflict that disputed maritime areas inherently bear is brought out into the open depends on the States concerned: will they exercise general restraint as far as taking acts that fall under coastal State authority is concerned? Will they bring the disputed area under the reach of a provisional arrangement? Or will there be a continuous willingness to act unilaterally, by authorising and undertaking acts under the authority of the coastal State, often with the result of creating a conflict with the other claimant? As is exemplified by State practice, various States do follow the path of unilateralism regularly. This suggests that the frequent occurrence of conflicts as a result thereof is not necessarily linked to the applicable international law, which lays down a variety of rules and obligations that, although more abstract in nature, similarly require restraint, but rather to individual claimants which disregard them, or, put more positively, interpret them to their advantage.

Index

www.ingramcontent.com/pod-product-compliance
Ingram Content Group UK Ltd.
Pitfield, Milton Keynes, MK11 3LW, UK
UKHW020244281225
466426UK00008B/509
* 9 7 8 1 1 0 8 8 3 0 1 0 2 *